Kamisama Kiss

Story & Art by
Julietta Suzuki

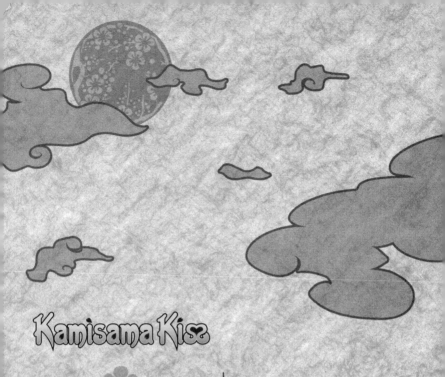

Kamisama Kiss

Volume 16
CONTENTS

CHARACTERS

Tomoe
The shinshi who serves Nanami now that she's a tochigami. Originally a wild fox ayakashi. He controls powerful kitsunebi.

Nanami Momozono
A high school student who was turned into a kamisama by the tochigami Mikage. She likes Tomoe.

Onikiri
Onibi-warashi, spirits of the shrine.

Kotetsu
Onibi-warashi, spirits of the shrine.

Mamoru
Nanami's shikigami. He can create a spiritual barrier to keep out evil.

Yukiji
A human woman from more than 500 years ago who was somehow connected to Tomoe.

Akura-oh
A great yokai and Tomoe's partner more than 500 years ago. He committed every evil act he possibly could.

Futa
An apprentice at Yukiji's residence. He is very attached to Yukiji.

Furball
An ayakashi who serves Akura-oh. He's always sent on errands and he stinks.

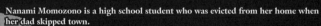

Nanami Momozono is a high school student who was evicted from her home when her dad skipped town.

She meets the tochigami Mikage in a park, and he leaves his shrine and his kami powers to her.

Now Nanami spends her days with Tomoe and Mizuki, her shinshi, and with Onikiri and Kotetsu, the onibi-warashi spirits of the shrine.

Nanami has been slowly gaining powers as a kamisama by holding a festival at her shrine, attending a big kami conference, and getting embroiled in the succession fight at the tengu village.

But mysterious marks have appeared on Tomoe's body, causing him to go into a coma. Mikage explains that the marks are part of a curse cast by a fallen kami.

So Nanami goes back in time to search for clues to break the curse. She learns that a fallen kami named "Kuromaro of Mount Ontake" is who she's looking for, but...

Story so far

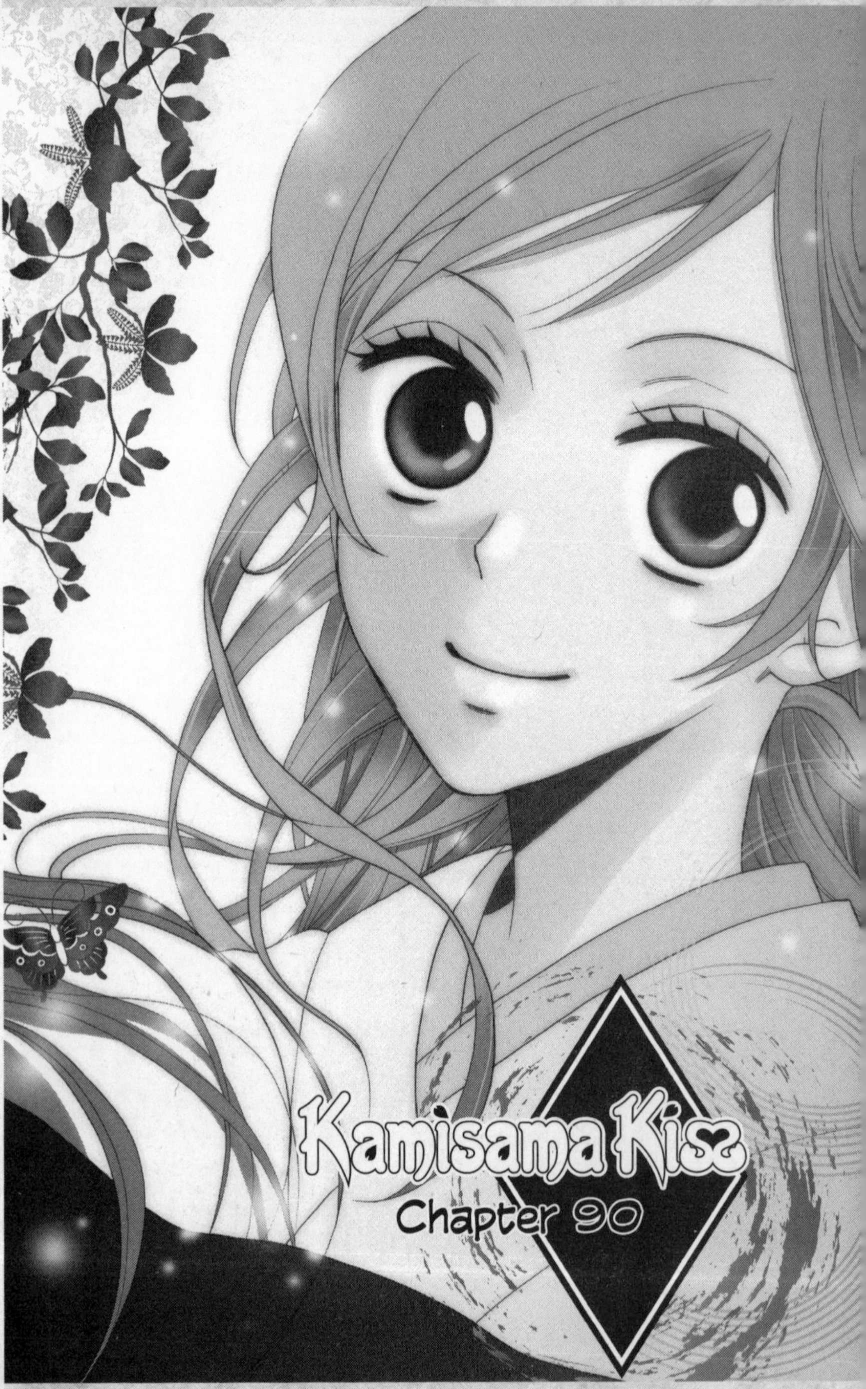
Kamisama Kiss
Chapter 90

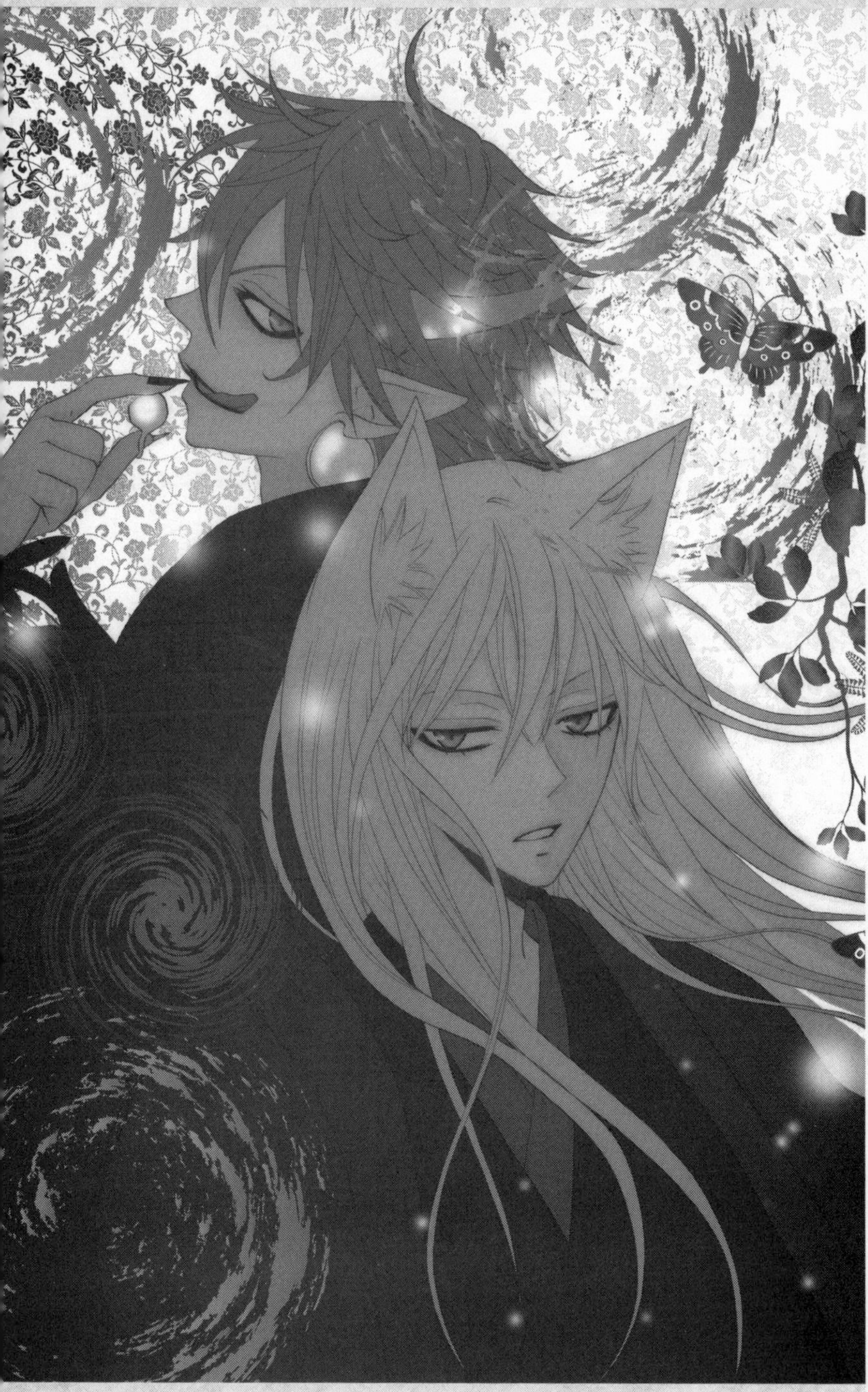

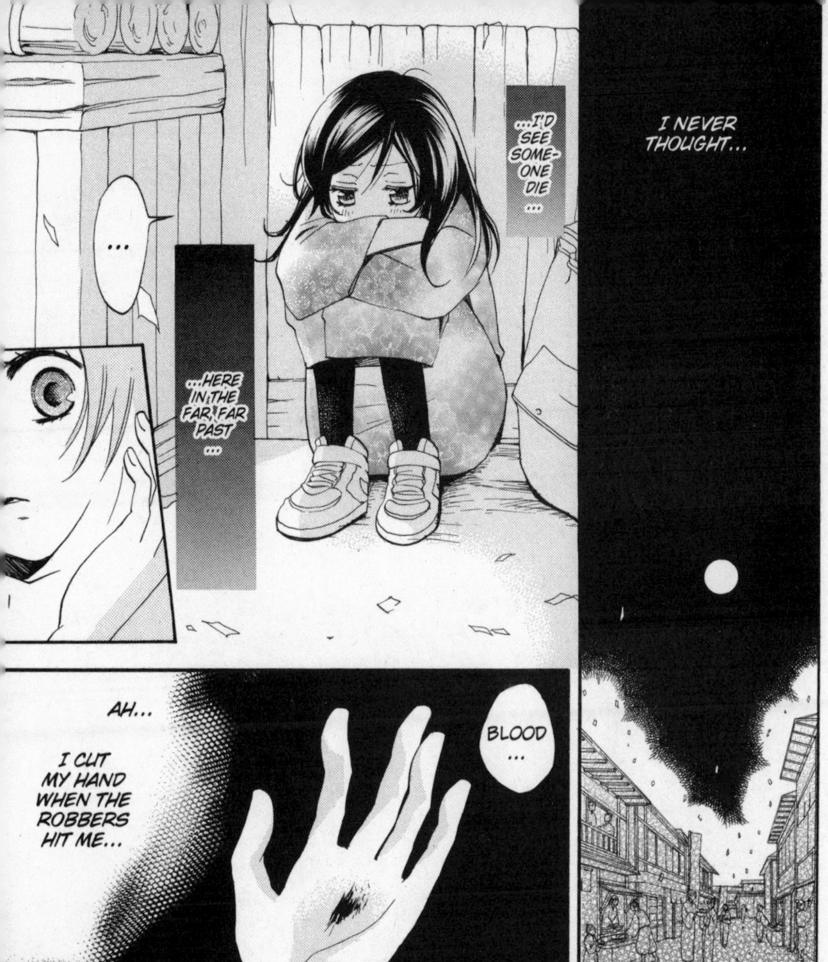
I NEVER THOUGHT...
...I'D SEE SOMEONE DIE...
...HERE IN THE FAR, FAR PAST...
...
BLOOD...
AH...
I CUT MY HAND WHEN THE ROBBERS HIT ME...

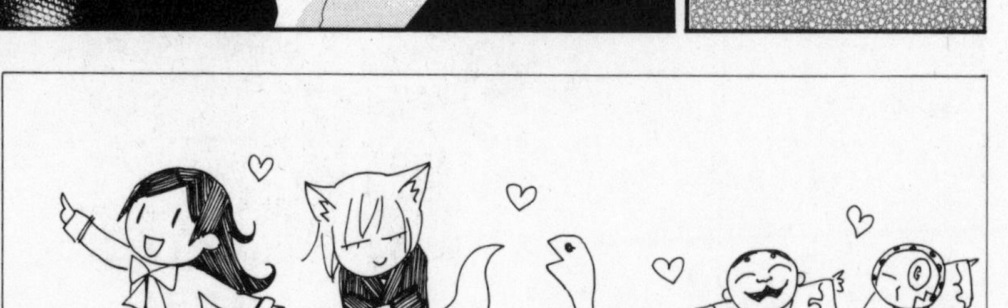

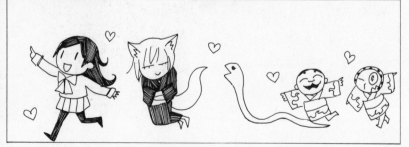

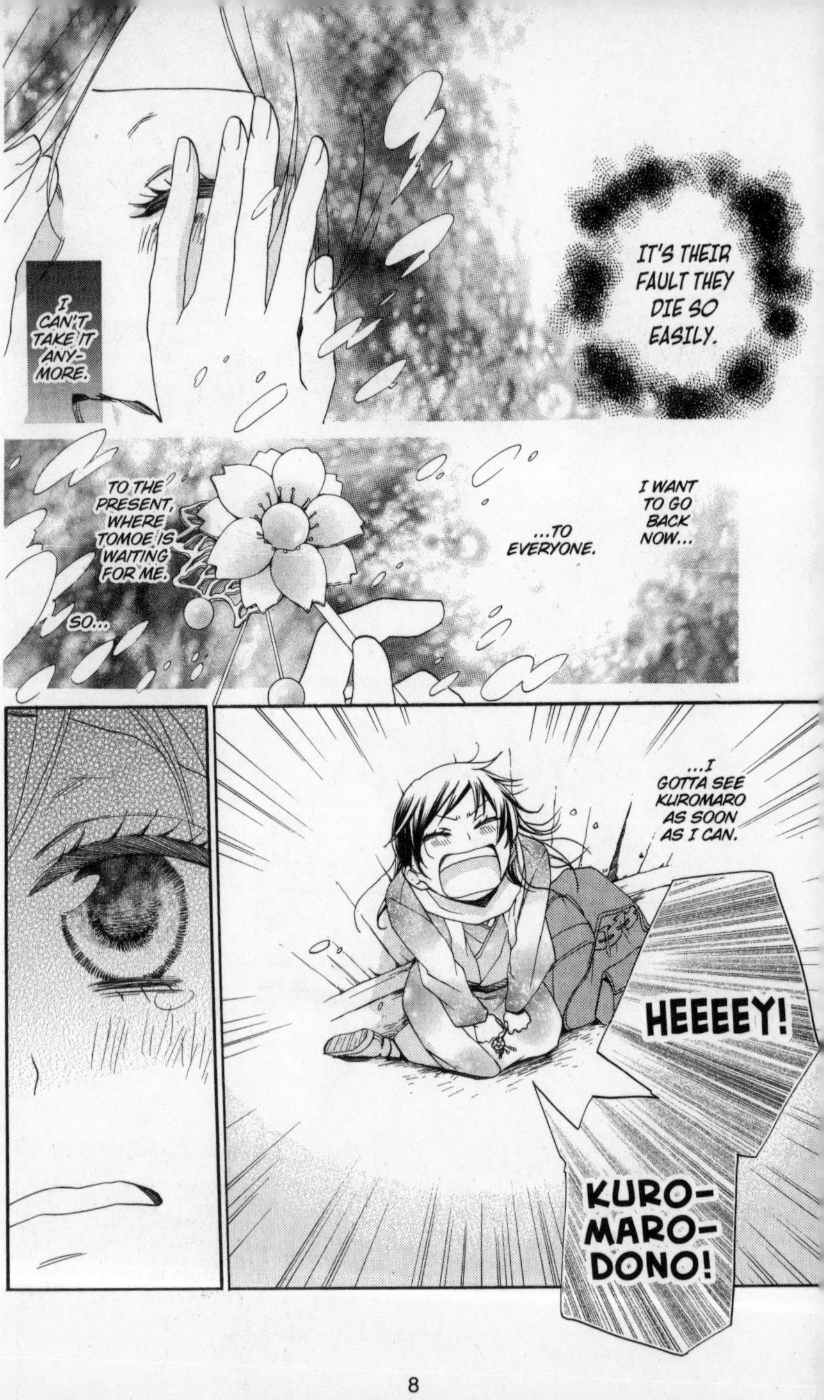
IT'S THEIR FAULT THEY DIE SO EASILY.
I CAN'T TAKE IT ANYMORE.
I WANT TO GO BACK NOW...
...TO EVERYONE.
TO THE PRESENT, WHERE TOMOE IS WAITING FOR ME.
SO...
...I GOTTA SEE KUROMARO AS SOON AS I CAN.
HEEEEY!
KURO-MARO-DONO!

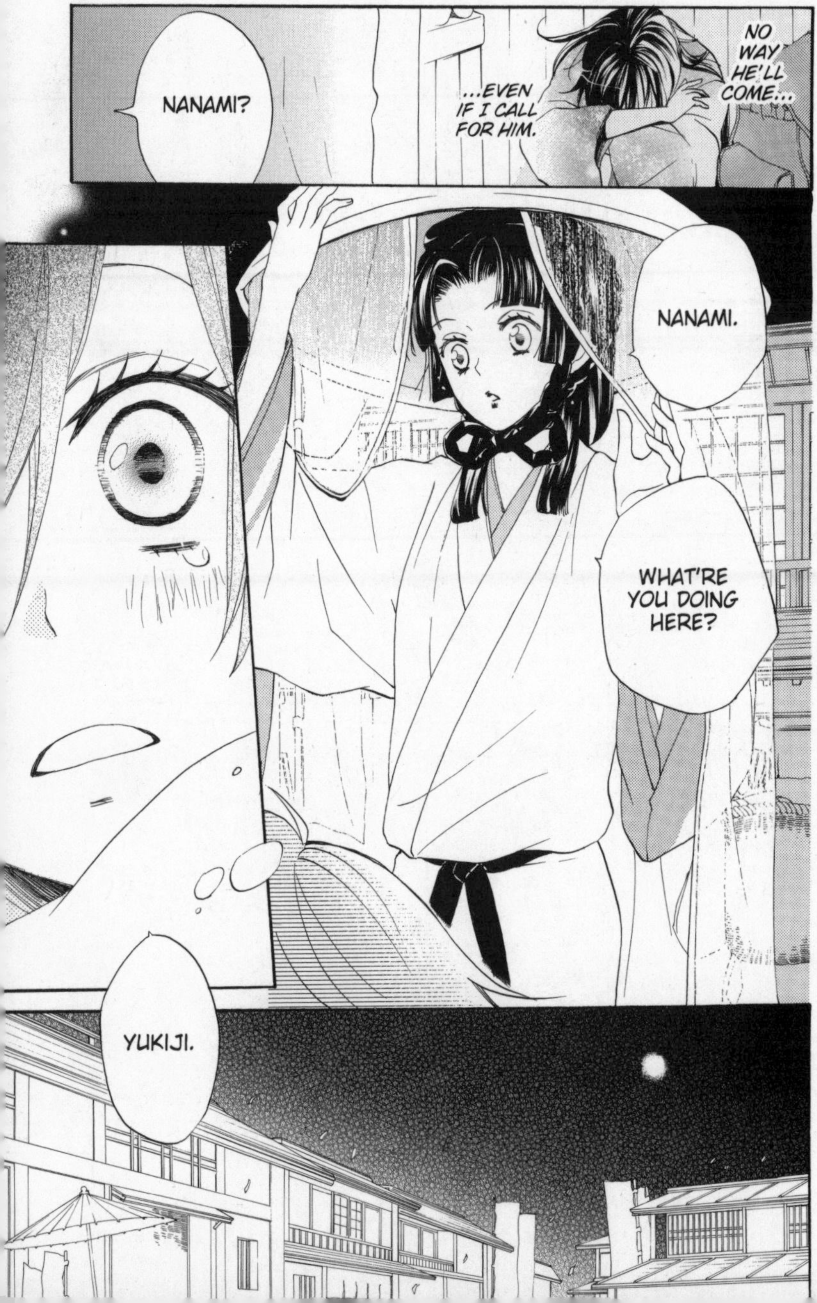
NO WAY HE'LL COME...
...EVEN IF I CALL FOR HIM.
NANAMI?
NANAMI.
WHAT'RE YOU DOING HERE?
YUKIJI.

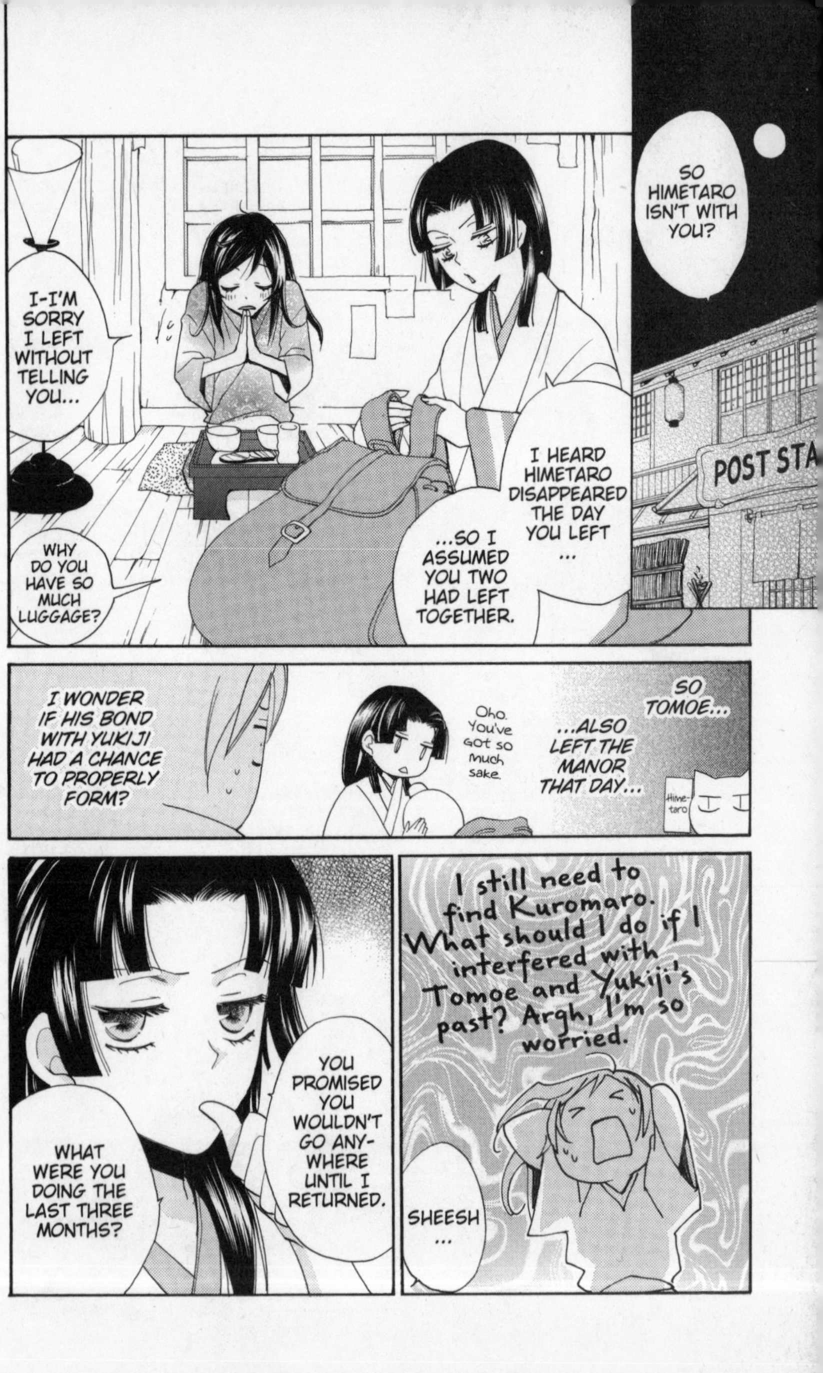
SO HIMETARO ISN'T WITH YOU?
POST STA
I HEARD HIMETARO DISAPPEARED THE DAY YOU LEFT ...
...SO I ASSUMED YOU TWO HAD LEFT TOGETHER.
I-I'M SORRY I LEFT WITHOUT TELLING YOU...
WHY DO YOU HAVE SO MUCH LUGGAGE?
SO TOMOE...
...ALSO LEFT THE MANOR THAT DAY...
Hime-taro
Oho. You've got so much sake.
I WONDER IF HIS BOND WITH YUKIJI HAD A CHANCE TO PROPERLY FORM?
I still need to find Kuromaro. What should I do if I interfered with Tomoe and Yukiji's past? Argh, I'm so worried.
SHEESH ...
YOU PROMISED YOU WOULDN'T GO ANYWHERE UNTIL I RETURNED.
WHAT WERE YOU DOING THE LAST THREE MONTHS?

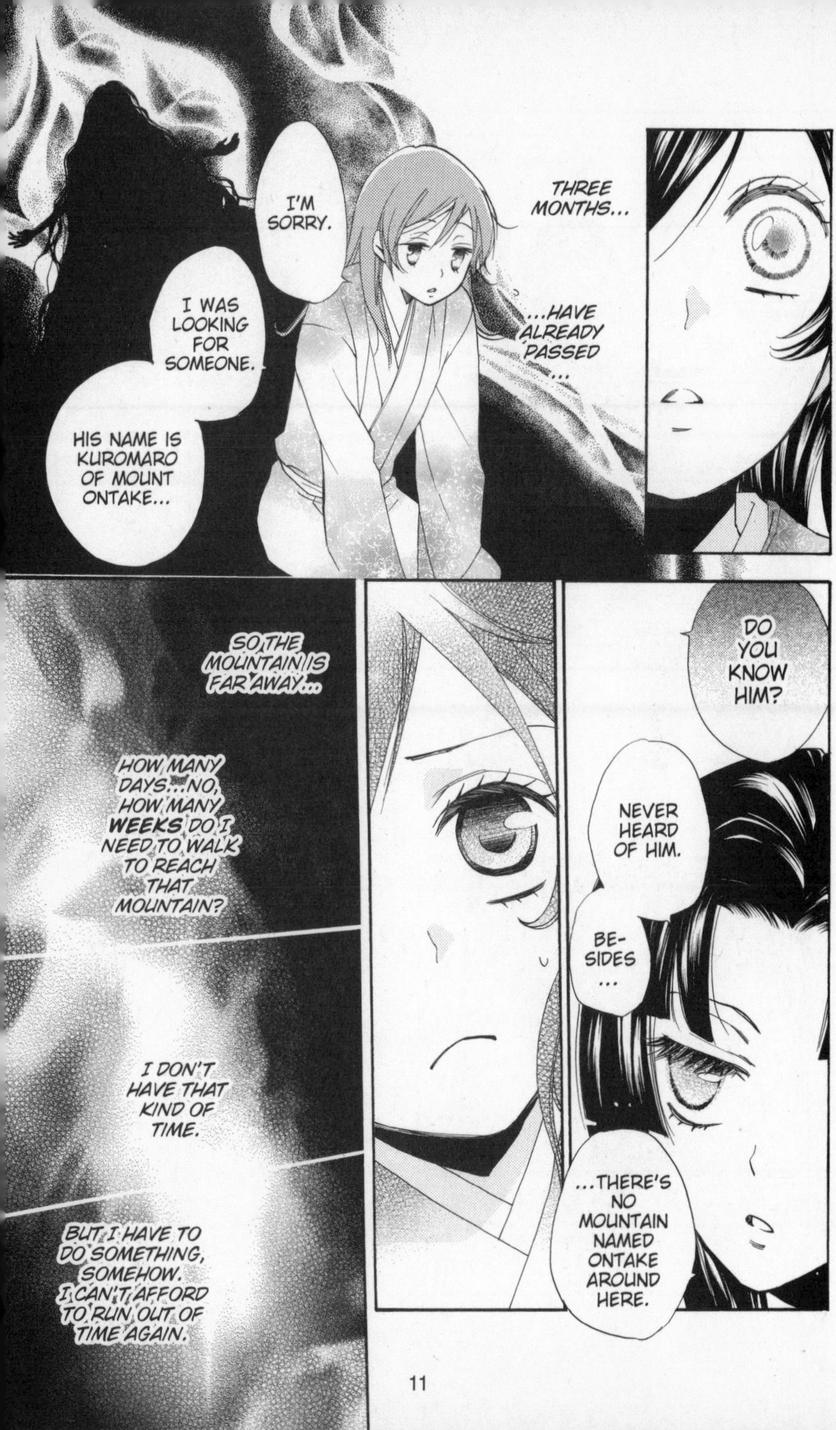
THREE MONTHS...
...HAVE ALREADY PASSED...
I'M SORRY.
I WAS LOOKING FOR SOMEONE.
HIS NAME IS KUROMARO OF MOUNT ONTAKE...
DO YOU KNOW HIM?
NEVER HEARD OF HIM.
BESIDES...
...THERE'S NO MOUNTAIN NAMED ONTAKE AROUND HERE.
SO THE MOUNTAIN IS FAR AWAY...
HOW MANY DAYS...NO, HOW MANY **WEEKS** DO I NEED TO WALK TO REACH THAT MOUNTAIN?
I DON'T HAVE THAT KIND OF TIME.
BUT I HAVE TO DO SOMETHING, SOMEHOW. I CAN'T AFFORD TO RUN OUT OF TIME AGAIN.

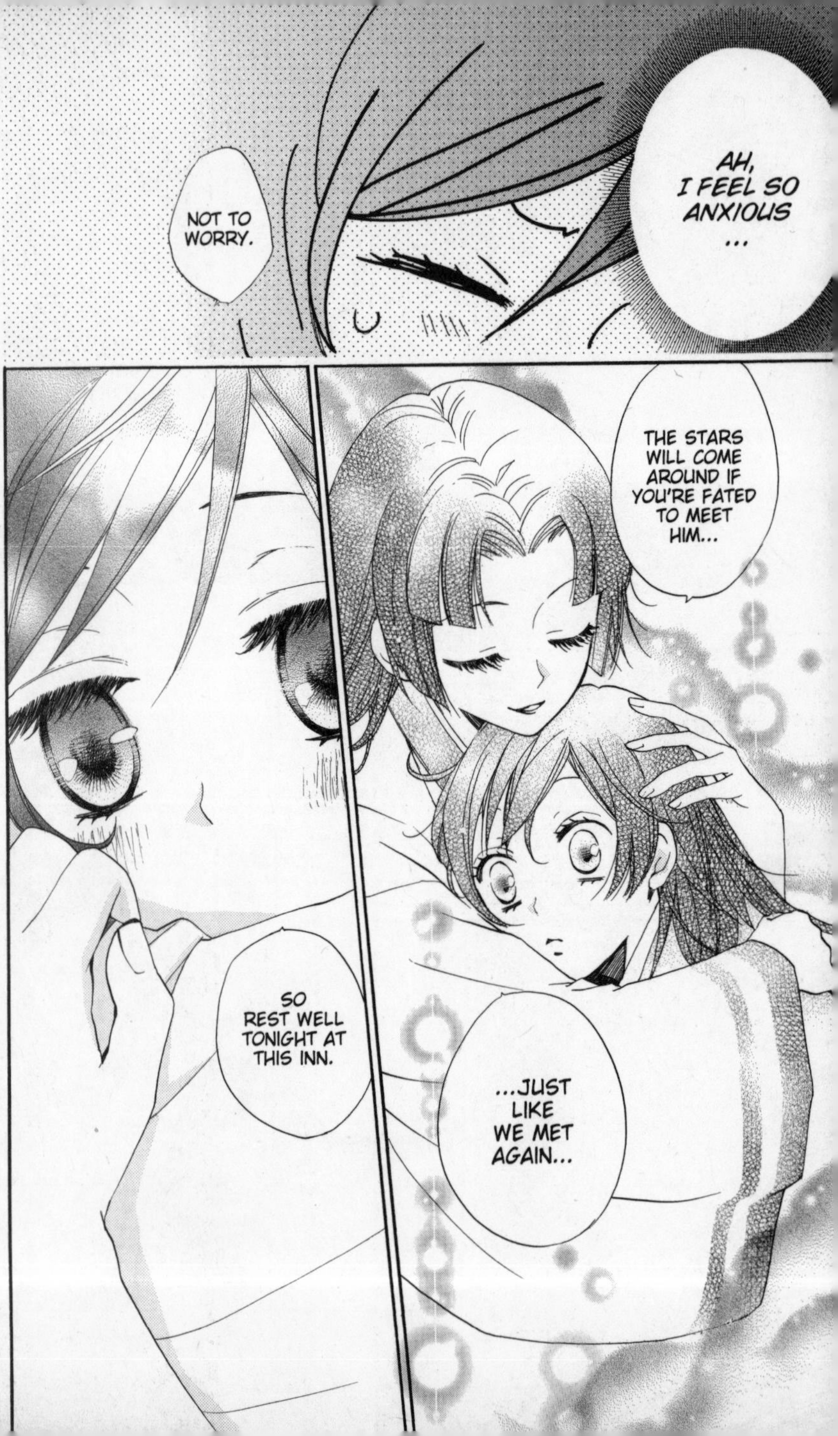
AH, I FEEL SO ANXIOUS ...
NOT TO WORRY.
THE STARS WILL COME AROUND IF YOU'RE FATED TO MEET HIM...
...JUST LIKE WE MET AGAIN...
SO REST WELL TONIGHT AT THIS INN.

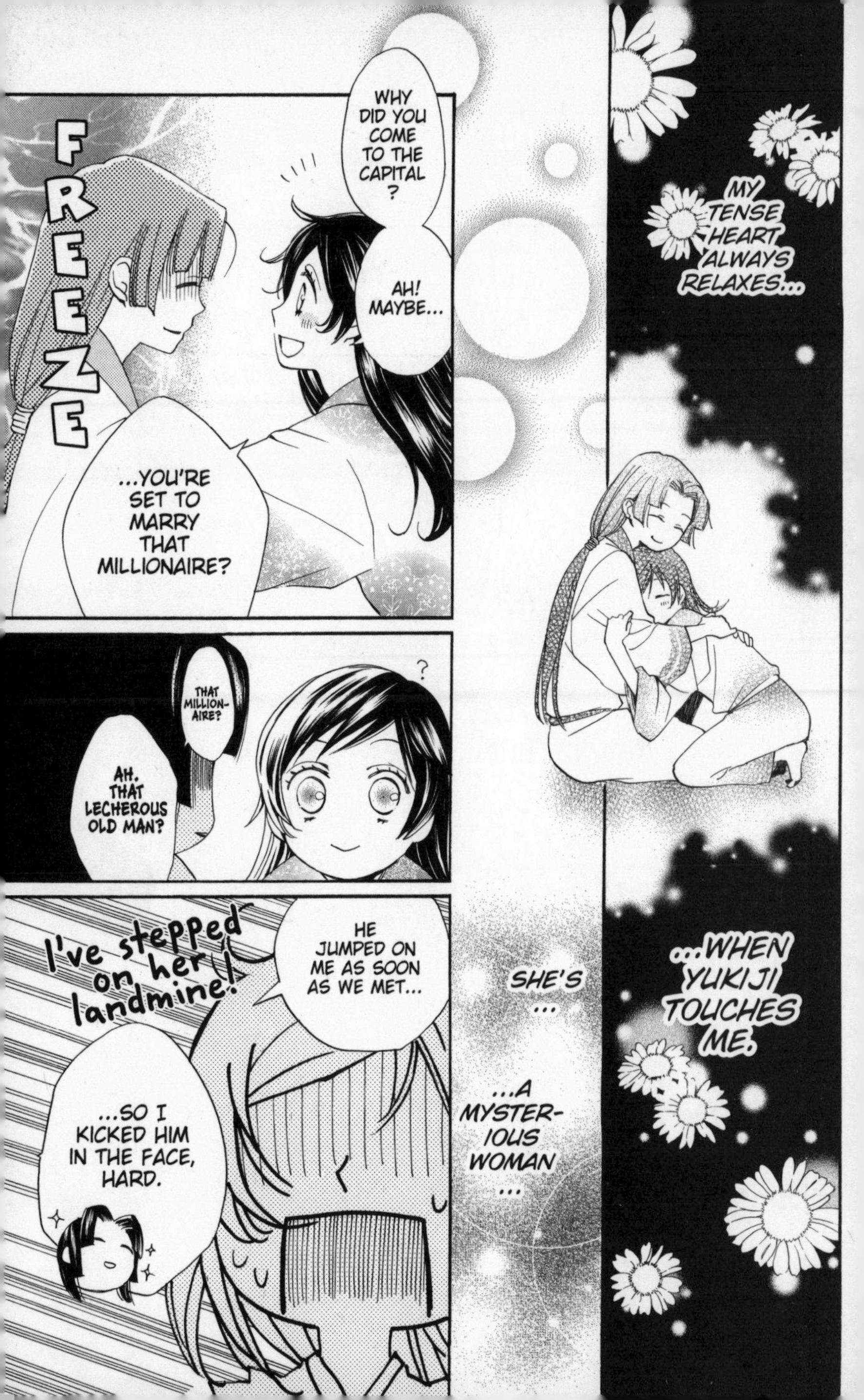
MY TENSE HEART ALWAYS RELAXES...
...WHEN YUKIJI TOUCHES ME.
WHY DID YOU COME TO THE CAPITAL?
AH! MAYBE...
...YOU'RE SET TO MARRY THAT MILLIONAIRE?
FREEZE
THAT MILLIONAIRE?
AH. THAT LECHEROUS OLD MAN?
?
HE JUMPED ON ME AS SOON AS WE MET...
...SO I KICKED HIM IN THE FACE, HARD.
I've stepped on her landmine!
SHE'S...
...A MYSTERIOUS WOMAN...

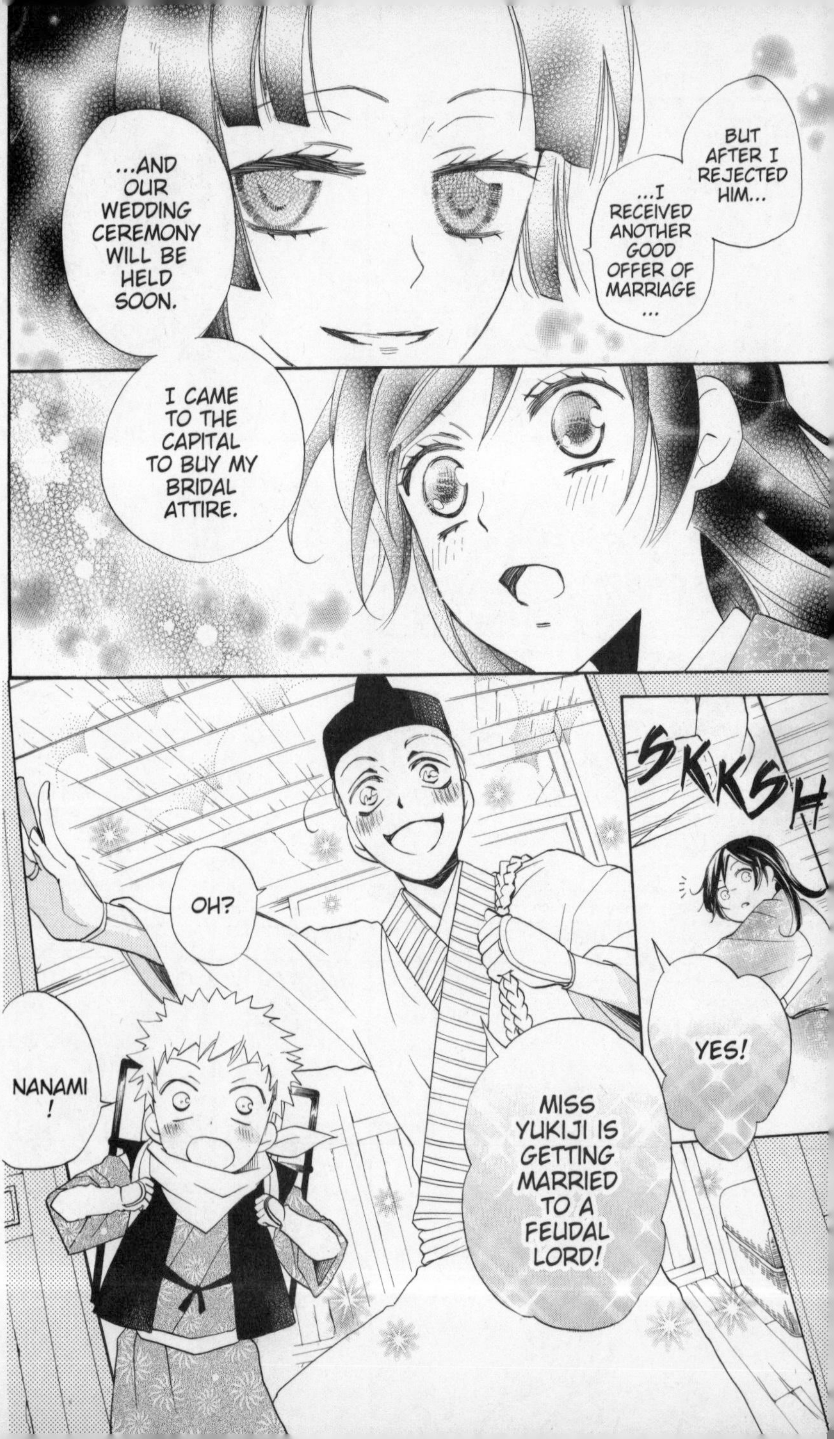
BUT AFTER I REJECTED HIM...
...I RECEIVED ANOTHER GOOD OFFER OF MARRIAGE...
...AND OUR WEDDING CEREMONY WILL BE HELD SOON.
I CAME TO THE CAPITAL TO BUY MY BRIDAL ATTIRE.
SKKSH
YES!
OH?
MISS YUKIJI IS GETTING MARRIED TO A FEUDAL LORD!
NANAMI!

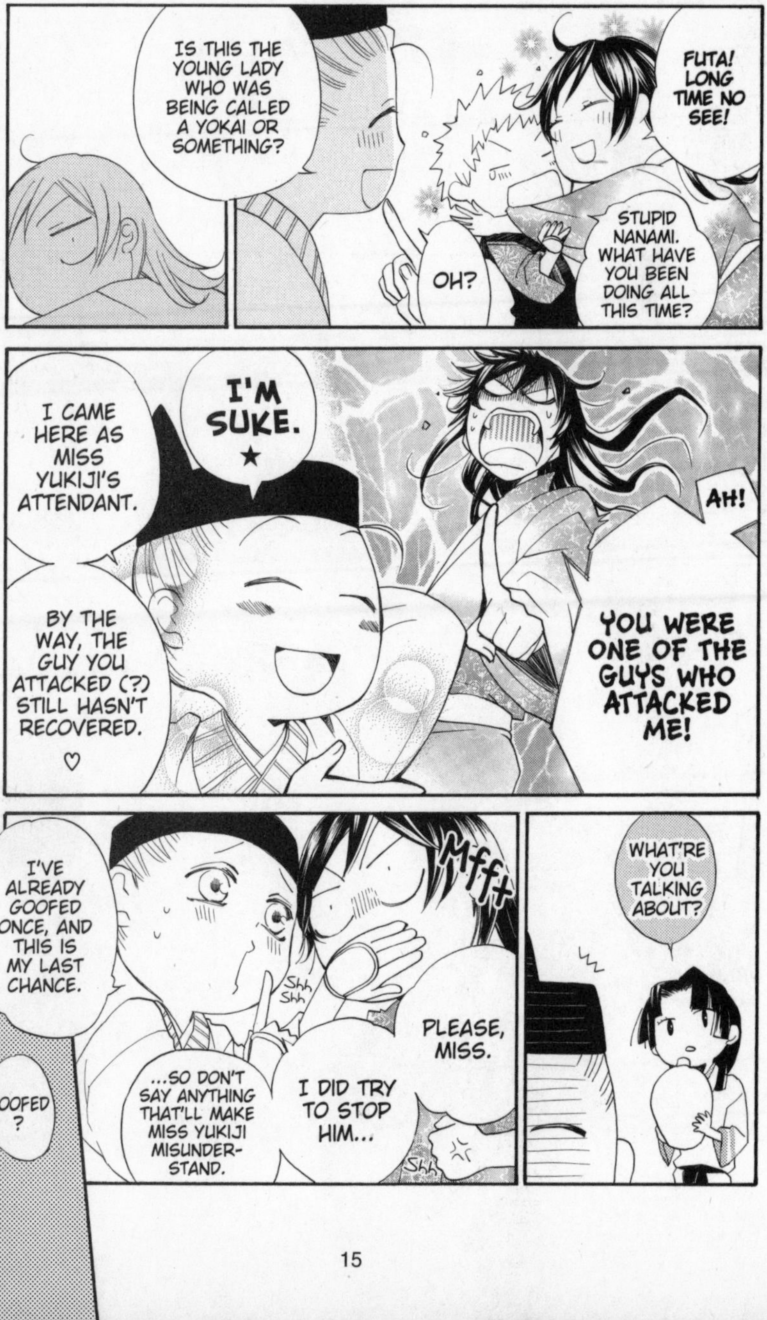
FUTA! LONG TIME NO SEE!
STUPID NANAMI. WHAT HAVE YOU BEEN DOING ALL THIS TIME?
OH?
IS THIS THE YOUNG LADY WHO WAS BEING CALLED A YOKAI OR SOMETHING?
AH!
YOU WERE ONE OF THE GUYS WHO ATTACKED ME!
I'M SUKE. ★
I CAME HERE AS MISS YUKIJI'S ATTENDANT.
BY THE WAY, THE GUY YOU ATTACKED (?) STILL HASN'T RECOVERED. ♡
WHAT'RE YOU TALKING ABOUT?
Mfft
I'VE ALREADY GOOFED ONCE, AND THIS IS MY LAST CHANCE.
Shh Shh
PLEASE, MISS.
I DID TRY TO STOP HIM...
...SO DON'T SAY ANYTHING THAT'LL MAKE MISS YUKIJI MISUNDER-STAND.
Shh
GOOFED?

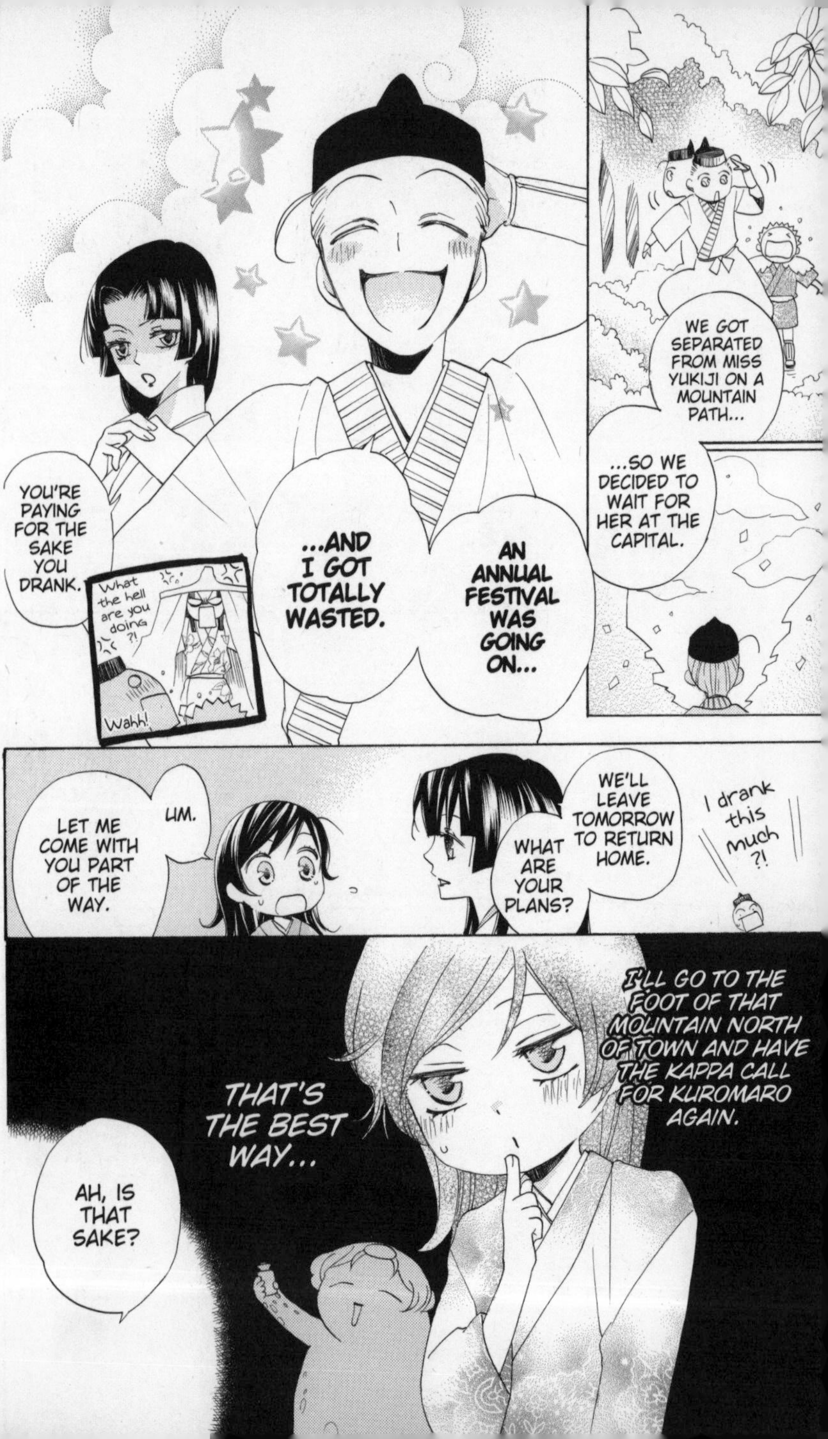

WE GOT SEPARATED FROM MISS YUKIJI ON A MOUNTAIN PATH...
...SO WE DECIDED TO WAIT FOR HER AT THE CAPITAL.
AN ANNUAL FESTIVAL WAS GOING ON...
...AND I GOT TOTALLY WASTED.
What the hell are you doing?!
Wahh!
YOU'RE PAYING FOR THE SAKE YOU DRANK.
I drank this much?!
WE'LL LEAVE TOMORROW TO RETURN HOME.
WHAT ARE YOUR PLANS?
UM.
LET ME COME WITH YOU PART OF THE WAY.
I'LL GO TO THE FOOT OF THAT MOUNTAIN NORTH OF TOWN AND HAVE THE KAPPA CALL FOR KUROMARO AGAIN.
THAT'S THE BEST WAY...
AH, IS THAT SAKE?

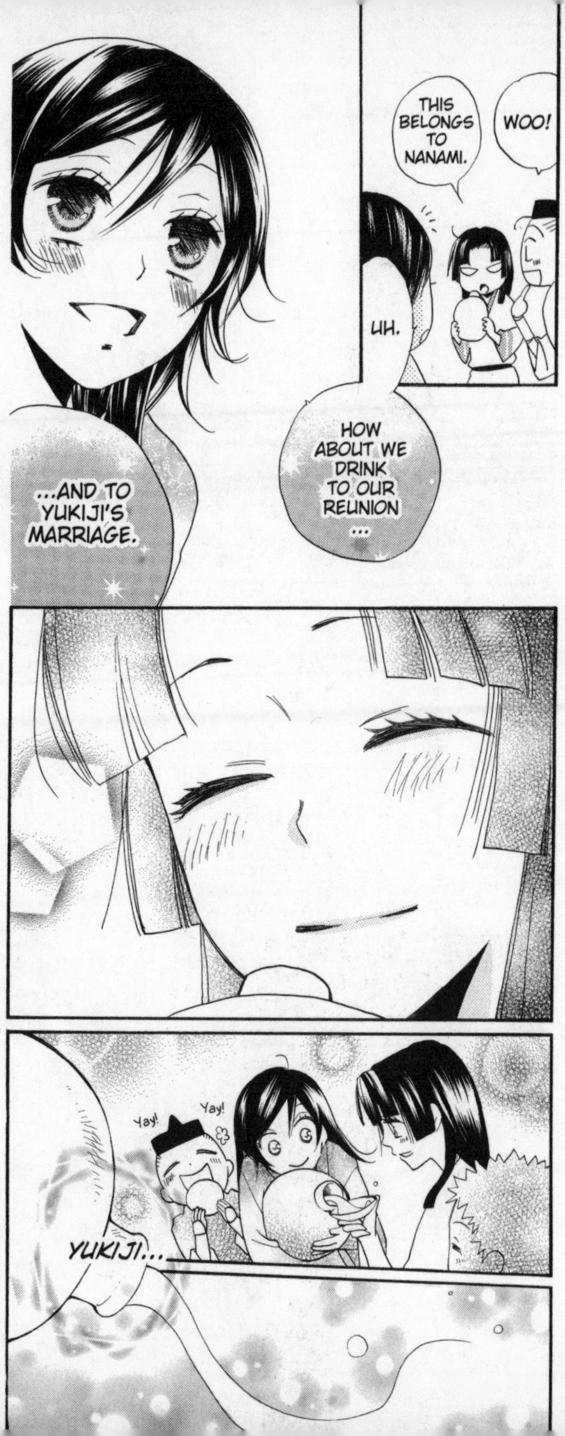
WOO!
THIS BELONGS TO NANAMI.
UH.
HOW ABOUT WE DRINK TO OUR REUNION ...
...AND TO YUKIJI'S MARRIAGE.
Yay!
Yay!
YUKIJI...

Thank you for picking up volume 16 of Kamisama Kiss!

This is the third tankobon set in the past. The next volume will finish off the past arc.

I'll be happy if you follow the story.

And I hope you'll enjoy volume 16...

Th-thump th-thump th-thump

See you later then!

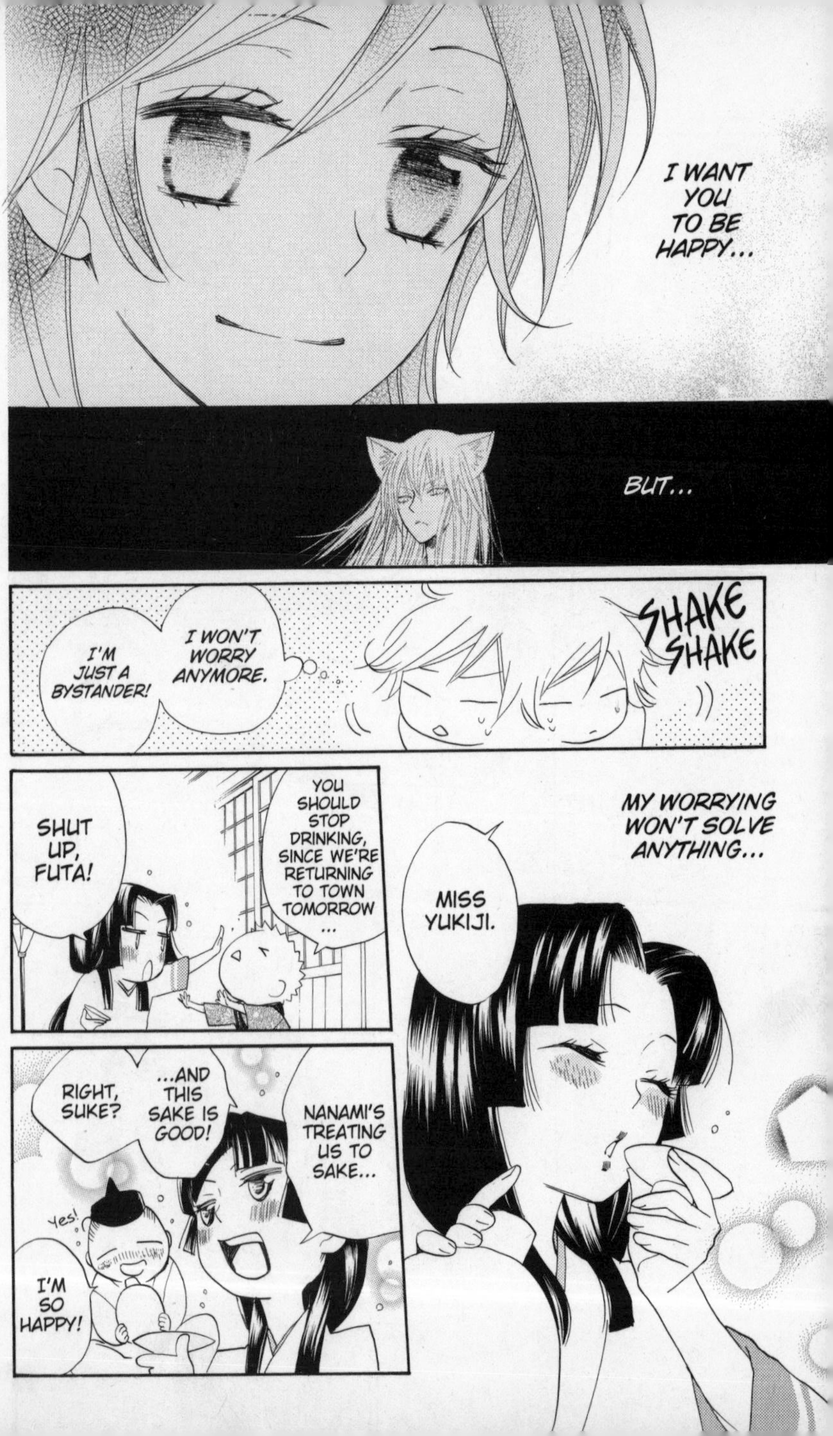
I WANT YOU TO BE HAPPY...
BUT...
SHAKE SHAKE
I WON'T WORRY ANYMORE.
I'M JUST A BYSTANDER!
MY WORRYING WON'T SOLVE ANYTHING...
MISS YUKIJI.
YOU SHOULD STOP DRINKING, SINCE WE'RE RETURNING TO TOWN TOMORROW ...
SHUT UP, FUTA!
NANAMI'S TREATING US TO SAKE...
...AND THIS SAKE IS GOOD!
RIGHT, SUKE?
Yes!
I'M SO HAPPY!

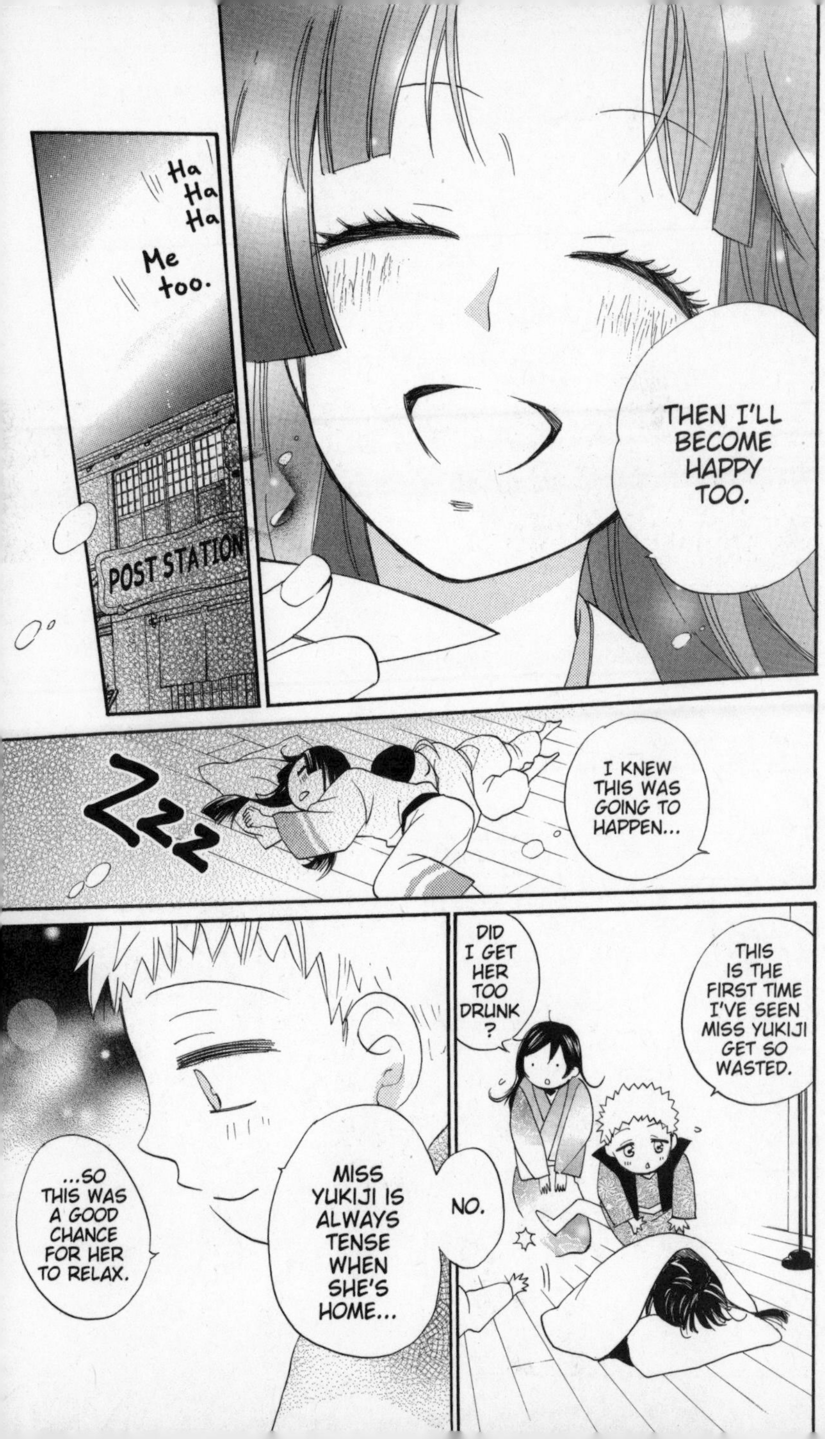
THEN I'LL BECOME HAPPY TOO.
Ha Ha Ha
Me too.
POST STATION
I KNEW THIS WAS GOING TO HAPPEN...
Zzz
THIS IS THE FIRST TIME I'VE SEEN MISS YUKIJI GET SO WASTED.
DID I GET HER TOO DRUNK?
NO.
MISS YUKIJI IS ALWAYS TENSE WHEN SHE'S HOME...
...SO THIS WAS A GOOD CHANCE FOR HER TO RELAX.

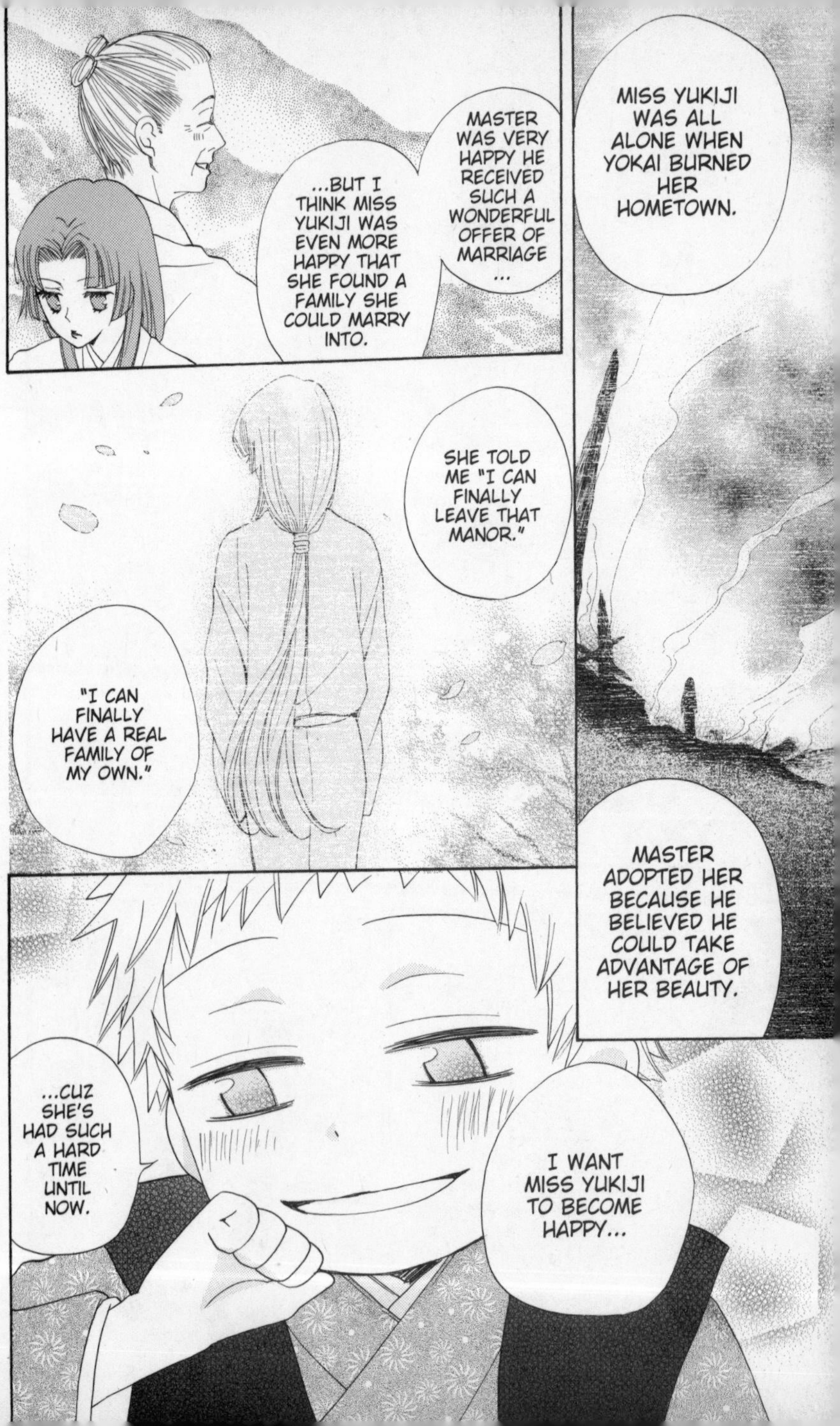
MISS YUKIJI WAS ALL ALONE WHEN YOKAI BURNED HER HOMETOWN.
MASTER ADOPTED HER BECAUSE HE BELIEVED HE COULD TAKE ADVANTAGE OF HER BEAUTY.
MASTER WAS VERY HAPPY HE RECEIVED SUCH A WONDERFUL OFFER OF MARRIAGE ...
...BUT I THINK MISS YUKIJI WAS EVEN MORE HAPPY THAT SHE FOUND A FAMILY SHE COULD MARRY INTO.
SHE TOLD ME "I CAN FINALLY LEAVE THAT MANOR."
"I CAN FINALLY HAVE A REAL FAMILY OF MY OWN."
I WANT MISS YUKIJI TO BECOME HAPPY...
...CUZ SHE'S HAD SUCH A HARD TIME UNTIL NOW.

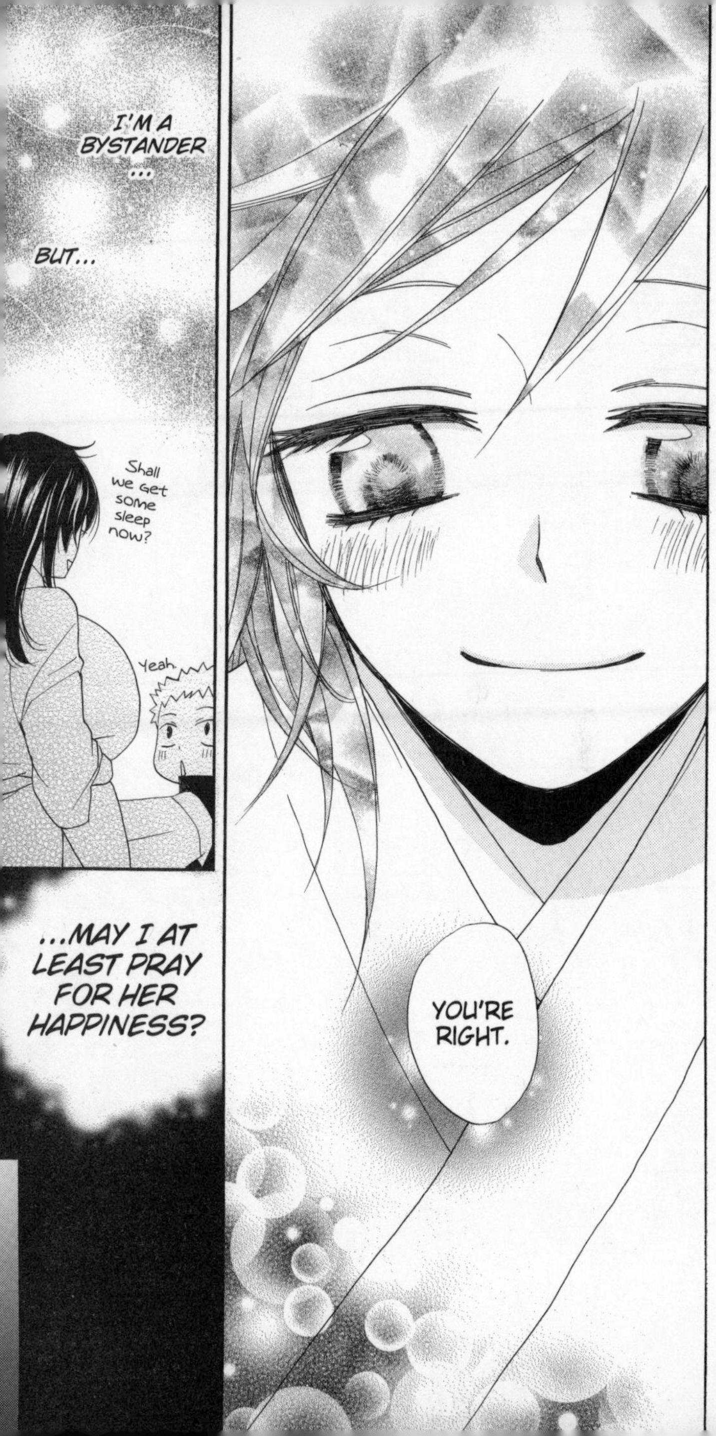

YOU'RE RIGHT.
I'M A BYSTANDER ...
BUT...
Shall we get some sleep now?
Yeah.
...MAY I AT LEAST PRAY FOR HER HAPPINESS?

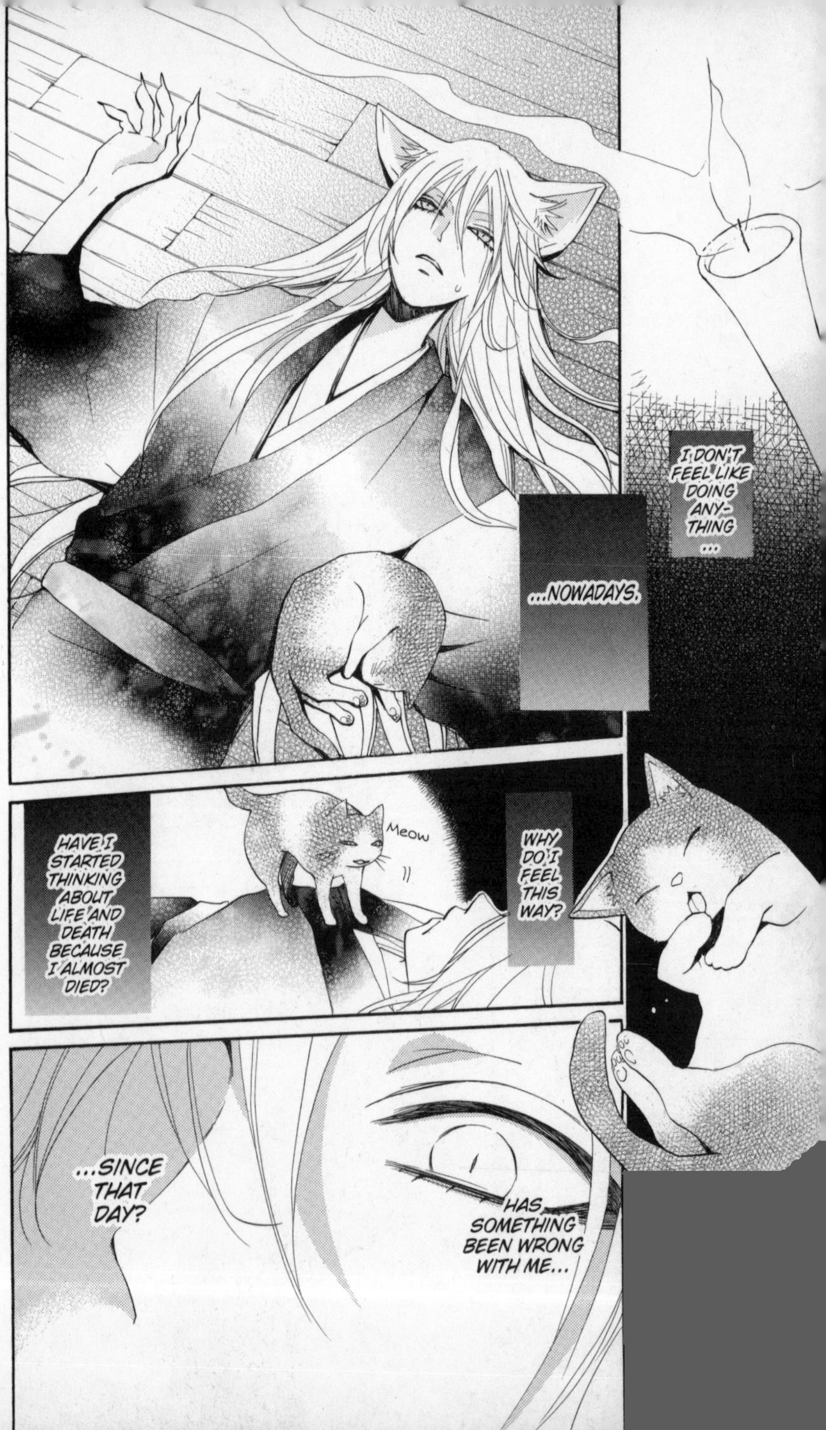
I DON'T FEEL LIKE DOING ANYTHING...
...NOWADAYS.
WHY DO I FEEL THIS WAY?
Meow
HAVE I STARTED THINKING ABOUT LIFE AND DEATH BECAUSE I ALMOST DIED?
HAS SOMETHING BEEN WRONG WITH ME...
...SINCE THAT DAY?

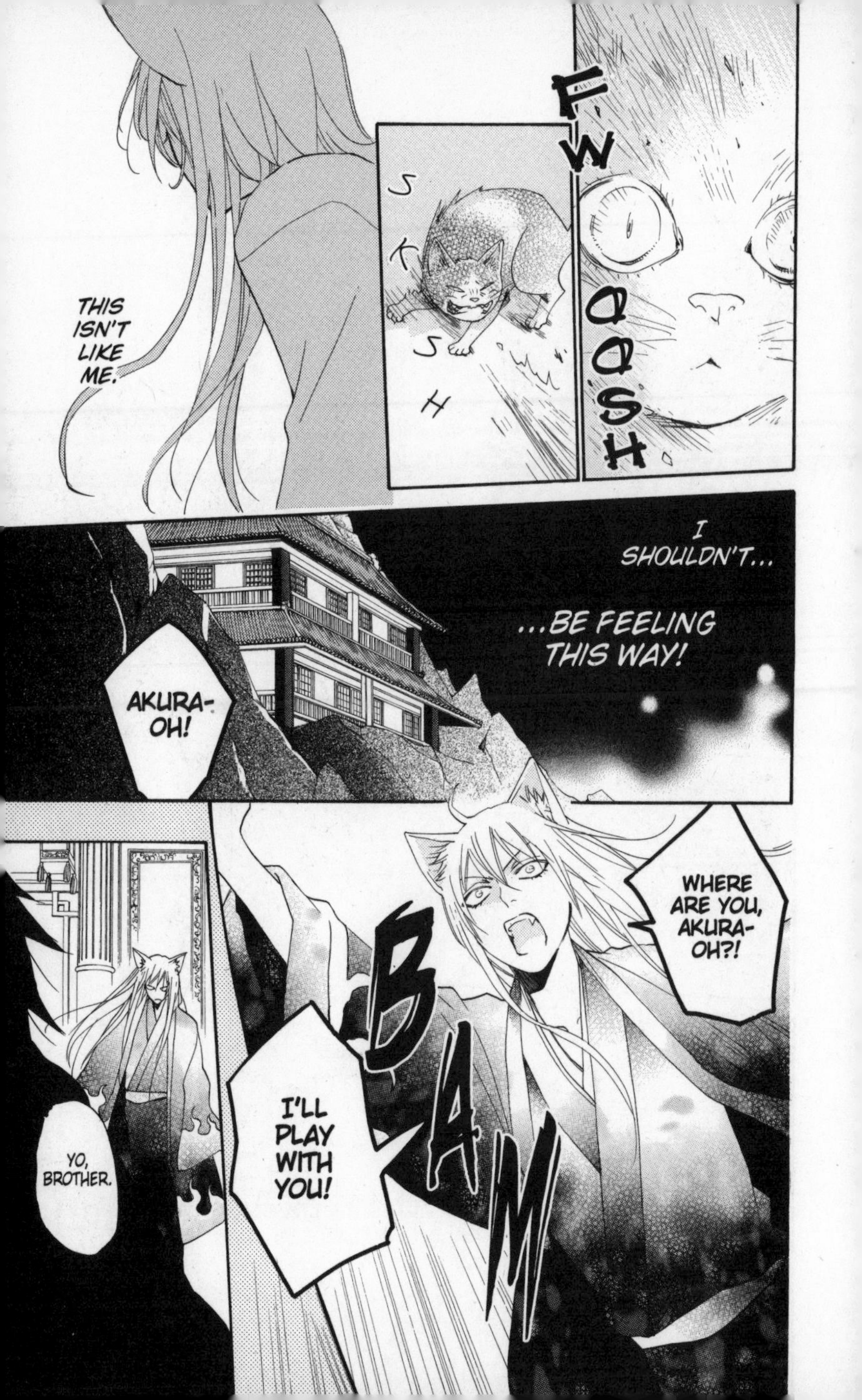
FWOOSH
SKSH
THIS ISN'T LIKE ME.
I SHOULDN'T...
...BE FEELING THIS WAY!
AKURA-OH!
WHERE ARE YOU, AKURA-OH?!
BAM
I'LL PLAY WITH YOU!
YO, BROTHER.

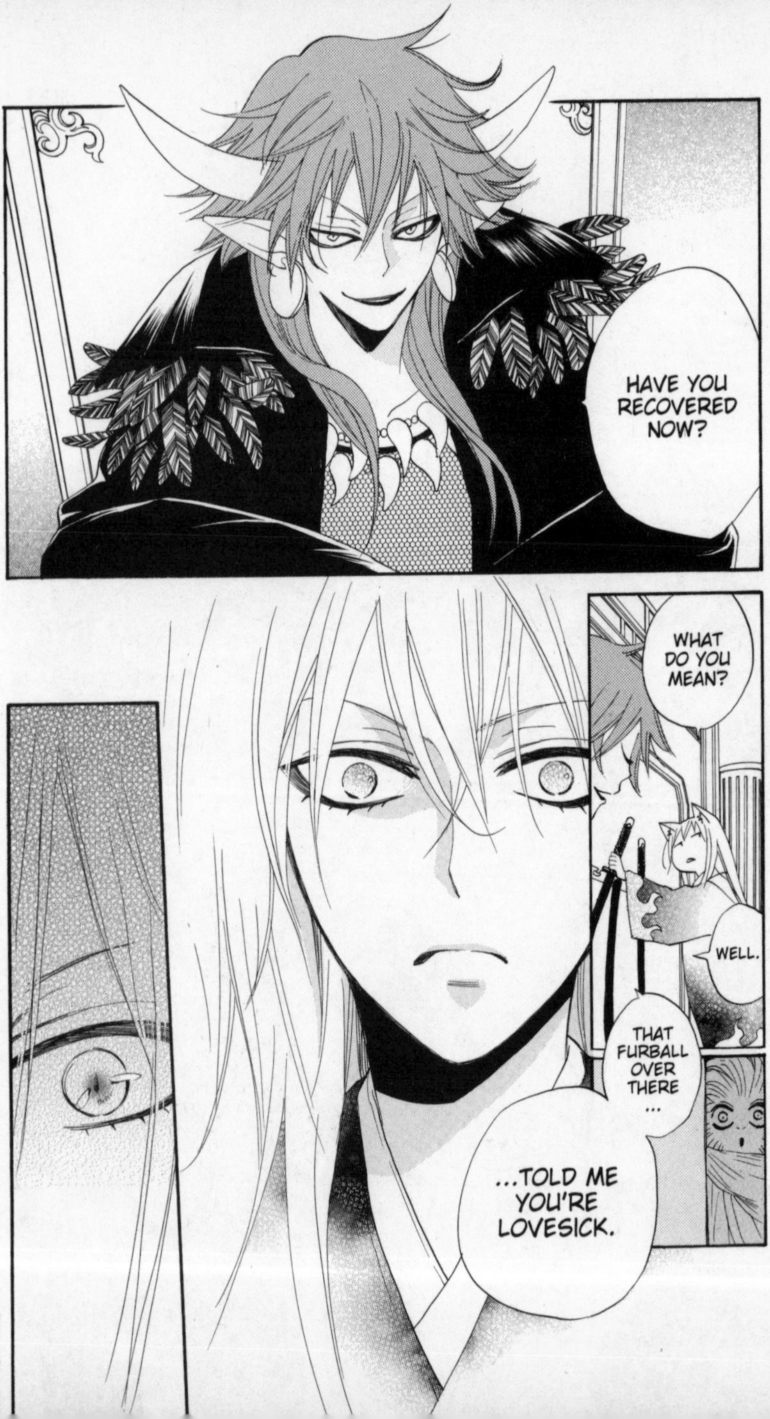
HAVE YOU RECOVERED NOW?
WHAT DO YOU MEAN?
WELL.
THAT FURBALL OVER THERE...
...TOLD ME YOU'RE LOVESICK.

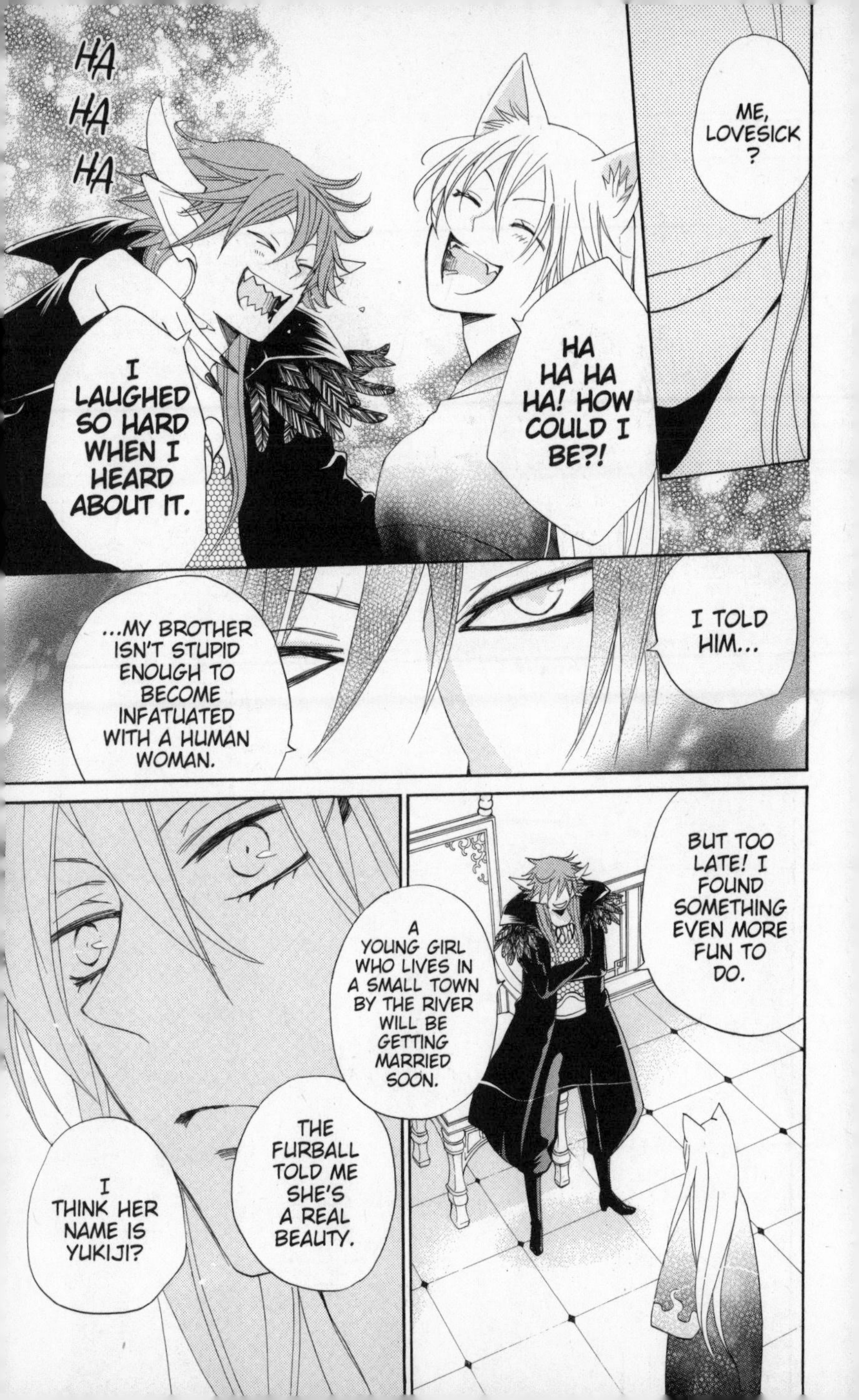
ME, LOVESICK?
HA HA HA HA! HOW COULD I BE?!
HA HA HA
I LAUGHED SO HARD WHEN I HEARD ABOUT IT.
I TOLD HIM...
...MY BROTHER ISN'T STUPID ENOUGH TO BECOME INFATUATED WITH A HUMAN WOMAN.
BUT TOO LATE! I FOUND SOMETHING EVEN MORE FUN TO DO.
A YOUNG GIRL WHO LIVES IN A SMALL TOWN BY THE RIVER WILL BE GETTING MARRIED SOON.
THE FURBALL TOLD ME SHE'S A REAL BEAUTY.
I THINK HER NAME IS YUKIJI?

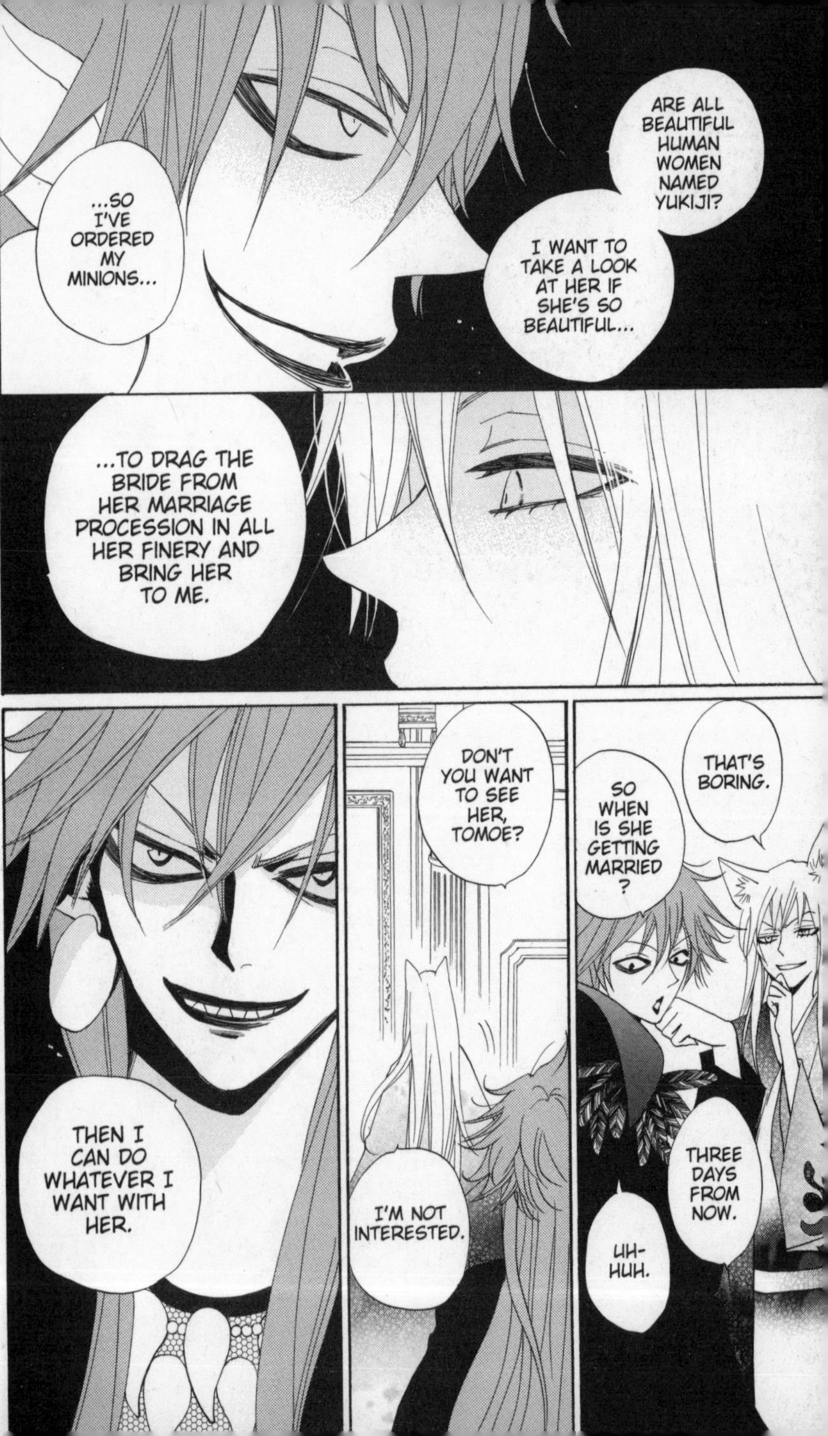
ARE ALL BEAUTIFUL HUMAN WOMEN NAMED YUKIJI?
I WANT TO TAKE A LOOK AT HER IF SHE'S SO BEAUTIFUL...
...SO I'VE ORDERED MY MINIONS...
...TO DRAG THE BRIDE FROM HER MARRIAGE PROCESSION IN ALL HER FINERY AND BRING HER TO ME.
THAT'S BORING.
SO WHEN IS SHE GETTING MARRIED?
THREE DAYS FROM NOW.
UH-HUH.
DON'T YOU WANT TO SEE HER, TOMOE?
I'M NOT INTERESTED.
THEN I CAN DO WHATEVER I WANT WITH HER.

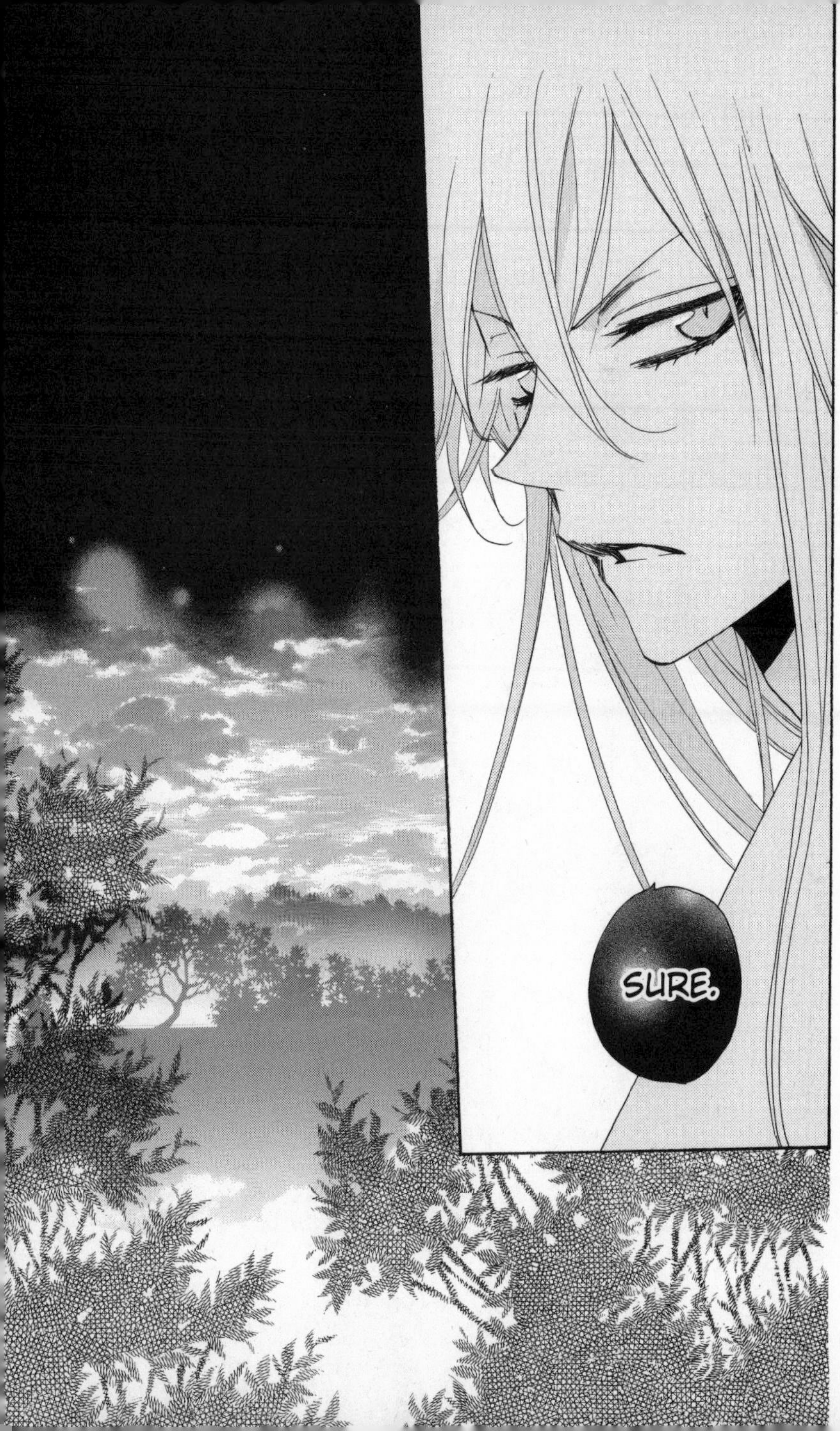
SURE.

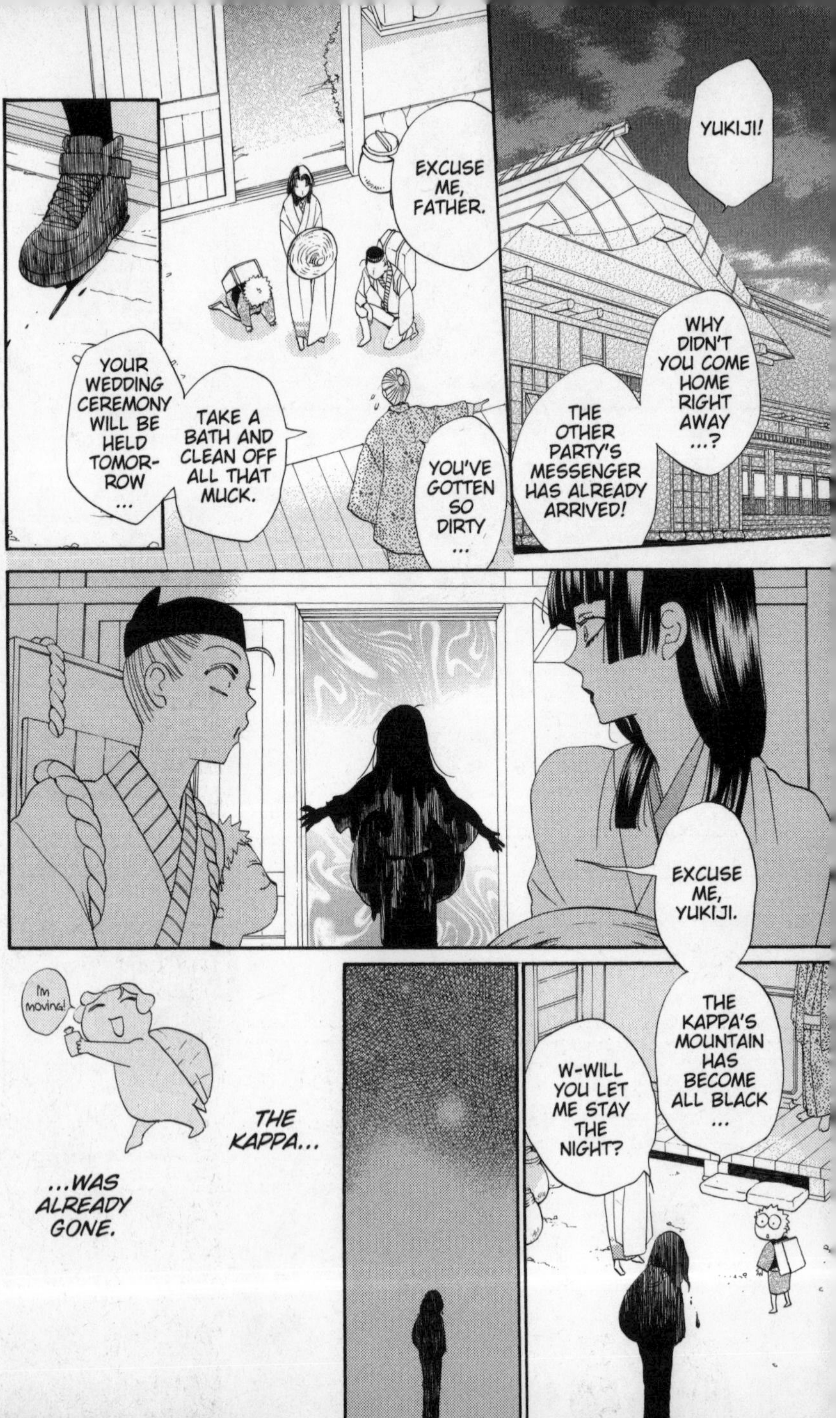
YUKIJI!
WHY DIDN'T YOU COME HOME RIGHT AWAY ...?
THE OTHER PARTY'S MESSENGER HAS ALREADY ARRIVED!
EXCUSE ME, FATHER.
YOU'VE GOTTEN SO DIRTY ...
TAKE A BATH AND CLEAN OFF ALL THAT MUCK.
YOUR WEDDING CEREMONY WILL BE HELD TOMORROW ...
EXCUSE ME, YUKIJI.
THE KAPPA'S MOUNTAIN HAS BECOME ALL BLACK ...
W-WILL YOU LET ME STAY THE NIGHT?
THE KAPPA...
...WAS ALREADY GONE.
I'm moving!

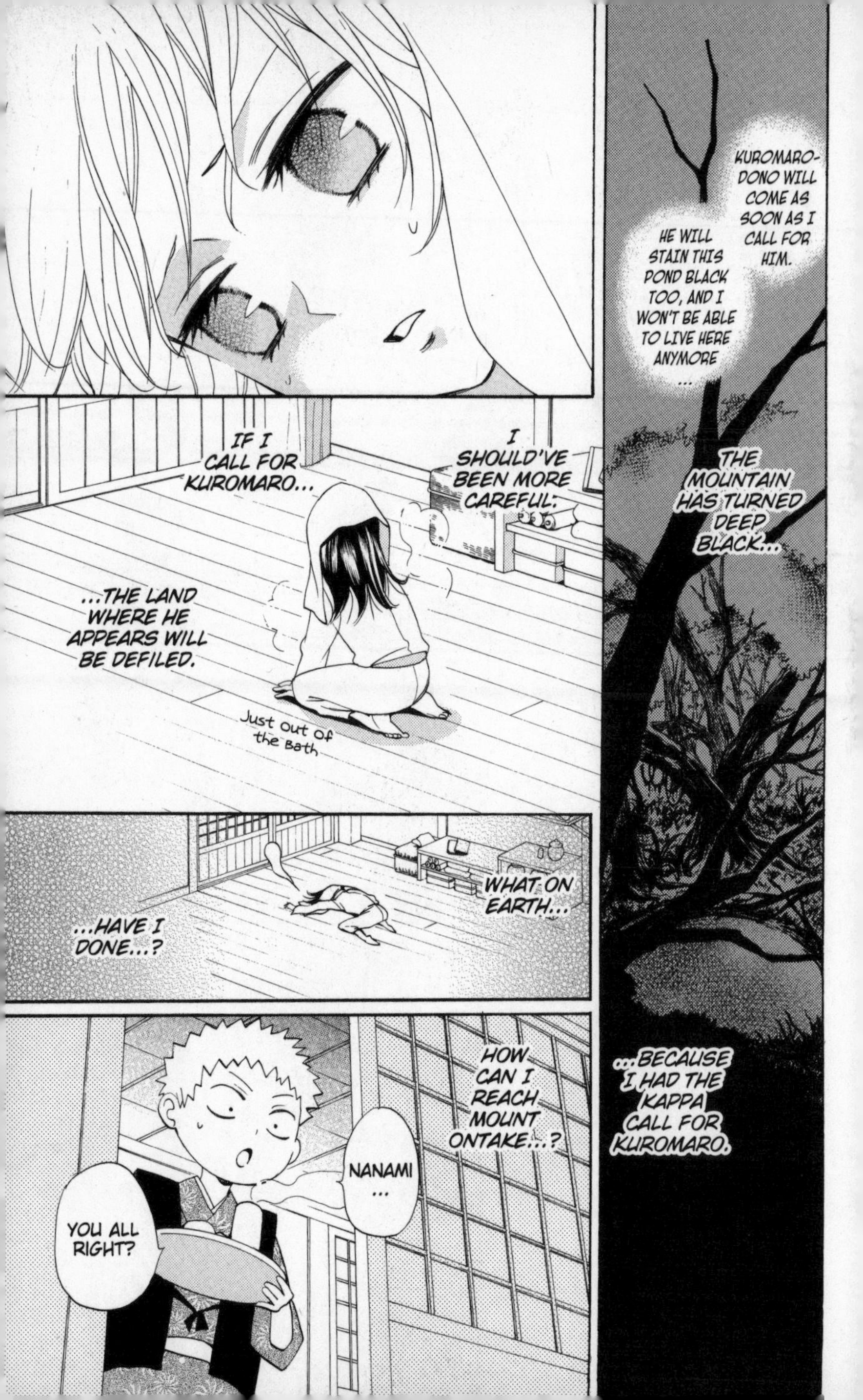
KUROMARO-DONO WILL COME AS SOON AS I CALL FOR HIM.
HE WILL STAIN THIS POND BLACK TOO, AND I WON'T BE ABLE TO LIVE HERE ANYMORE...
THE MOUNTAIN HAS TURNED DEEP BLACK...
...BECAUSE I HAD THE KAPPA CALL FOR KUROMARO.
I SHOULD'VE BEEN MORE CAREFUL.
IF I CALL FOR KUROMARO...
...THE LAND WHERE HE APPEARS WILL BE DEFILED.
Just out of the Bath
WHAT ON EARTH...
...HAVE I DONE...?
HOW CAN I REACH MOUNT ONTAKE...?
NANAMI...
YOU ALL RIGHT?

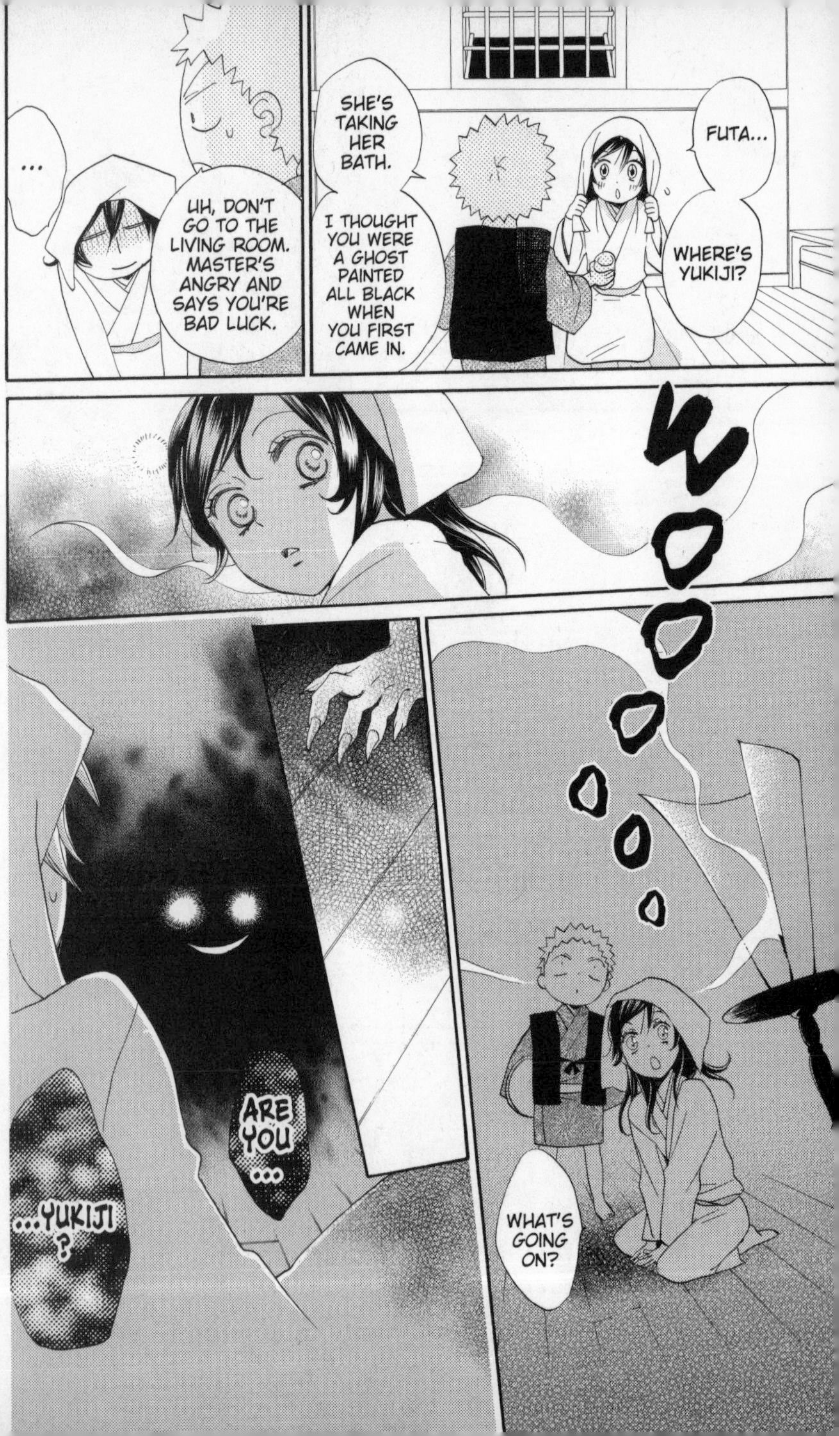
FUTA...
WHERE'S YUKIJI?
SHE'S TAKING HER BATH.
I THOUGHT YOU WERE A GHOST PAINTED ALL BLACK WHEN YOU FIRST CAME IN.
UH, DON'T GO TO THE LIVING ROOM. MASTER'S ANGRY AND SAYS YOU'RE BAD LUCK.
...
WOOOOOOOO
WHAT'S GOING ON?
ARE YOU...
...YUKIJI?

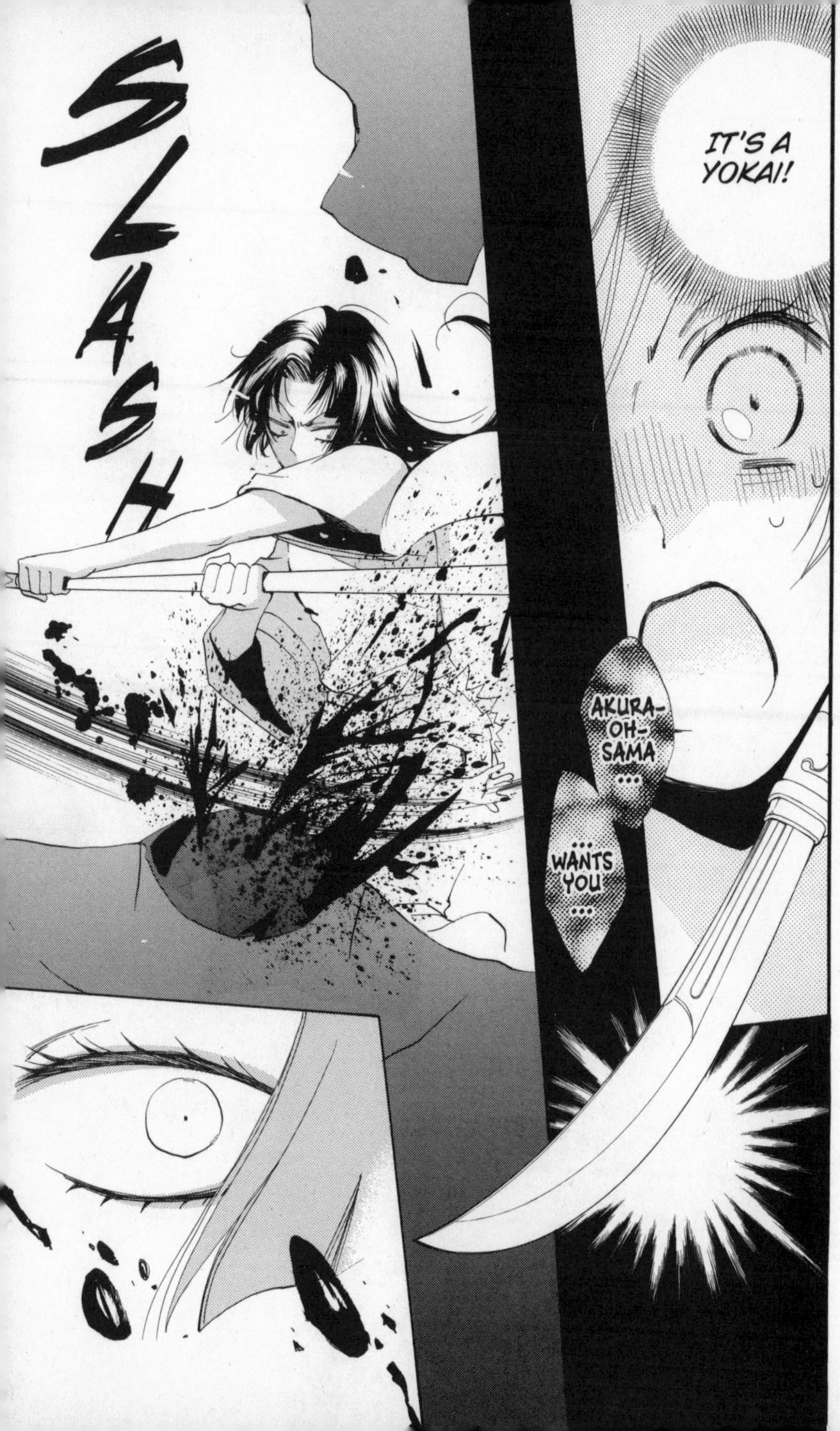
IT'S A YOKAI!
AKURA-OH-SAMA...
...WANTS YOU...
SLASH

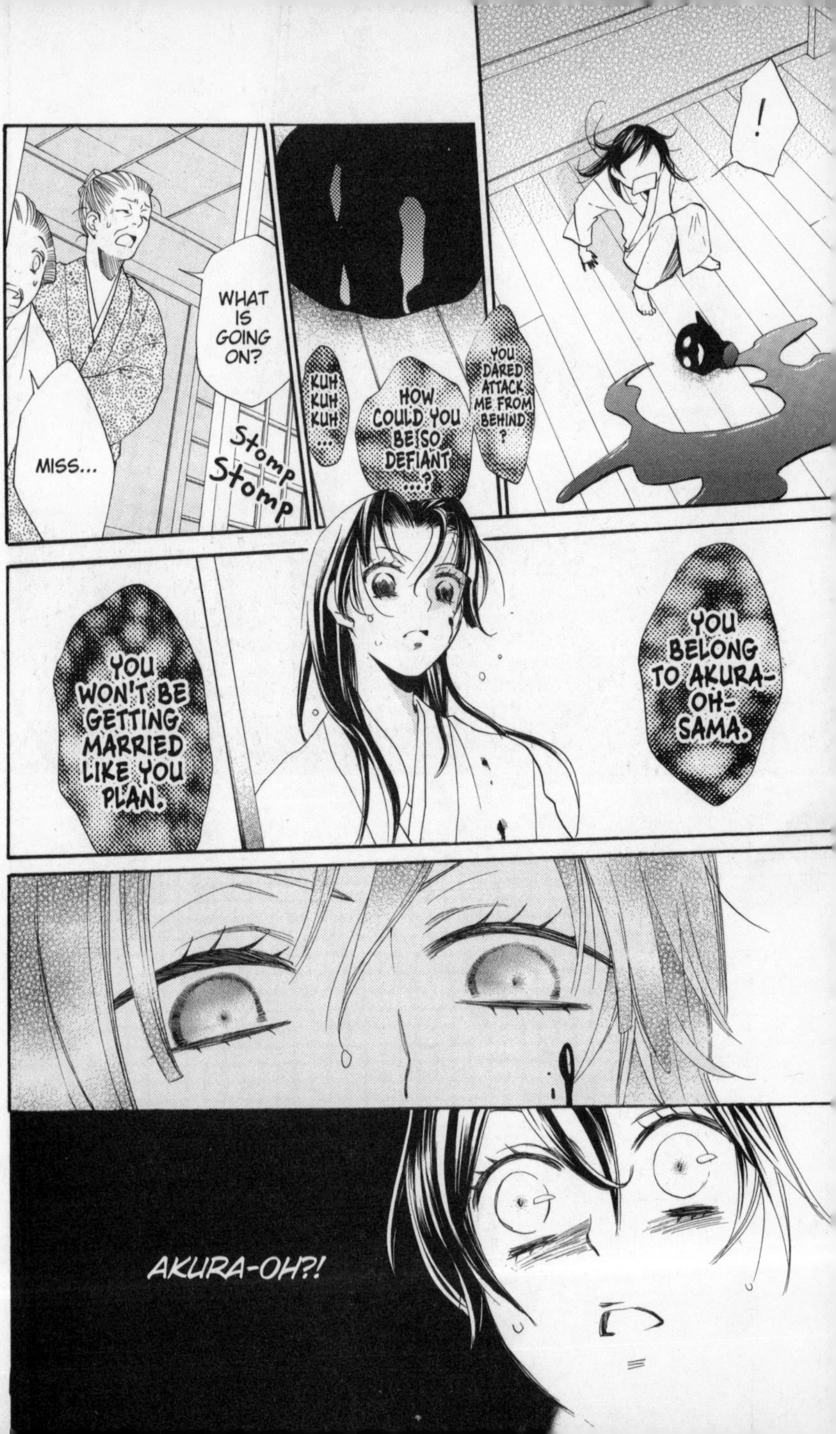
!
YOU DARED ATTACK ME FROM BEHIND?
HOW COULD YOU BE SO DEFIANT...?
KUH KUH KUH...
WHAT IS GOING ON?
Stomp Stomp
MISS...
YOU BELONG TO AKURA-OH-SAMA.
YOU WON'T BE GETTING MARRIED LIKE YOU PLAN.
AKURA-OH?!

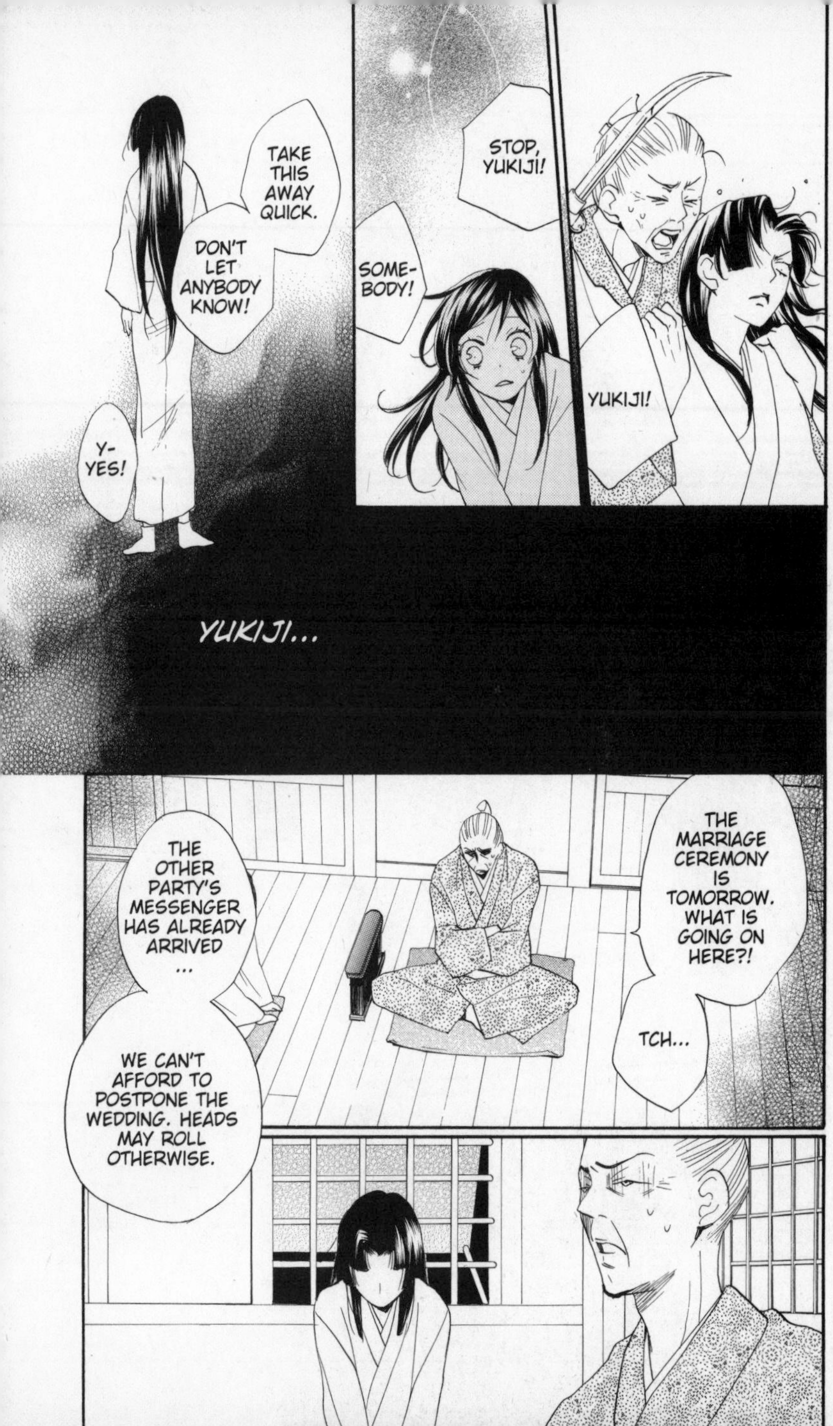
STOP, YUKIJI!
SOME-BODY!
YUKIJI!
TAKE THIS AWAY QUICK.
DON'T LET ANYBODY KNOW!
Y-YES!
YUKIJI...
THE MARRIAGE CEREMONY IS TOMORROW. WHAT IS GOING ON HERE?!
TCH...
THE OTHER PARTY'S MESSENGER HAS ALREADY ARRIVED...
WE CAN'T AFFORD TO POSTPONE THE WEDDING. HEADS MAY ROLL OTHERWISE.

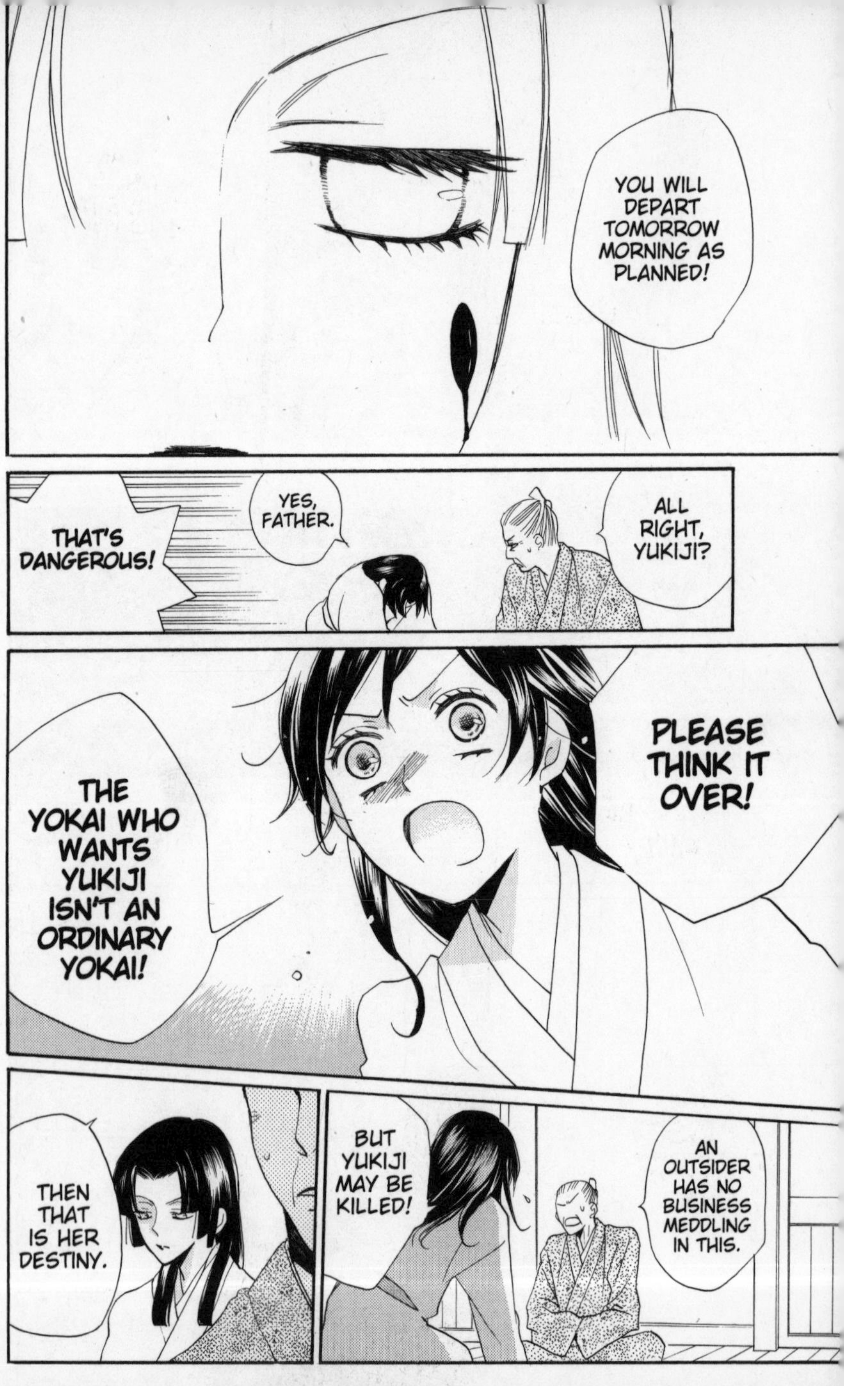
YOU WILL DEPART TOMORROW MORNING AS PLANNED!
ALL RIGHT, YUKIJI?
YES, FATHER.
THAT'S DANGEROUS!
PLEASE THINK IT OVER!
THE YOKAI WHO WANTS YUKIJI ISN'T AN ORDINARY YOKAI!
AN OUTSIDER HAS NO BUSINESS MEDDLING IN THIS.
BUT YUKIJI MAY BE KILLED!
THEN THAT IS HER DESTINY.

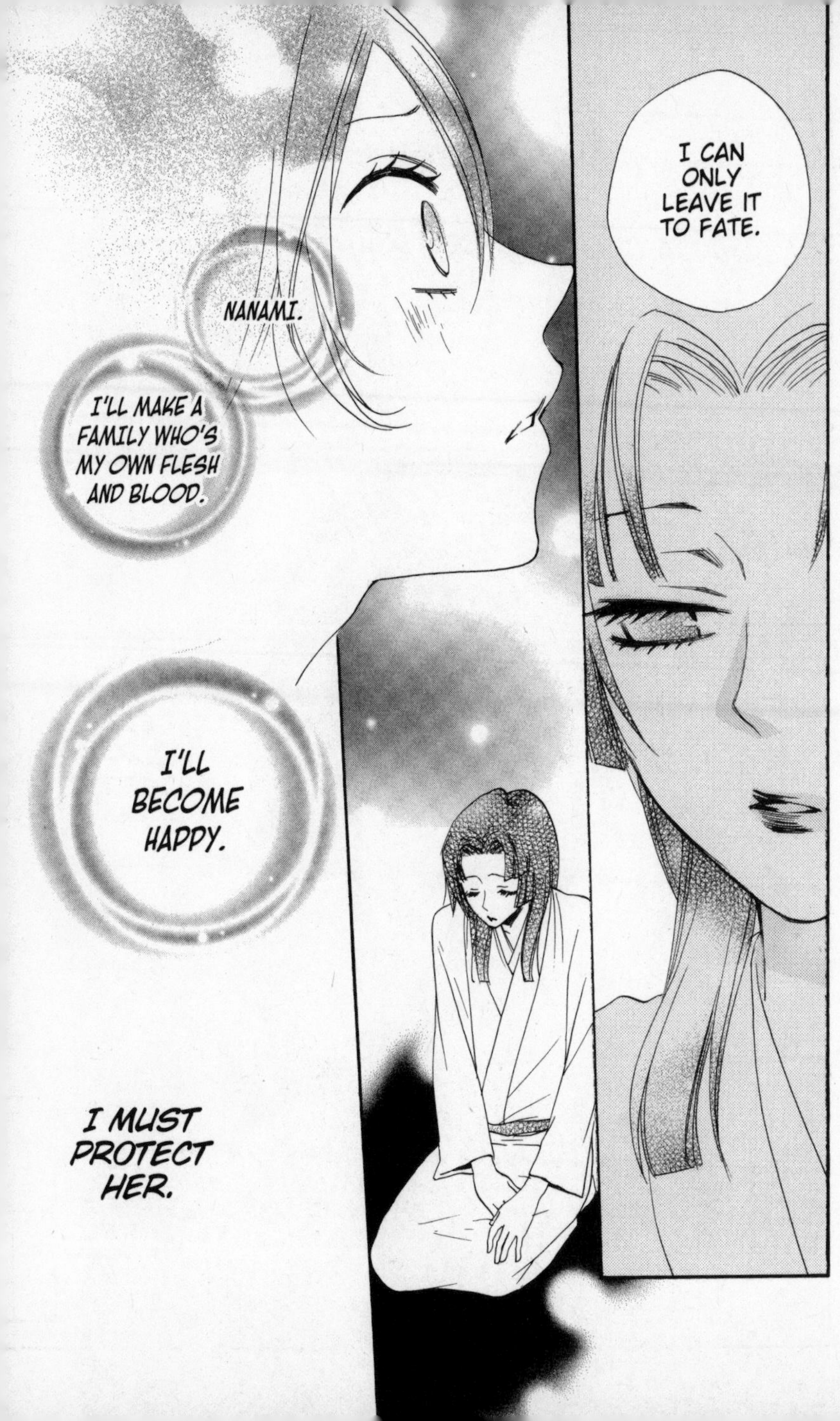
I CAN ONLY LEAVE IT TO FATE.
NANAMI.
I'LL MAKE A FAMILY WHO'S MY OWN FLESH AND BLOOD.
I'LL BECOME HAPPY.
I MUST PROTECT HER.

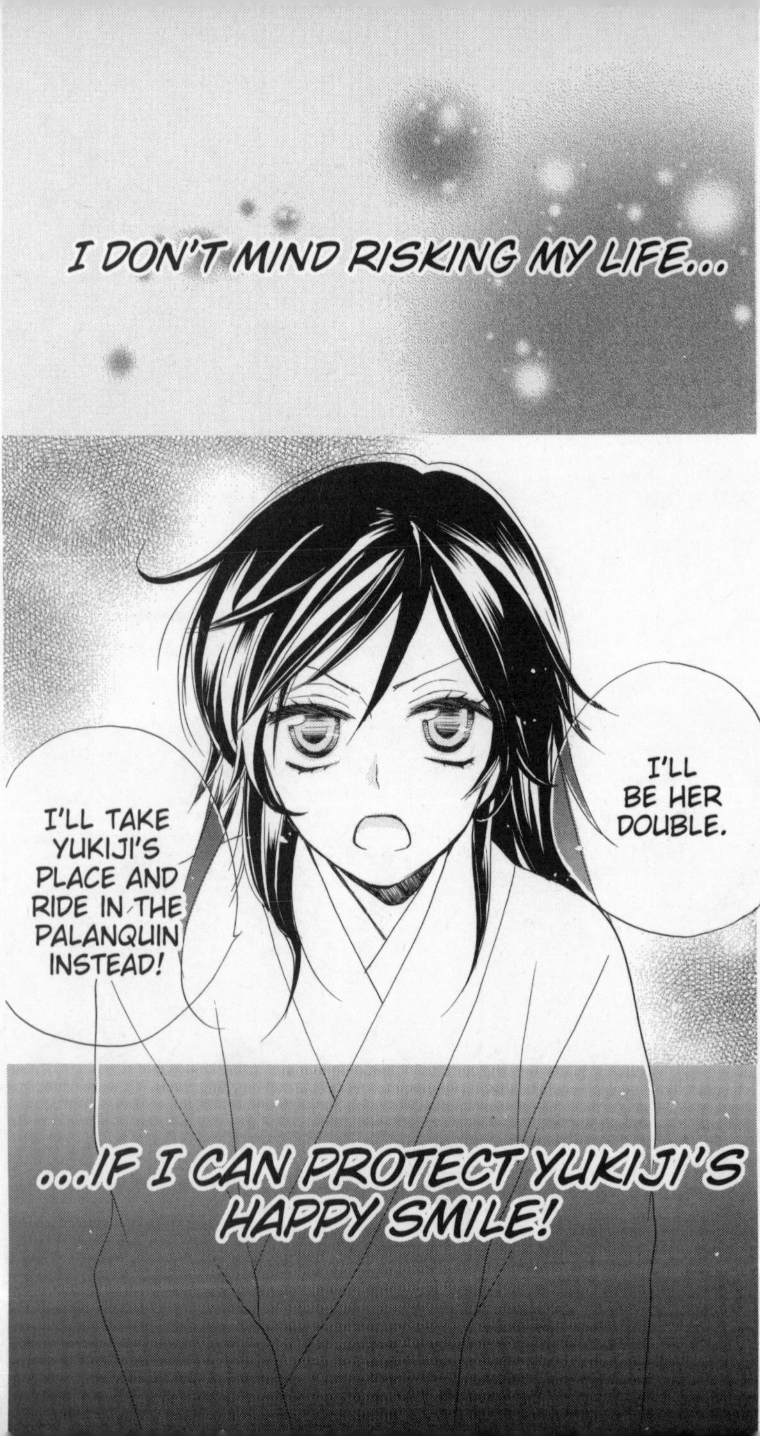
I DON'T MIND RISKING MY LIFE...
I'LL BE HER DOUBLE.
I'LL TAKE YUKIJI'S PLACE AND RIDE IN THE PALANQUIN INSTEAD!
...IF I CAN PROTECT YUKIJI'S HAPPY SMILE!

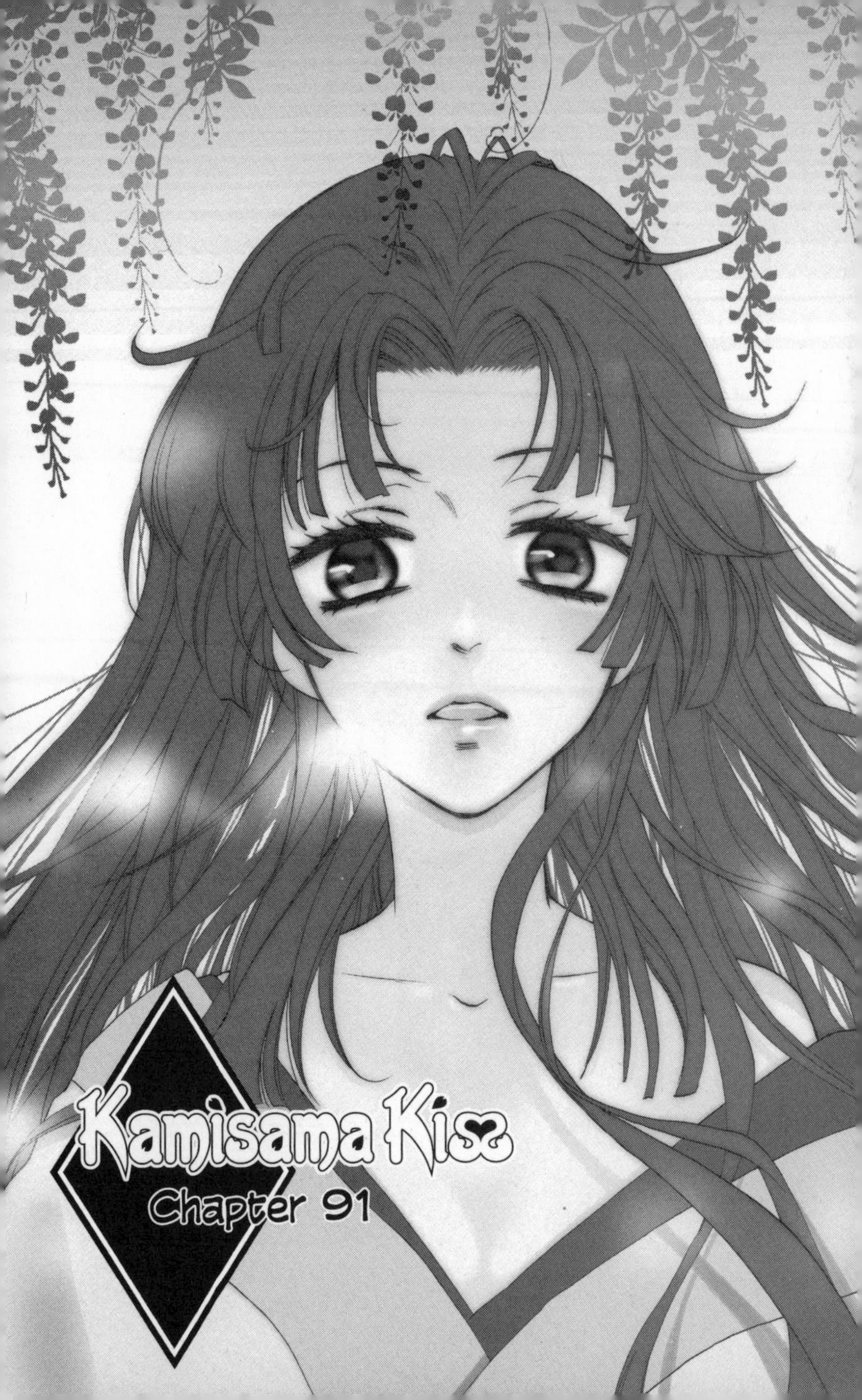
Kamisama Kiss
Chapter 91

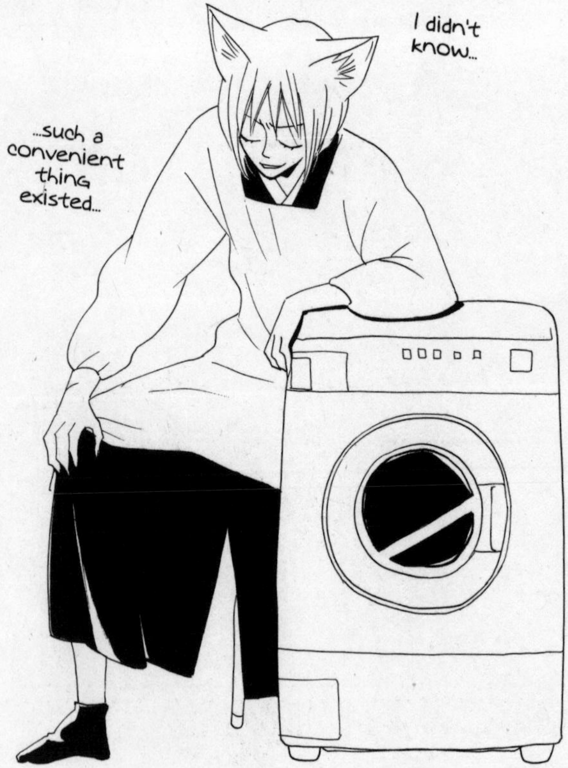
I didn't know...
...such a convenient thing existed...

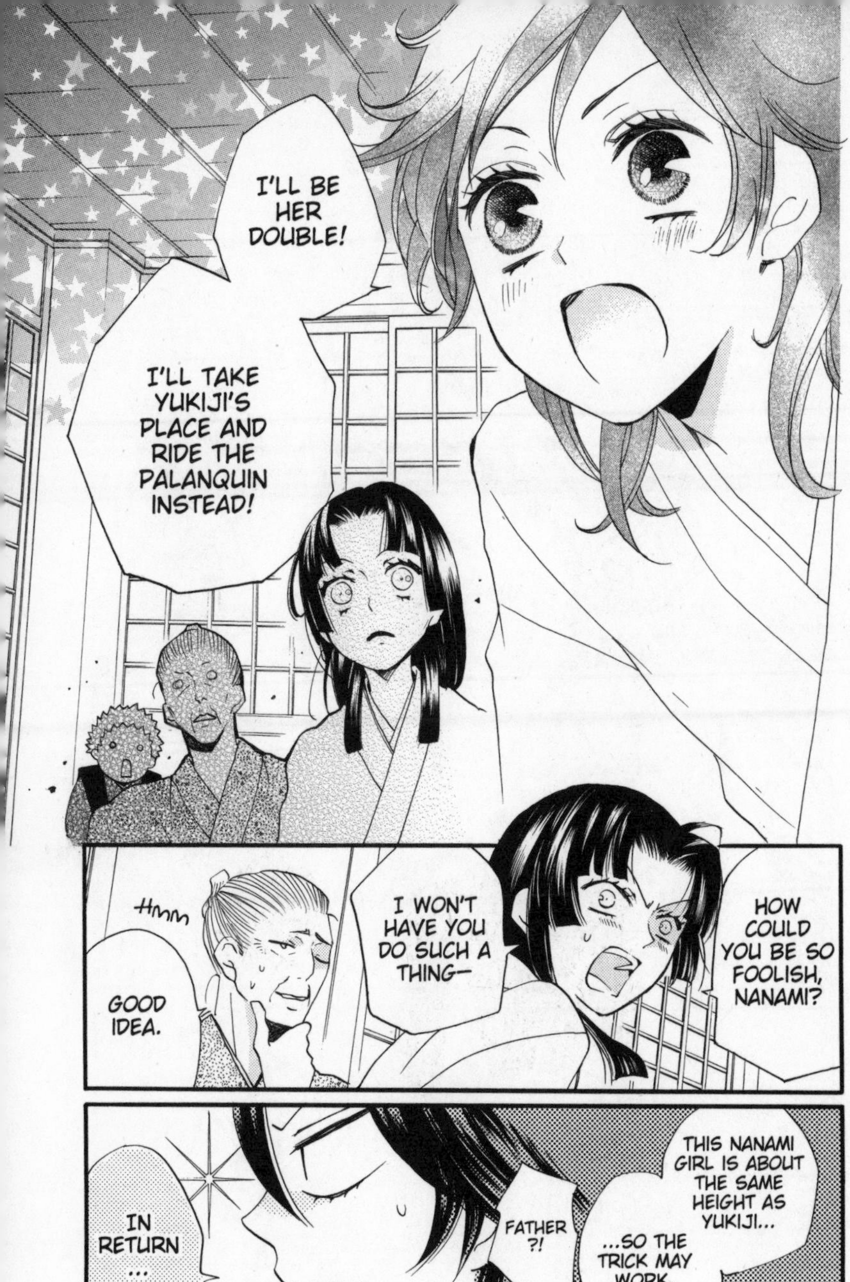
I'LL BE HER DOUBLE!
I'LL TAKE YUKIJI'S PLACE AND RIDE THE PALANQUIN INSTEAD!
HOW COULD YOU BE SO FOOLISH, NANAMI?
I WON'T HAVE YOU DO SUCH A THING—
Hmm
GOOD IDEA.
THIS NANAMI GIRL IS ABOUT THE SAME HEIGHT AS YUKIJI...
...SO THE TRICK MAY WORK.
FATHER ?!
IN RETURN ...

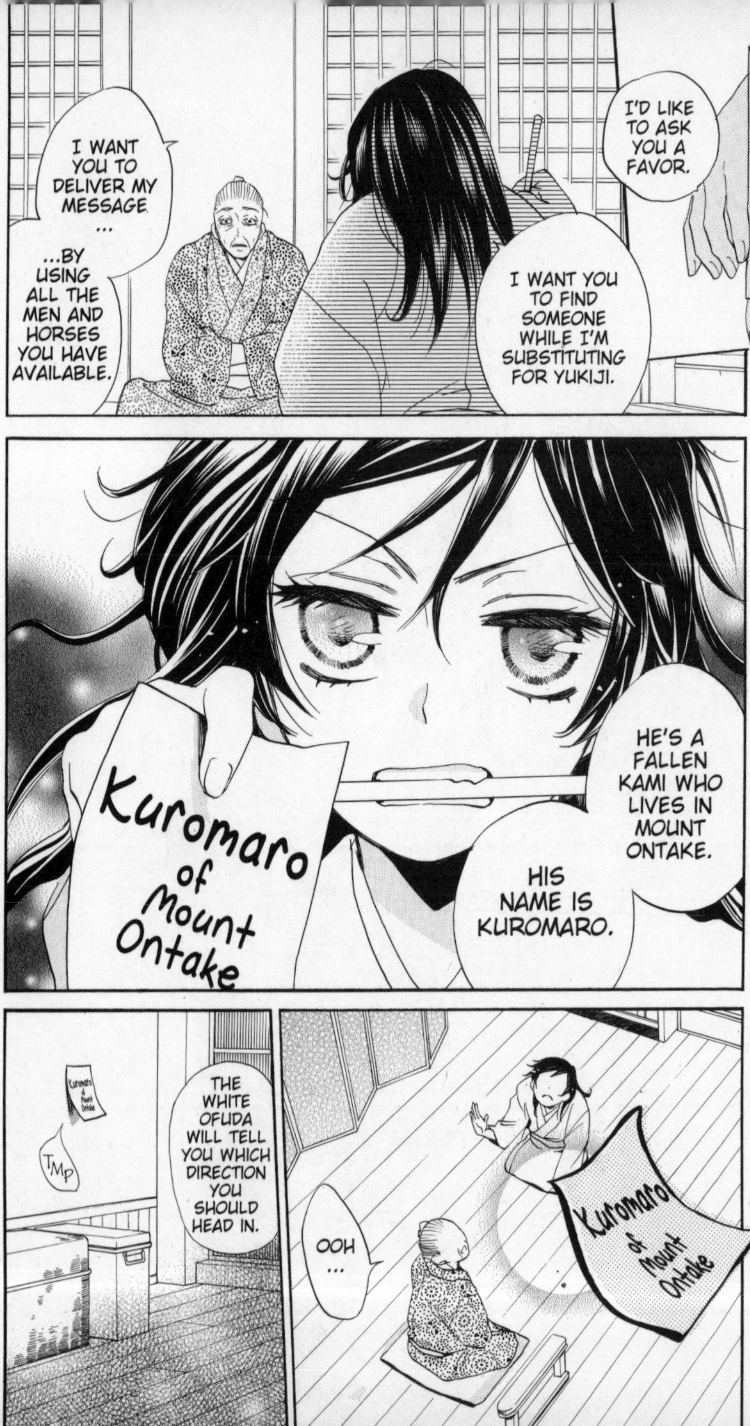
I'D LIKE TO ASK YOU A FAVOR.
I WANT YOU TO FIND SOMEONE WHILE I'M SUBSTITUTING FOR YUKIJI.
I WANT YOU TO DELIVER MY MESSAGE ...
...BY USING ALL THE MEN AND HORSES YOU HAVE AVAILABLE.
HE'S A FALLEN KAMI WHO LIVES IN MOUNT ONTAKE.
HIS NAME IS KUROMARO.
Kuromaro of Mount Ontake
Kuromaro of Mount Ontake
OOH ...
THE WHITE OFUDA WILL TELL YOU WHICH DIRECTION YOU SHOULD HEAD IN.
TMP

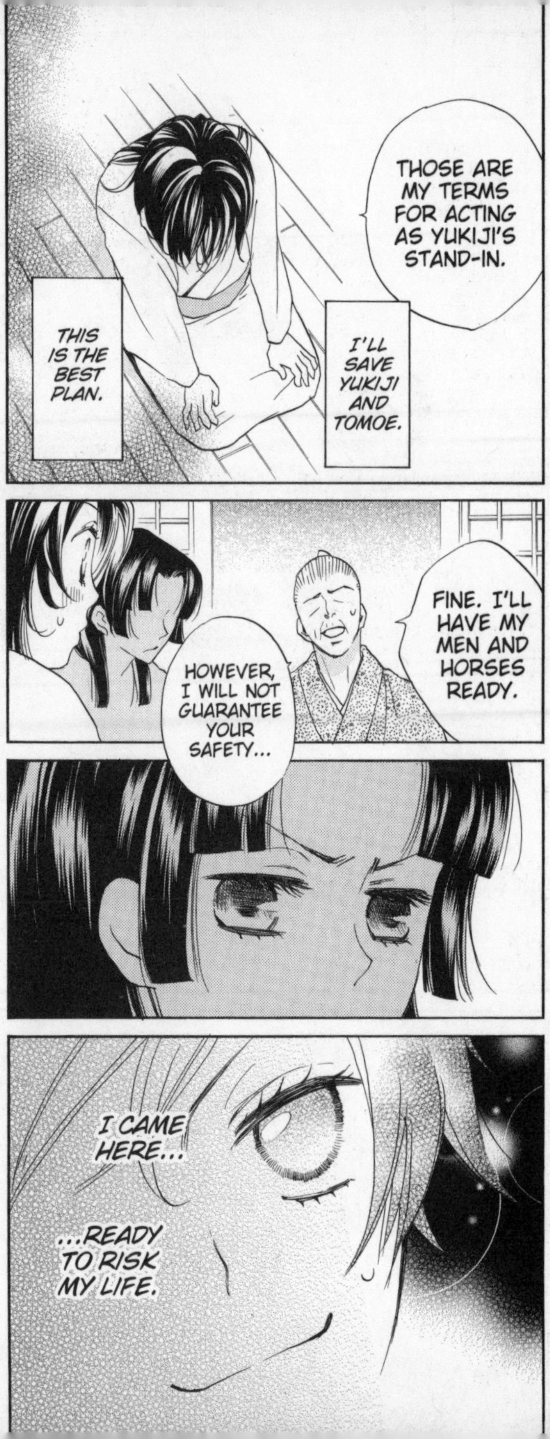
THOSE ARE MY TERMS FOR ACTING AS YUKIJI'S STAND-IN.
I'LL SAVE YUKIJI AND TOMOE.
THIS IS THE BEST PLAN.
FINE. I'LL HAVE MY MEN AND HORSES READY.
HOWEVER, I WILL NOT GUARANTEE YOUR SAFETY...
I CAME HERE...
...READY TO RISK MY LIFE.

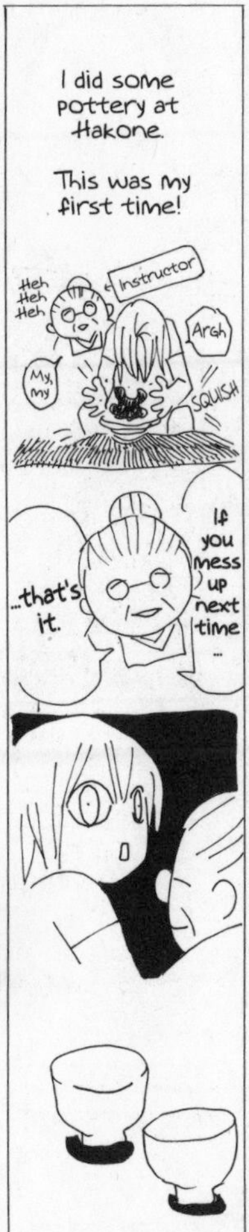
I did some pottery at Hakone.
This was my first time!
Instructor
Heh Heh Heh
Argh
My, my
SQUISH
If you mess up next time...
...that's it.
I made two sake cups.

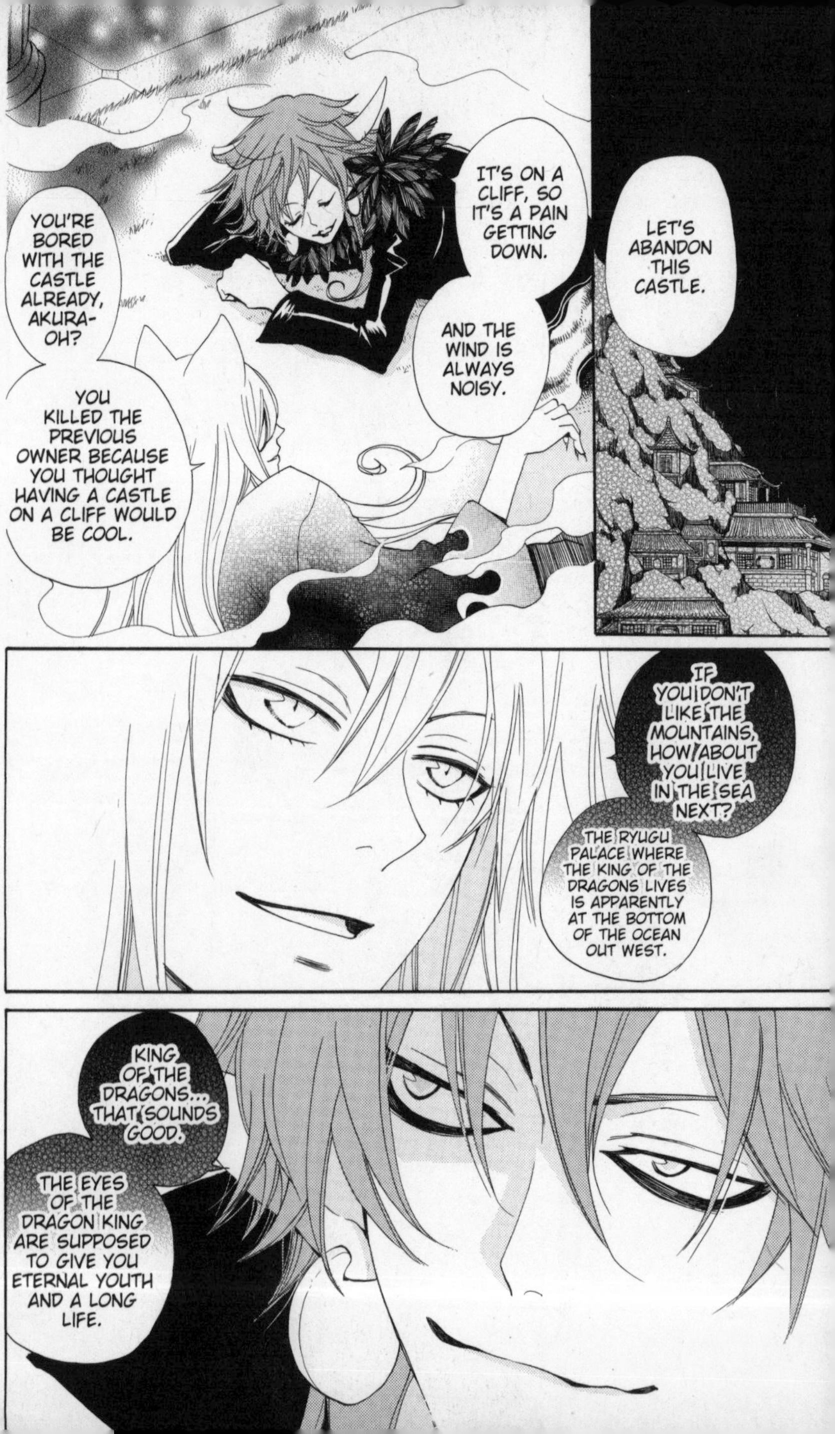
LET'S ABANDON THIS CASTLE.
IT'S ON A CLIFF, SO IT'S A PAIN GETTING DOWN.
AND THE WIND IS ALWAYS NOISY.
YOU'RE BORED WITH THE CASTLE ALREADY, AKURA-OH?
YOU KILLED THE PREVIOUS OWNER BECAUSE YOU THOUGHT HAVING A CASTLE ON A CLIFF WOULD BE COOL.
IF YOU DON'T LIKE THE MOUNTAINS, HOW ABOUT YOU LIVE IN THE SEA NEXT?
THE RYUGU PALACE WHERE THE KING OF THE DRAGONS LIVES IS APPARENTLY AT THE BOTTOM OF THE OCEAN OUT WEST.
KING OF THE DRAGONS... THAT SOUNDS GOOD.
THE EYES OF THE DRAGON KING ARE SUPPOSED TO GIVE YOU ETERNAL YOUTH AND A LONG LIFE.

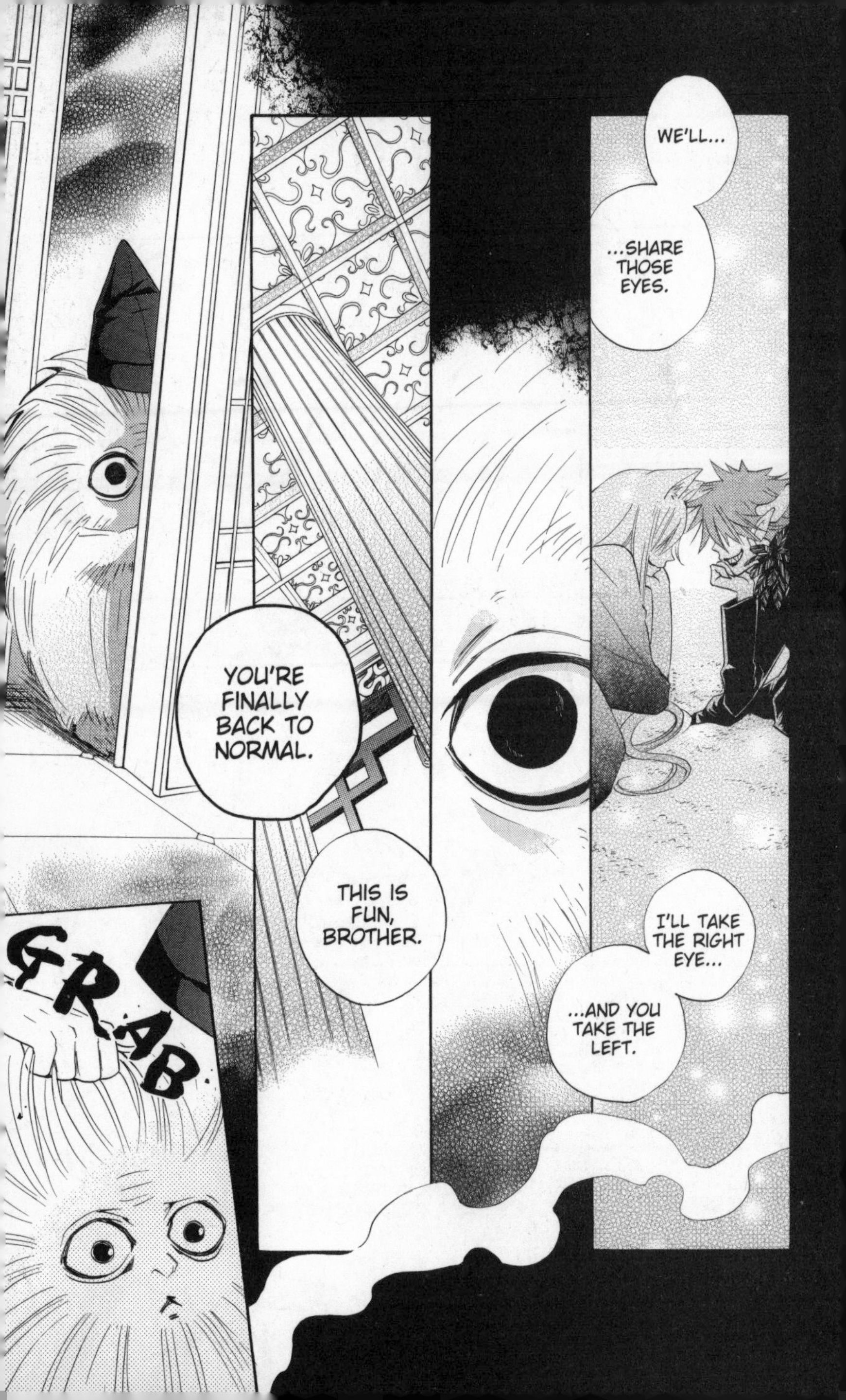
WE'LL...
...SHARE THOSE EYES.
I'LL TAKE THE RIGHT EYE...
...AND YOU TAKE THE LEFT.
YOU'RE FINALLY BACK TO NORMAL.
THIS IS FUN, BROTHER.
GRAB

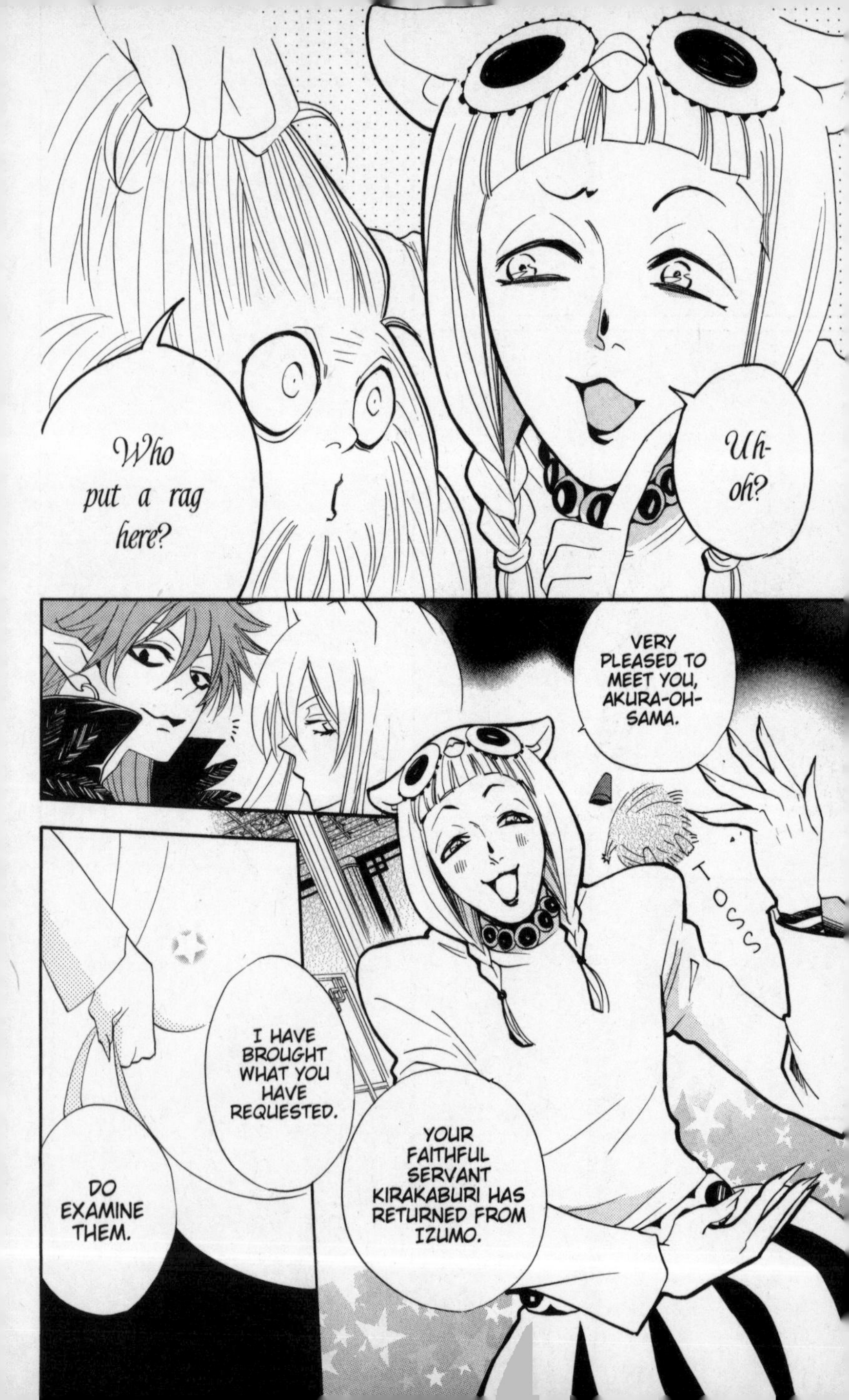
Uh-oh?
Who put a rag here?
VERY PLEASED TO MEET YOU, AKURA-OH-SAMA.
TOSS
YOUR FAITHFUL SERVANT KIRAKABURI HAS RETURNED FROM IZUMO.
I HAVE BROUGHT WHAT YOU HAVE REQUESTED.
DO EXAMINE THEM.

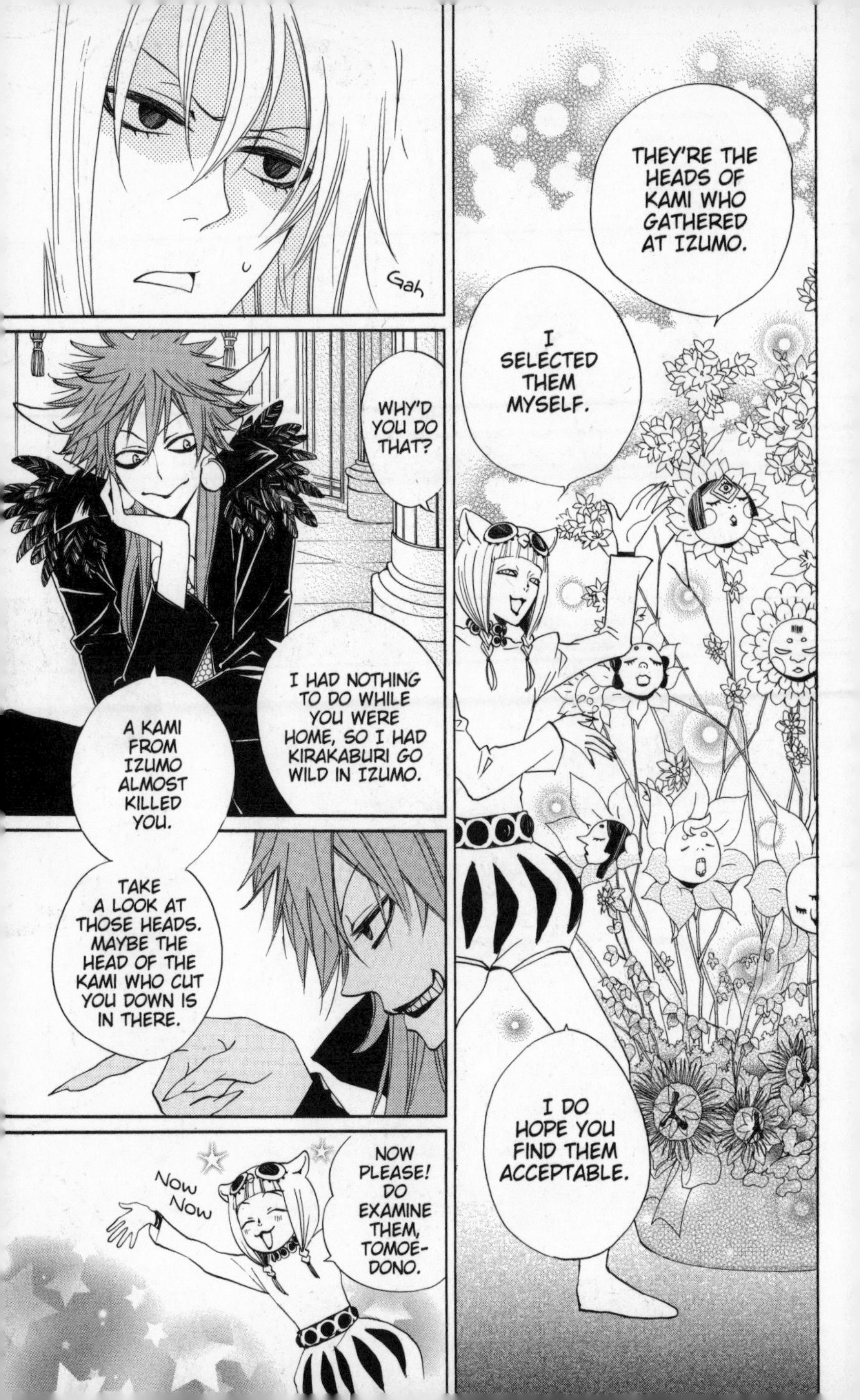
THEY'RE THE HEADS OF KAMI WHO GATHERED AT IZUMO.
I SELECTED THEM MYSELF.
I DO HOPE YOU FIND THEM ACCEPTABLE.
Gah
WHY'D YOU DO THAT?
I HAD NOTHING TO DO WHILE YOU WERE HOME, SO I HAD KIRAKABURI GO WILD IN IZUMO.
A KAMI FROM IZUMO ALMOST KILLED YOU.
TAKE A LOOK AT THOSE HEADS. MAYBE THE HEAD OF THE KAMI WHO CUT YOU DOWN IS IN THERE.
NOW PLEASE! DO EXAMINE THEM, TOMOE-DONO.
Now Now

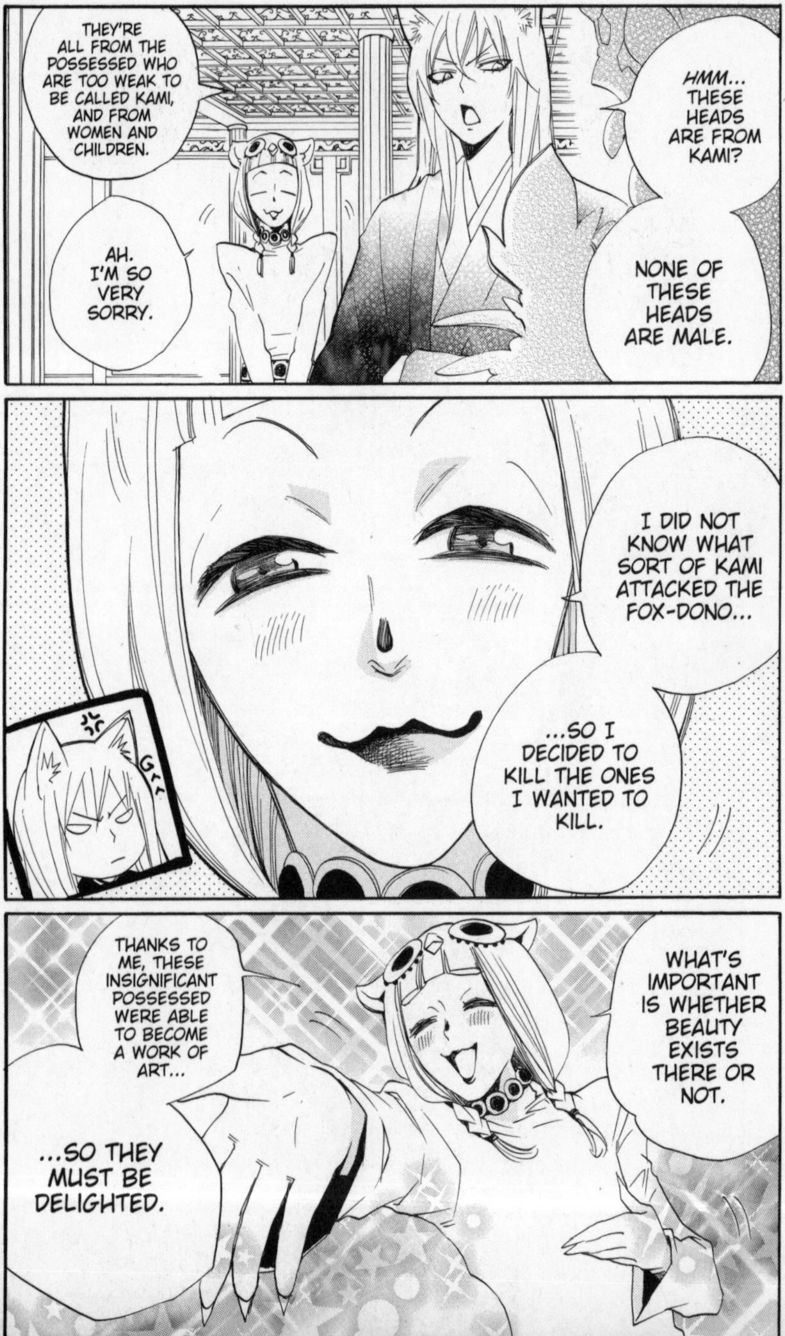
HMM... THESE HEADS ARE FROM KAMI?
NONE OF THESE HEADS ARE MALE.
THEY'RE ALL FROM THE POSSESSED WHO ARE TOO WEAK TO BE CALLED KAMI, AND FROM WOMEN AND CHILDREN.
AH. I'M SO VERY SORRY.
I DID NOT KNOW WHAT SORT OF KAMI ATTACKED THE FOX-DONO...
...SO I DECIDED TO KILL THE ONES I WANTED TO KILL.
Grr
WHAT'S IMPORTANT IS WHETHER BEAUTY EXISTS THERE OR NOT.
THANKS TO ME, THESE INSIGNIFICANT POSSESSED WERE ABLE TO BECOME A WORK OF ART...
...SO THEY MUST BE DELIGHTED.

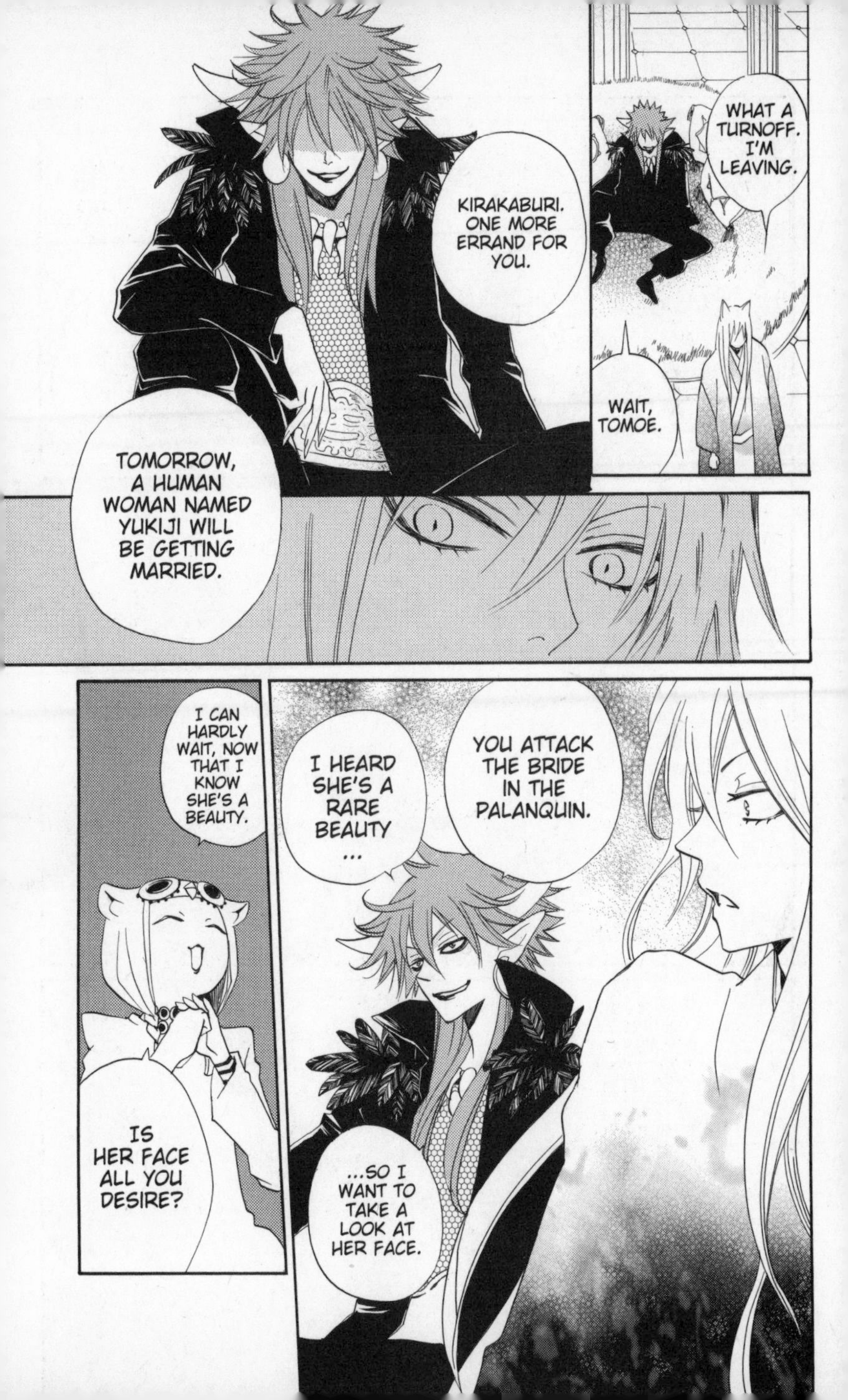
WHAT A TURNOFF. I'M LEAVING.
WAIT, TOMOE.
KIRAKABURI. ONE MORE ERRAND FOR YOU.
TOMORROW, A HUMAN WOMAN NAMED YUKIJI WILL BE GETTING MARRIED.
YOU ATTACK THE BRIDE IN THE PALANQUIN.
I HEARD SHE'S A RARE BEAUTY ...
...SO I WANT TO TAKE A LOOK AT HER FACE.
I CAN HARDLY WAIT, NOW THAT I KNOW SHE'S A BEAUTY.
IS HER FACE ALL YOU DESIRE?

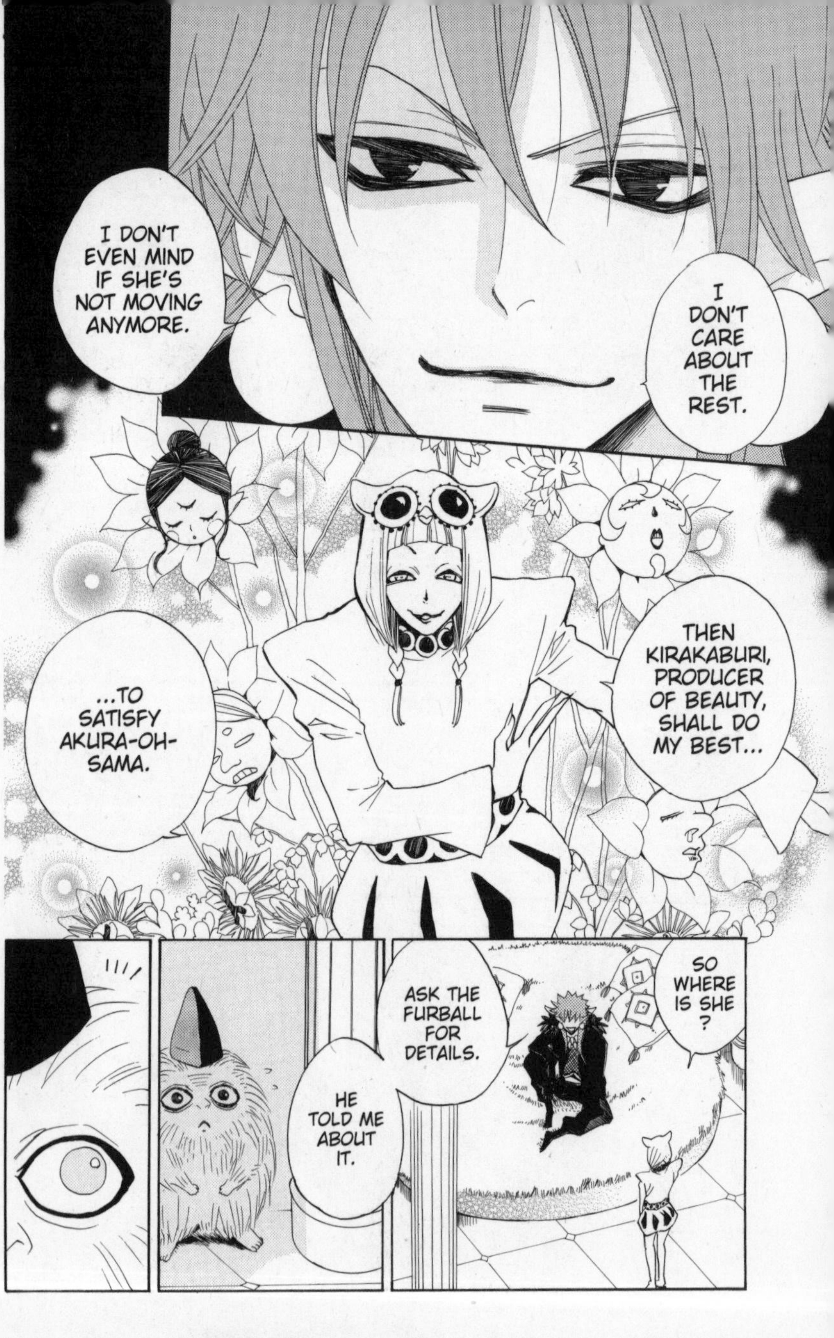
I DON'T CARE ABOUT THE REST.
I DON'T EVEN MIND IF SHE'S NOT MOVING ANYMORE.
THEN KIRAKABURI, PRODUCER OF BEAUTY, SHALL DO MY BEST...
...TO SATISFY AKURA-OH-SAMA.
SO WHERE IS SHE?
ASK THE FURBALL FOR DETAILS.
HE TOLD ME ABOUT IT.

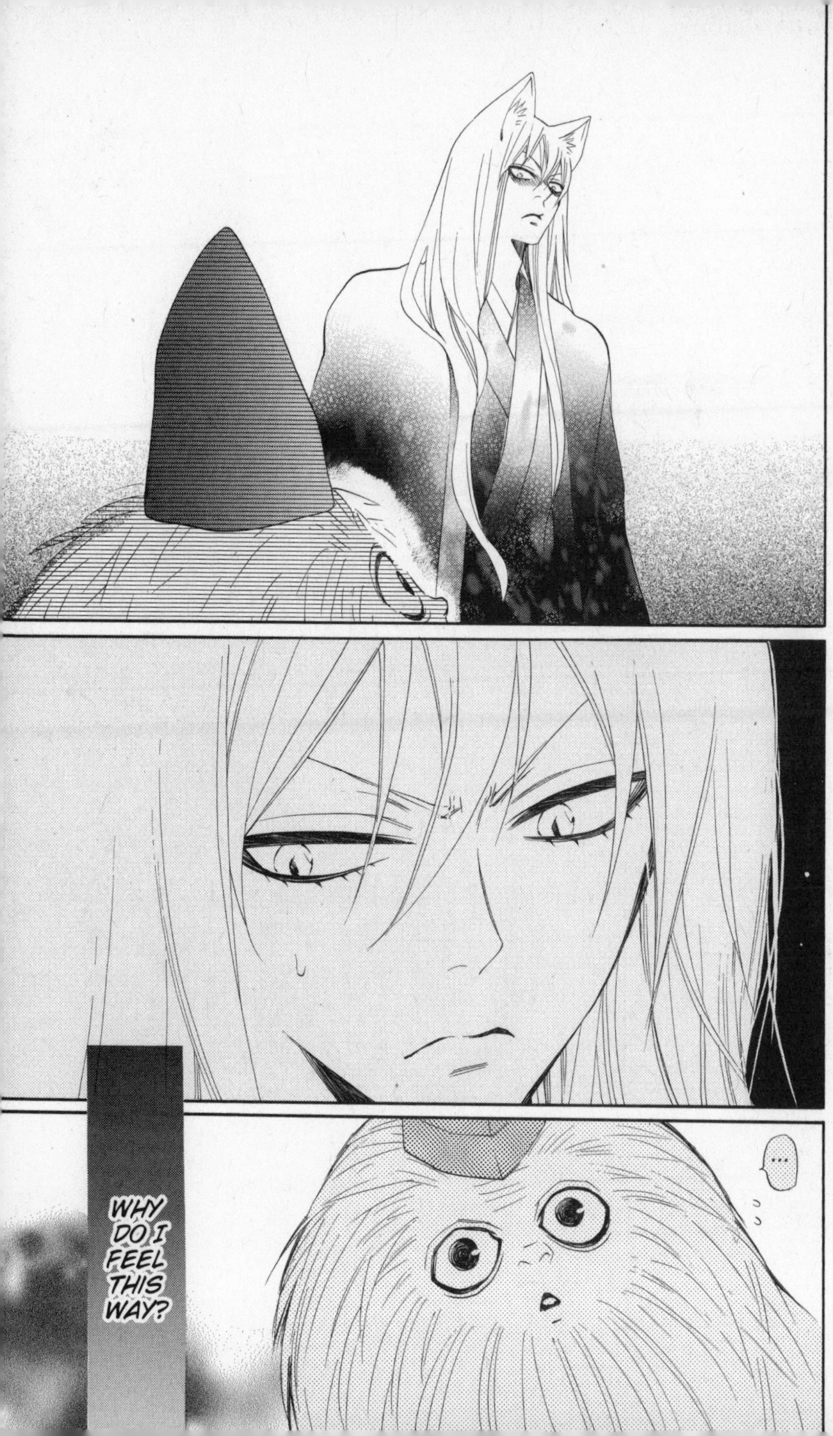
WHY DO I FEEL THIS WAY?
...

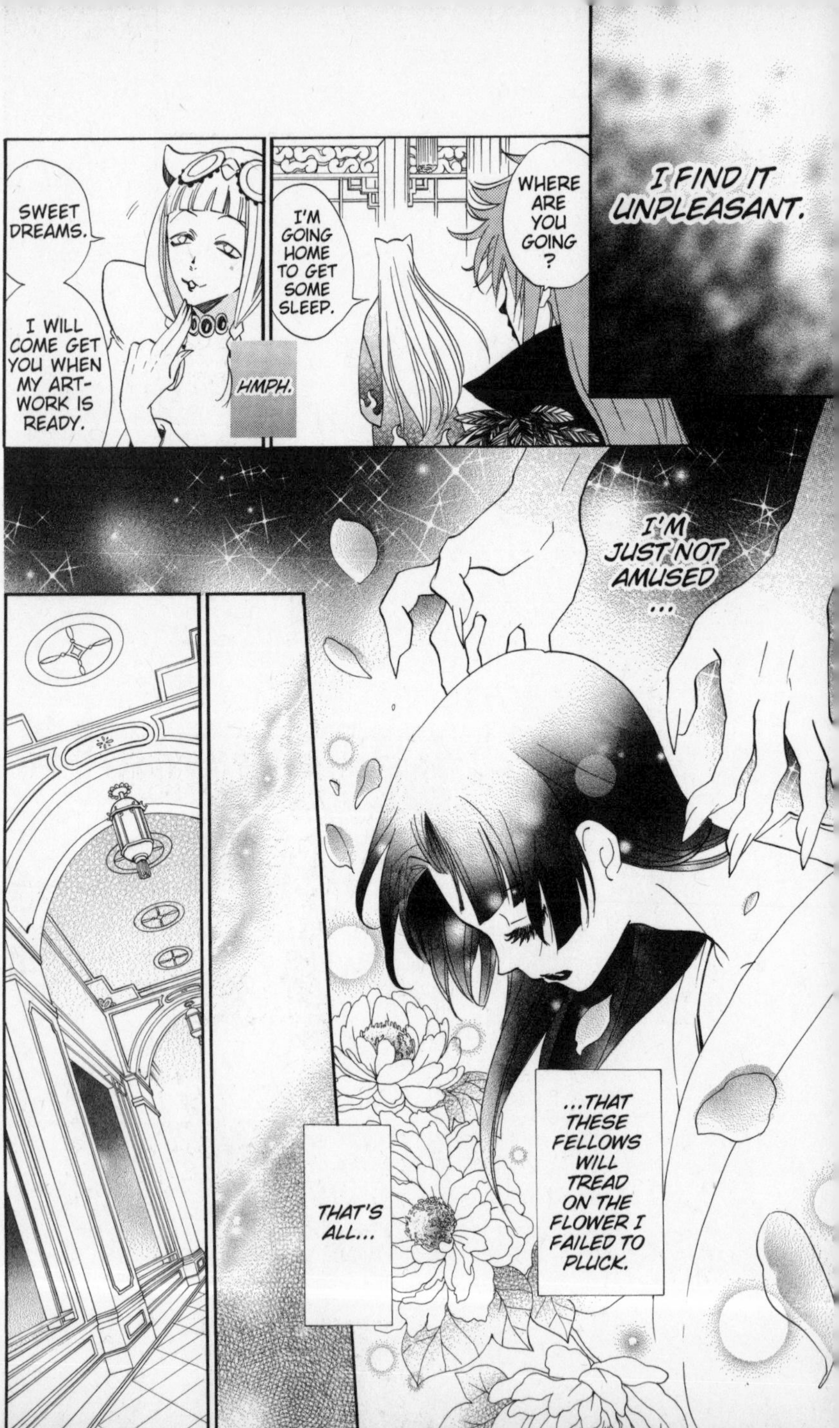
I FIND IT UNPLEASANT.
WHERE ARE YOU GOING?
I'M GOING HOME TO GET SOME SLEEP.
HMPH.
SWEET DREAMS.
I WILL COME GET YOU WHEN MY ART-WORK IS READY.
I'M JUST NOT AMUSED...
...THAT THESE FELLOWS WILL TREAD ON THE FLOWER I FAILED TO PLUCK.
THAT'S ALL...

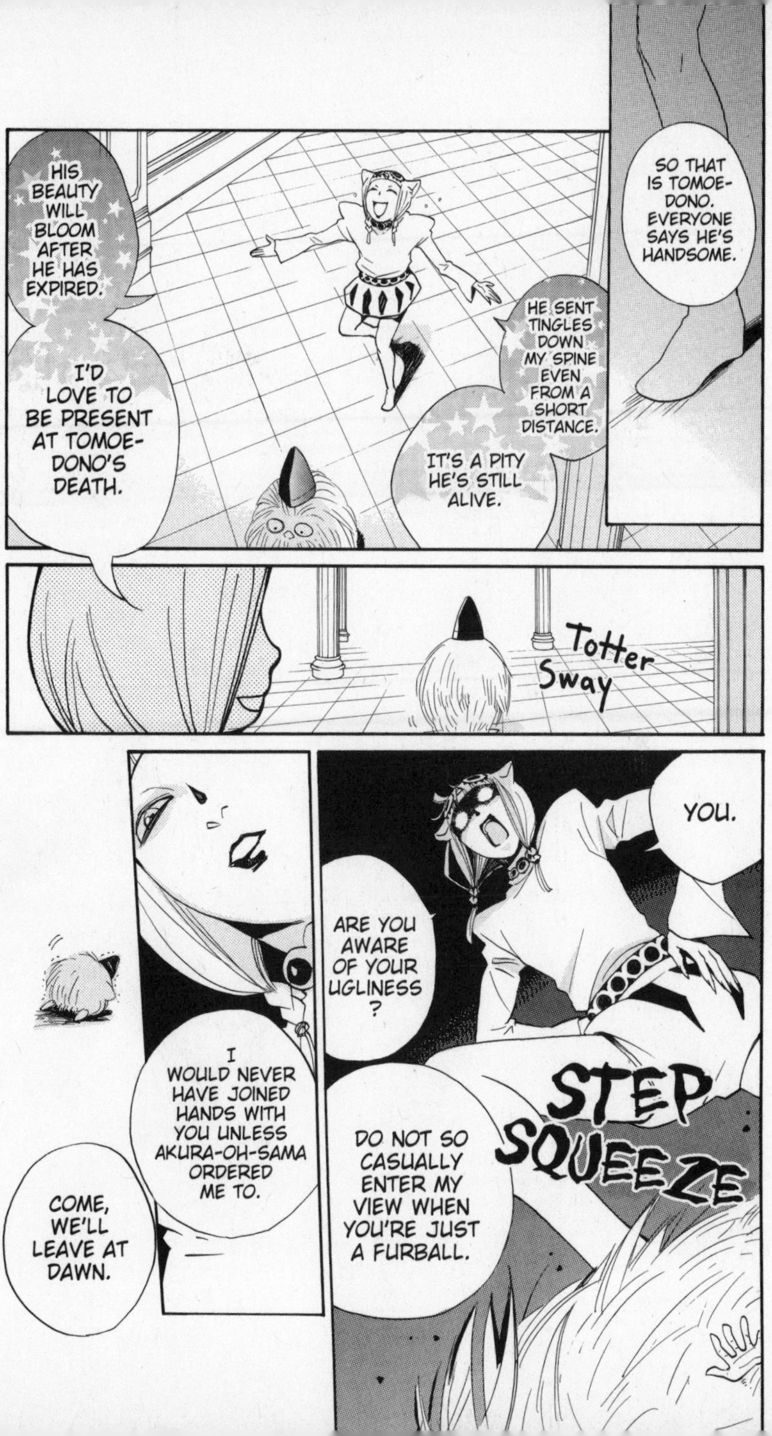
SO THAT IS TOMOE-DONO. EVERYONE SAYS HE'S HANDSOME.
HE SENT TINGLES DOWN MY SPINE EVEN FROM A SHORT DISTANCE.
IT'S A PITY HE'S STILL ALIVE.
HIS BEAUTY WILL BLOOM AFTER HE HAS EXPIRED.
I'D LOVE TO BE PRESENT AT TOMOE-DONO'S DEATH.
Totter Sway
YOU.
ARE YOU AWARE OF YOUR UGLINESS?
STEP SQUEEZE
DO NOT SO CASUALLY ENTER MY VIEW WHEN YOU'RE JUST A FURBALL.
I WOULD NEVER HAVE JOINED HANDS WITH YOU UNLESS AKURA-OH-SAMA ORDERED ME TO.
COME, WE'LL LEAVE AT DAWN.

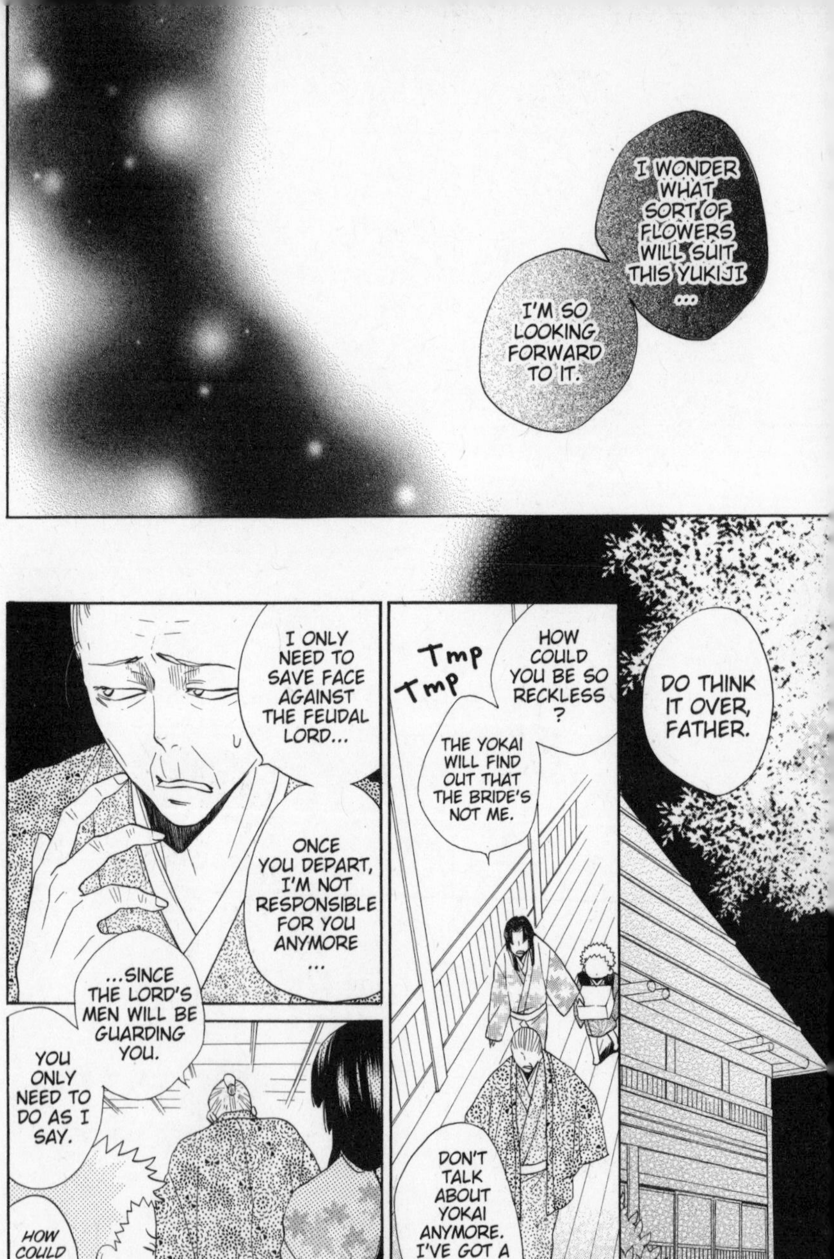
I WONDER WHAT SORT OF FLOWERS WILL SUIT THIS YUKIJI ...
I'M SO LOOKING FORWARD TO IT.
DO THINK IT OVER, FATHER.
Tmp Tmp
HOW COULD YOU BE SO RECKLESS ?
THE YOKAI WILL FIND OUT THAT THE BRIDE'S NOT ME.
DON'T TALK ABOUT YOKAI ANYMORE. I'VE GOT A HEADACHE.
I ONLY NEED TO SAVE FACE AGAINST THE FEUDAL LORD...
ONCE YOU DEPART, I'M NOT RESPONSIBLE FOR YOU ANYMORE ...
...SINCE THE LORD'S MEN WILL BE GUARDING YOU.
YOU ONLY NEED TO DO AS I SAY.
HOW COULD HE ...?

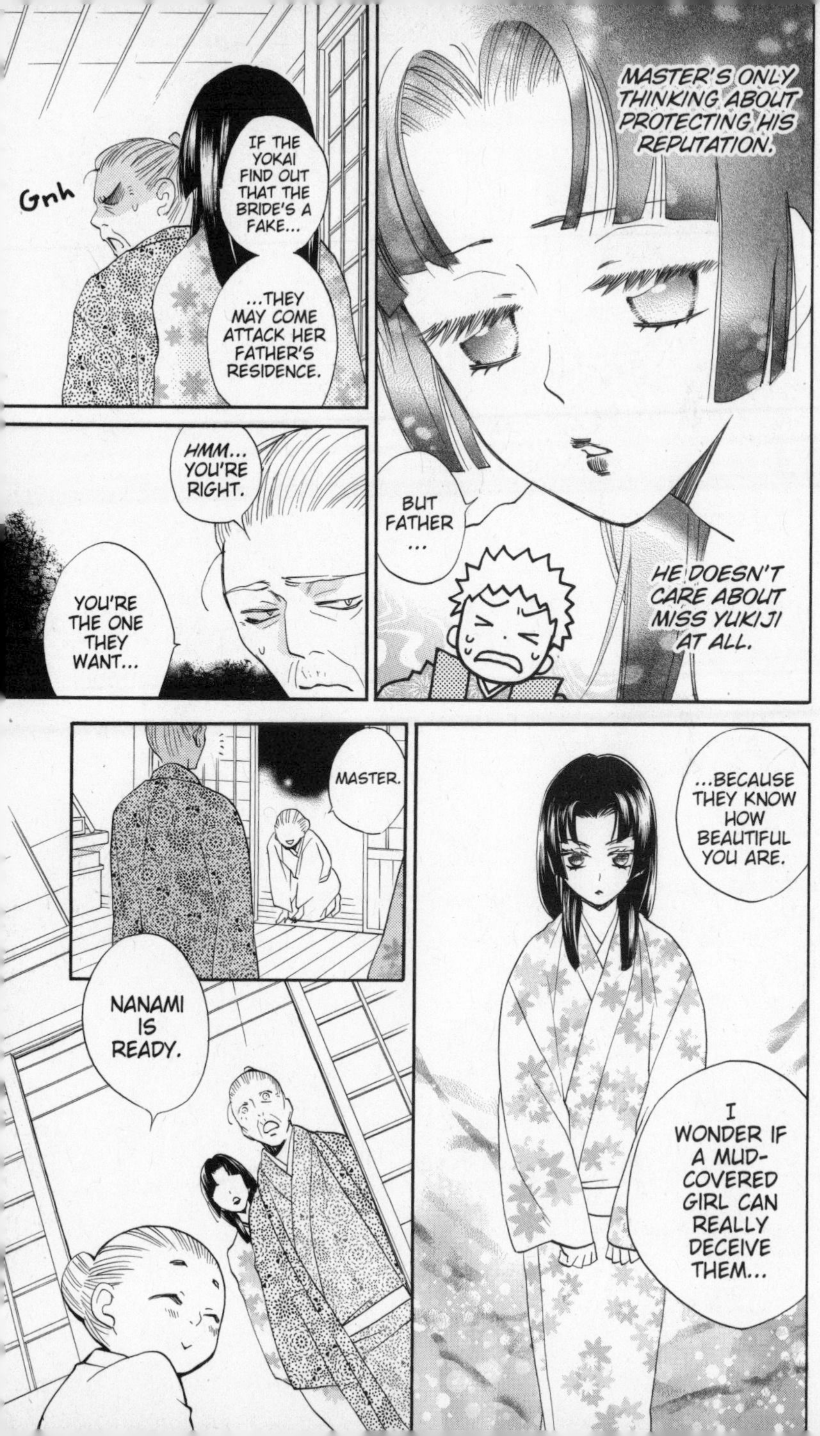
MASTER'S ONLY THINKING ABOUT PROTECTING HIS REPUTATION.
BUT FATHER...
HE DOESN'T CARE ABOUT MISS YUKIJI AT ALL.
IF THE YOKAI FIND OUT THAT THE BRIDE'S A FAKE...
...THEY MAY COME ATTACK HER FATHER'S RESIDENCE.
Gnh
HMM... YOU'RE RIGHT.
YOU'RE THE ONE THEY WANT...
...BECAUSE THEY KNOW HOW BEAUTIFUL YOU ARE.
I WONDER IF A MUD-COVERED GIRL CAN REALLY DECEIVE THEM...
MASTER.
NANAMI IS READY.

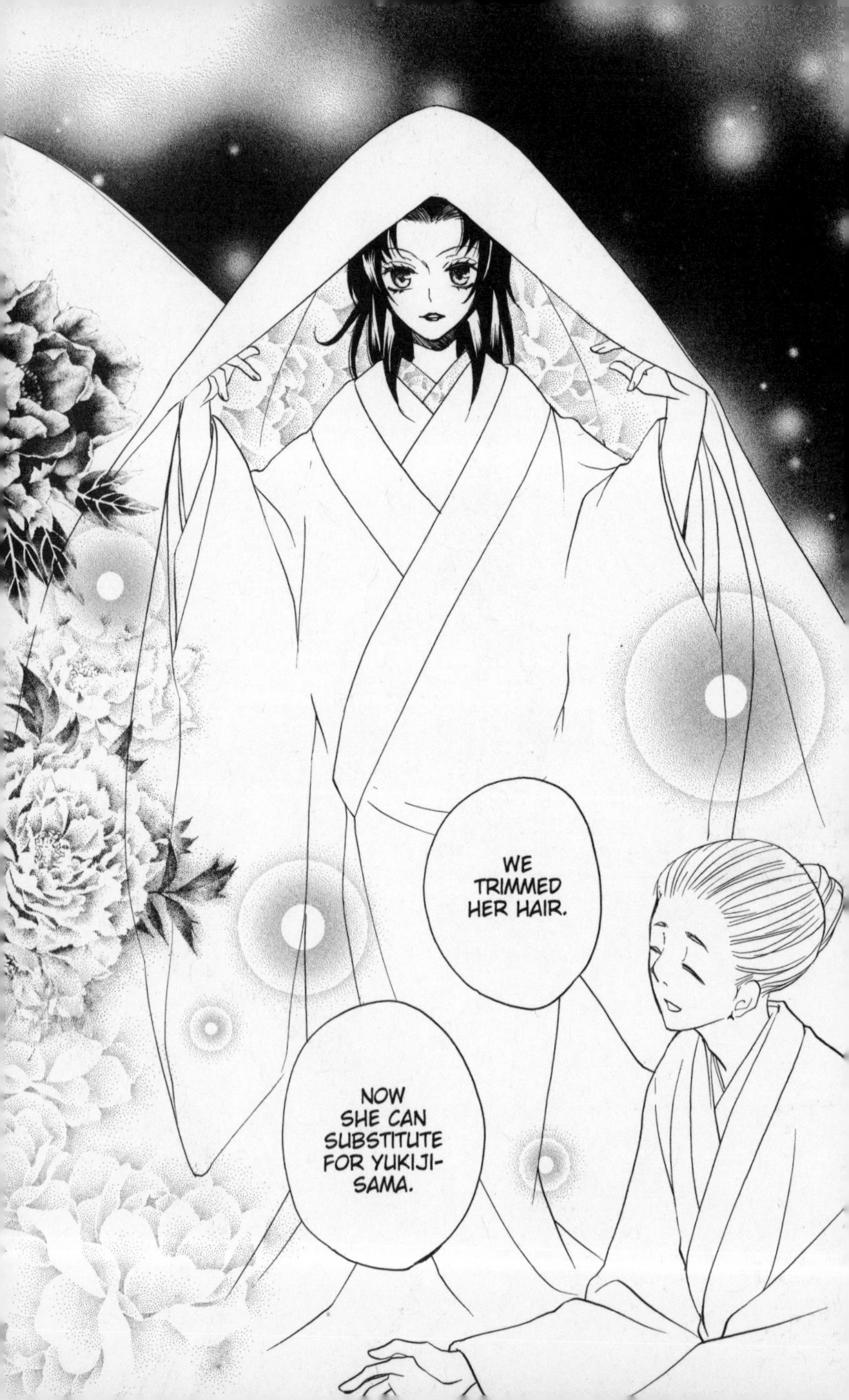
WE TRIMMED HER HAIR.
NOW SHE CAN SUBSTITUTE FOR YUKIJI-SAMA.

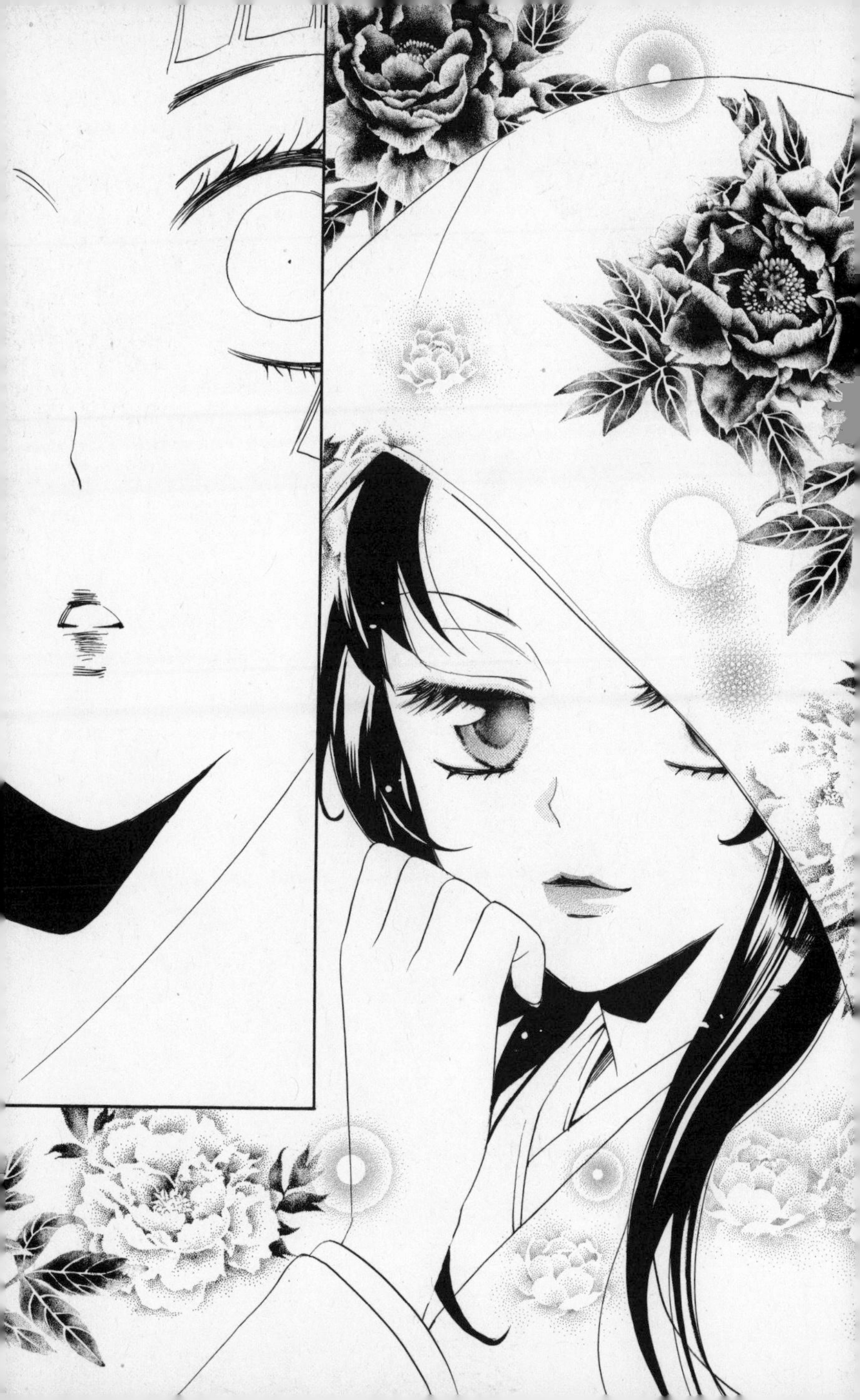

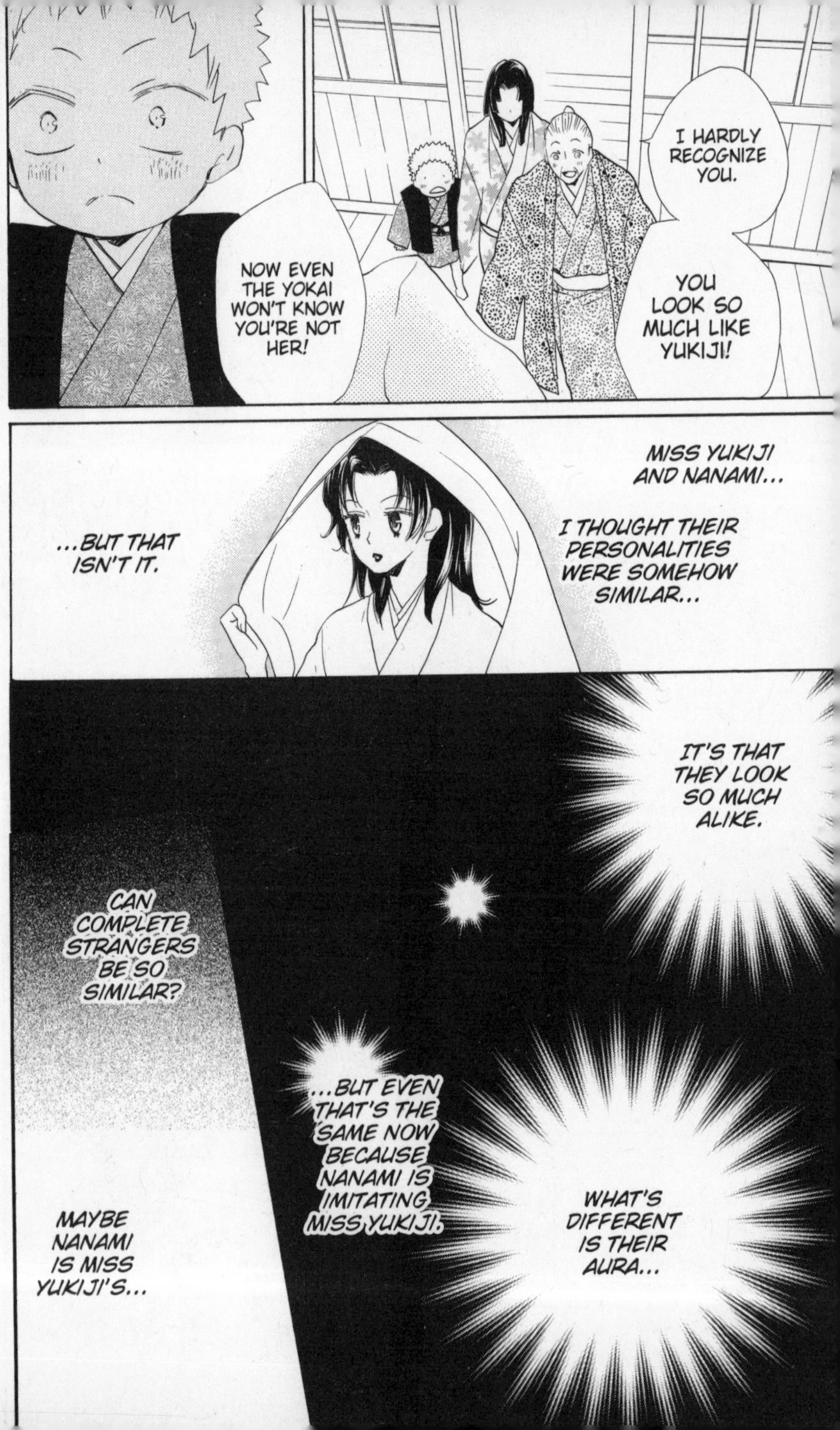

I HARDLY RECOGNIZE YOU.
YOU LOOK SO MUCH LIKE YUKIJI!
NOW EVEN THE YOKAI WON'T KNOW YOU'RE NOT HER!
MISS YUKIJI AND NANAMI...
I THOUGHT THEIR PERSONALITIES WERE SOMEHOW SIMILAR...
...BUT THAT ISN'T IT.
IT'S THAT THEY LOOK SO MUCH ALIKE.
CAN COMPLETE STRANGERS BE SO SIMILAR?
...BUT EVEN THAT'S THE SAME NOW BECAUSE NANAMI IS IMITATING MISS YUKIJI.
WHAT'S DIFFERENT IS THEIR AURA...
MAYBE NANAMI IS MISS YUKIJI'S...

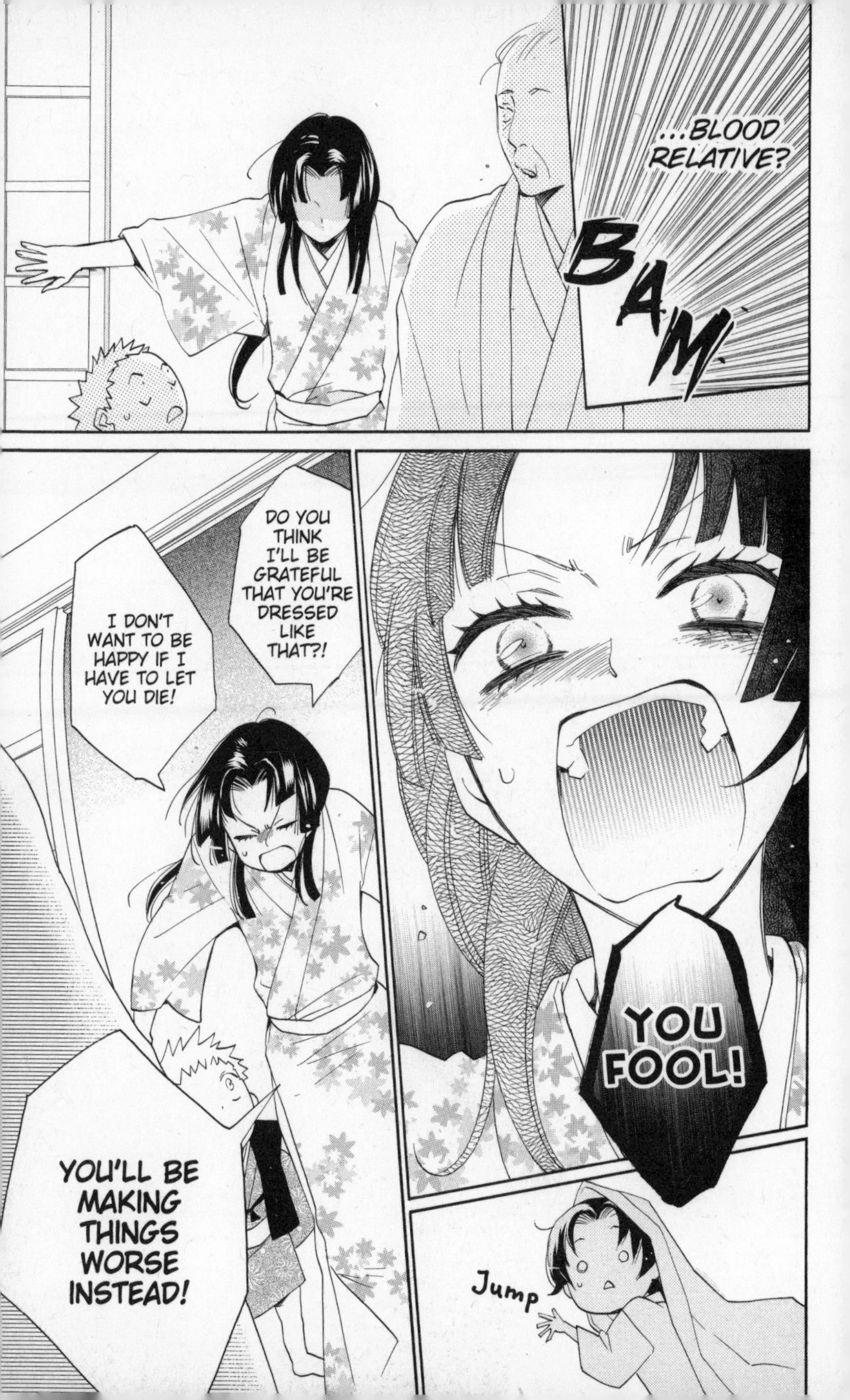
...BLOOD RELATIVE?
BAM
YOU FOOL!
Jump
DO YOU THINK I'LL BE GRATEFUL THAT YOU'RE DRESSED LIKE THAT?!
I DON'T WANT TO BE HAPPY IF I HAVE TO LET YOU DIE!
YOU'LL BE MAKING THINGS WORSE INSTEAD!

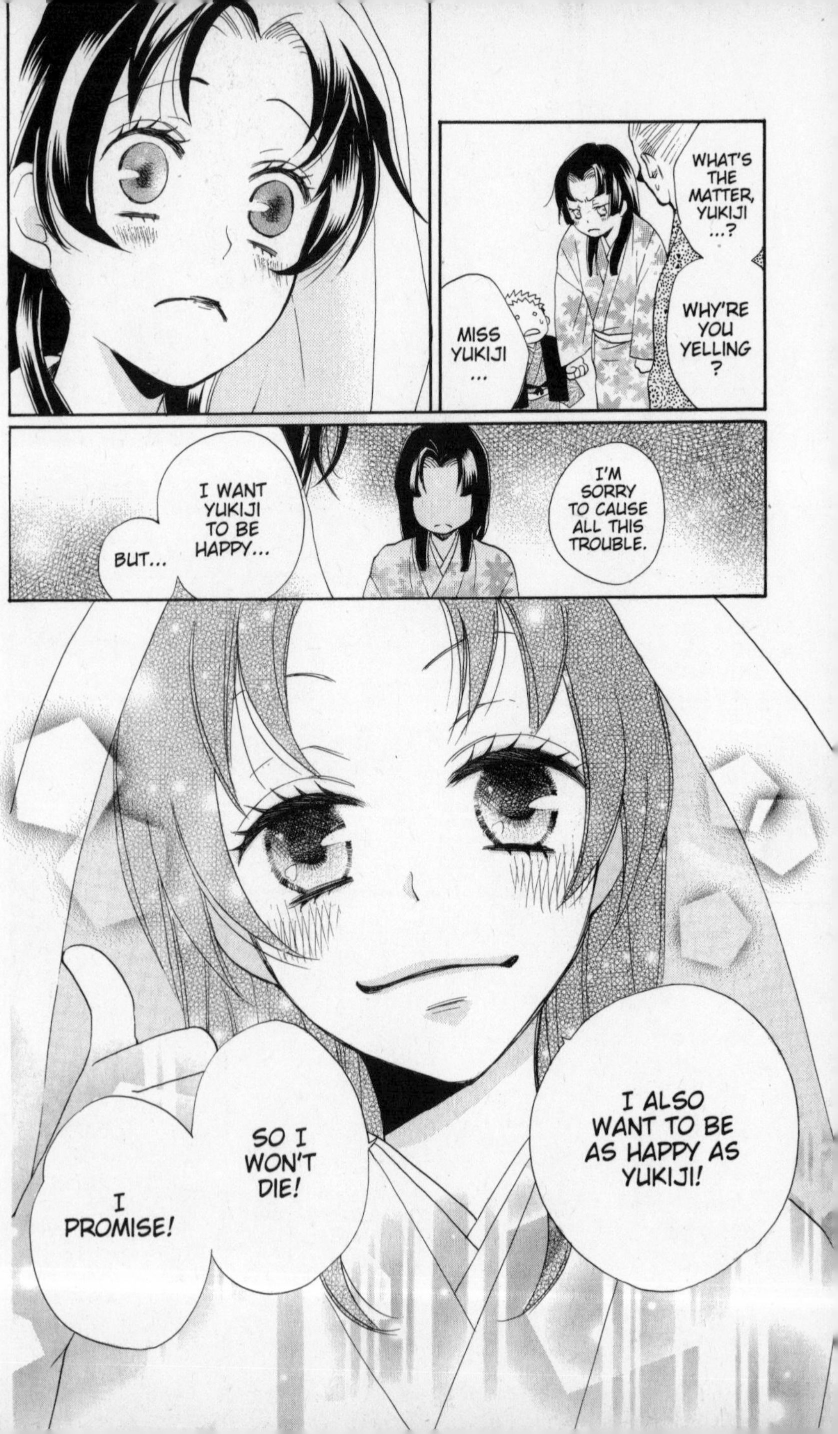
WHAT'S THE MATTER, YUKIJI ...?
WHY'RE YOU YELLING ?
MISS YUKIJI ...
I'M SORRY TO CAUSE ALL THIS TROUBLE.
I WANT YUKIJI TO BE HAPPY... BUT...
I ALSO WANT TO BE AS HAPPY AS YUKIJI!
SO I WON'T DIE! I PROMISE!

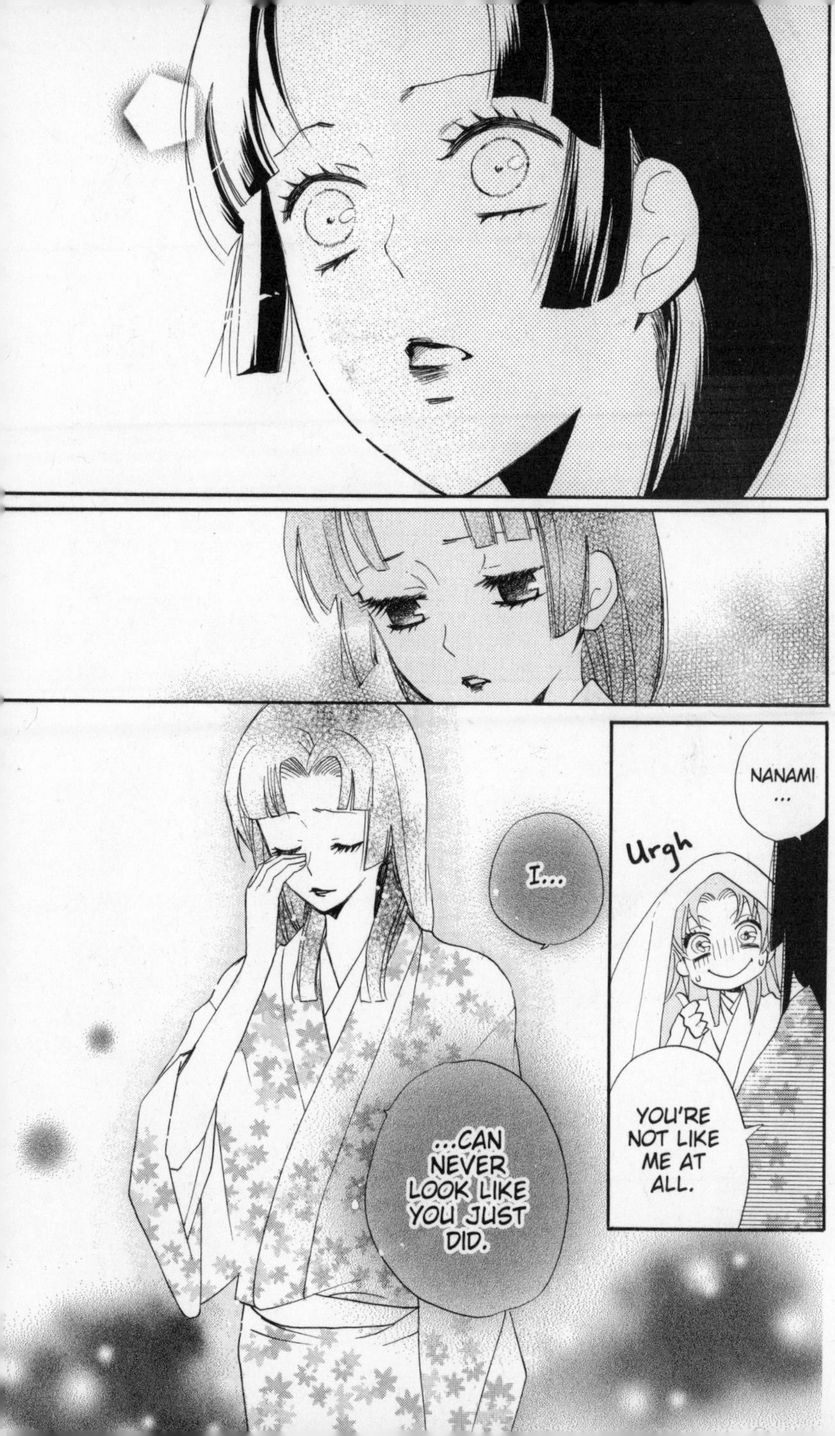
NANAMI ...
Urgh
YOU'RE NOT LIKE ME AT ALL.
I...
...CAN NEVER LOOK LIKE YOU JUST DID.

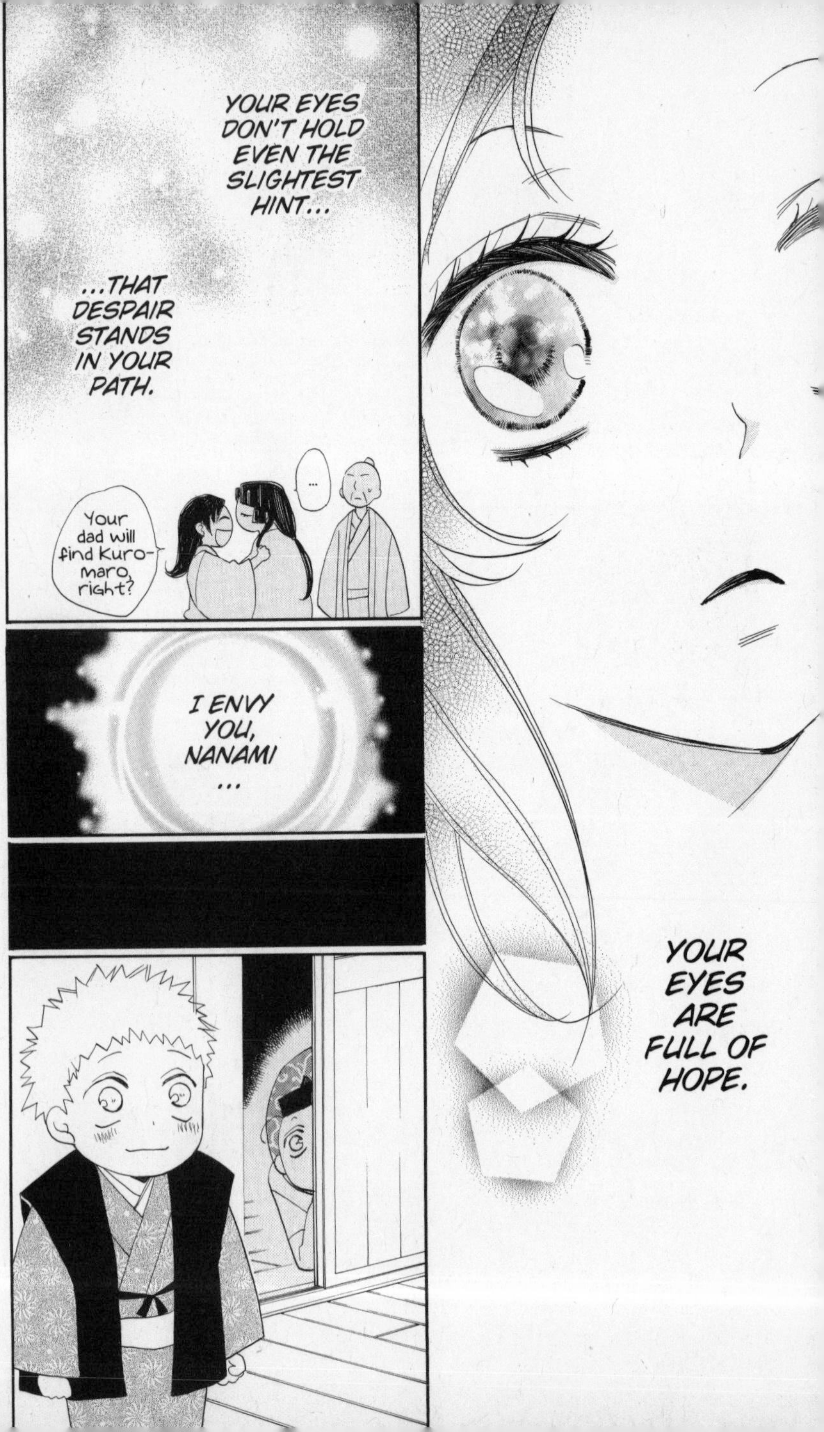
YOUR EYES ARE FULL OF HOPE.
YOUR EYES DON'T HOLD EVEN THE SLIGHTEST HINT...
...THAT DESPAIR STANDS IN YOUR PATH.
...
Your dad will find Kuro-maro, right?
I ENVY YOU, NANAMI ...

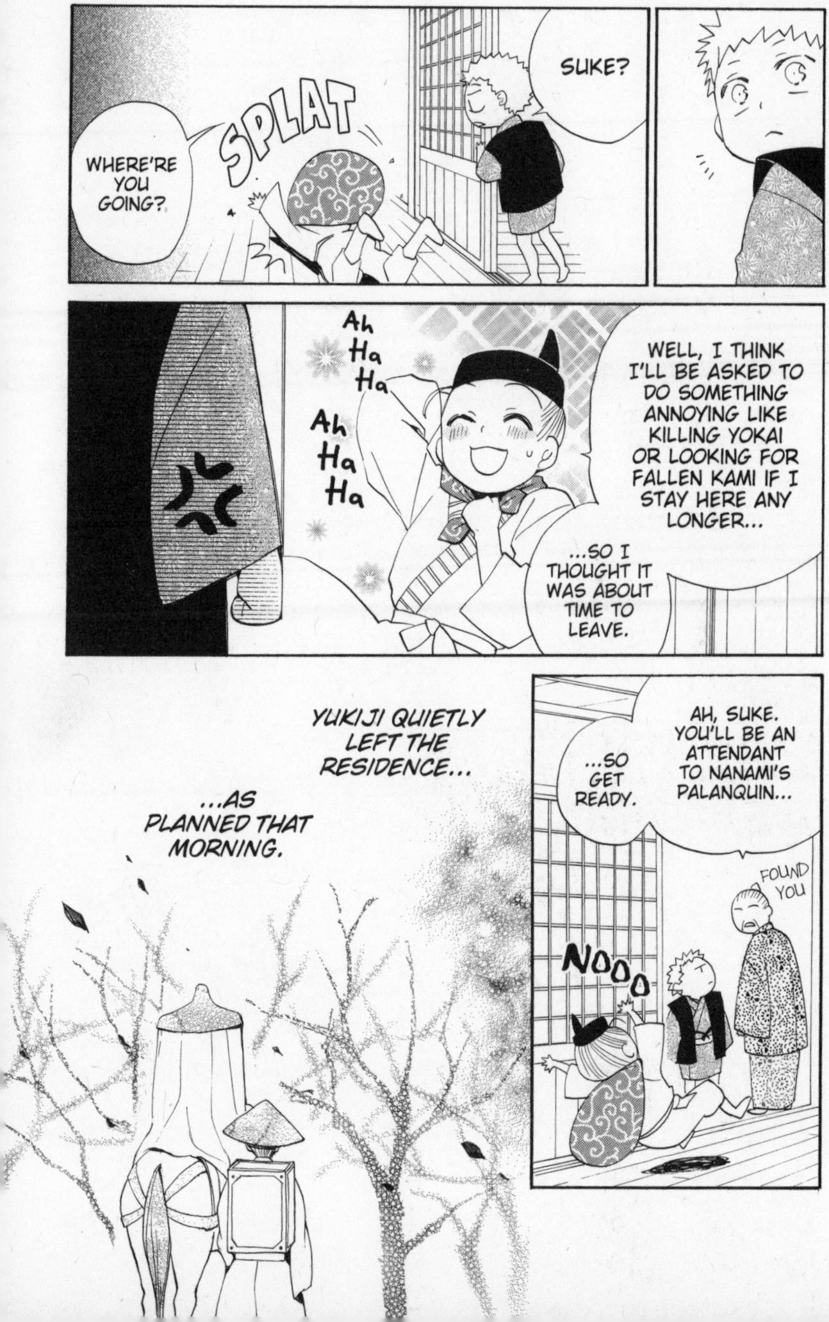
SUKE?
SPLAT
WHERE'RE YOU GOING?
WELL, I THINK I'LL BE ASKED TO DO SOMETHING ANNOYING LIKE KILLING YOKAI OR LOOKING FOR FALLEN KAMI IF I STAY HERE ANY LONGER...
...SO I THOUGHT IT WAS ABOUT TIME TO LEAVE.
Ah Ha Ha
Ah Ha Ha
AH, SUKE. YOU'LL BE AN ATTENDANT TO NANAMI'S PALANQUIN...
...SO GET READY.
FOUND YOU
NOOO
YUKIJI QUIETLY LEFT THE RESIDENCE...
...AS PLANNED THAT MORNING.

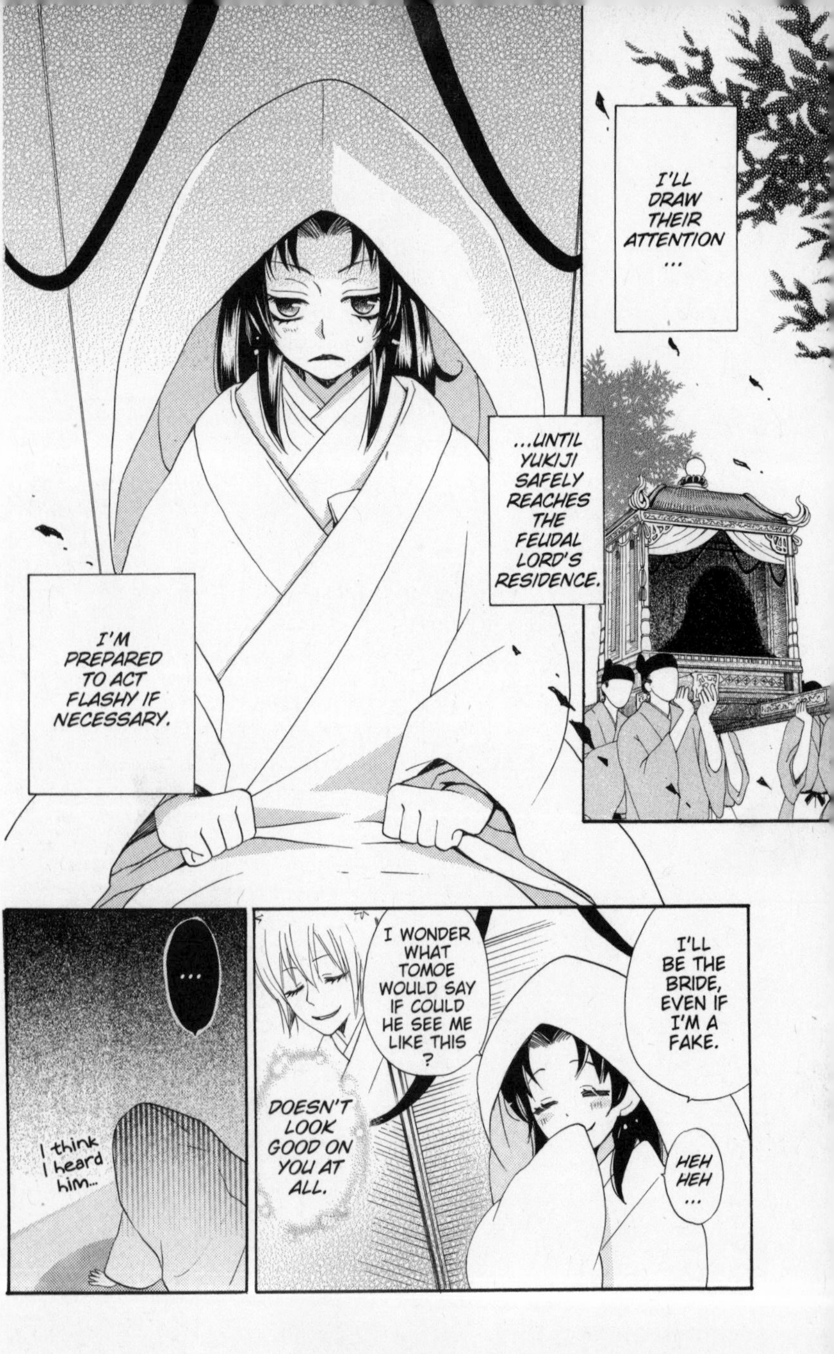
I'LL DRAW THEIR ATTENTION ...
...UNTIL YUKIJI SAFELY REACHES THE FEUDAL LORD'S RESIDENCE.
I'M PREPARED TO ACT FLASHY IF NECESSARY.
I'LL BE THE BRIDE, EVEN IF I'M A FAKE.
I WONDER WHAT TOMOE WOULD SAY IF COULD HE SEE ME LIKE THIS ?
HEH HEH ...
DOESN'T LOOK GOOD ON YOU AT ALL.
...
I think I heard him...

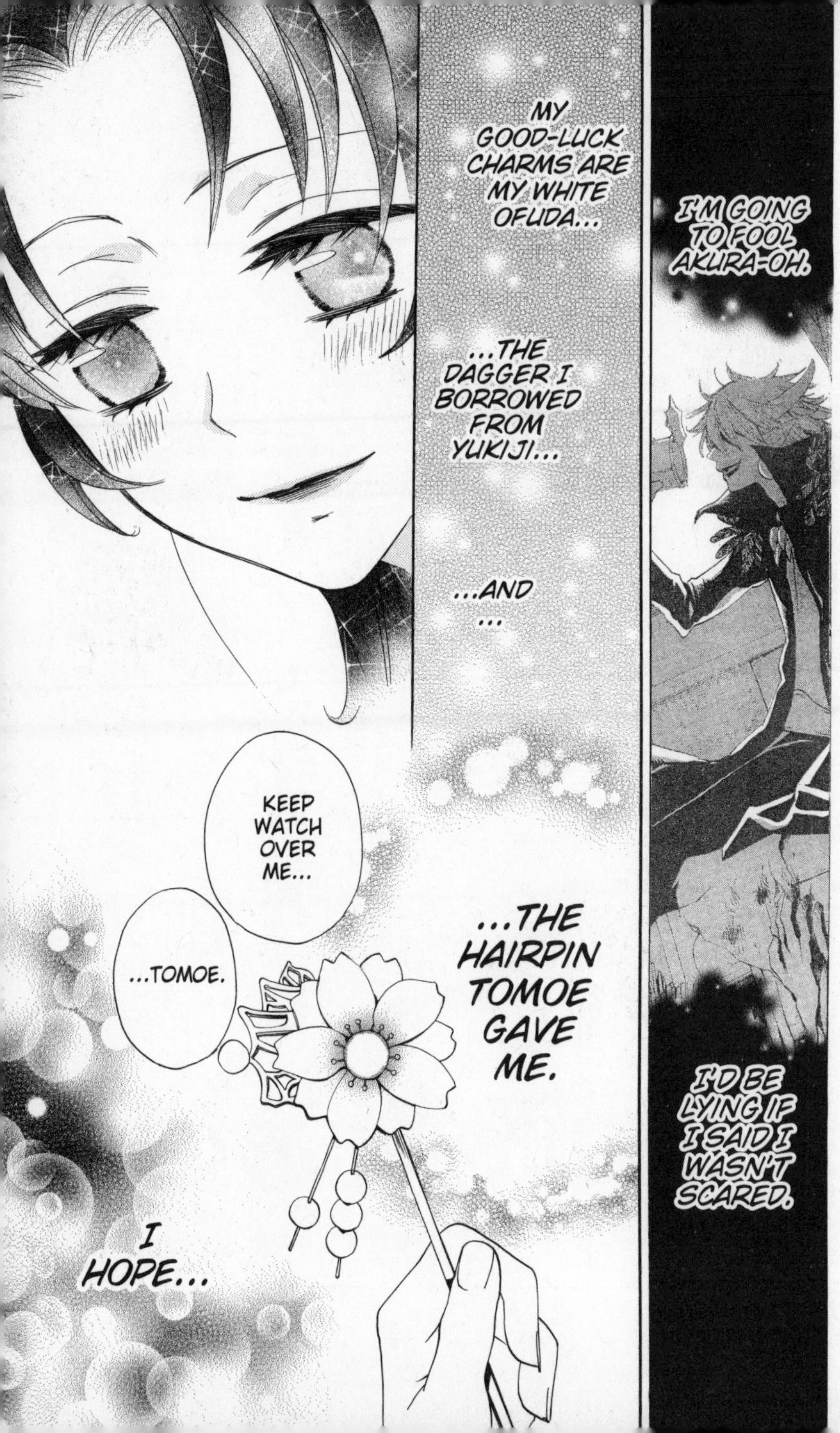
I'M GOING TO FOOL AKURA-OH.
I'D BE LYING IF I SAID I WASN'T SCARED.
MY GOOD-LUCK CHARMS ARE MY WHITE OFUDA...
...THE DAGGER I BORROWED FROM YUKIJI...
...AND ...
...THE HAIRPIN TOMOE GAVE ME.
I HOPE...
KEEP WATCH OVER ME...
...TOMOE.

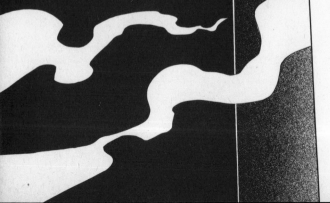

...EVERYTHING
GOES
WELL...

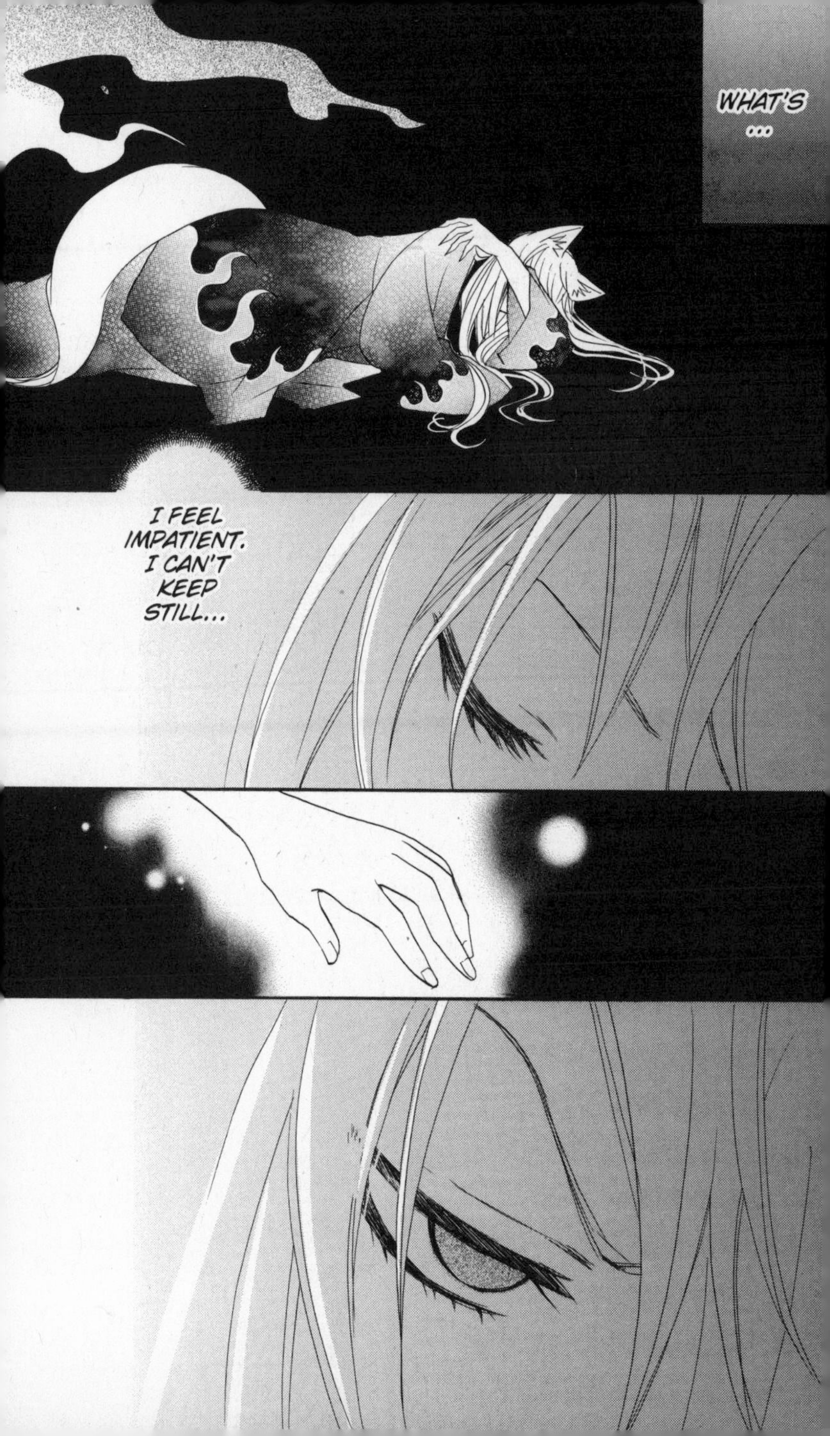
WHAT'S ...
I FEEL IMPATIENT. I CAN'T KEEP STILL...

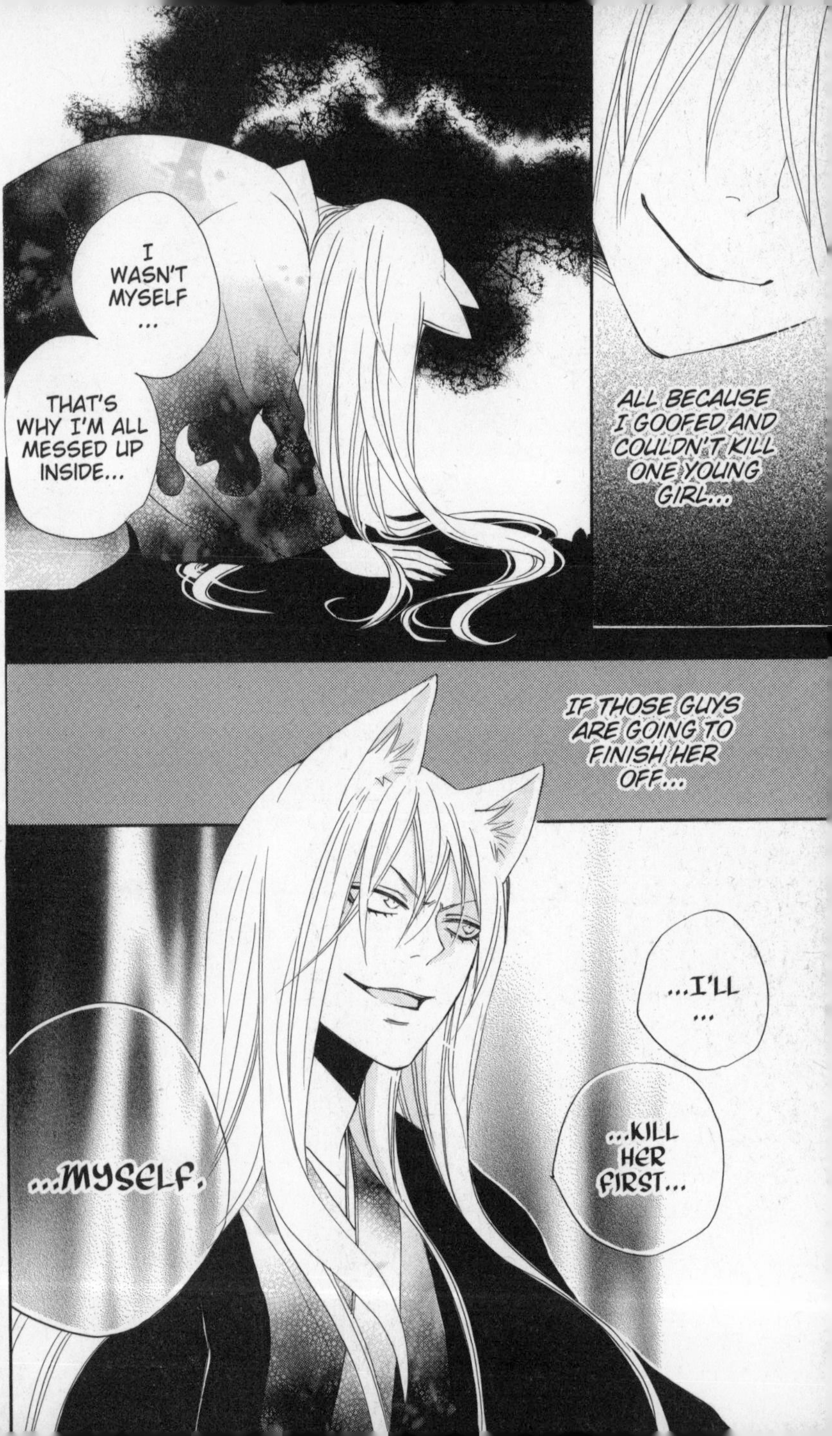
ALL BECAUSE I GOOFED AND COULDN'T KILL ONE YOUNG GIRL...
I WASN'T MYSELF...
THAT'S WHY I'M ALL MESSED UP INSIDE...
IF THOSE GUYS ARE GOING TO FINISH HER OFF...
...I'LL...
...KILL HER FIRST...
...MYSELF.

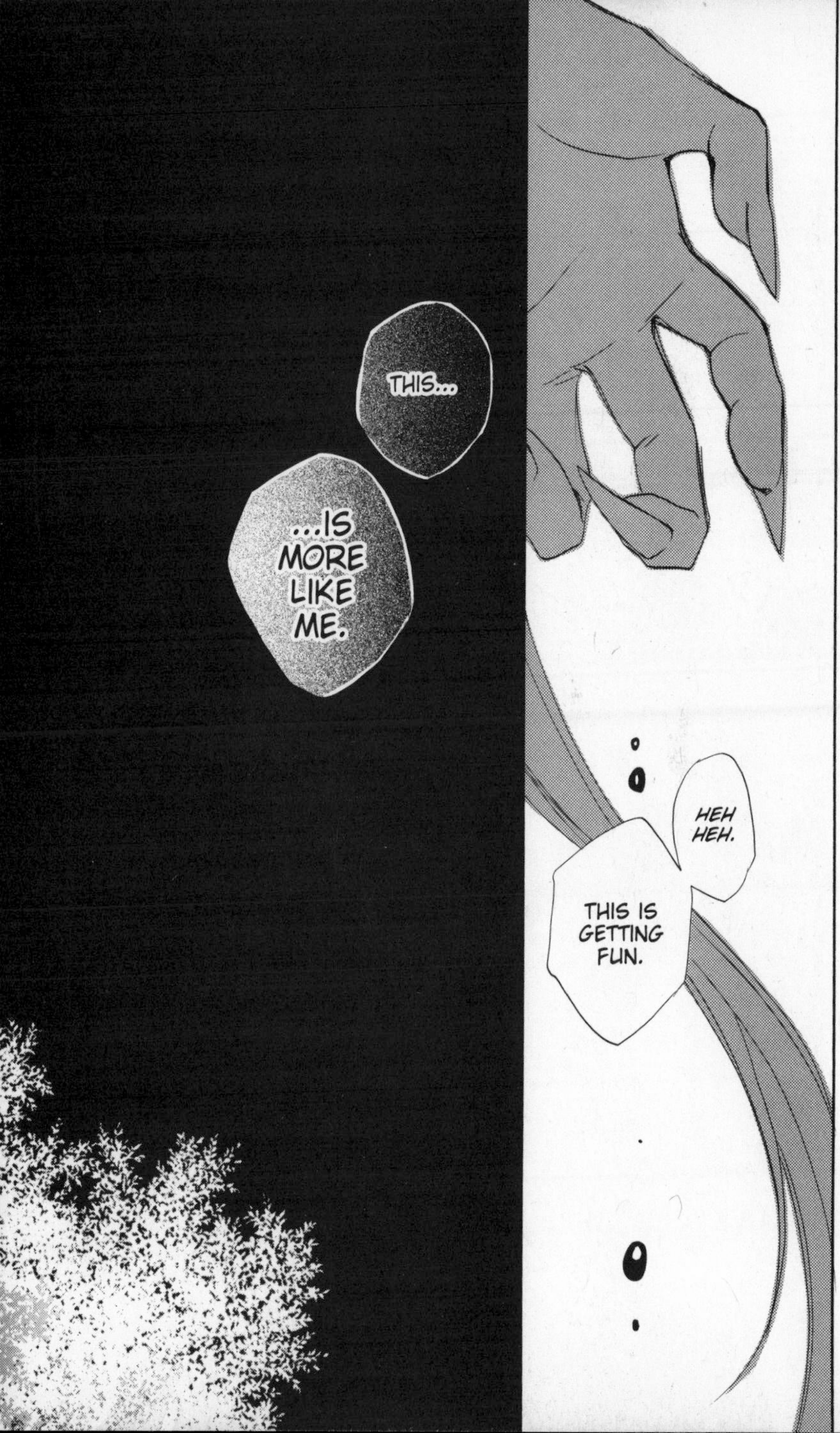
HEH HEH.
THIS IS GETTING FUN.
THIS...
...IS MORE LIKE ME.

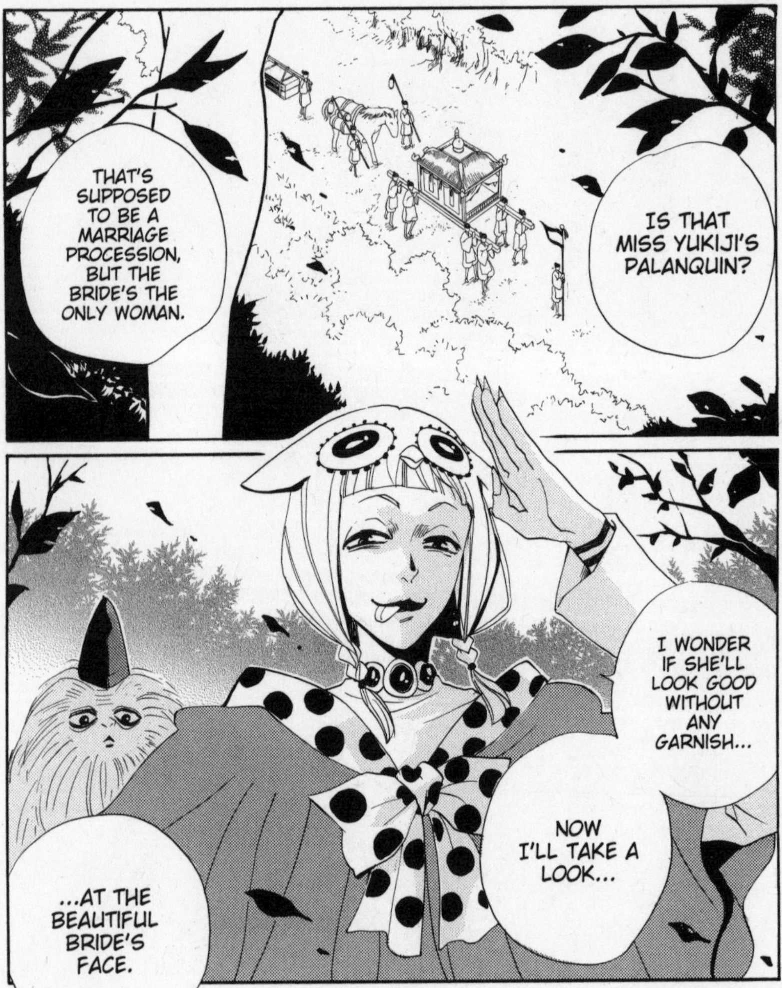
IS THAT MISS YUKIJI'S PALANQUIN?
THAT'S SUPPOSED TO BE A MARRIAGE PROCESSION, BUT THE BRIDE'S THE ONLY WOMAN.
I WONDER IF SHE'LL LOOK GOOD WITHOUT ANY GARNISH...
NOW I'LL TAKE A LOOK...
...AT THE BEAUTIFUL BRIDE'S FACE.

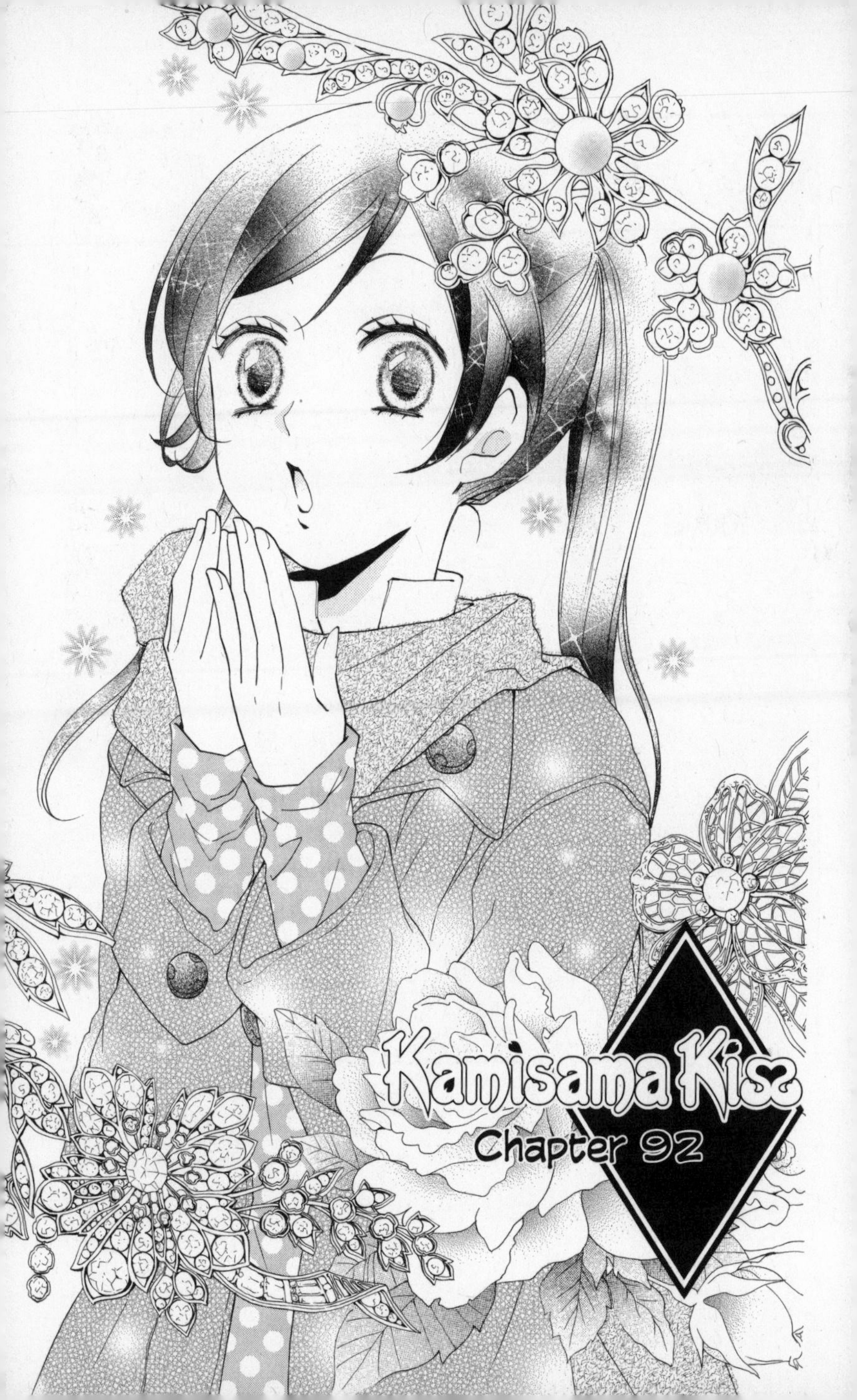
Kamisama Kiss
Chapter 92

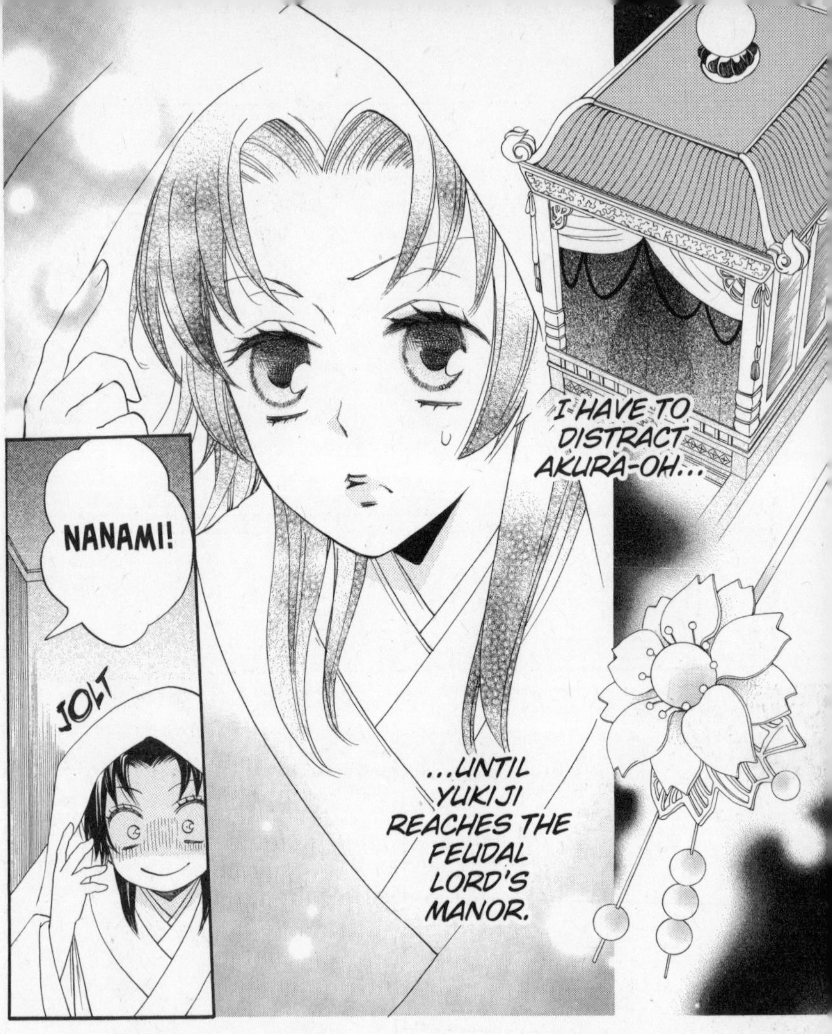
I HAVE TO DISTRACT AKURA-OH...
...UNTIL YUKIJI REACHES THE FEUDAL LORD'S MANOR.
NANAMI!
JOLT

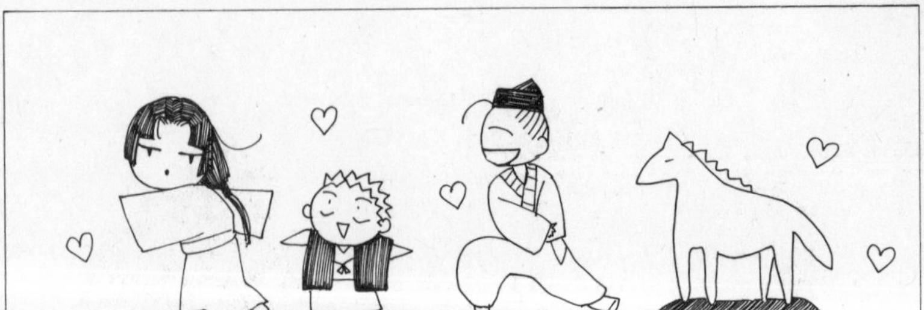

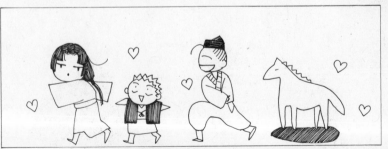

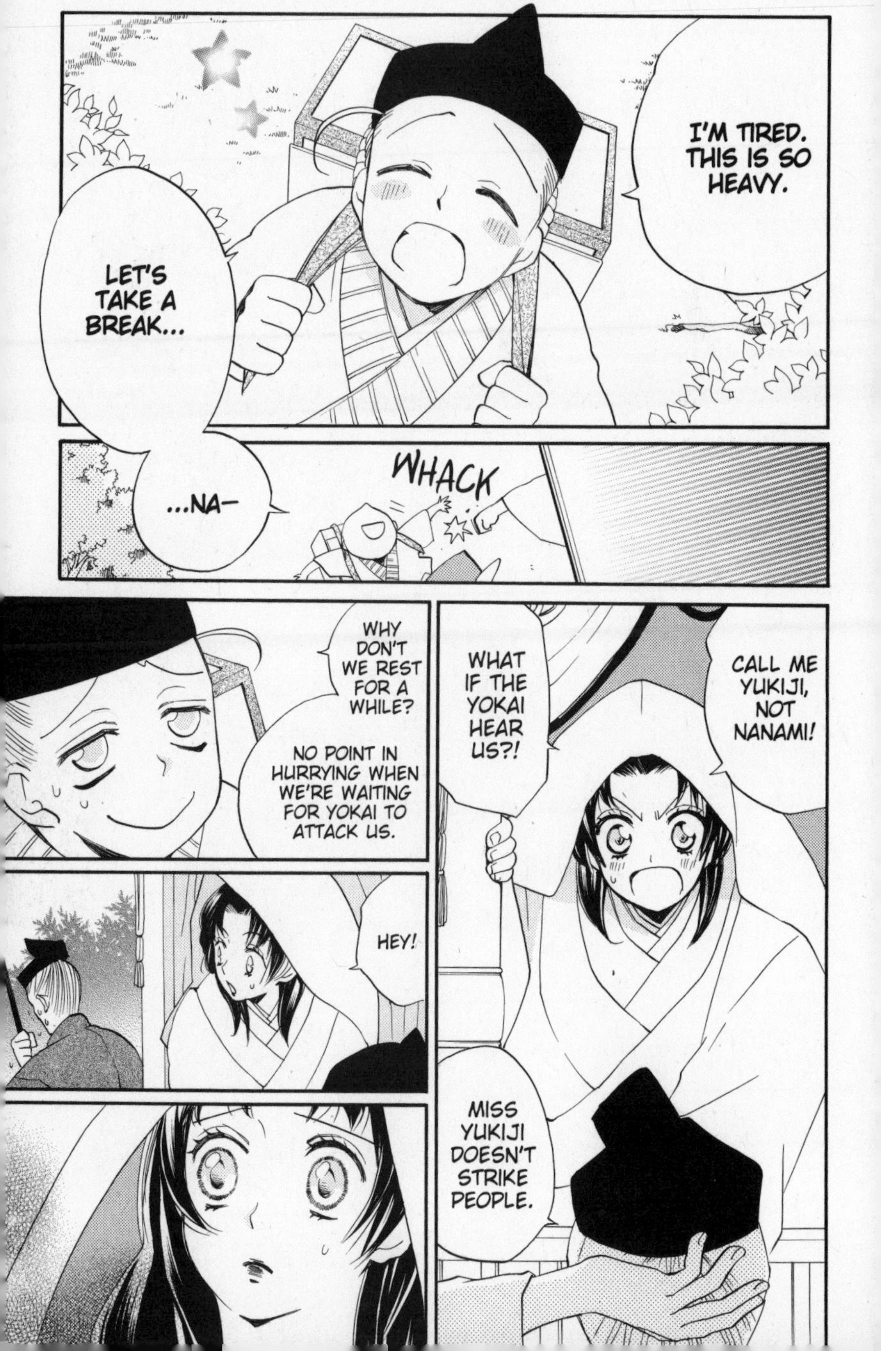
I'M TIRED. THIS IS SO HEAVY.
LET'S TAKE A BREAK...
...NA-
WHACK
CALL ME YUKIJI, NOT NANAMI!
WHAT IF THE YOKAI HEAR US?!
MISS YUKIJI DOESN'T STRIKE PEOPLE.
WHY DON'T WE REST FOR A WHILE?
NO POINT IN HURRYING WHEN WE'RE WAITING FOR YOKAI TO ATTACK US.
HEY!

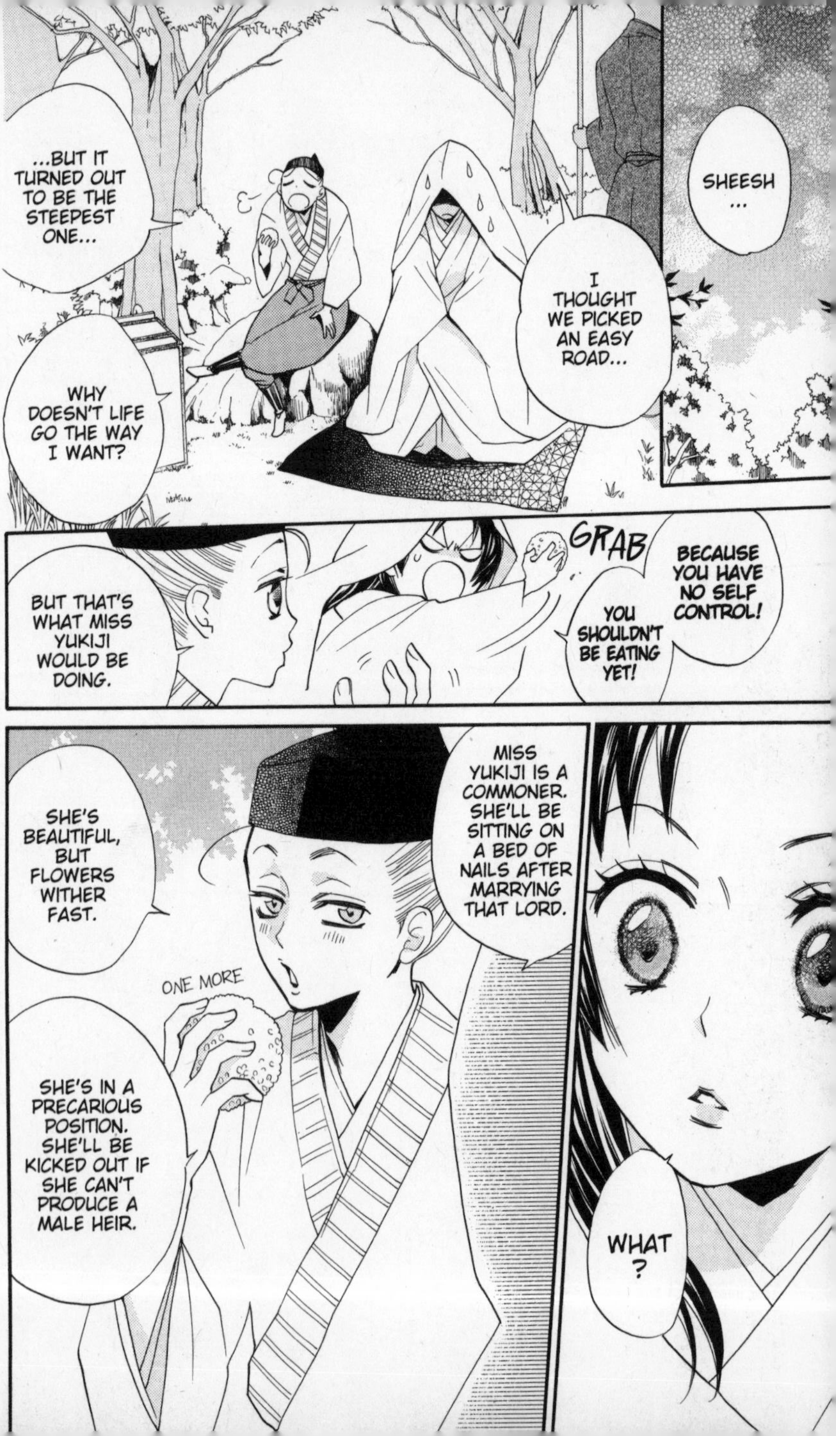
SHEESH ...
I THOUGHT WE PICKED AN EASY ROAD...
...BUT IT TURNED OUT TO BE THE STEEPEST ONE...
WHY DOESN'T LIFE GO THE WAY I WANT?
BECAUSE YOU HAVE NO SELF CONTROL!
YOU SHOULDN'T BE EATING YET!
GRAB
BUT THAT'S WHAT MISS YUKIJI WOULD BE DOING.
WHAT ?
MISS YUKIJI IS A COMMONER. SHE'LL BE SITTING ON A BED OF NAILS AFTER MARRYING THAT LORD.
SHE'S BEAUTIFUL, BUT FLOWERS WITHER FAST.
ONE MORE
SHE'S IN A PRECARIOUS POSITION. SHE'LL BE KICKED OUT IF SHE CAN'T PRODUCE A MALE HEIR.

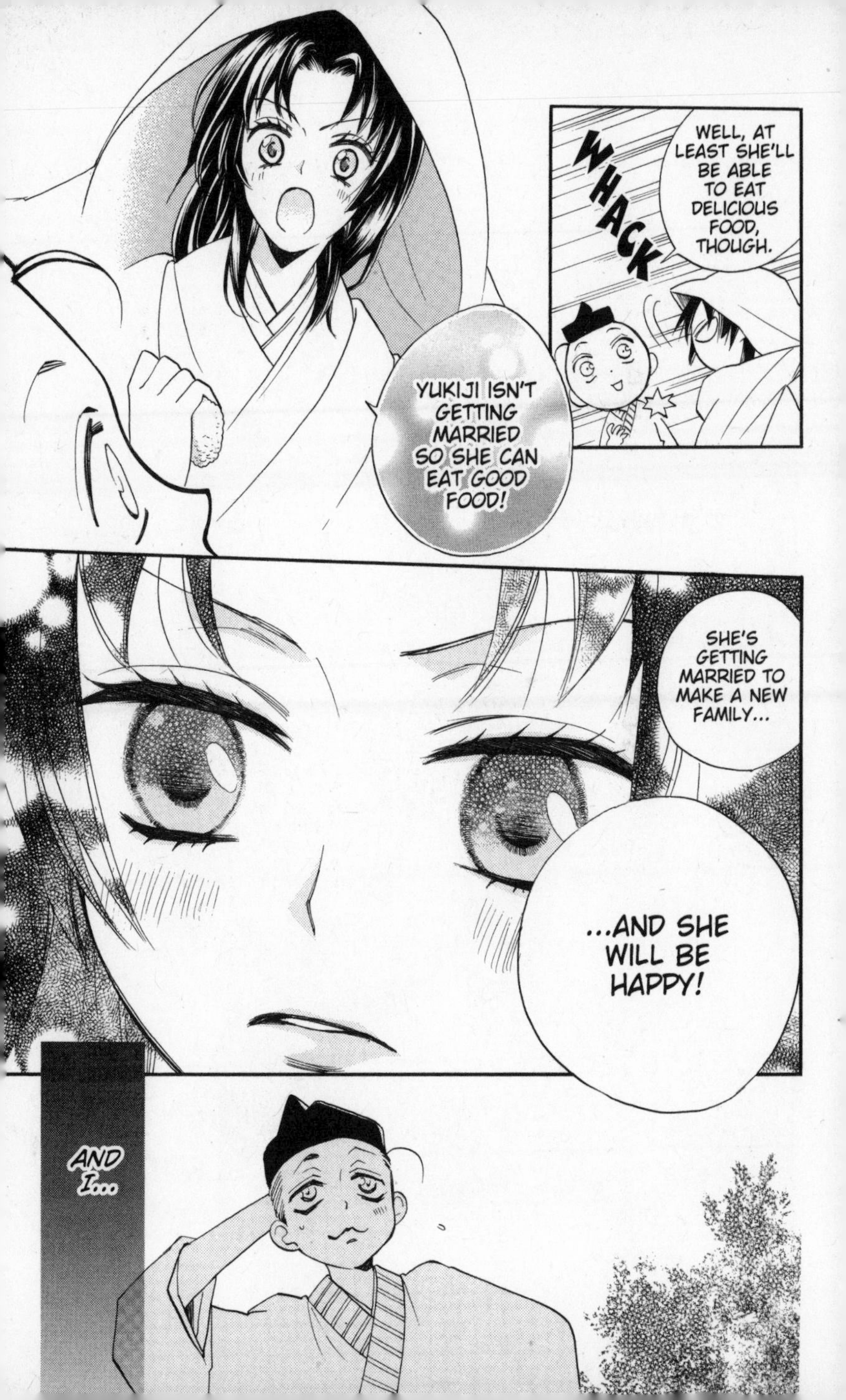
WELL, AT LEAST SHE'LL BE ABLE TO EAT DELICIOUS FOOD, THOUGH.
WHACK
YUKIJI ISN'T GETTING MARRIED SO SHE CAN EAT GOOD FOOD!
SHE'S GETTING MARRIED TO MAKE A NEW FAMILY...
...AND SHE WILL BE HAPPY!
AND I...

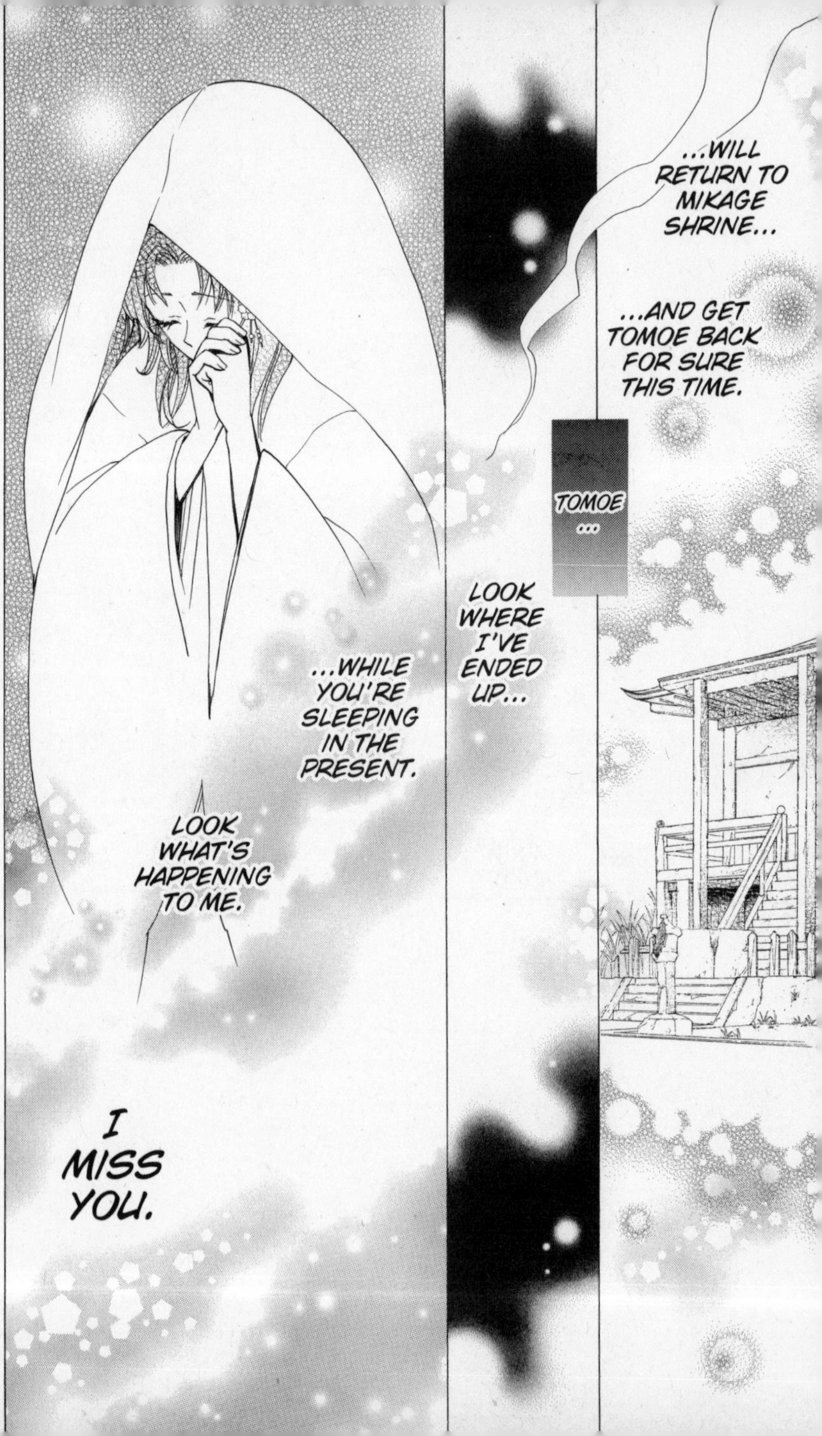
...WILL RETURN TO MIKAGE SHRINE...
...AND GET TOMOE BACK FOR SURE THIS TIME.
TOMOE ...
LOOK WHERE I'VE ENDED UP...
...WHILE YOU'RE SLEEPING IN THE PRESENT.
LOOK WHAT'S HAPPENING TO ME.
I MISS YOU.

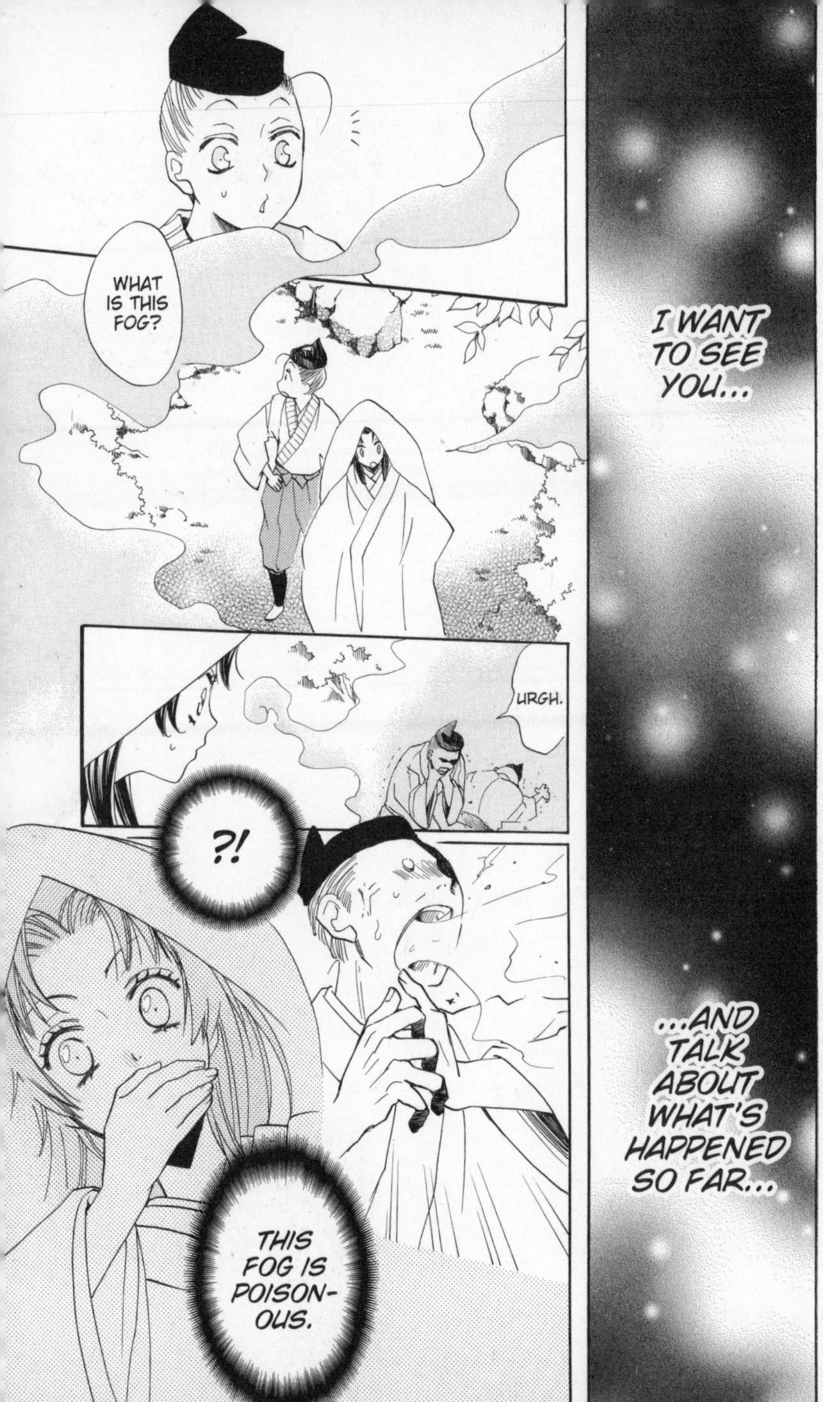
I WANT TO SEE YOU...
...AND TALK ABOUT WHAT'S HAPPENED SO FAR...
WHAT IS THIS FOG?
URGH.
?!
THIS FOG IS POISON-OUS.

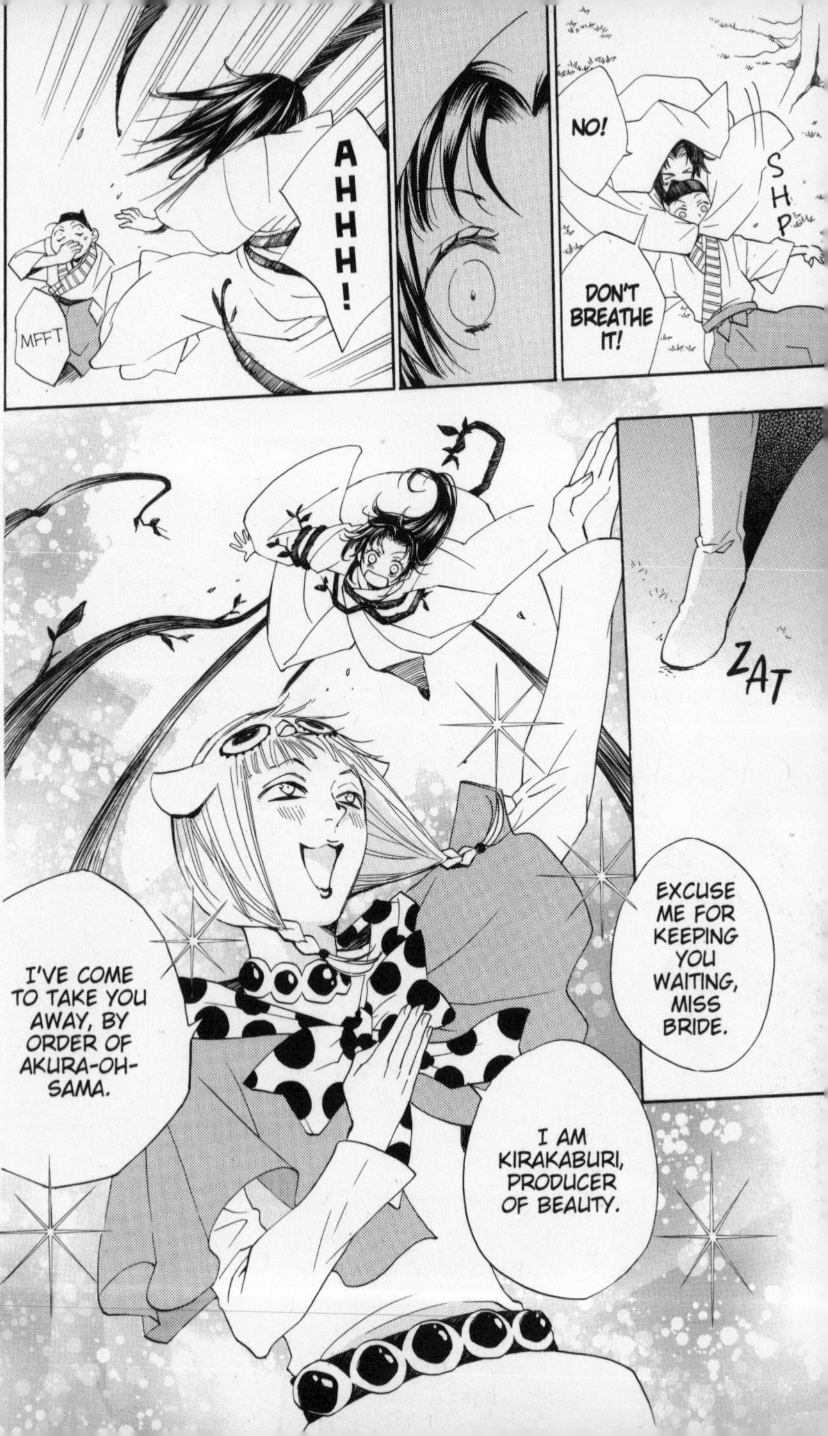
NO!
SHP
DON'T BREATHE IT!
AHHHH!
MFFT
ZAT
EXCUSE ME FOR KEEPING YOU WAITING, MISS BRIDE.
I AM KIRAKABURI, PRODUCER OF BEAUTY.
I'VE COME TO TAKE YOU AWAY, BY ORDER OF AKURA-OH-SAMA.

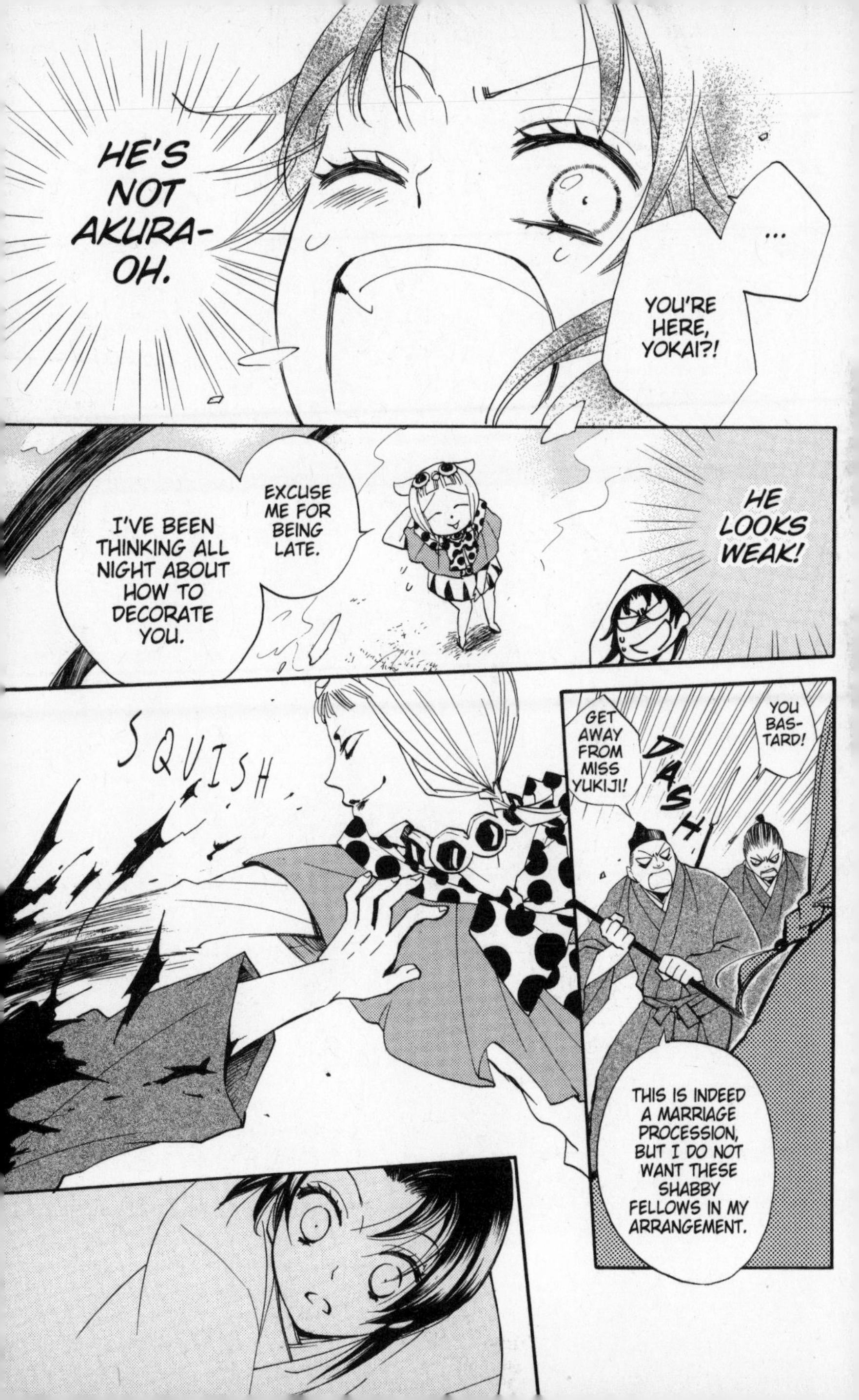
...
YOU'RE HERE, YOKAI?!
HE'S NOT AKURA-OH.
HE LOOKS WEAK!
EXCUSE ME FOR BEING LATE.
I'VE BEEN THINKING ALL NIGHT ABOUT HOW TO DECORATE YOU.
YOU BASTARD!
DASH
GET AWAY FROM MISS YUKIJI!
SQUISH
THIS IS INDEED A MARRIAGE PROCESSION, BUT I DO NOT WANT THESE SHABBY FELLOWS IN MY ARRANGEMENT.

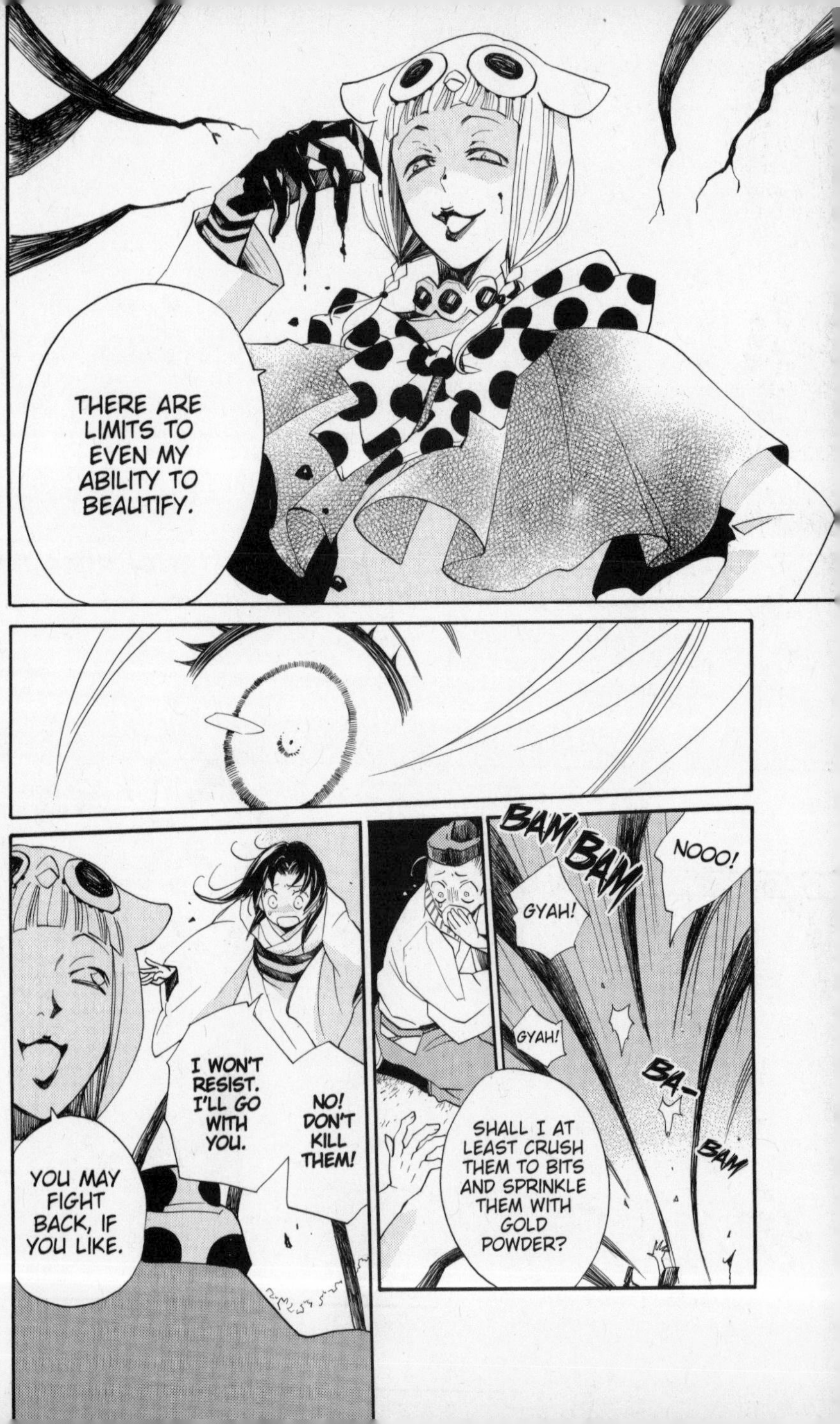
THERE ARE LIMITS TO EVEN MY ABILITY TO BEAUTIFY.
BAM BAM
NOOO!
GYAH!
GYAH!
BA-BAM
SHALL I AT LEAST CRUSH THEM TO BITS AND SPRINKLE THEM WITH GOLD POWDER?
NO! DON'T KILL THEM!
I WON'T RESIST. I'LL GO WITH YOU.
YOU MAY FIGHT BACK, IF YOU LIKE.

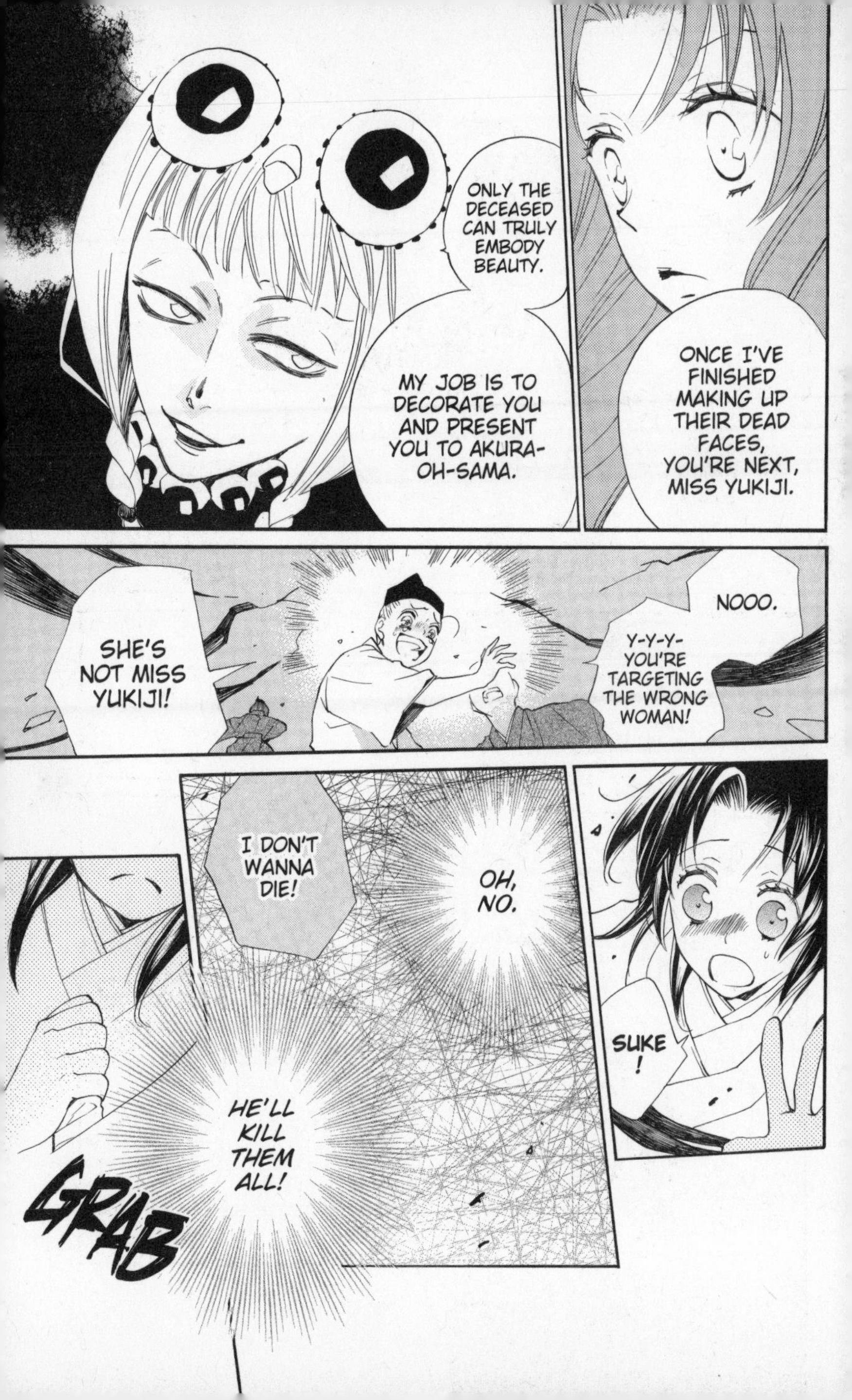
ONCE I'VE FINISHED MAKING UP THEIR DEAD FACES, YOU'RE NEXT, MISS YUKIJI.
ONLY THE DECEASED CAN TRULY EMBODY BEAUTY.
MY JOB IS TO DECORATE YOU AND PRESENT YOU TO AKURA-OH-SAMA.
NOOO.
Y-Y-Y-YOU'RE TARGETING THE WRONG WOMAN!
SHE'S NOT MISS YUKIJI!
SUKE!
I DON'T WANNA DIE!
OH, NO.
HE'LL KILL THEM ALL!
GRAB

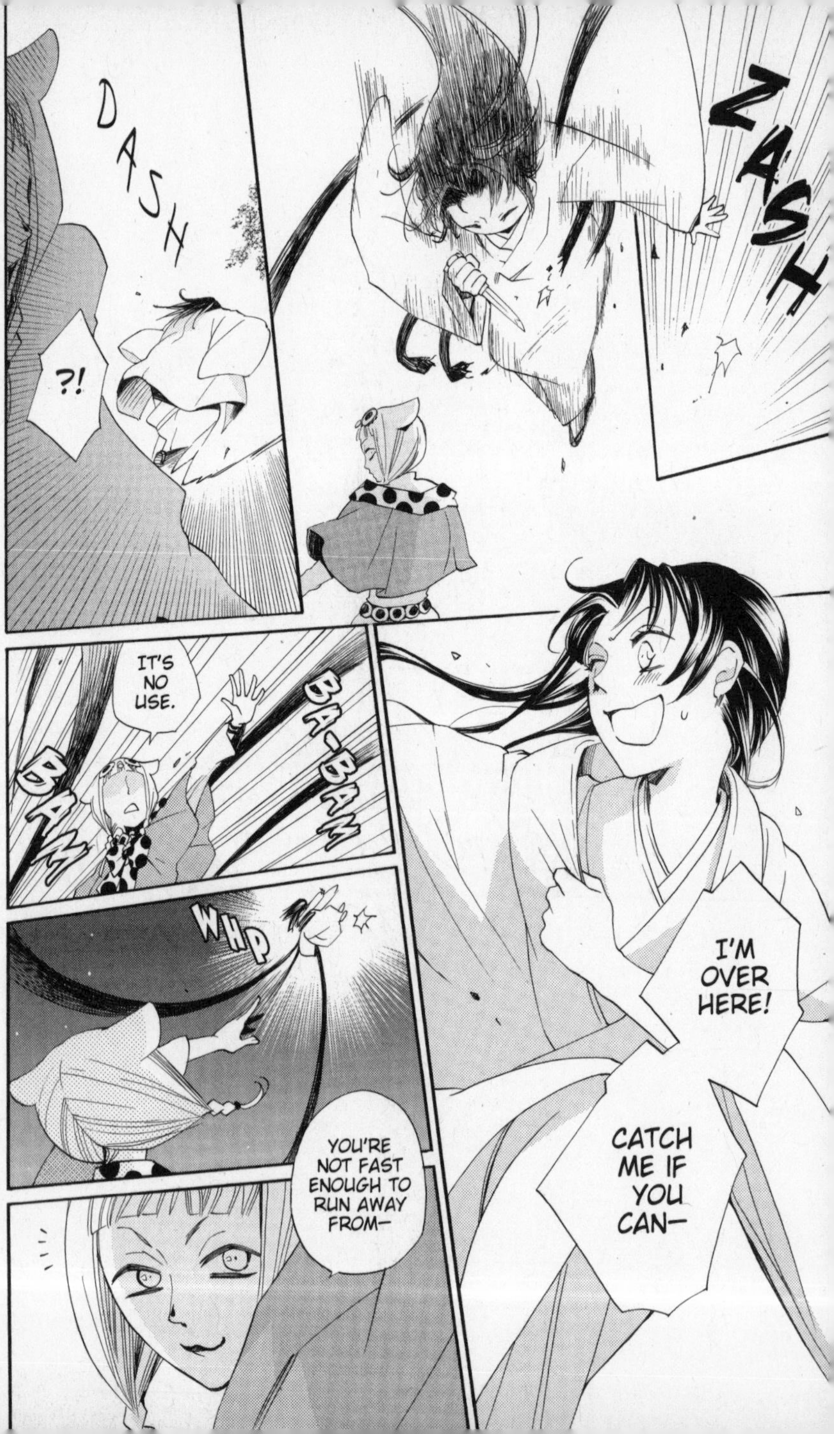
ZASH
DASH
?!
I'M OVER HERE!
CATCH ME IF YOU CAN—
IT'S NO USE.
BA-BAM
BAM
WHP
YOU'RE NOT FAST ENOUGH TO RUN AWAY FROM—

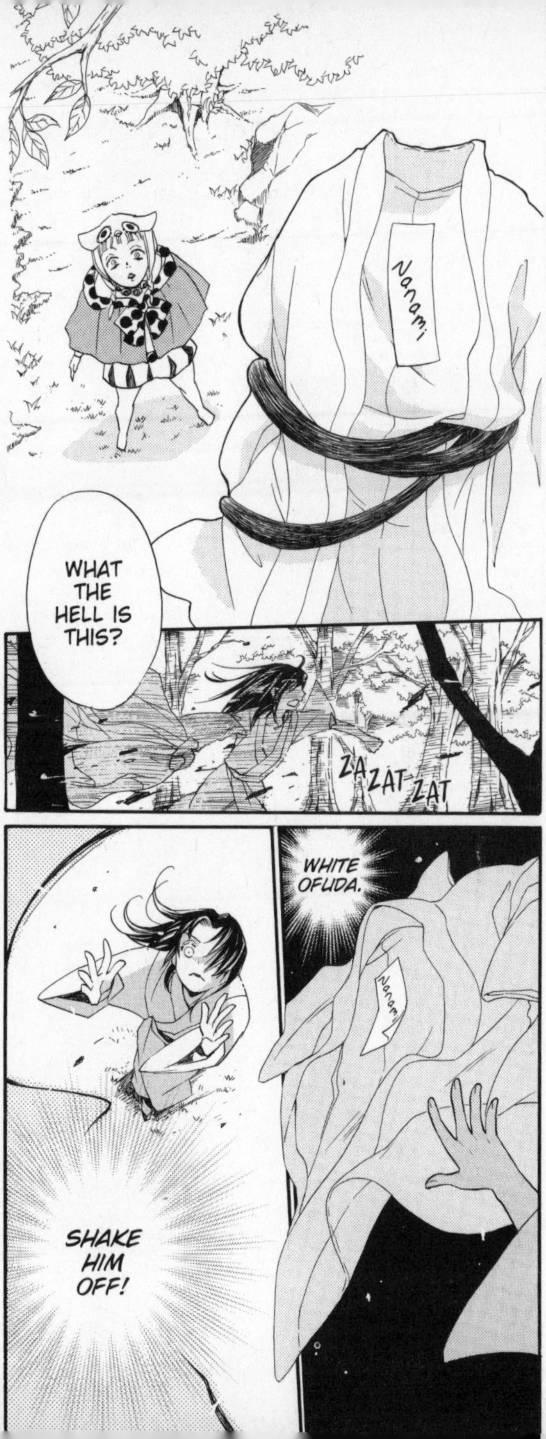
Nanami
WHAT THE HELL IS THIS?
ZA ZAT ZAT
WHITE OFUDA.
Nanami
SHAKE HIM OFF!

I'm on a diet nowadays. However, maybe because of that, things haven't been too good. I've gotten ill, my shoulders have gotten stiff, ← ?! and I've lost my strength.

I've been eating tofu instead of rice, for example, but do I need to eat rice after all? All right, I'll eat lots of rice then! No, no. If I do that, I'll suffer rebound effects. All right, then I'll take the calo-limit supplements!

And so I'm taking FANCL's calo-limit, a diet supplement.

I'll take calo-limit and eat rice... will it work? I hope it works... But dieting doesn't reduce my body size much. Dieting is difficult.

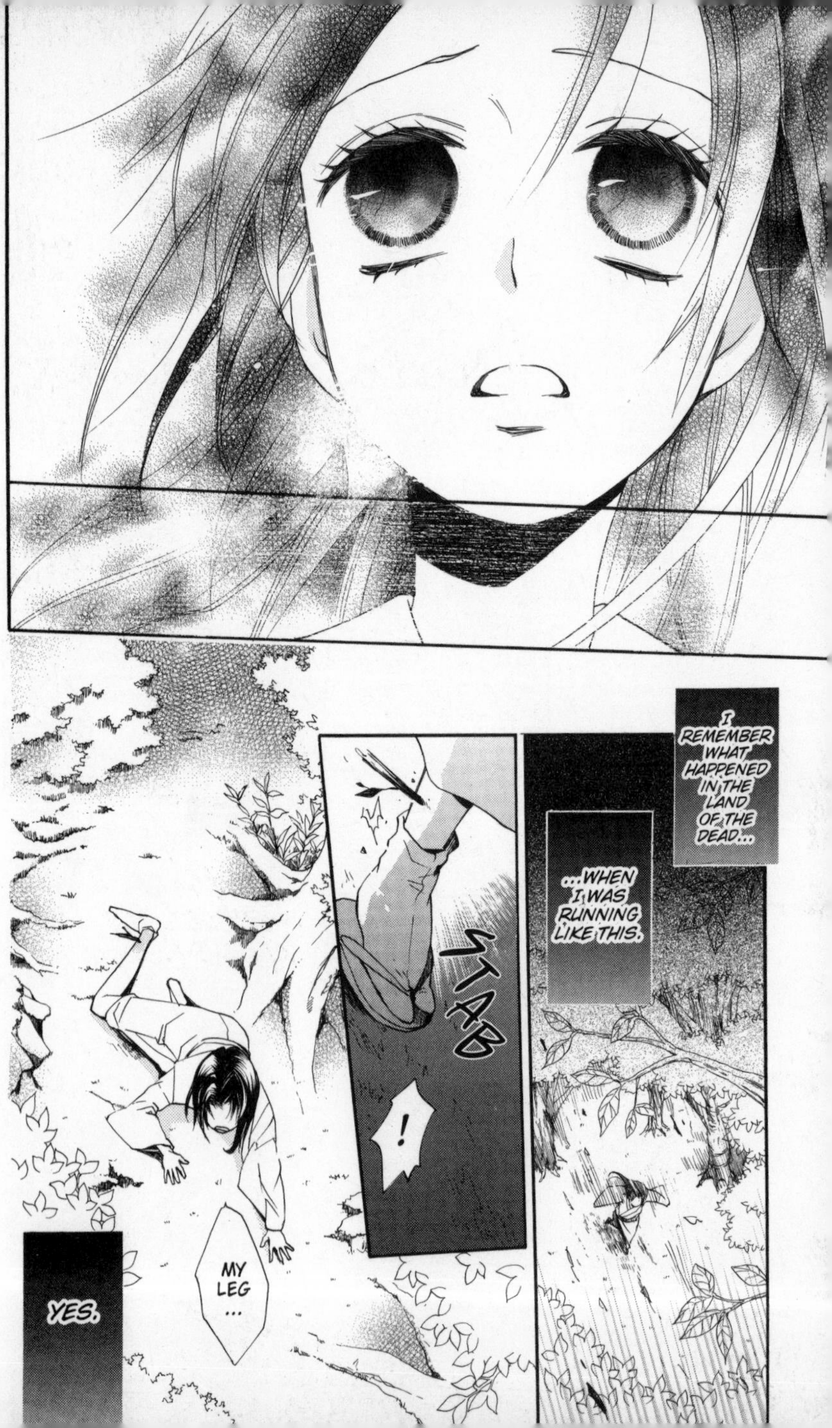
I REMEMBER WHAT HAPPENED IN THE LAND OF THE DEAD...
...WHEN I WAS RUNNING LIKE THIS.
STAB
!
MY LEG ...
YES.

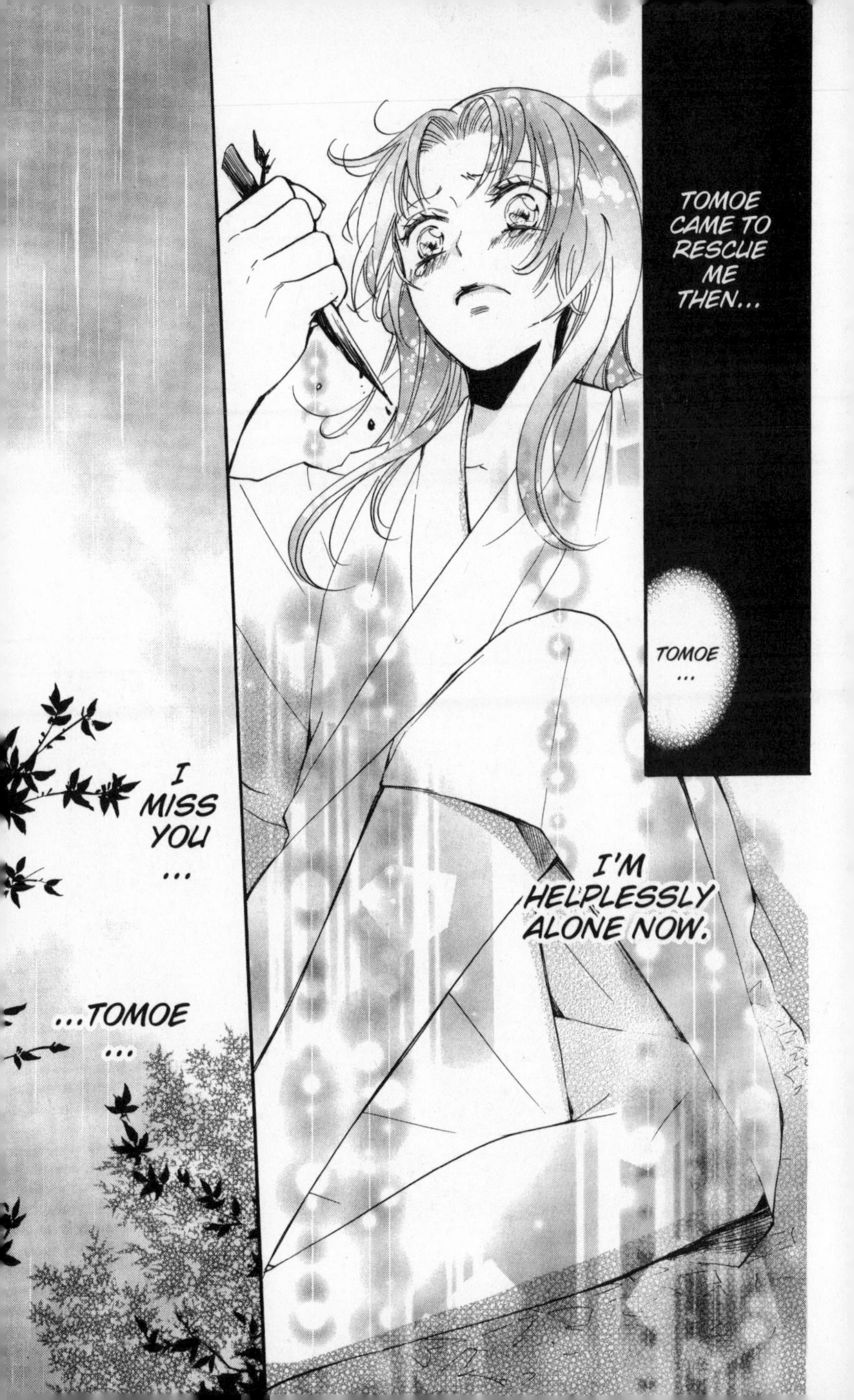
TOMOE CAME TO RESCUE ME THEN...
TOMOE ...
I'M HELPLESSLY ALONE NOW.
I MISS YOU ...
...TOMOE ...

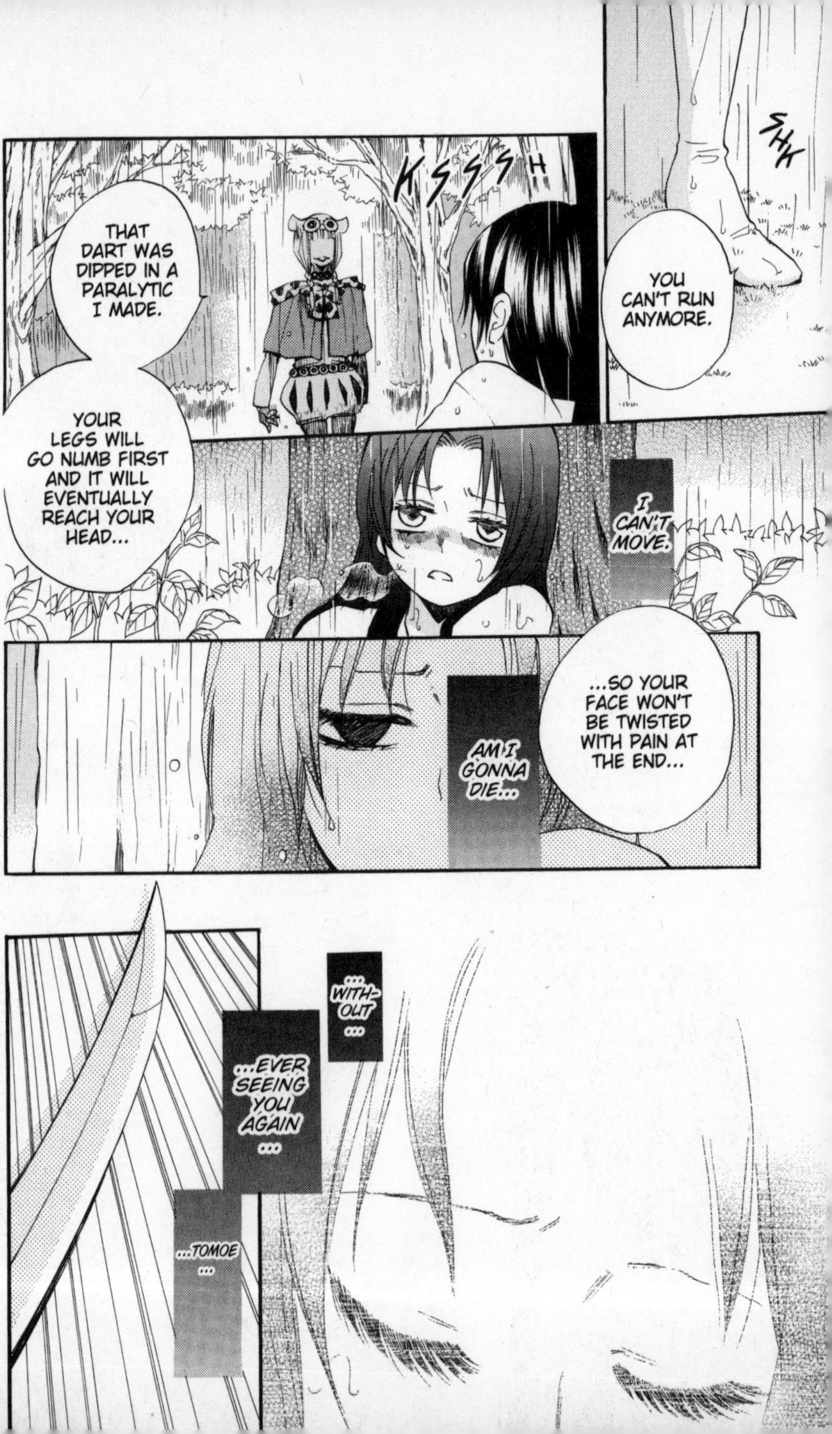
SHK
YOU CAN'T RUN ANYMORE.
KSSSH
THAT DART WAS DIPPED IN A PARALYTIC I MADE.
YOUR LEGS WILL GO NUMB FIRST AND IT WILL EVENTUALLY REACH YOUR HEAD...
I CAN'T MOVE.
...SO YOUR FACE WON'T BE TWISTED WITH PAIN AT THE END...
AM I GONNA DIE...
...WITH-OUT...
...EVER SEEING YOU AGAIN...
...TOMOE...

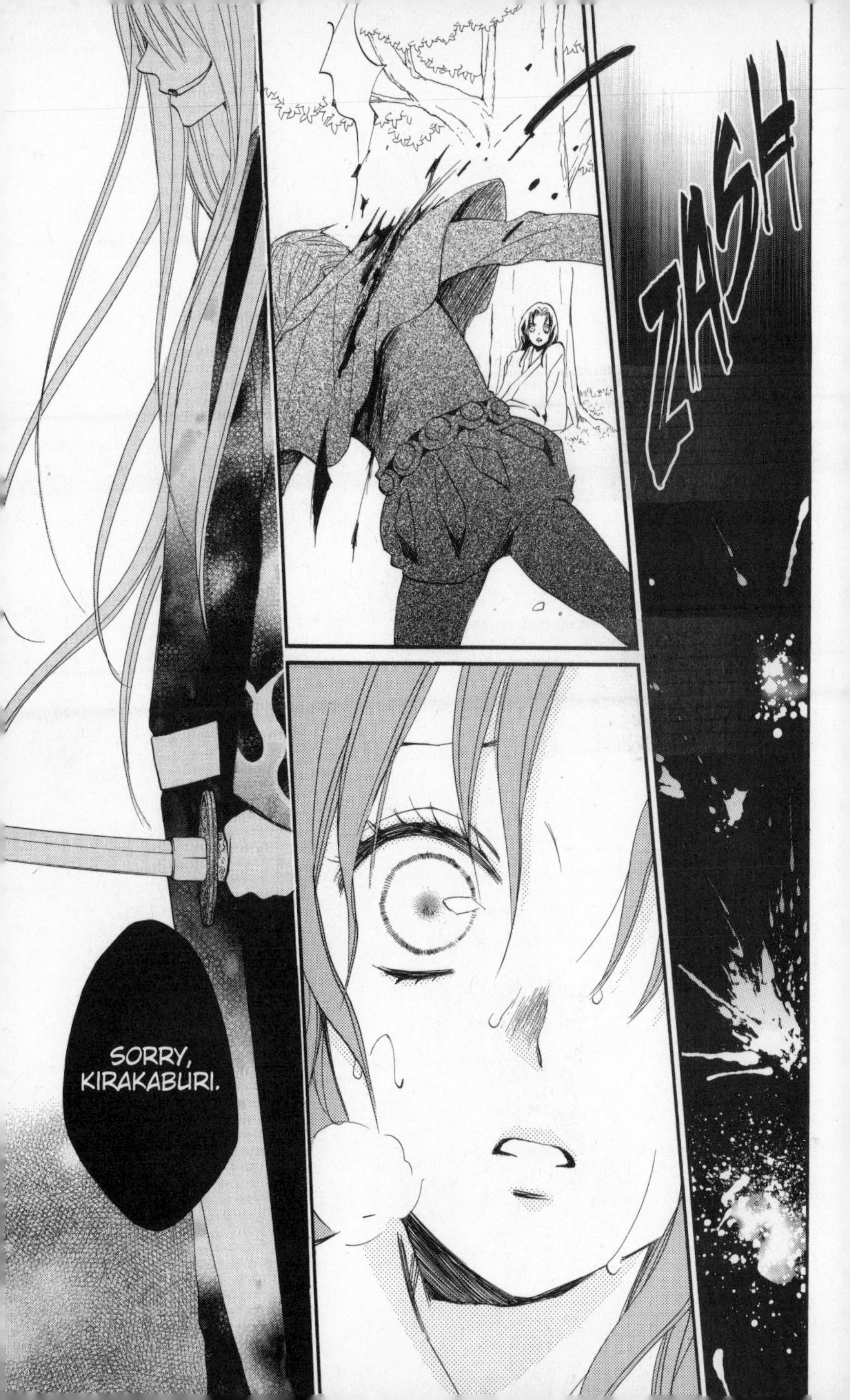
ZASH
SORRY, KIRAKABURI.

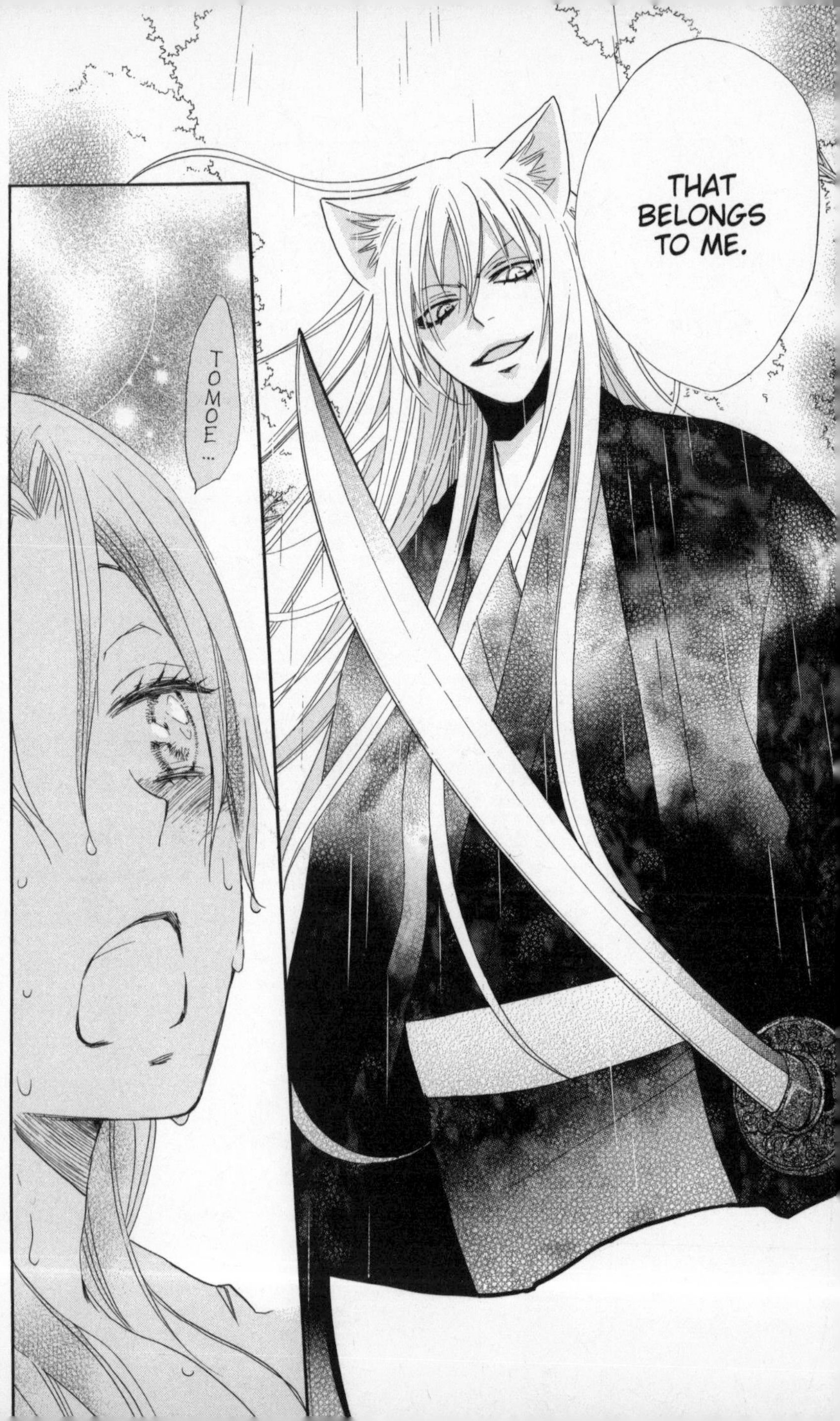
THAT BELONGS TO ME.
TOMOE...

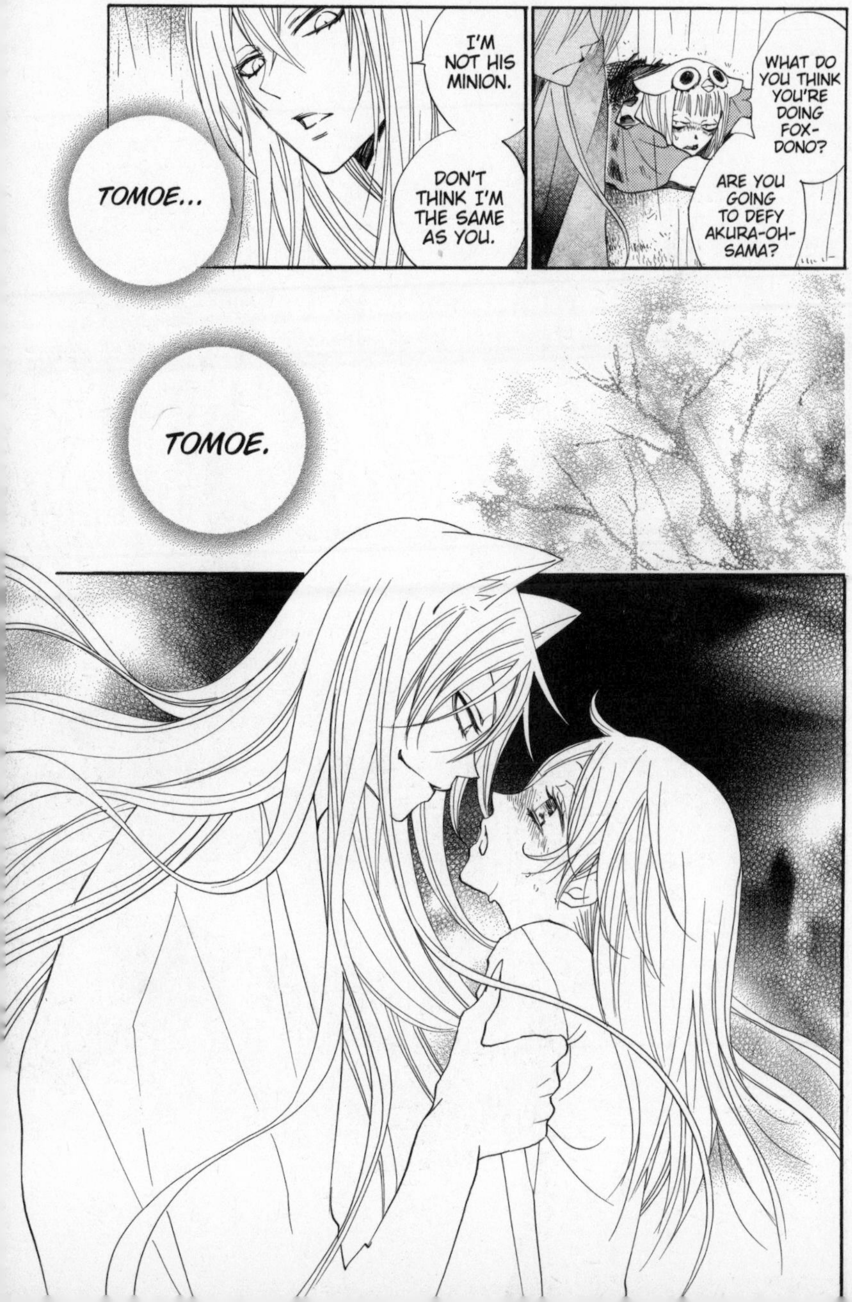
WHAT DO YOU THINK YOU'RE DOING FOX-DONO?
ARE YOU GOING TO DEFY AKURA-OH-SAMA?
I'M NOT HIS MINION.
DON'T THINK I'M THE SAME AS YOU.
TOMOE...
TOMOE.

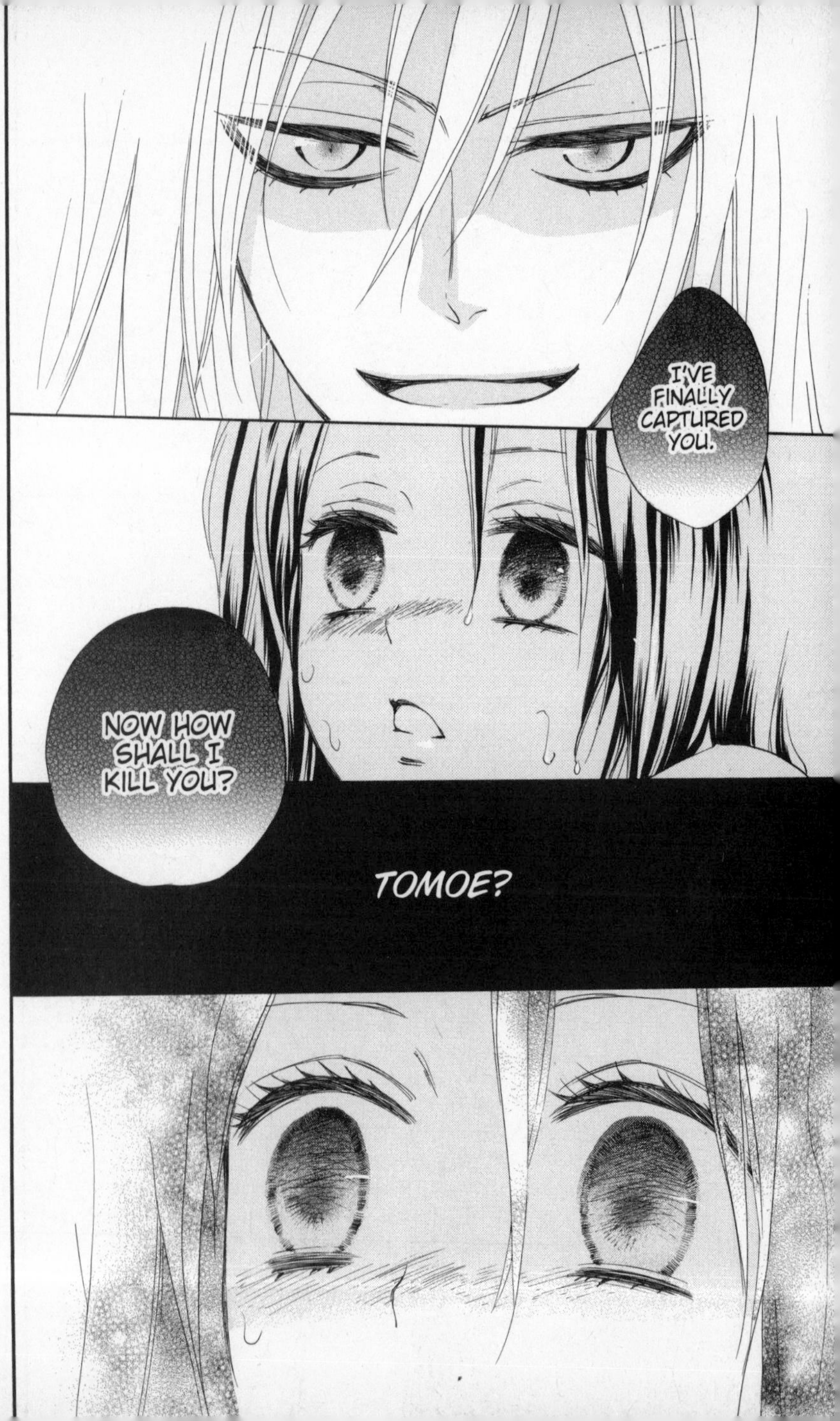
I'VE FINALLY CAPTURED YOU.
NOW HOW SHALL I KILL YOU?
TOMOE?

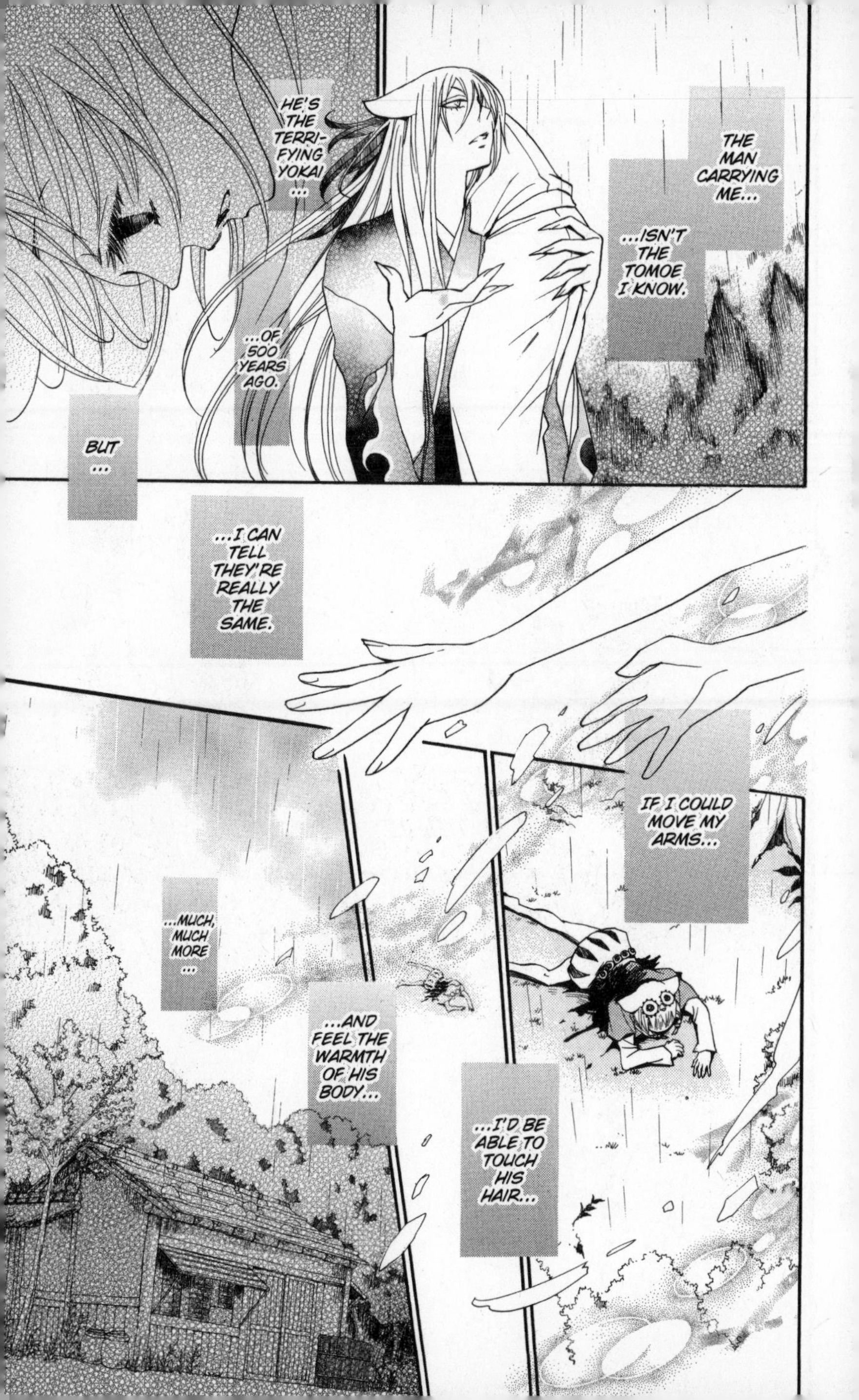

THE MAN CARRYING ME...
...ISN'T THE TOMOE I KNOW.
HE'S THE TERRI-FYING YOKAI...
...OF 500 YEARS AGO.
BUT...
...I CAN TELL THEY'RE REALLY THE SAME.
IF I COULD MOVE MY ARMS...
...I'D BE ABLE TO TOUCH HIS HAIR...
...AND FEEL THE WARMTH OF HIS BODY...
...MUCH, MUCH MORE...

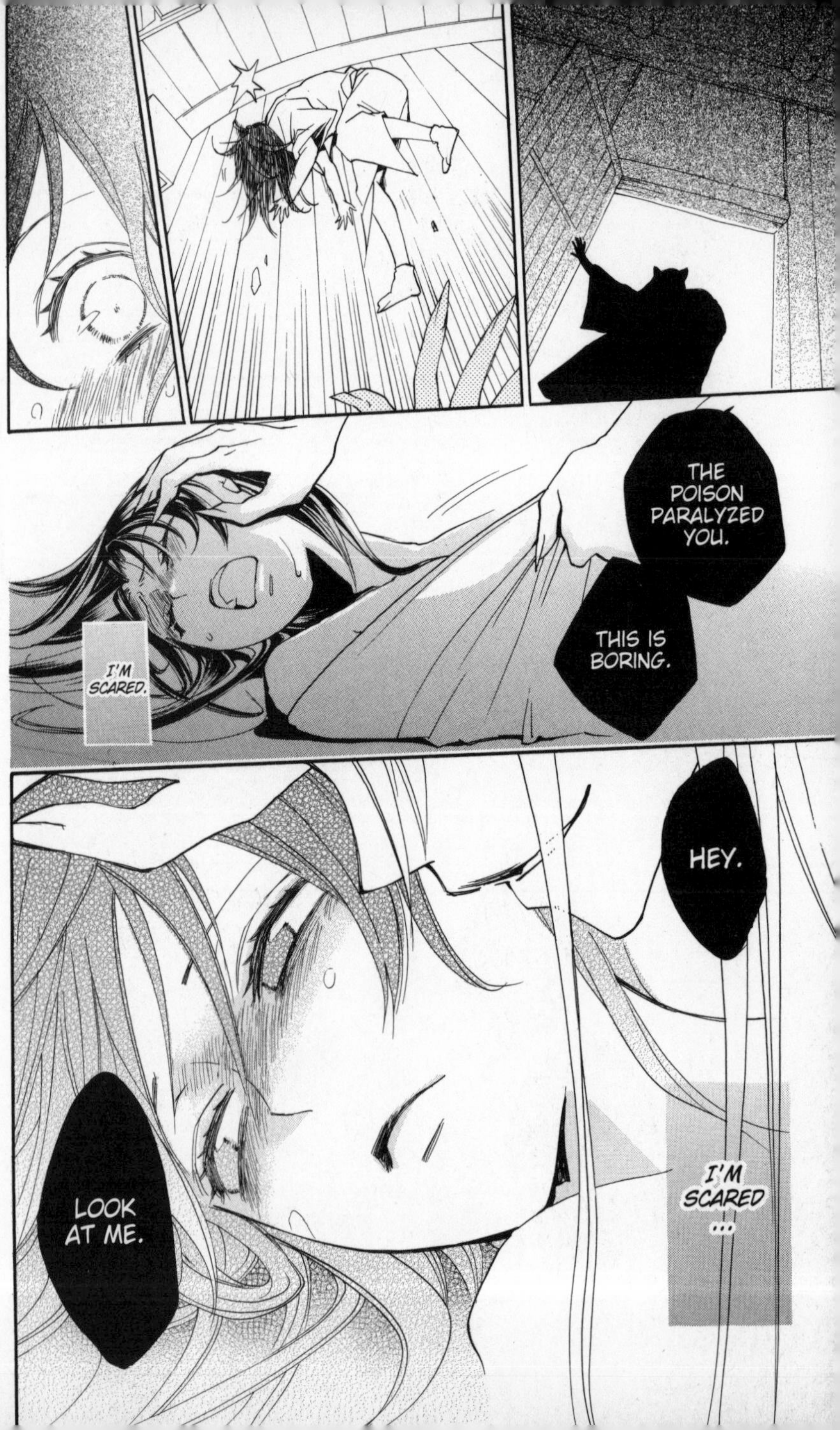

THE POISON PARALYZED YOU.
THIS IS BORING.
I'M SCARED.
HEY.
I'M SCARED ...
LOOK AT ME.

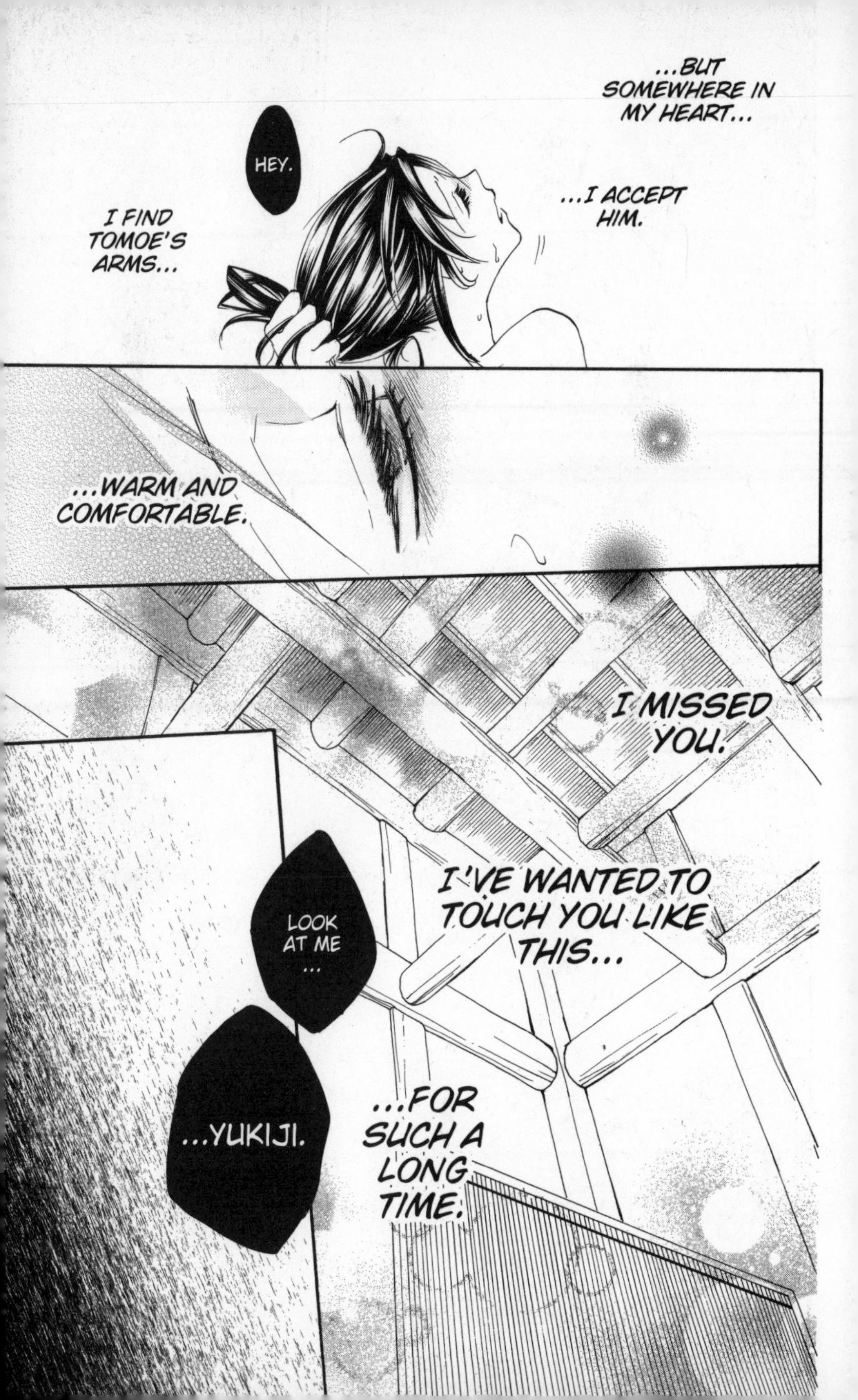
...BUT SOMEWHERE IN MY HEART...
...I ACCEPT HIM.
HEY.
I FIND TOMOE'S ARMS...
...WARM AND COMFORTABLE.
I MISSED YOU.
I'VE WANTED TO TOUCH YOU LIKE THIS...
...FOR SUCH A LONG TIME.
LOOK AT ME ...
...YUKIJI.

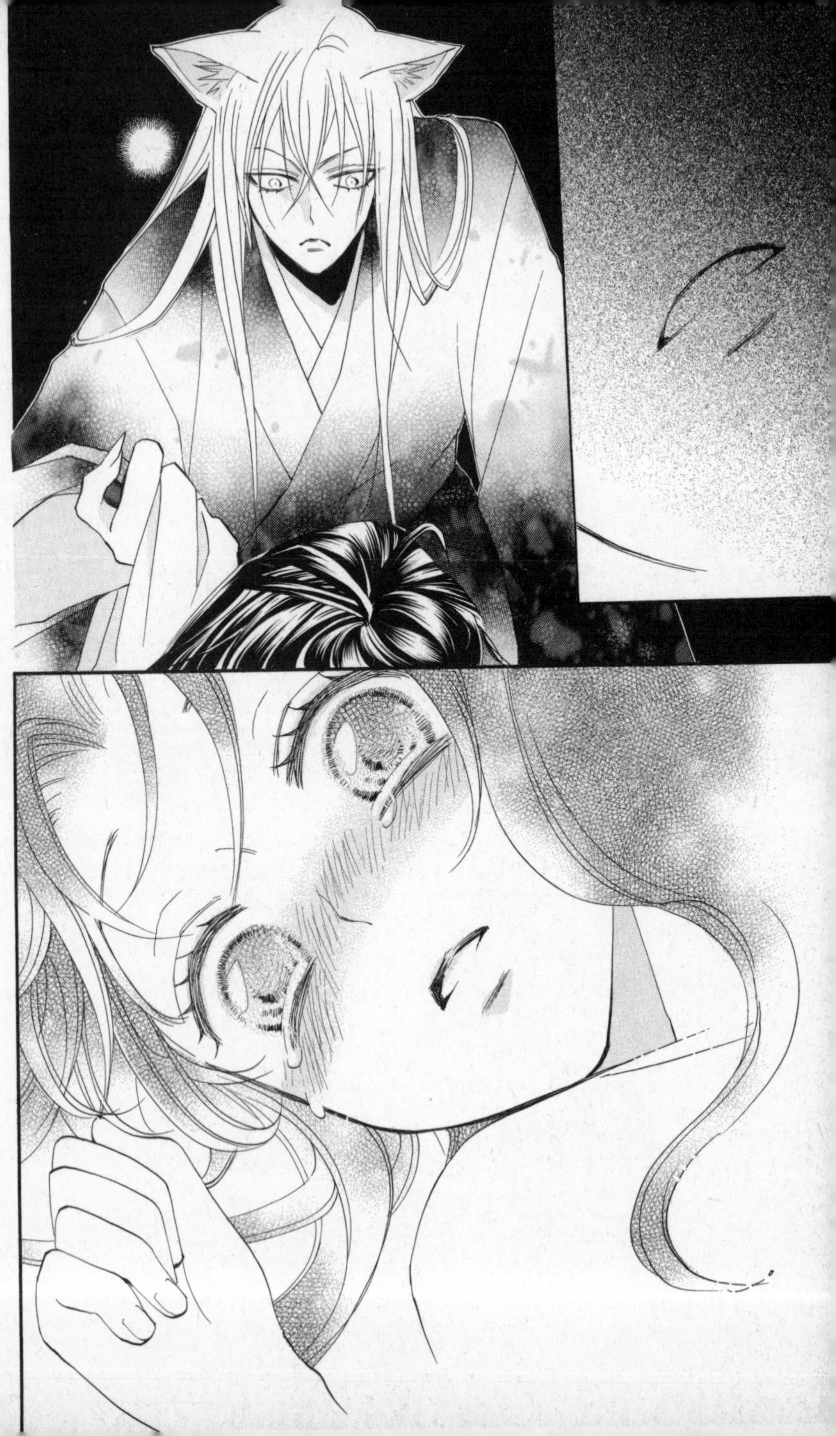

YUKIJI.

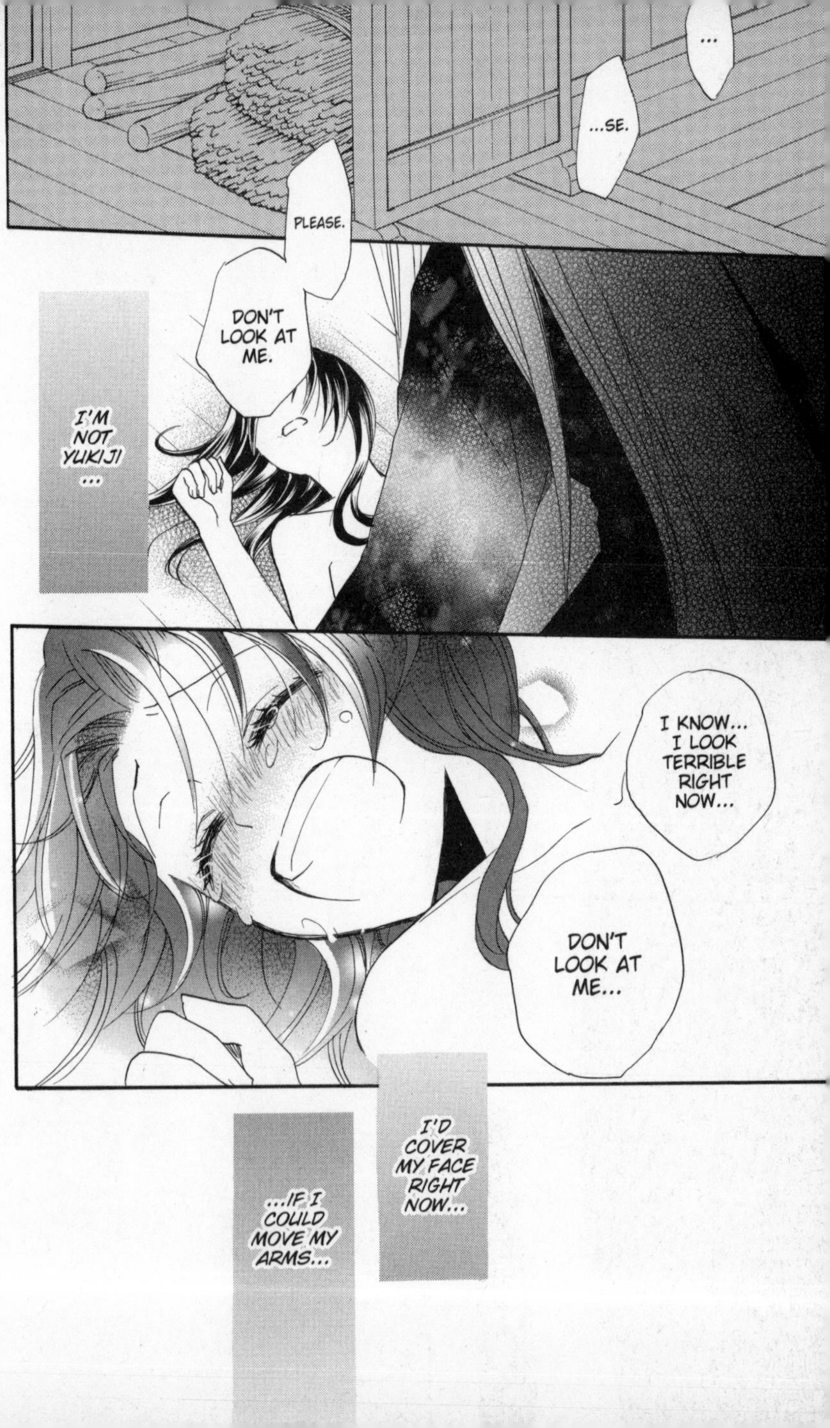
...
...SE.
PLEASE.
DON'T LOOK AT ME.
I'M NOT YUKIJI ...
I KNOW... I LOOK TERRIBLE RIGHT NOW...
DON'T LOOK AT ME...
I'D COVER MY FACE RIGHT NOW...
...IF I COULD MOVE MY ARMS...

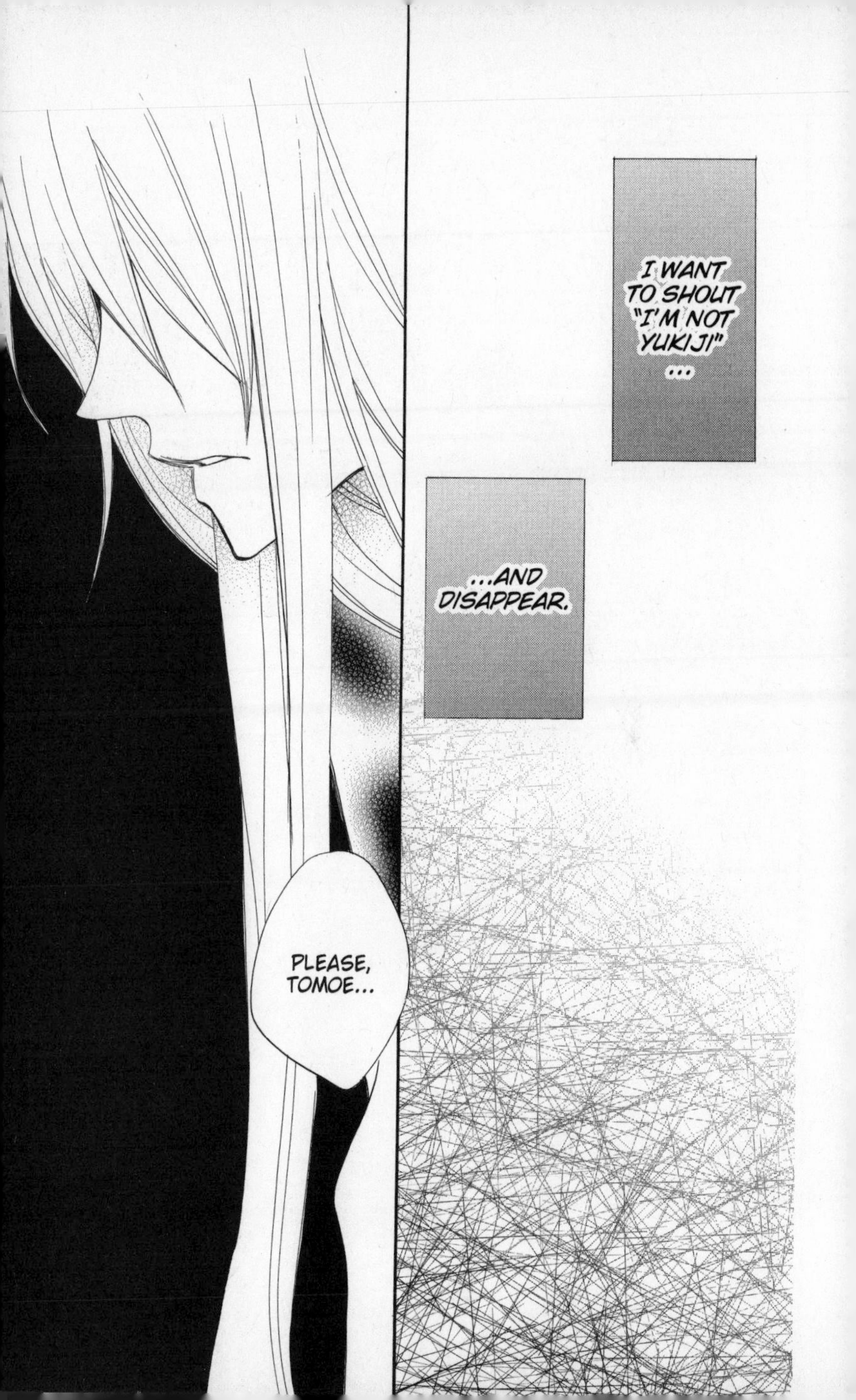
I WANT TO SHOUT "I'M NOT YUKIJI"...
...AND DISAPPEAR.
PLEASE, TOMOE...

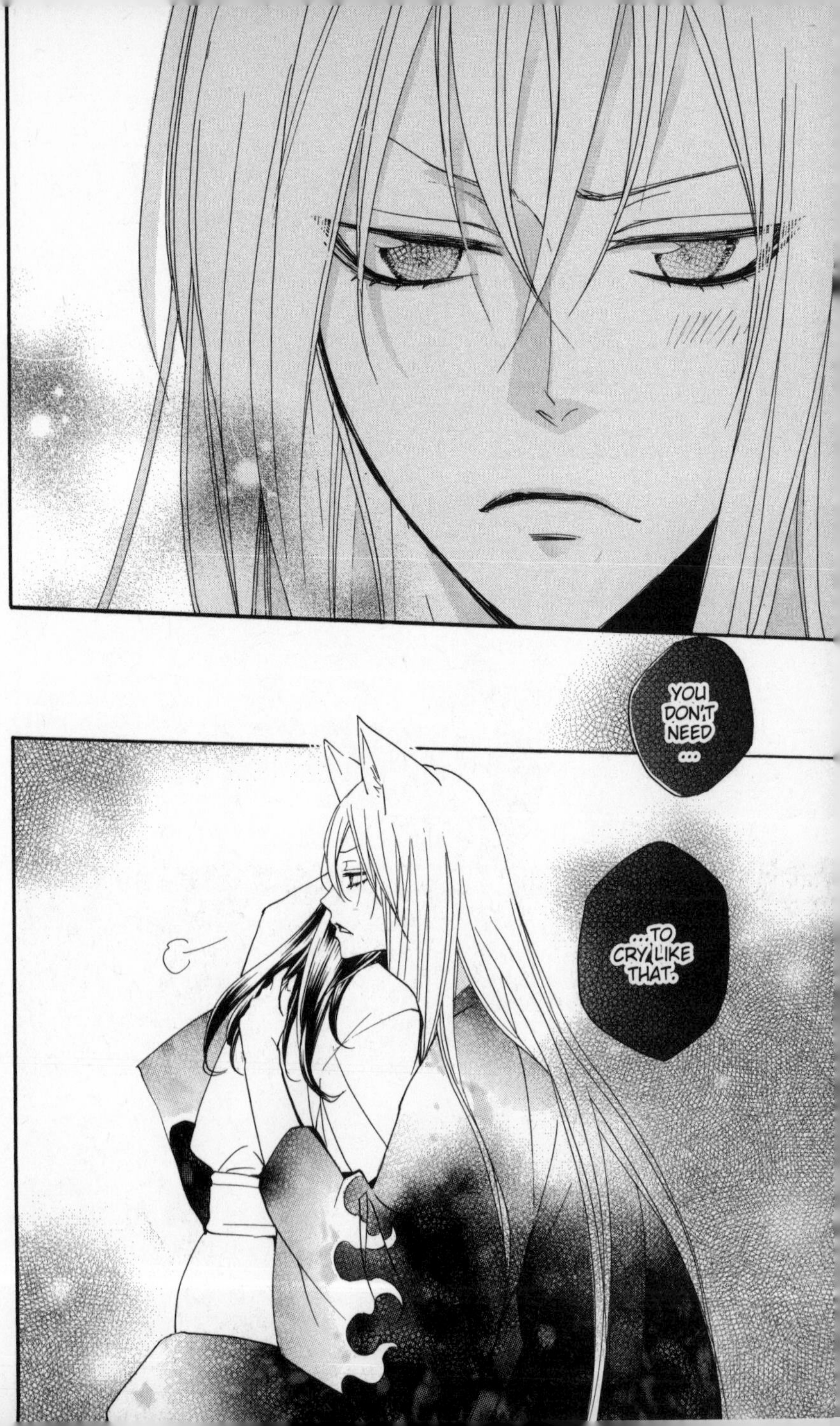
YOU DON'T NEED ...
...TO CRY LIKE THAT.

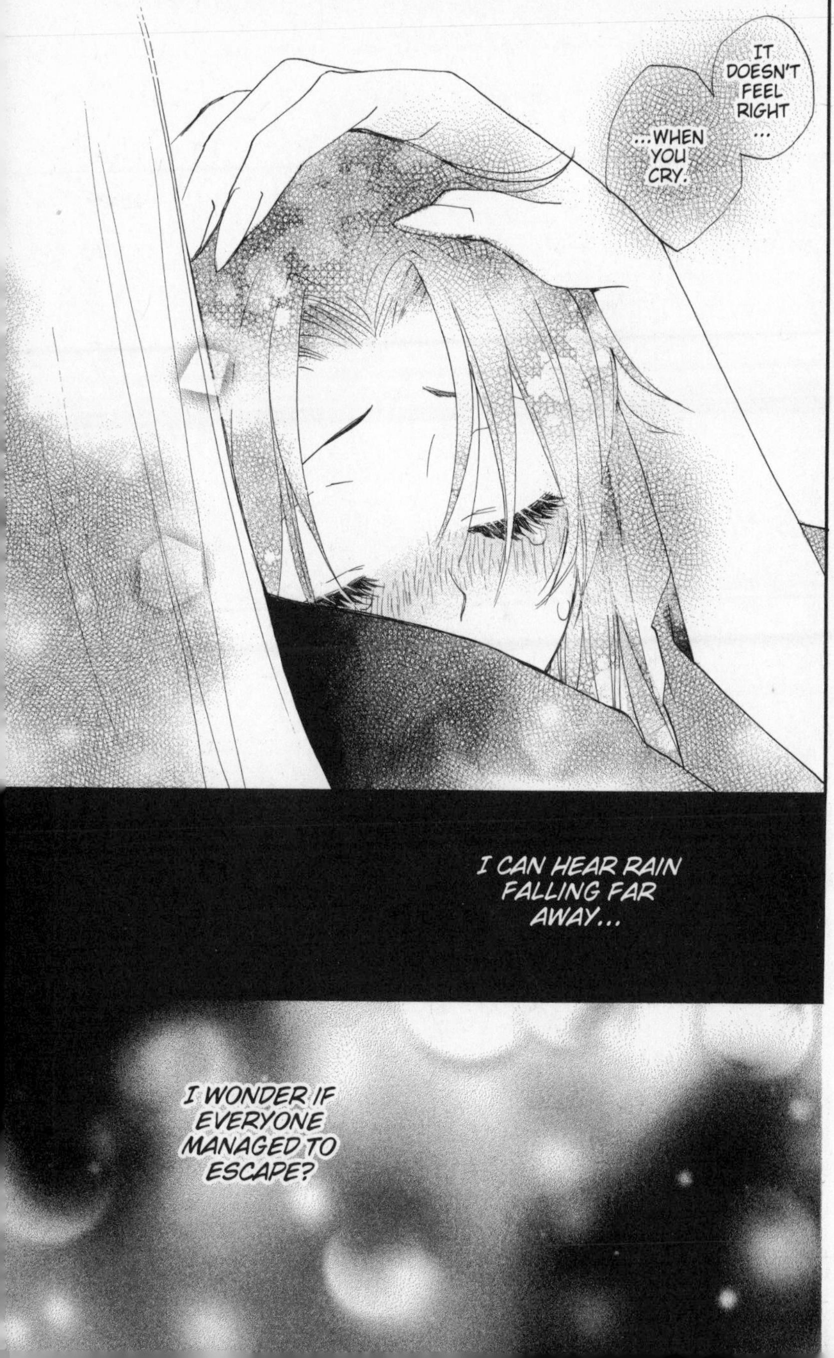
IT DOESN'T FEEL RIGHT ...
...WHEN YOU CRY.
I CAN HEAR RAIN FALLING FAR AWAY...
I WONDER IF EVERYONE MANAGED TO ESCAPE?

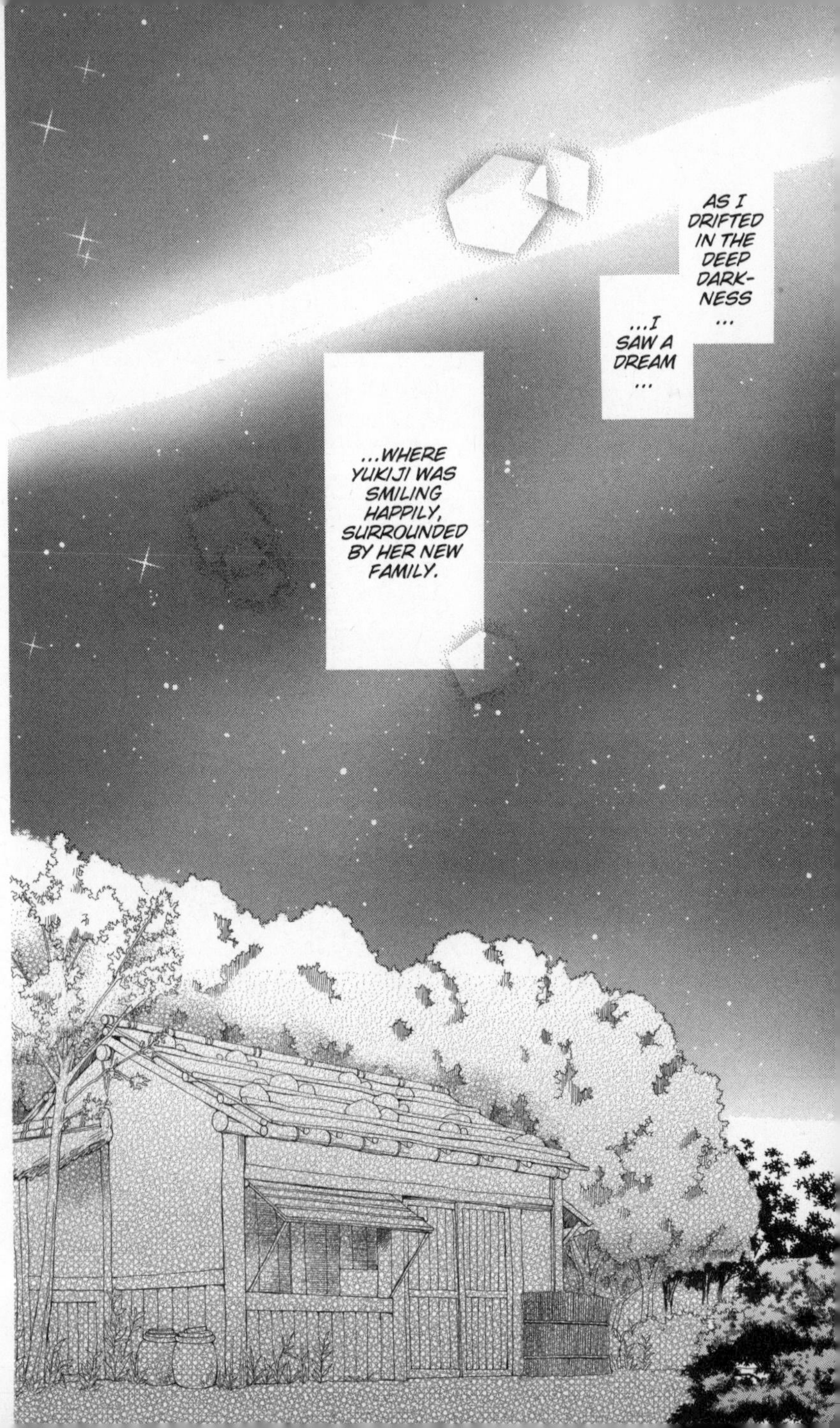
AS I DRIFTED IN THE DEEP DARK-NESS...
...I SAW A DREAM...
...WHERE YUKIJI WAS SMILING HAPPILY, SURROUNDED BY HER NEW FAMILY.

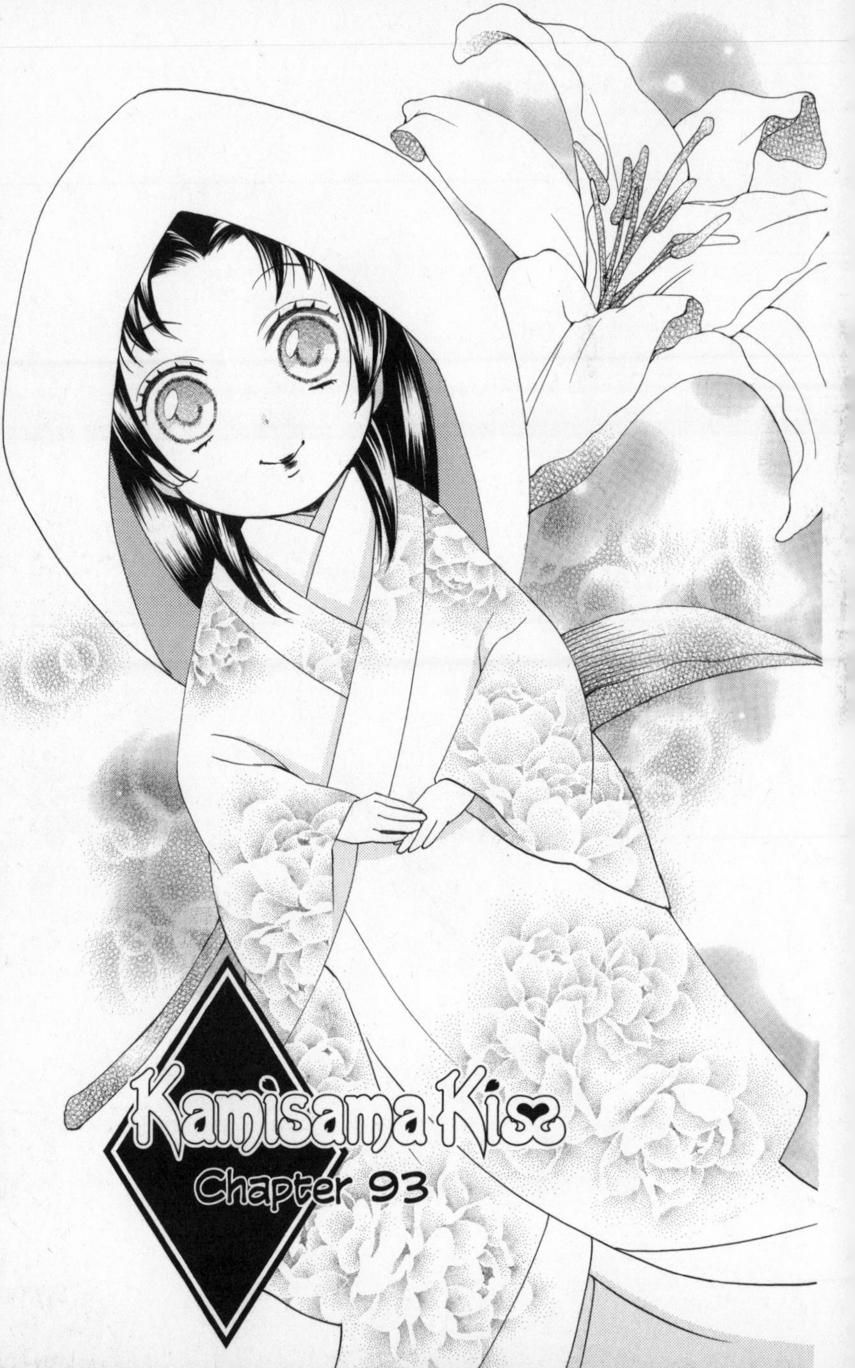
Kamisama Kiss
Chapter 93

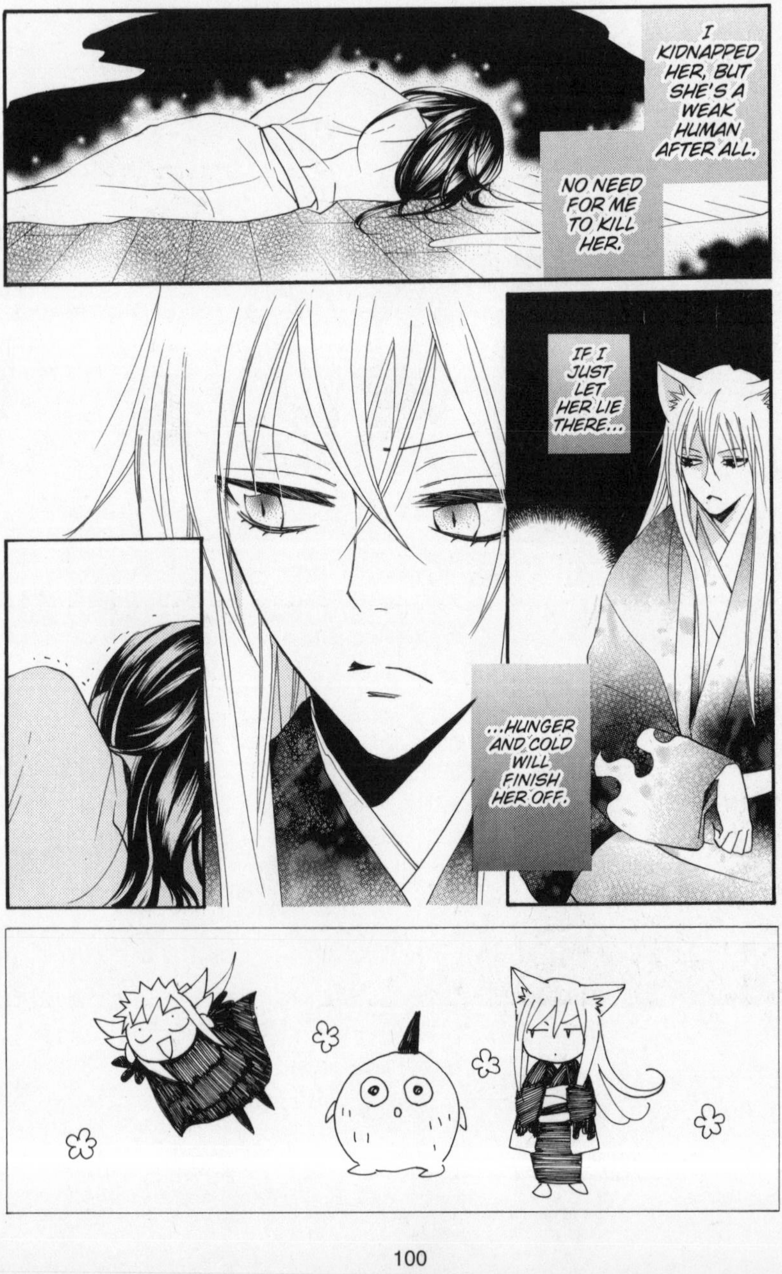
I KIDNAPPED HER, BUT SHE'S A WEAK HUMAN AFTER ALL.
NO NEED FOR ME TO KILL HER.
IF I JUST LET HER LIE THERE...
...HUNGER AND COLD WILL FINISH HER OFF.

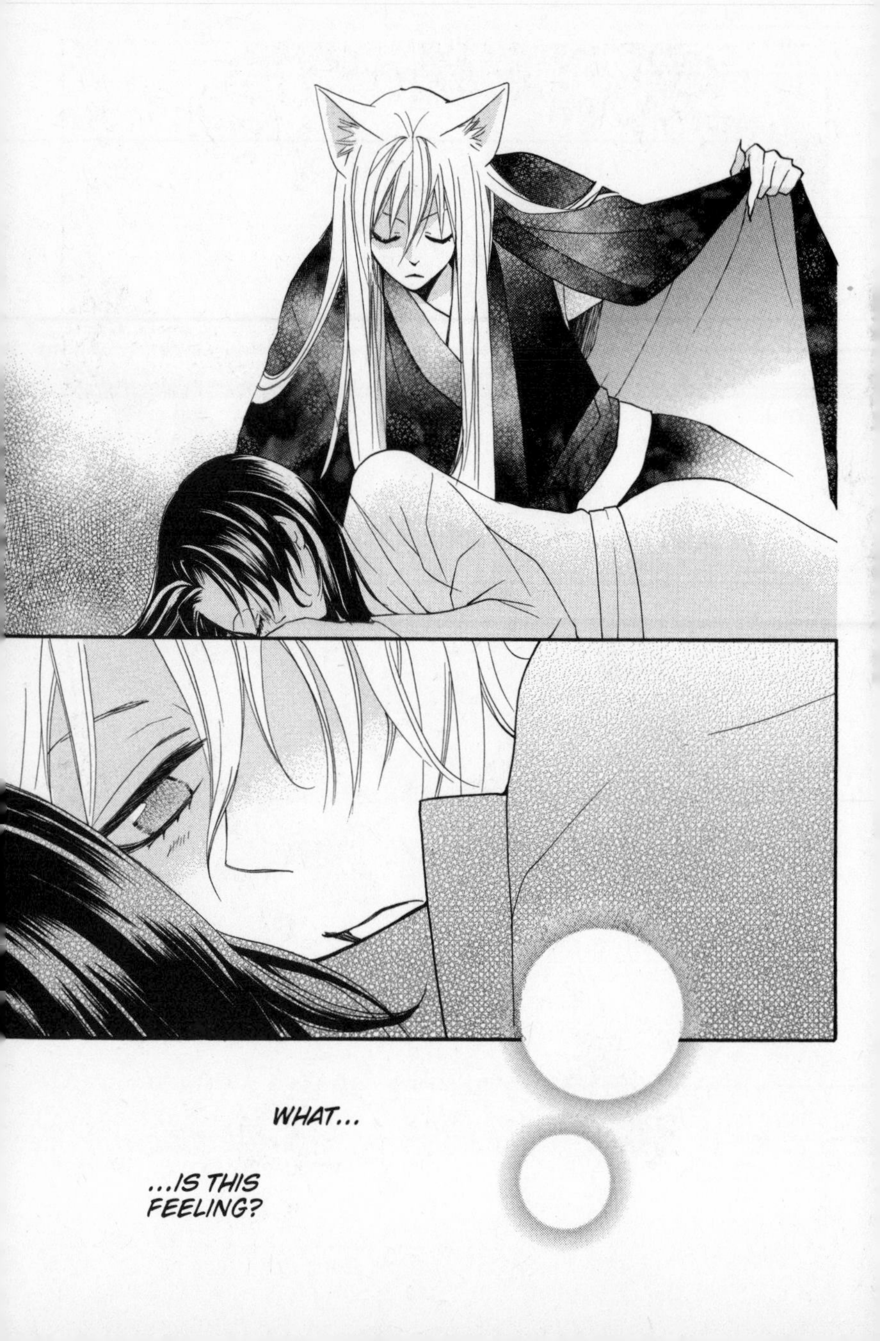
WHAT...
...IS THIS FEELING?

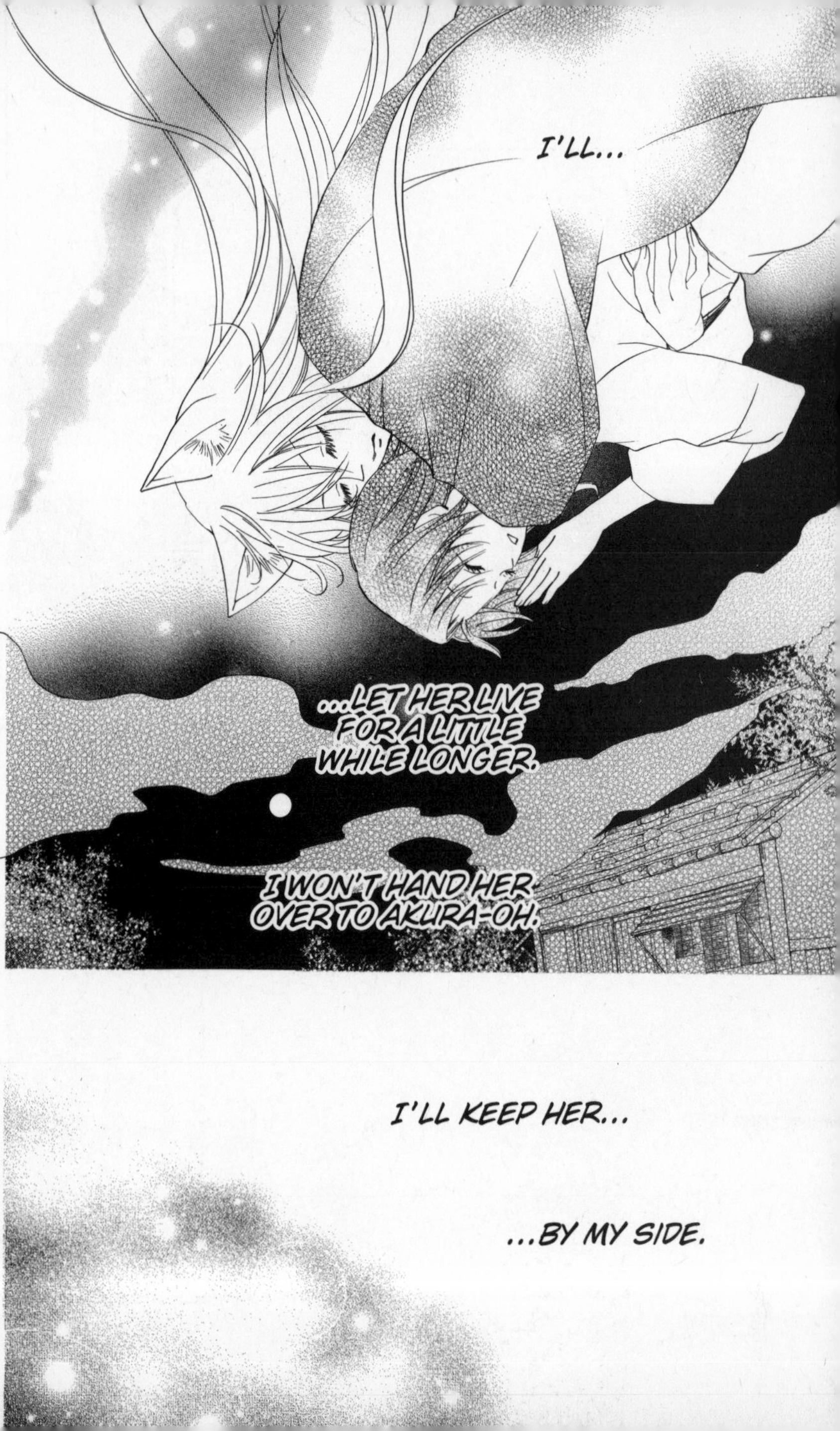
I'LL...
...LET HER LIVE FOR A LITTLE WHILE LONGER.
I WON'T HAND HER OVER TO AKURA-OH.
I'LL KEEP HER...
...BY MY SIDE.

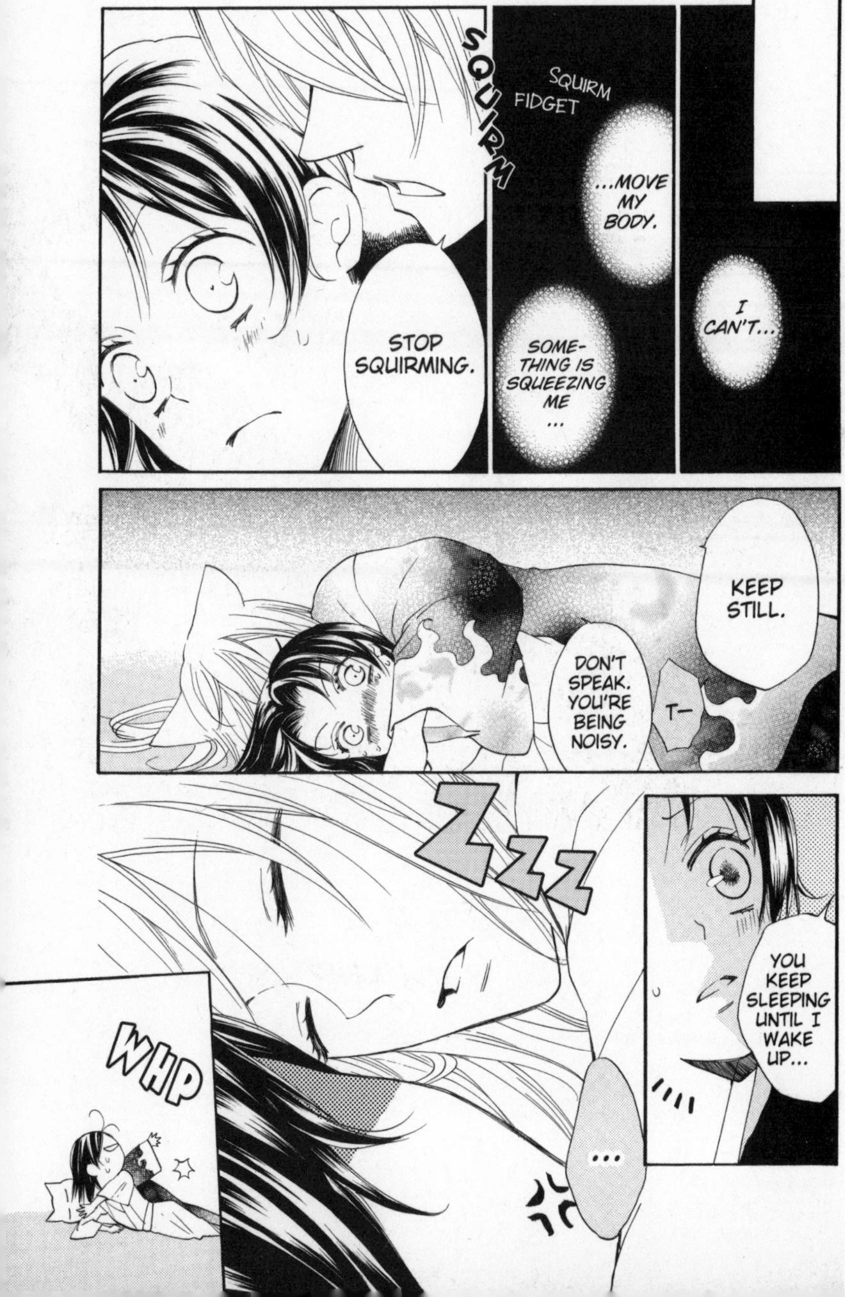
I CAN'T...
...MOVE MY BODY.
SQUIRM
FIDGET
SOME-THING IS SQUEEZING ME...
SQUIRM
STOP SQUIRMING.
KEEP STILL.
T—
DON'T SPEAK. YOU'RE BEING NOISY.
YOU KEEP SLEEPING UNTIL I WAKE UP...
ZZZ
...
WHP

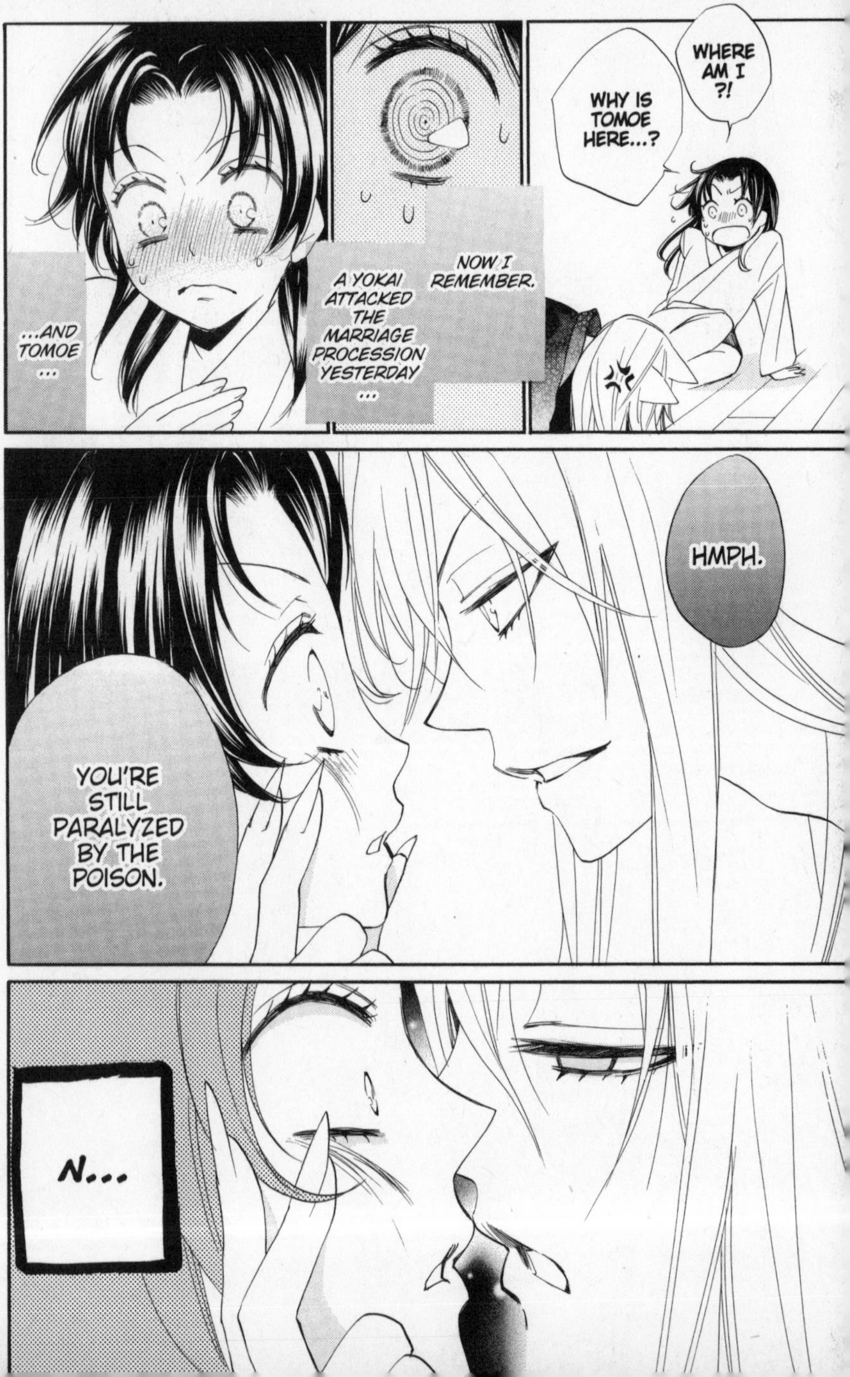
WHERE AM I ?!
WHY IS TOMOE HERE...?
NOW I REMEMBER.
A YOKAI ATTACKED THE MARRIAGE PROCESSION YESTERDAY ...
...AND TOMOE ...
HMPH.
YOU'RE STILL PARALYZED BY THE POISON.
N...

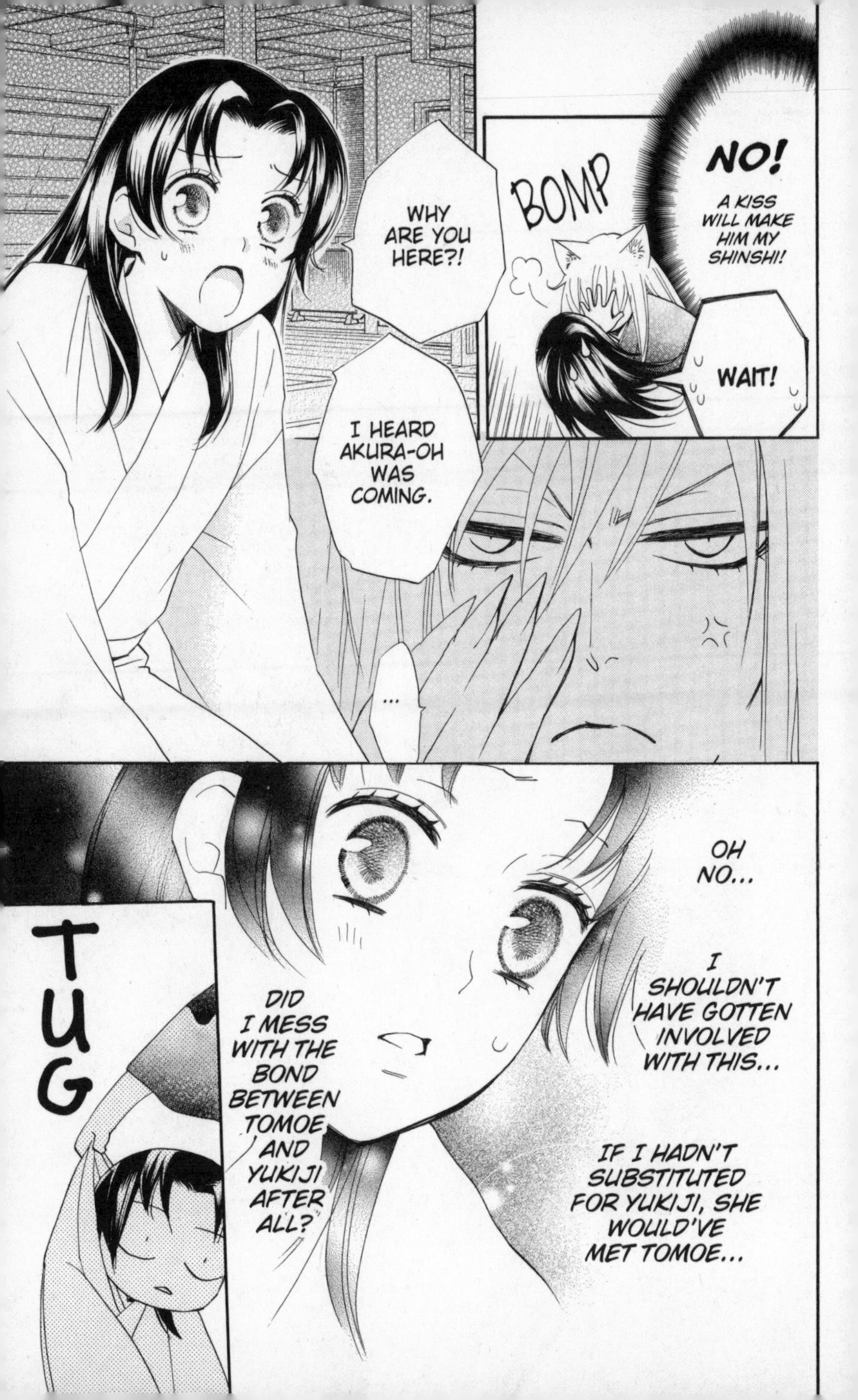
NO!
A KISS WILL MAKE HIM MY SHINSHI!
WAIT!
BOMP
...
WHY ARE YOU HERE?!
I HEARD AKURA-OH WAS COMING.
OH NO...
I SHOULDN'T HAVE GOTTEN INVOLVED WITH THIS...
IF I HADN'T SUBSTITUTED FOR YUKIJI, SHE WOULD'VE MET TOMOE...
DID I MESS WITH THE BOND BETWEEN TOMOE AND YUKIJI AFTER ALL?
TUG

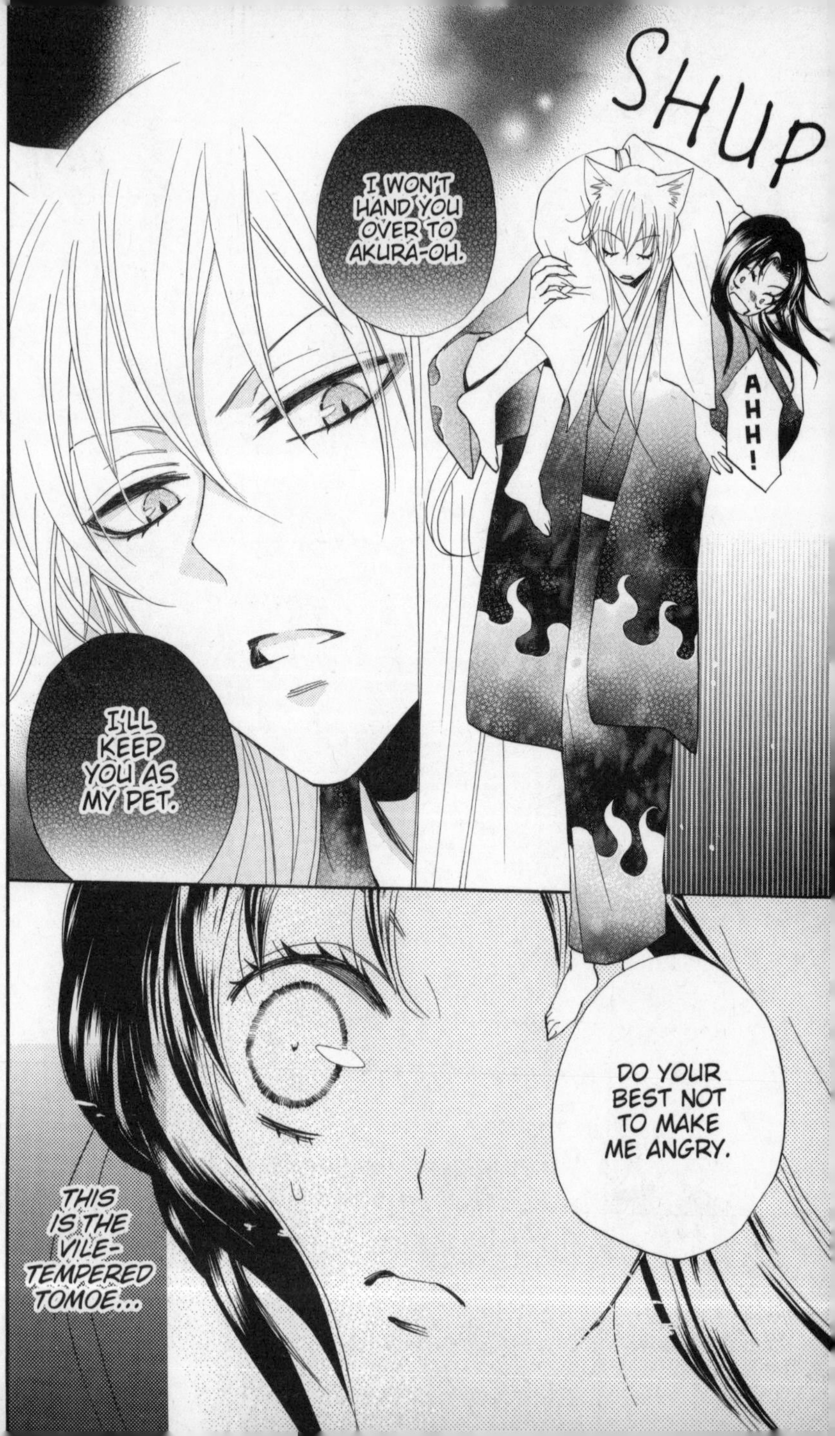
SHUP
AHH!
I WON'T HAND YOU OVER TO AKURA-OH.
I'LL KEEP YOU AS MY PET.
DO YOUR BEST NOT TO MAKE ME ANGRY.
THIS IS THE VILE-TEMPERED TOMOE...

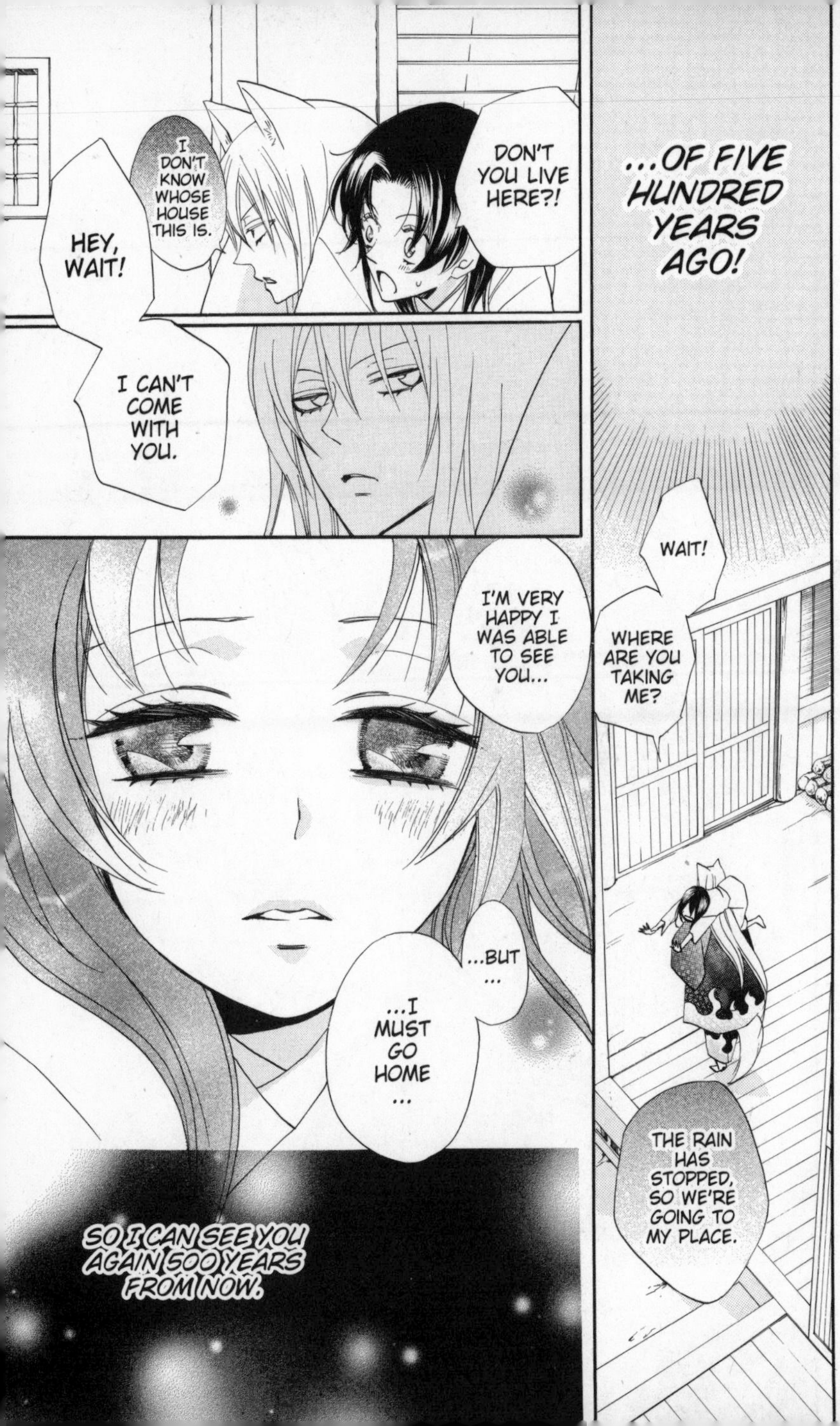
...OF FIVE HUNDRED YEARS AGO!
WAIT!
WHERE ARE YOU TAKING ME?
THE RAIN HAS STOPPED, SO WE'RE GOING TO MY PLACE.
DON'T YOU LIVE HERE?!
I DON'T KNOW WHOSE HOUSE THIS IS.
HEY, WAIT!
I CAN'T COME WITH YOU.
I'M VERY HAPPY I WAS ABLE TO SEE YOU...
...BUT ...
...I MUST GO HOME ...
SO I CAN SEE YOU AGAIN 500 YEARS FROM NOW.

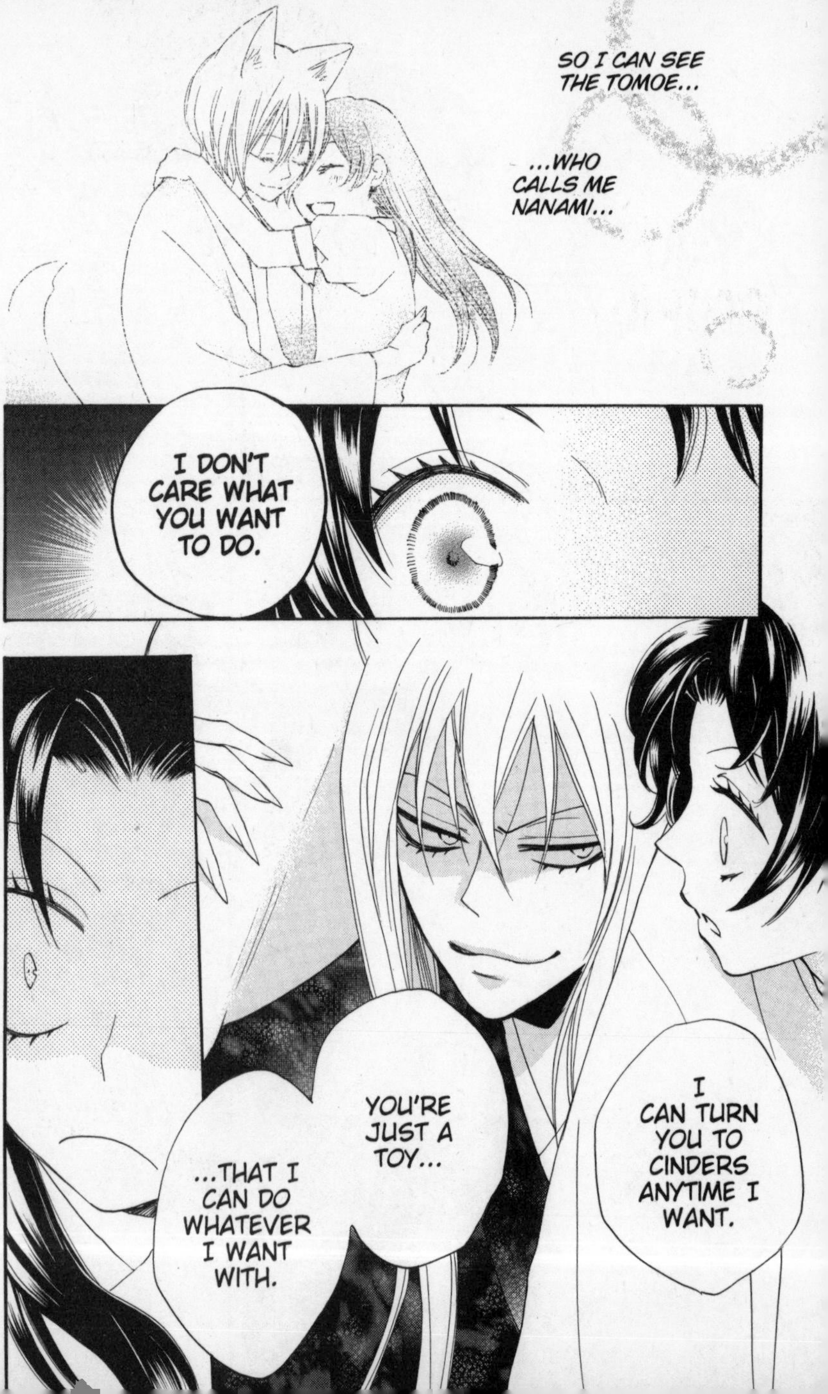
SO I CAN SEE THE TOMOE...
...WHO CALLS ME NANAMI...
I DON'T CARE WHAT YOU WANT TO DO.
I CAN TURN YOU TO CINDERS ANYTIME I WANT.
YOU'RE JUST A TOY...
...THAT I CAN DO WHATEVER I WANT WITH.

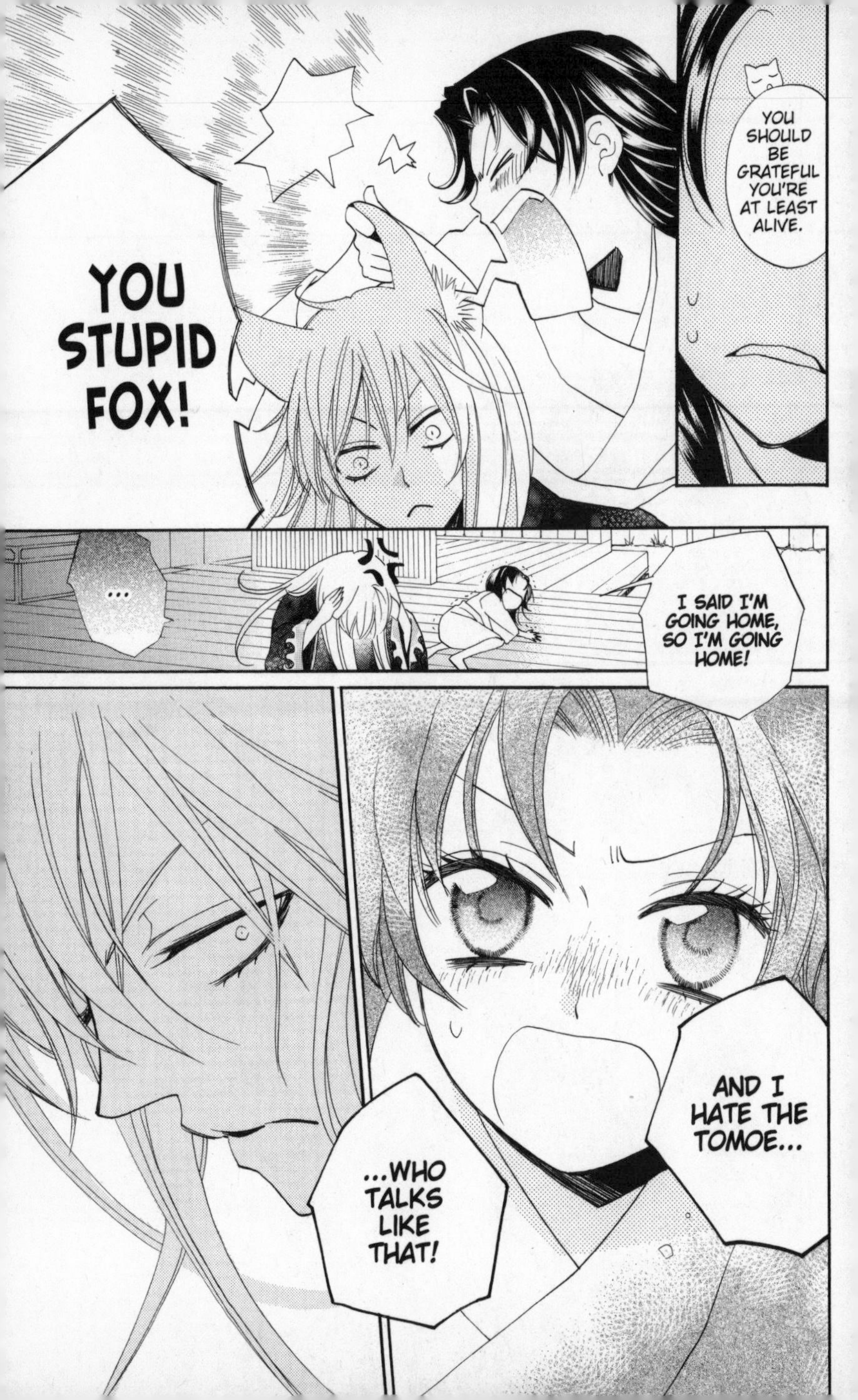
YOU SHOULD BE GRATEFUL YOU'RE AT LEAST ALIVE.
YOU STUPID FOX!
I SAID I'M GOING HOME, SO I'M GOING HOME!
...
AND I HATE THE TOMOE...
...WHO TALKS LIKE THAT!

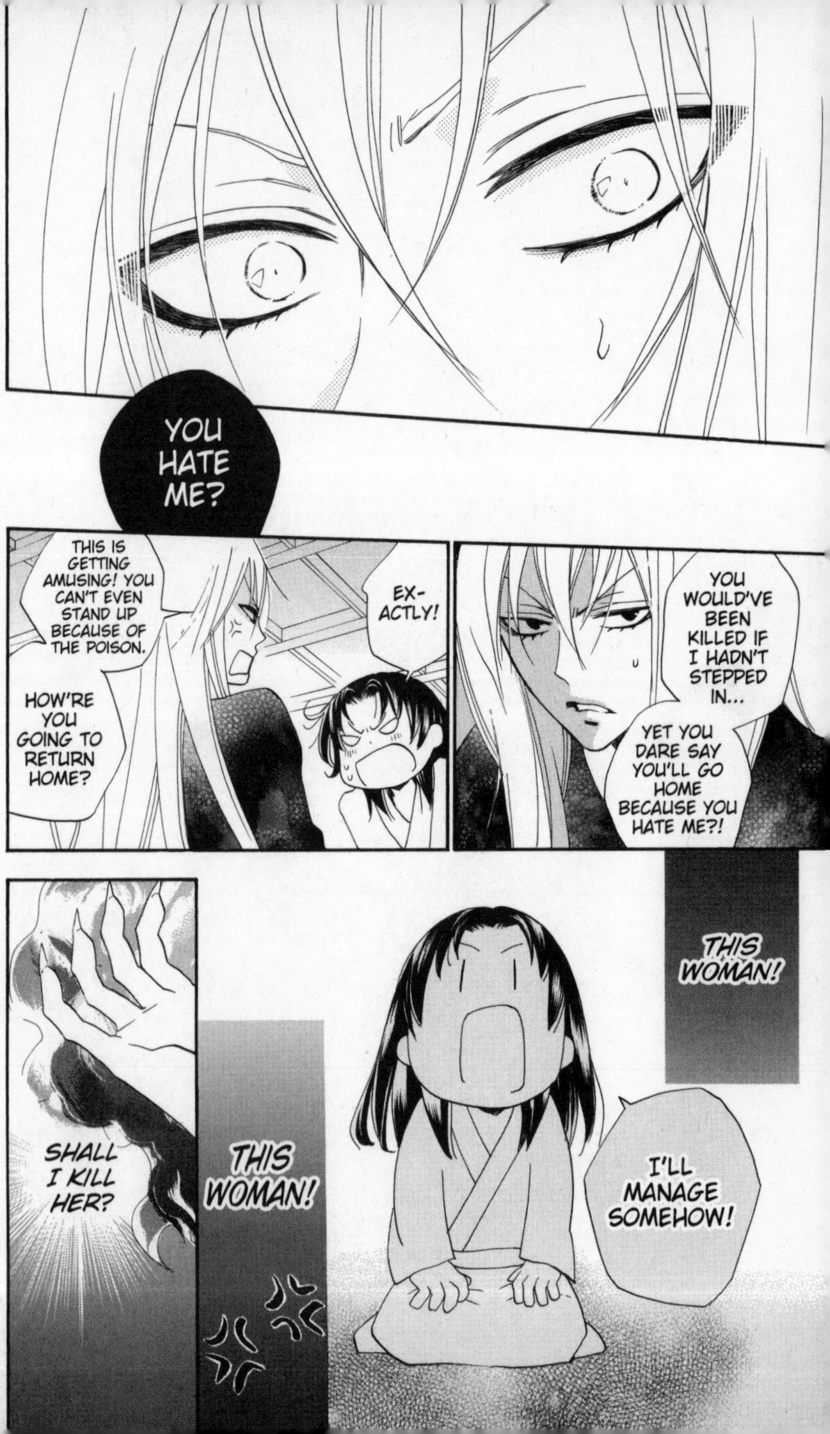

YOU HATE ME?
YOU WOULD'VE BEEN KILLED IF I HADN'T STEPPED IN...
YET YOU DARE SAY YOU'LL GO HOME BECAUSE YOU HATE ME?!
EX-ACTLY!
THIS IS GETTING AMUSING! YOU CAN'T EVEN STAND UP BECAUSE OF THE POISON.
HOW'RE YOU GOING TO RETURN HOME?
THIS WOMAN!
I'LL MANAGE SOMEHOW!
THIS WOMAN!
SHALL I KILL HER?

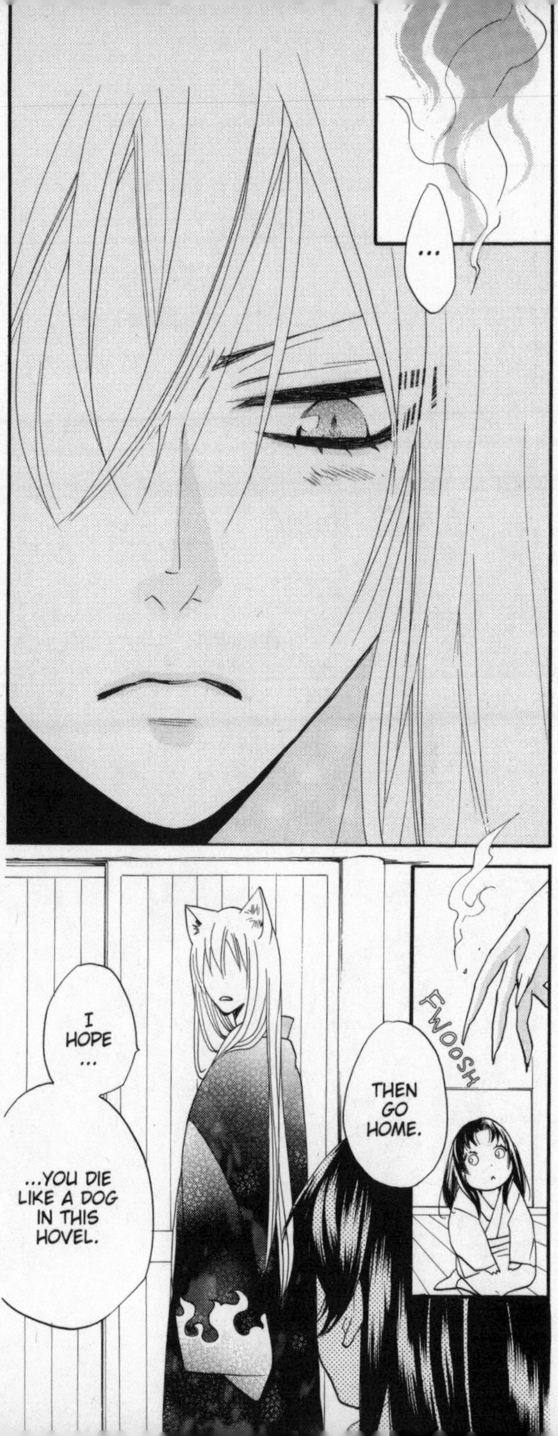
...
FWOOSH
THEN GO HOME.
I HOPE...
...YOU DIE LIKE A DOG IN THIS HOVEL.

I went to Aizu-wakamatsu.

This was my first time!

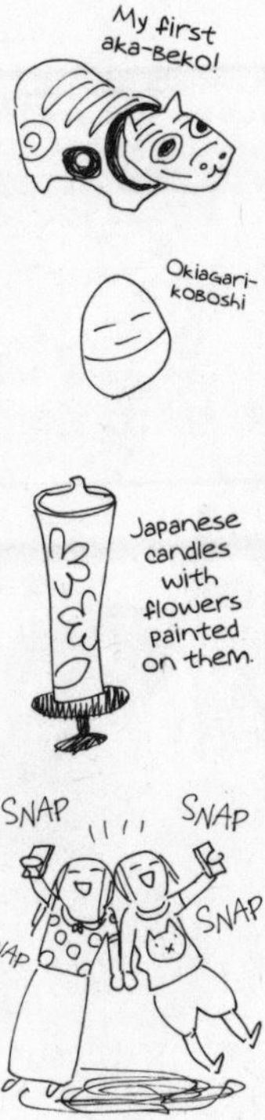
My first aka-beko!
Okiagari-koboshi
Japanese candles with flowers painted on them.
SNAP
SNAP
SNAP
SNAP

I took lots of photos with my iPhone.

I enjoyed my trip!

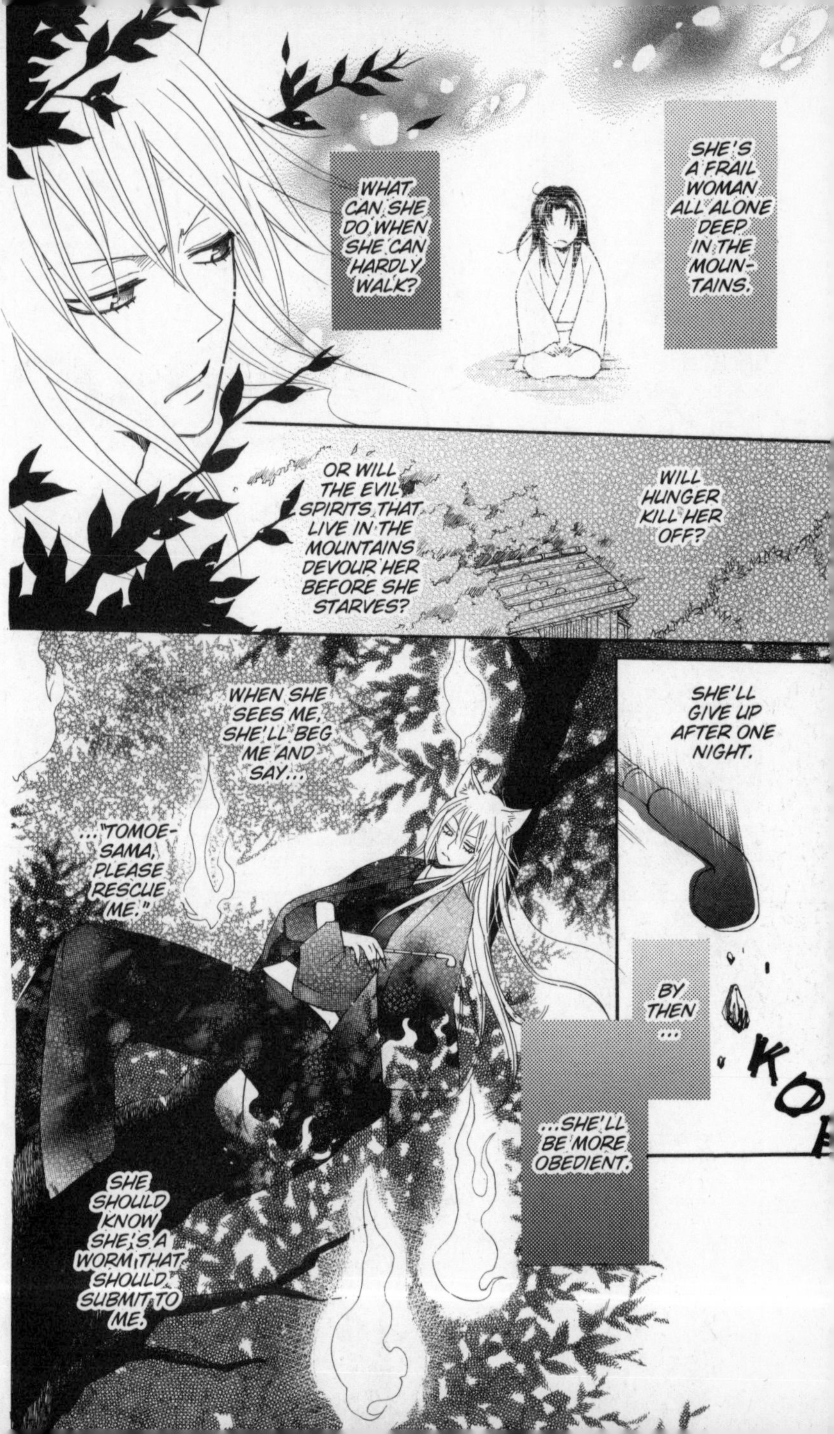
SHE'S A FRAIL WOMAN ALL ALONE DEEP IN THE MOUN-TAINS.
WHAT CAN SHE DO WHEN SHE CAN HARDLY WALK?
WILL HUNGER KILL HER OFF?
OR WILL THE EVIL SPIRITS THAT LIVE IN THE MOUNTAINS DEVOUR HER BEFORE SHE STARVES?
SHE'LL GIVE UP AFTER ONE NIGHT.
KO
BY THEN...
...SHE'LL BE MORE OBEDIENT.
WHEN SHE SEES ME, SHE'LL BEG ME AND SAY...
..."TOMOE-SAMA, PLEASE RESCUE ME."
SHE SHOULD KNOW SHE'S A WORM THAT SHOULD SUBMIT TO ME.

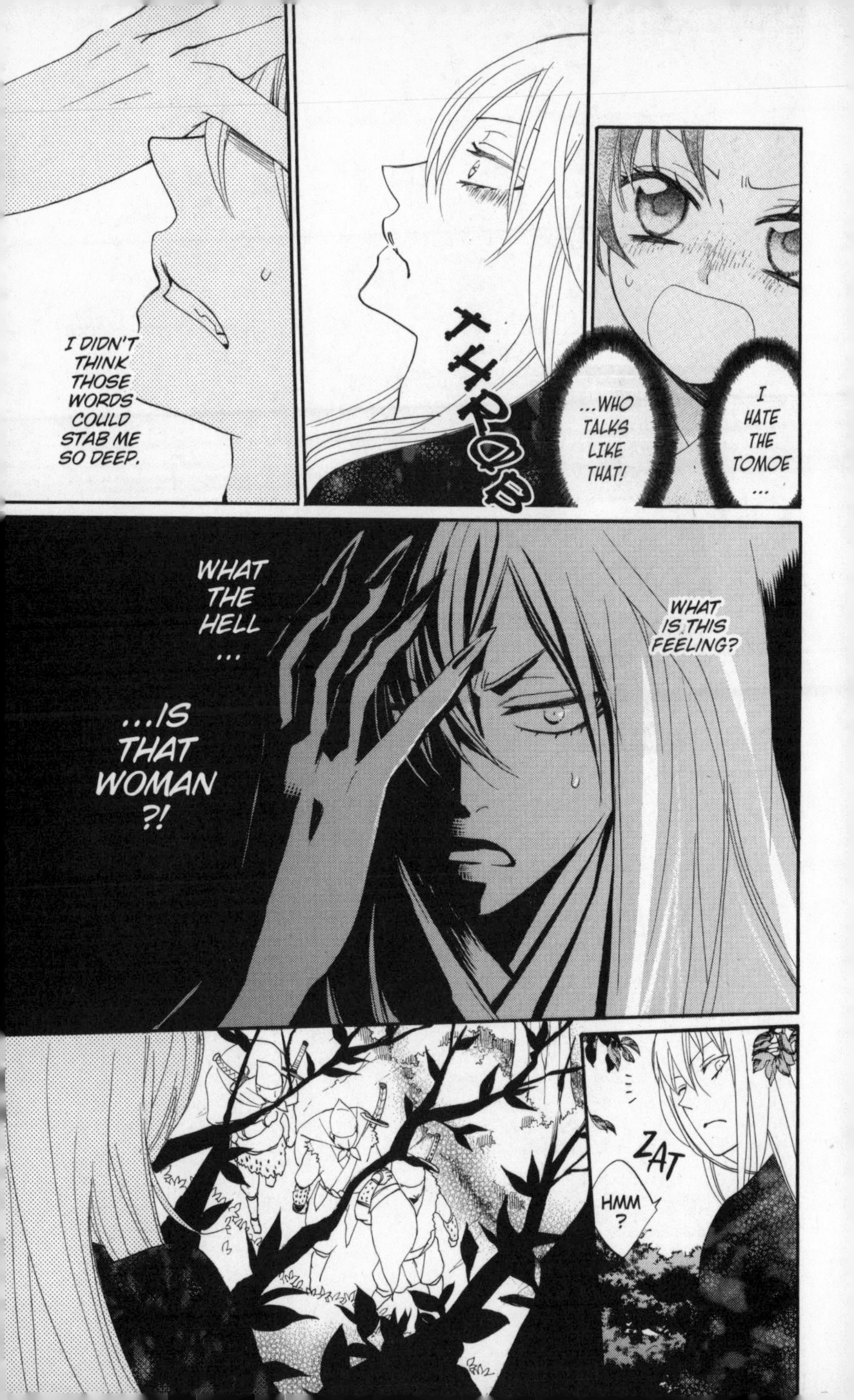
I HATE THE TOMOE ...
...WHO TALKS LIKE THAT!
THROB
I DIDN'T THINK THOSE WORDS COULD STAB ME SO DEEP.
WHAT IS THIS FEELING?
WHAT THE HELL ...
...IS THAT WOMAN ?!
ZAT
HMM ?

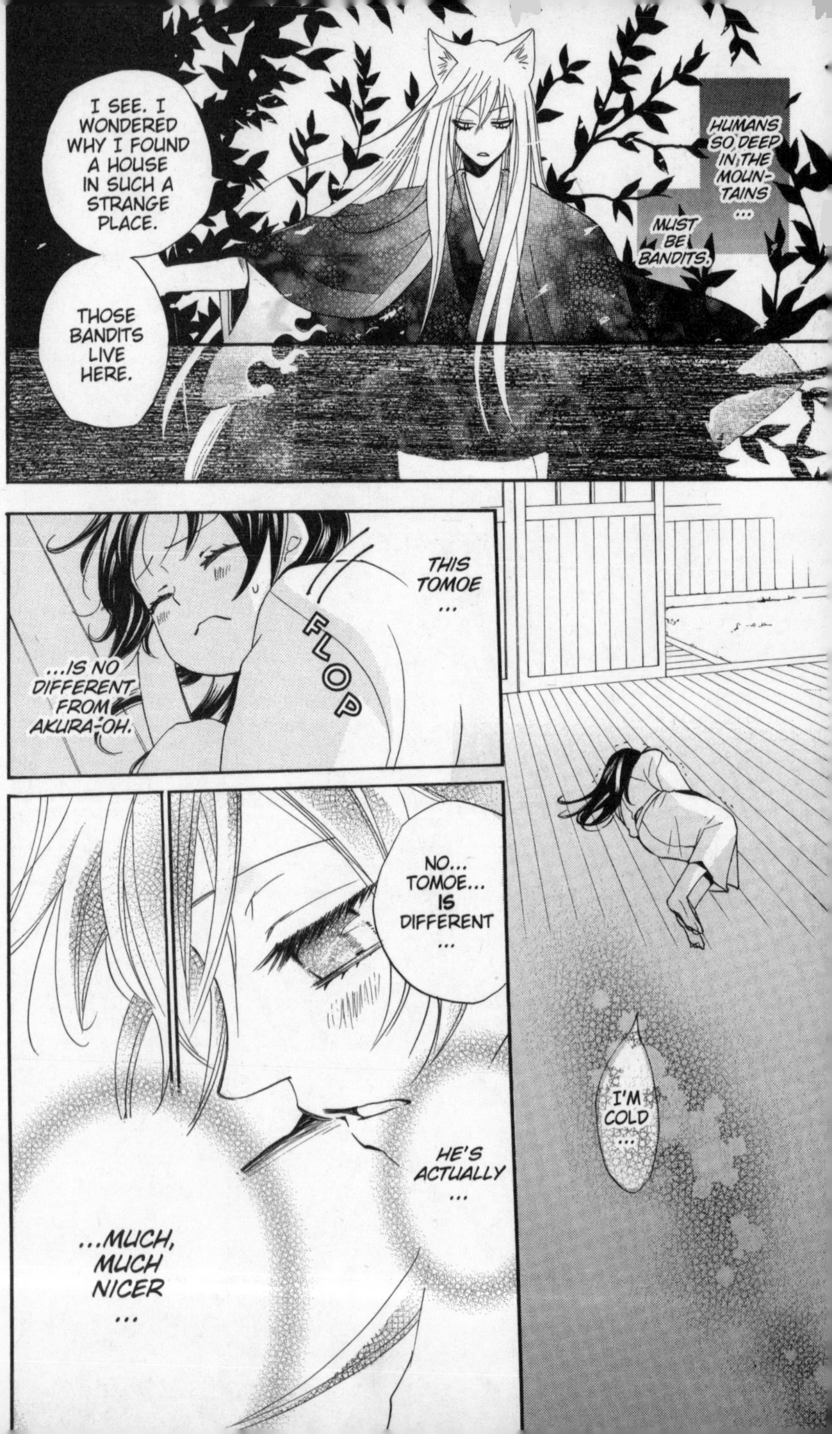
HUMANS SO DEEP IN THE MOUNTAINS ...
MUST BE BANDITS.
I SEE. I WONDERED WHY I FOUND A HOUSE IN SUCH A STRANGE PLACE.
THOSE BANDITS LIVE HERE.
I'M COLD ...
THIS TOMOE ...
FLOP
...IS NO DIFFERENT FROM AKURA-OH.
NO... TOMOE... IS DIFFERENT ...
HE'S ACTUALLY ...
...MUCH, MUCH NICER ...

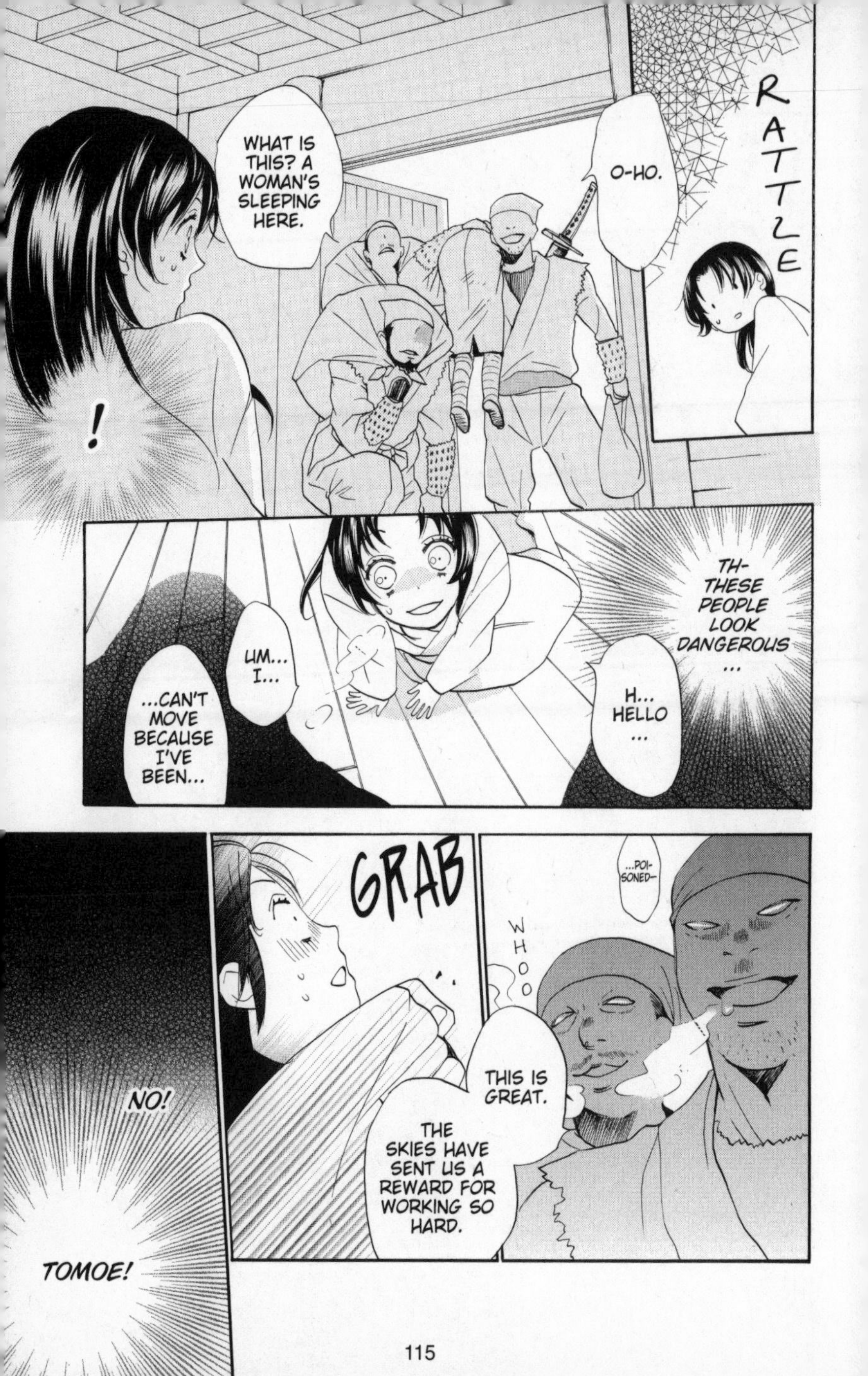
RATTLE
O-HO.
WHAT IS THIS? A WOMAN'S SLEEPING HERE.
!
TH-THESE PEOPLE LOOK DANGEROUS...
H... HELLO...
UM... I...
...CAN'T MOVE BECAUSE I'VE BEEN...
...POI-SONED—
WHOO
THIS IS GREAT.
THE SKIES HAVE SENT US A REWARD FOR WORKING SO HARD.
GRAB
NO!
TOMOE!

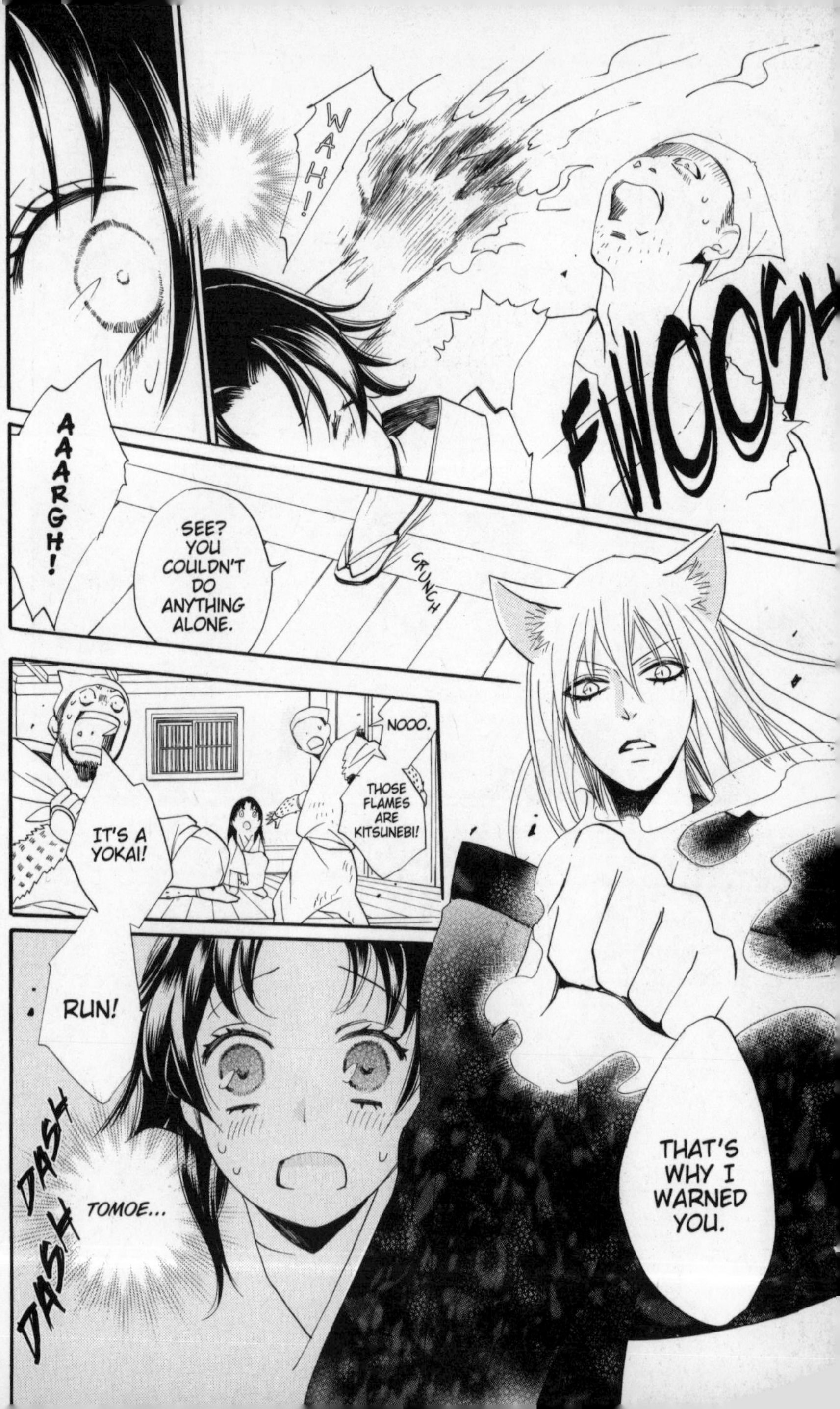
FWOOSH
WAH!
SEE? YOU COULDN'T DO ANYTHING ALONE.
CRUNCH
AAAARGH!
NOOO.
THOSE FLAMES ARE KITSUNEBI!
IT'S A YOKAI!
RUN!
THAT'S WHY I WARNED YOU.
DASH DASH
TOMOE...

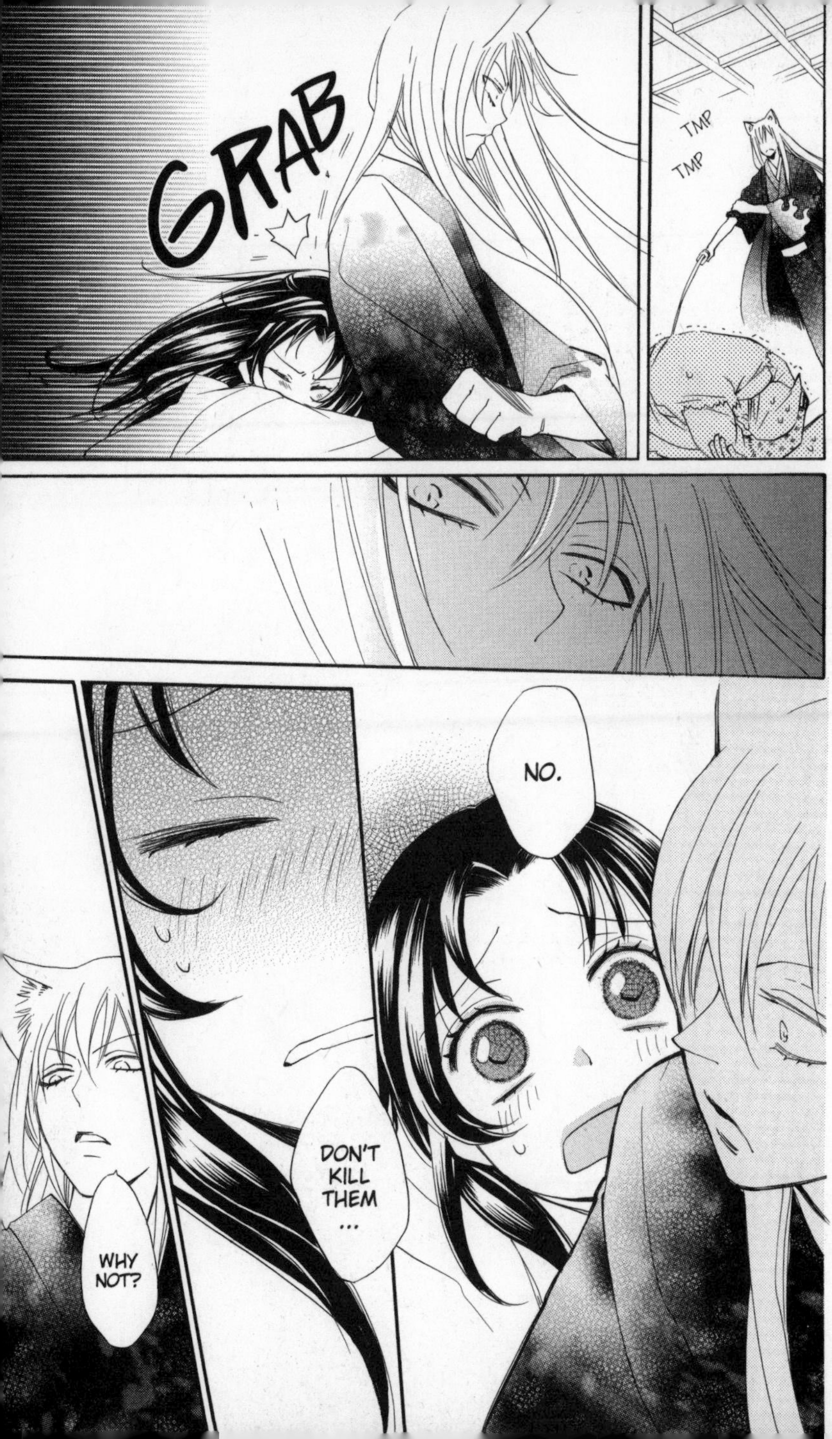
TMP
TMP
GRAB
NO.
DON'T KILL THEM ...
WHY NOT?

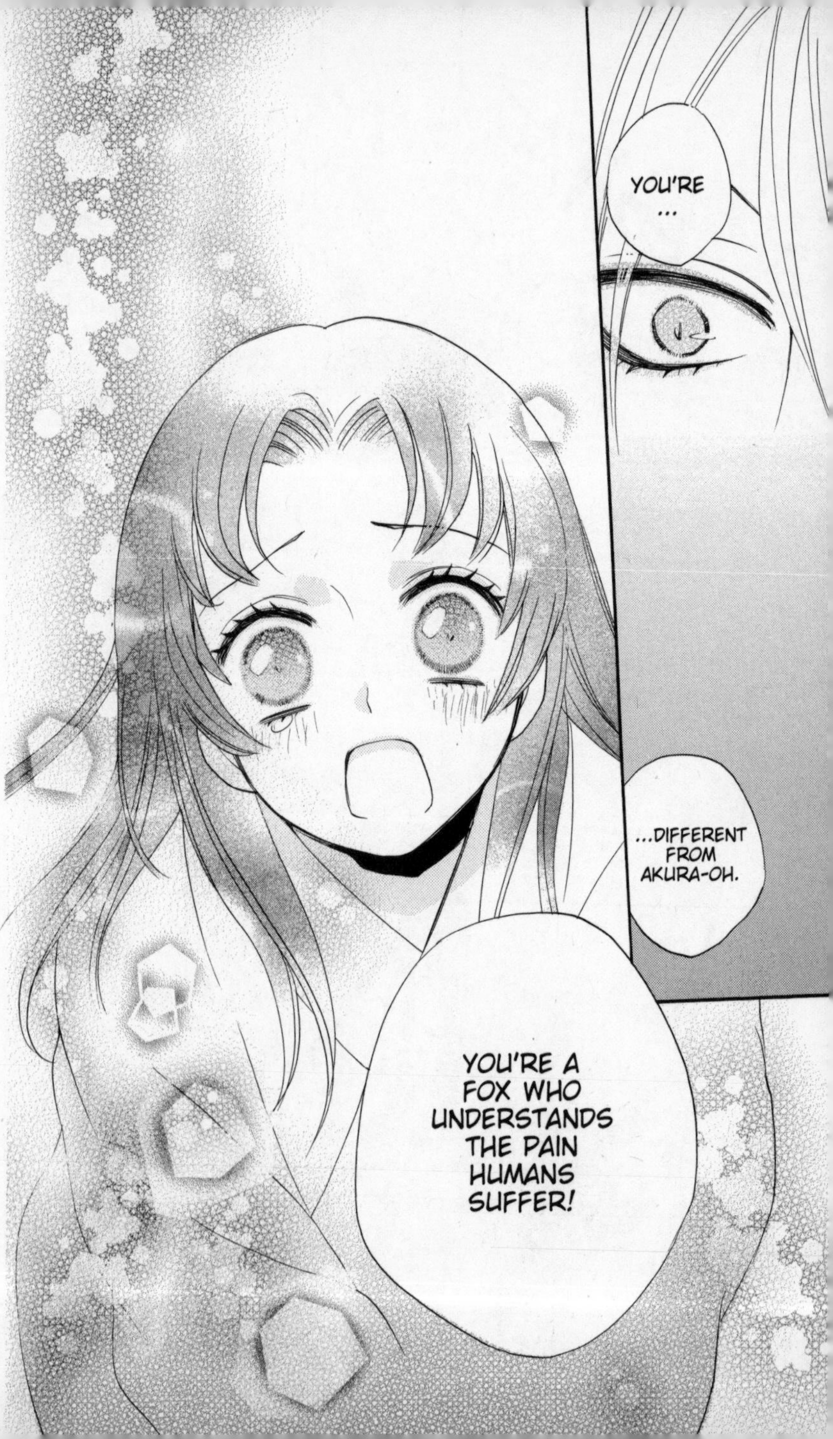
YOU'RE ...
...DIFFERENT FROM AKURA-OH.
YOU'RE A FOX WHO UNDERSTANDS THE PAIN HUMANS SUFFER!

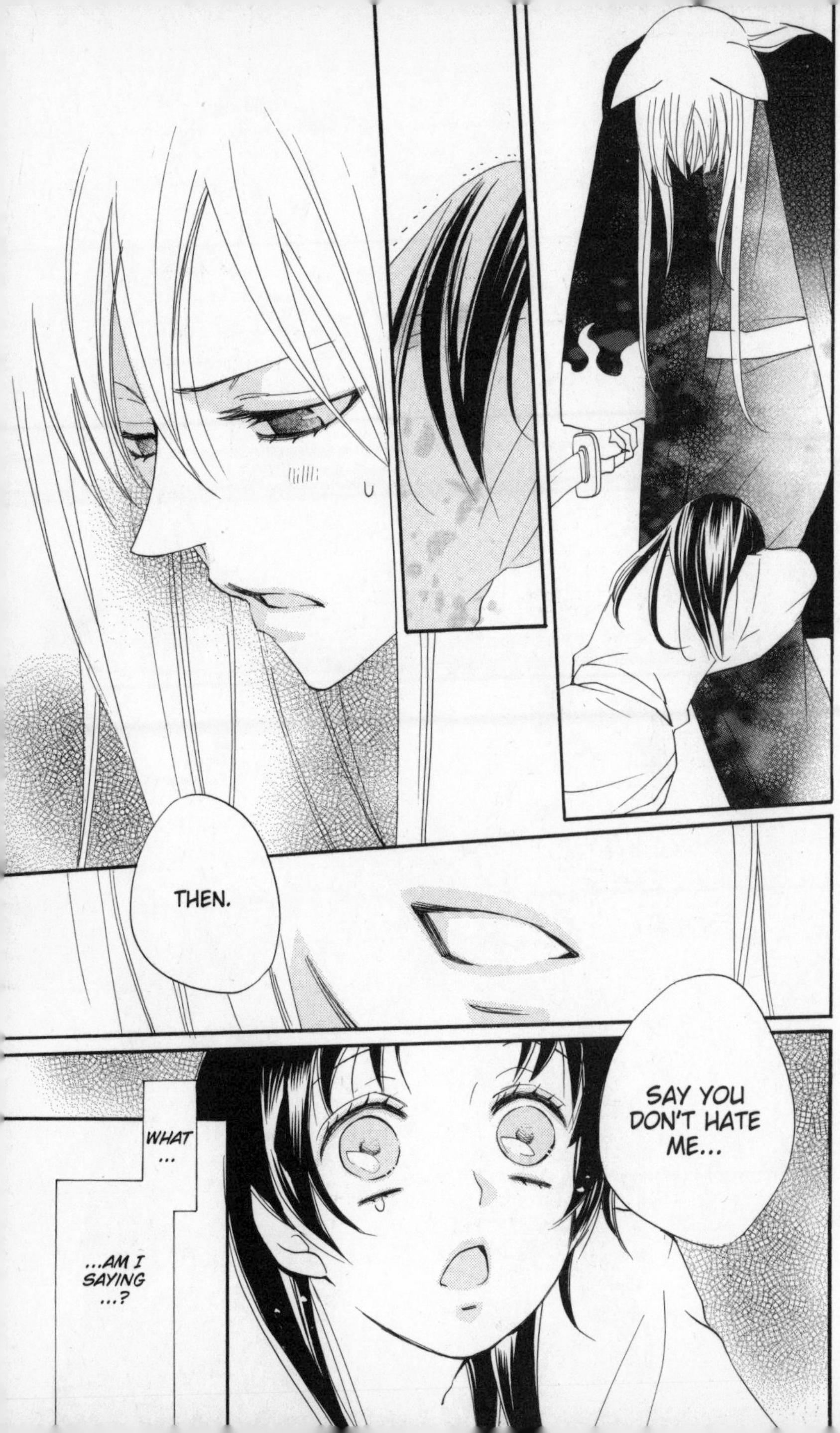
THEN.
SAY YOU DON'T HATE ME...
WHAT ...
...AM I SAYING ...?

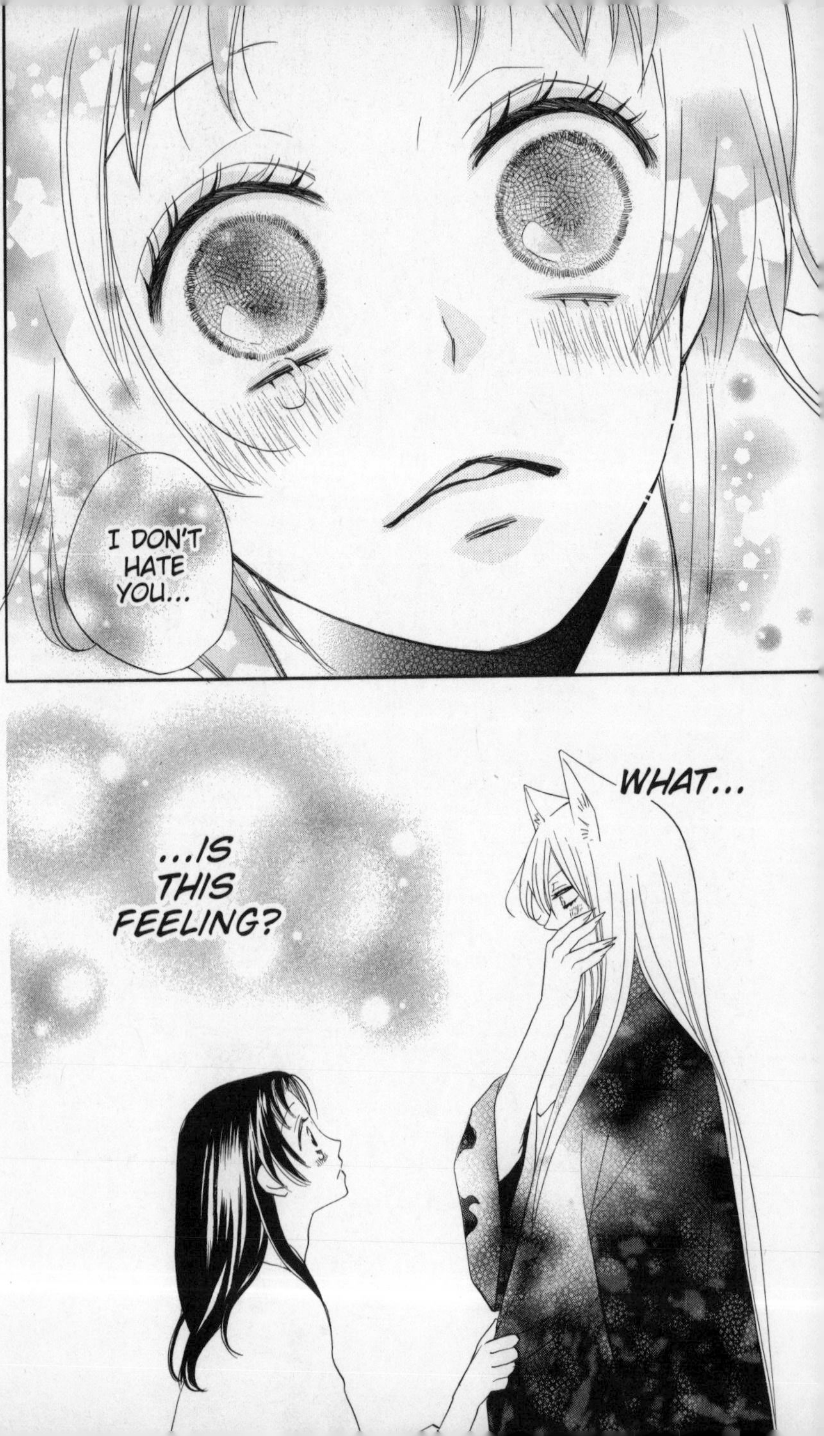
I DON'T HATE YOU...
WHAT...
...IS THIS FEELING?

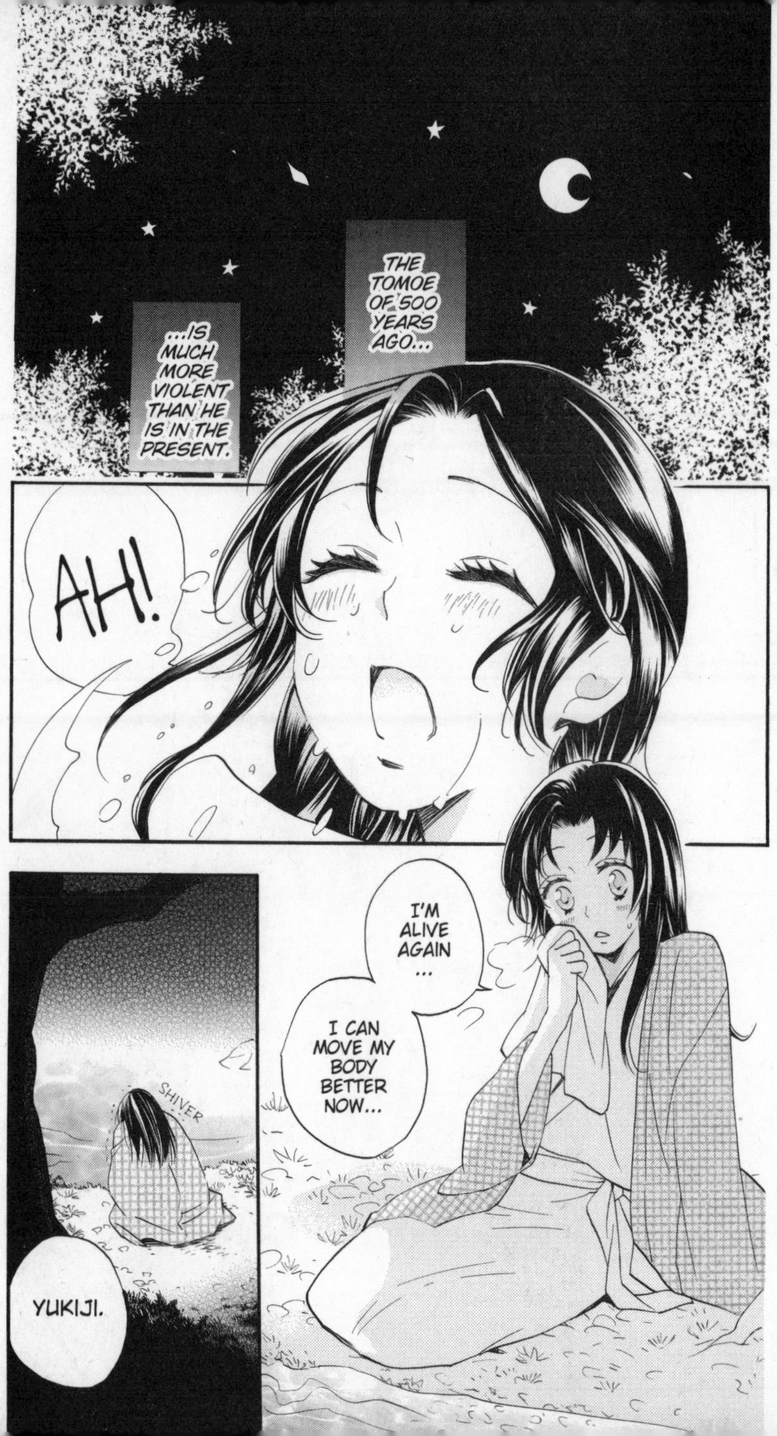
THE TOMOE OF 500 YEARS AGO...
...IS MUCH MORE VIOLENT THAN HE IS IN THE PRESENT.
AH!
I'M ALIVE AGAIN ...
I CAN MOVE MY BODY BETTER NOW...
SHIVER
YUKIJI.

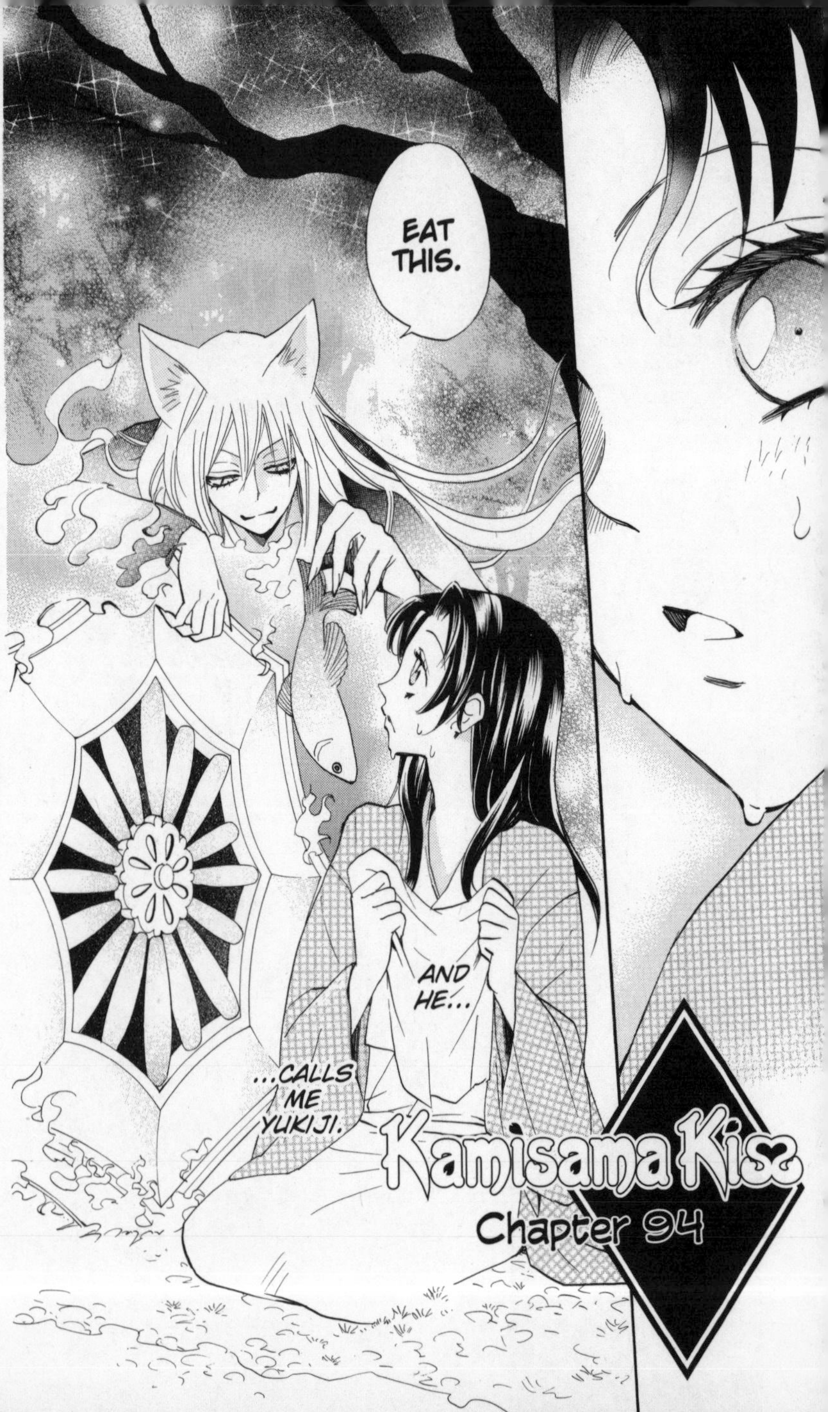
EAT THIS.
AND HE...
...CALLS ME YUKIJI.
Kamisama Kiss
Chapter 94

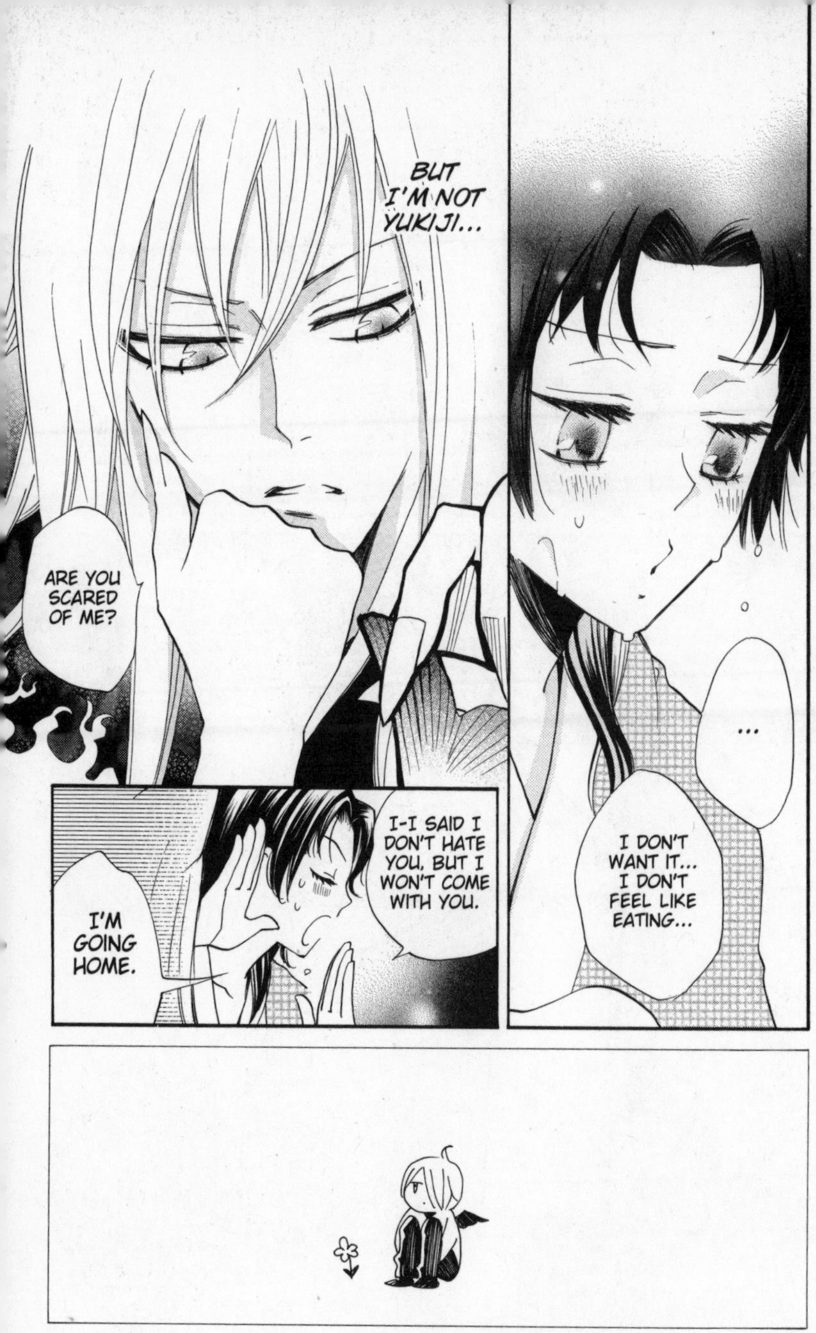
...
I DON'T WANT IT... I DON'T FEEL LIKE EATING...
BUT I'M NOT YUKIJI...
ARE YOU SCARED OF ME?
I-I SAID I DON'T HATE YOU, BUT I WON'T COME WITH YOU.
I'M GOING HOME.

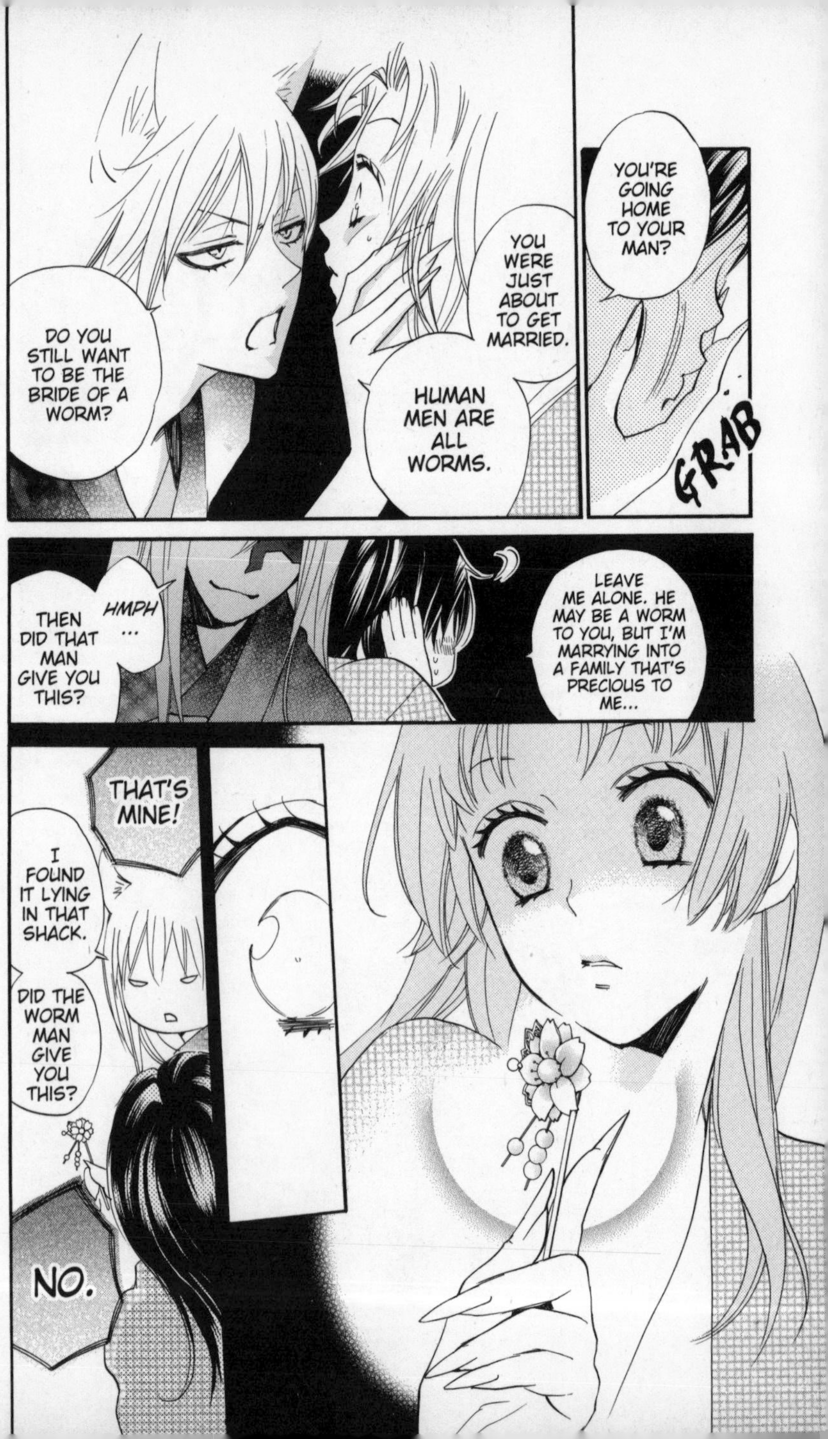
YOU'RE GOING HOME TO YOUR MAN?
GRAB
YOU WERE JUST ABOUT TO GET MARRIED.
HUMAN MEN ARE ALL WORMS.
DO YOU STILL WANT TO BE THE BRIDE OF A WORM?
LEAVE ME ALONE. HE MAY BE A WORM TO YOU, BUT I'M MARRYING INTO A FAMILY THAT'S PRECIOUS TO ME...
HMPH ...
THEN DID THAT MAN GIVE YOU THIS?
THAT'S MINE!
I FOUND IT LYING IN THAT SHACK.
DID THE WORM MAN GIVE YOU THIS?
NO.

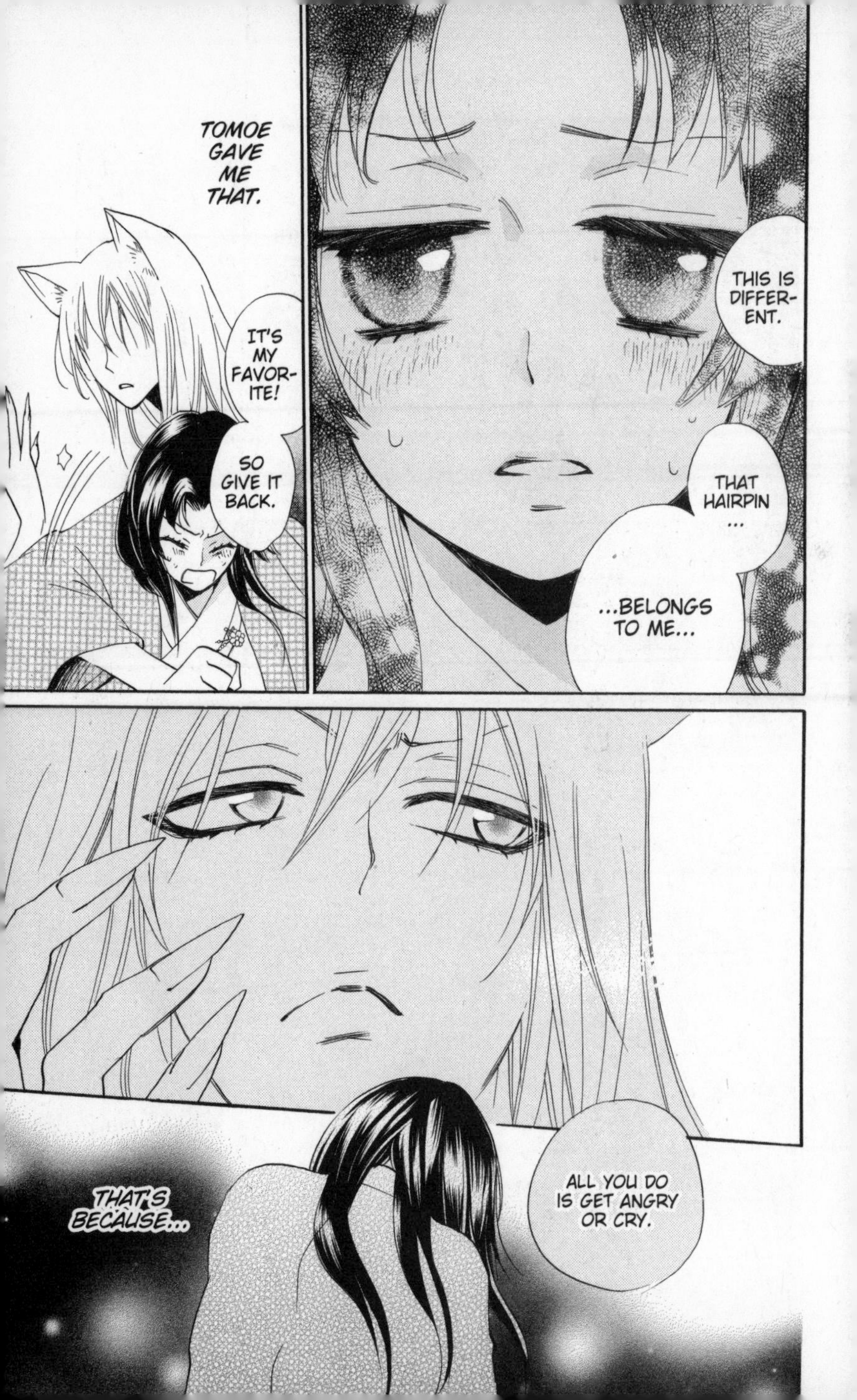
THIS IS DIFFERENT.
THAT HAIRPIN...
...BELONGS TO ME...
TOMOE GAVE ME THAT.
IT'S MY FAVORITE!
SO GIVE IT BACK.
ALL YOU DO IS GET ANGRY OR CRY.
THAT'S BECAUSE...

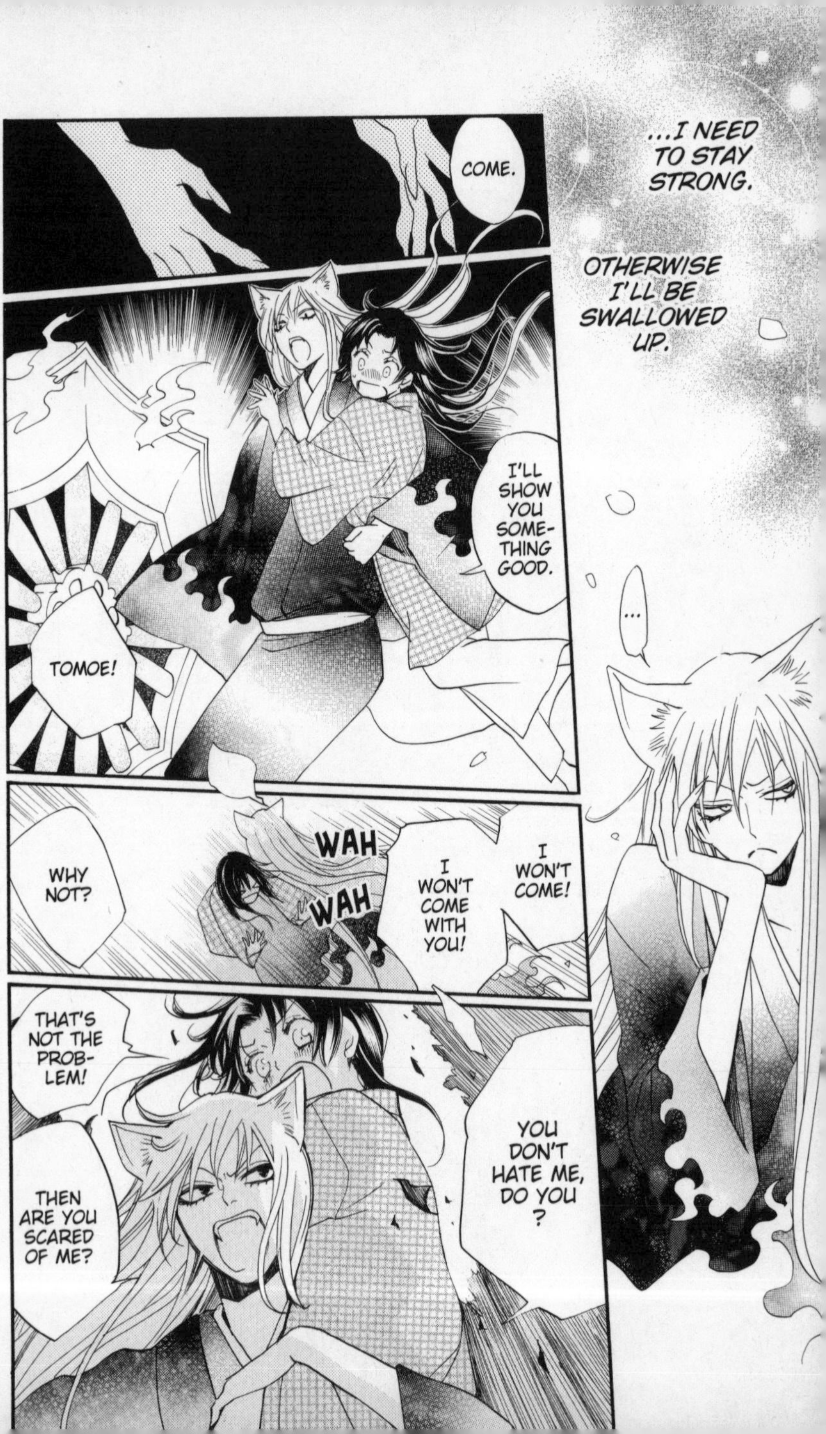
...I NEED TO STAY STRONG.
OTHERWISE I'LL BE SWALLOWED UP.
...
COME.
I'LL SHOW YOU SOME-THING GOOD.
TOMOE!
I WON'T COME!
I WON'T COME WITH YOU!
WAH WAH
WHY NOT?
YOU DON'T HATE ME, DO YOU?
THAT'S NOT THE PROB-LEM!
THEN ARE YOU SCARED OF ME?

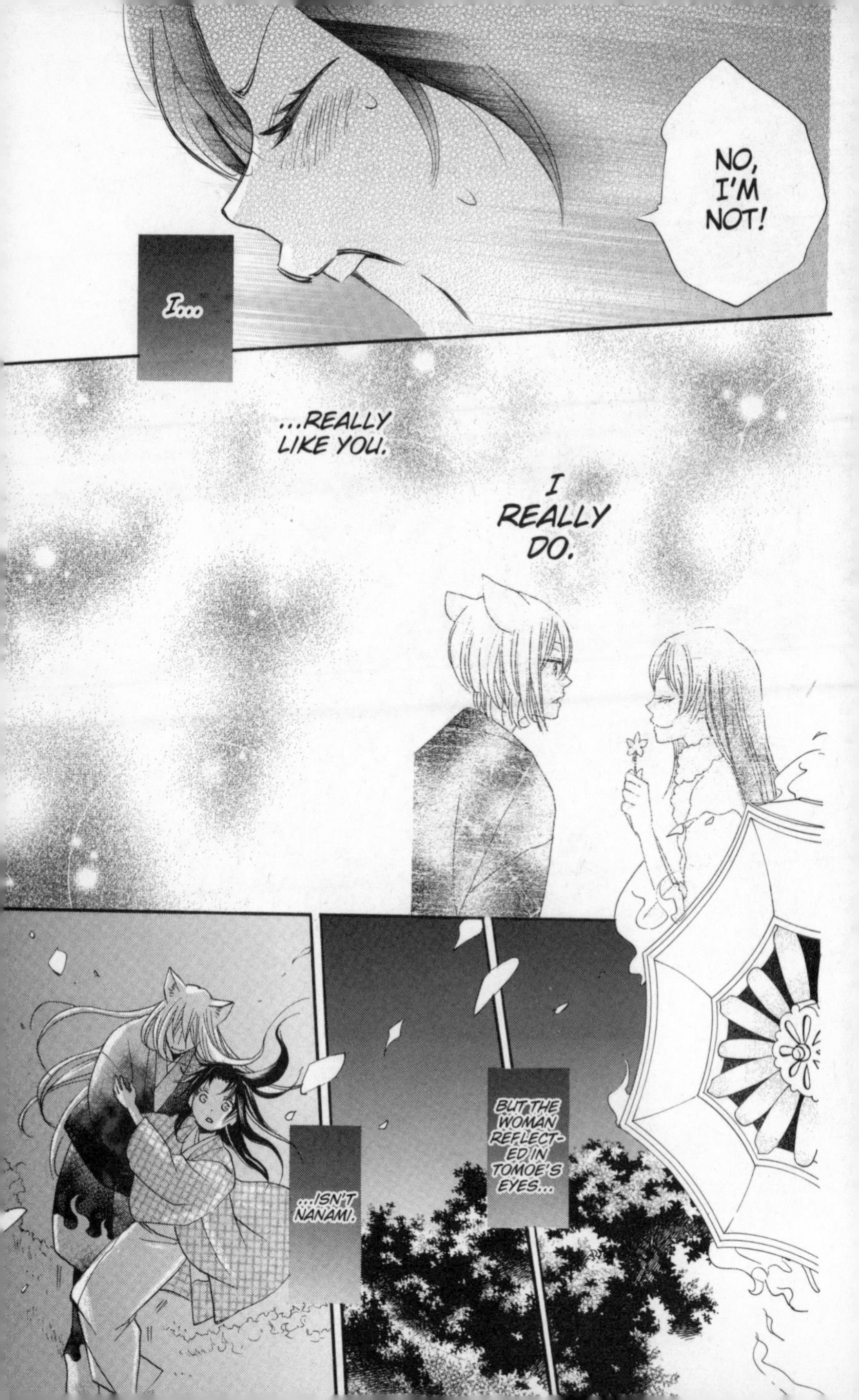
NO, I'M NOT!
I...
...REALLY LIKE YOU.
I REALLY DO.
BUT THE WOMAN REFLECT-ED IN TOMOE'S EYES...
...ISN'T NANAMI.

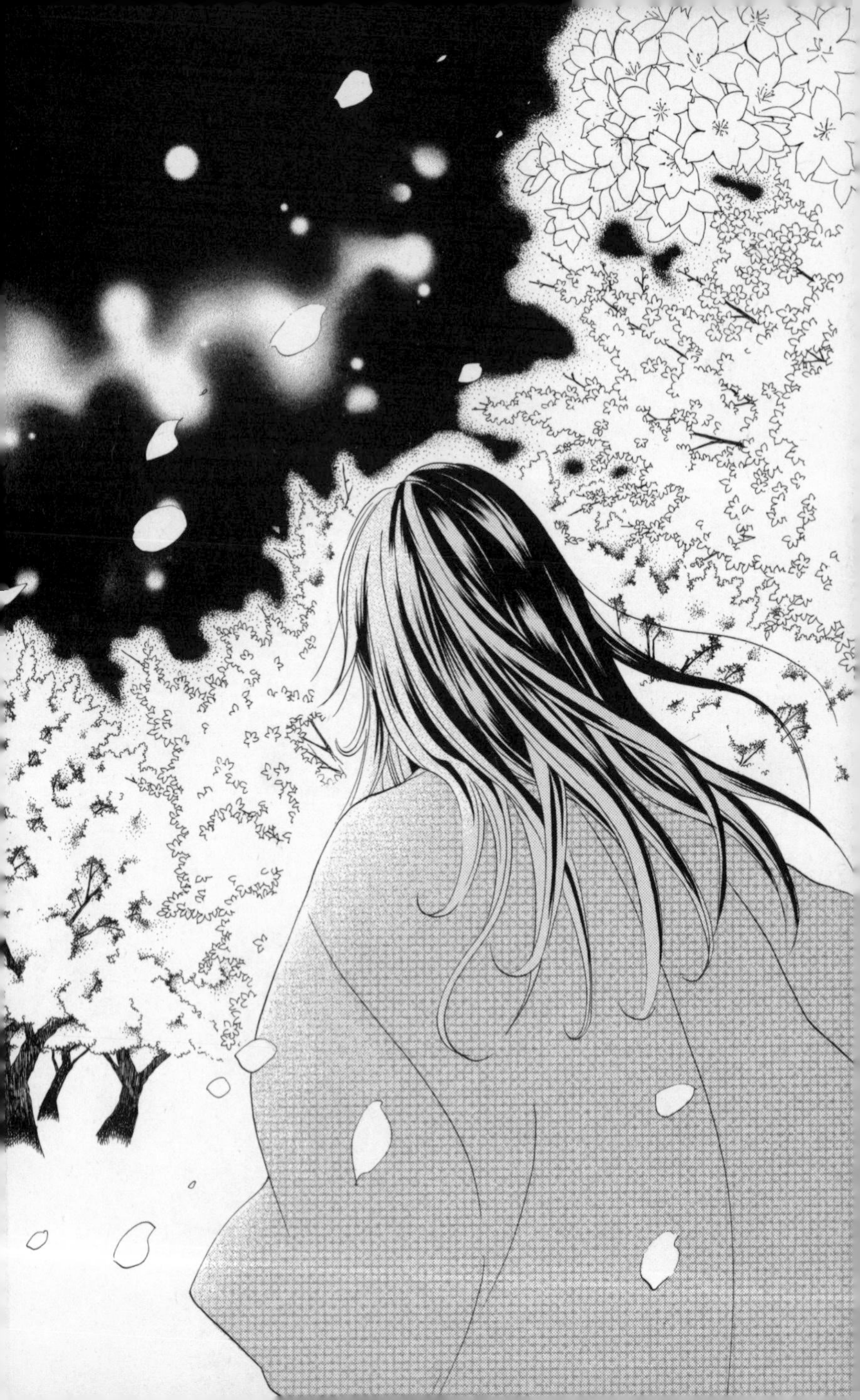

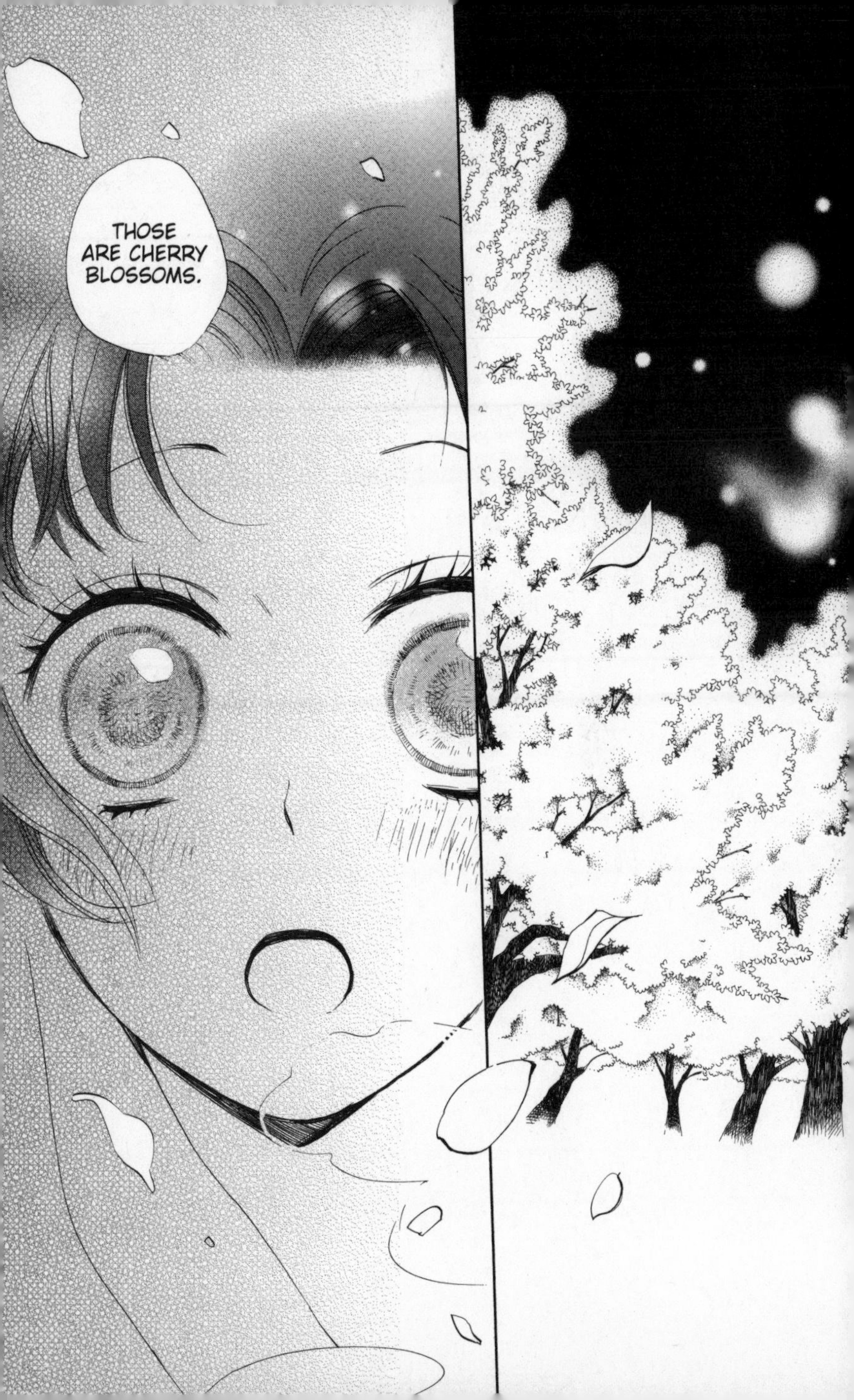
THOSE ARE CHERRY BLOSSOMS.

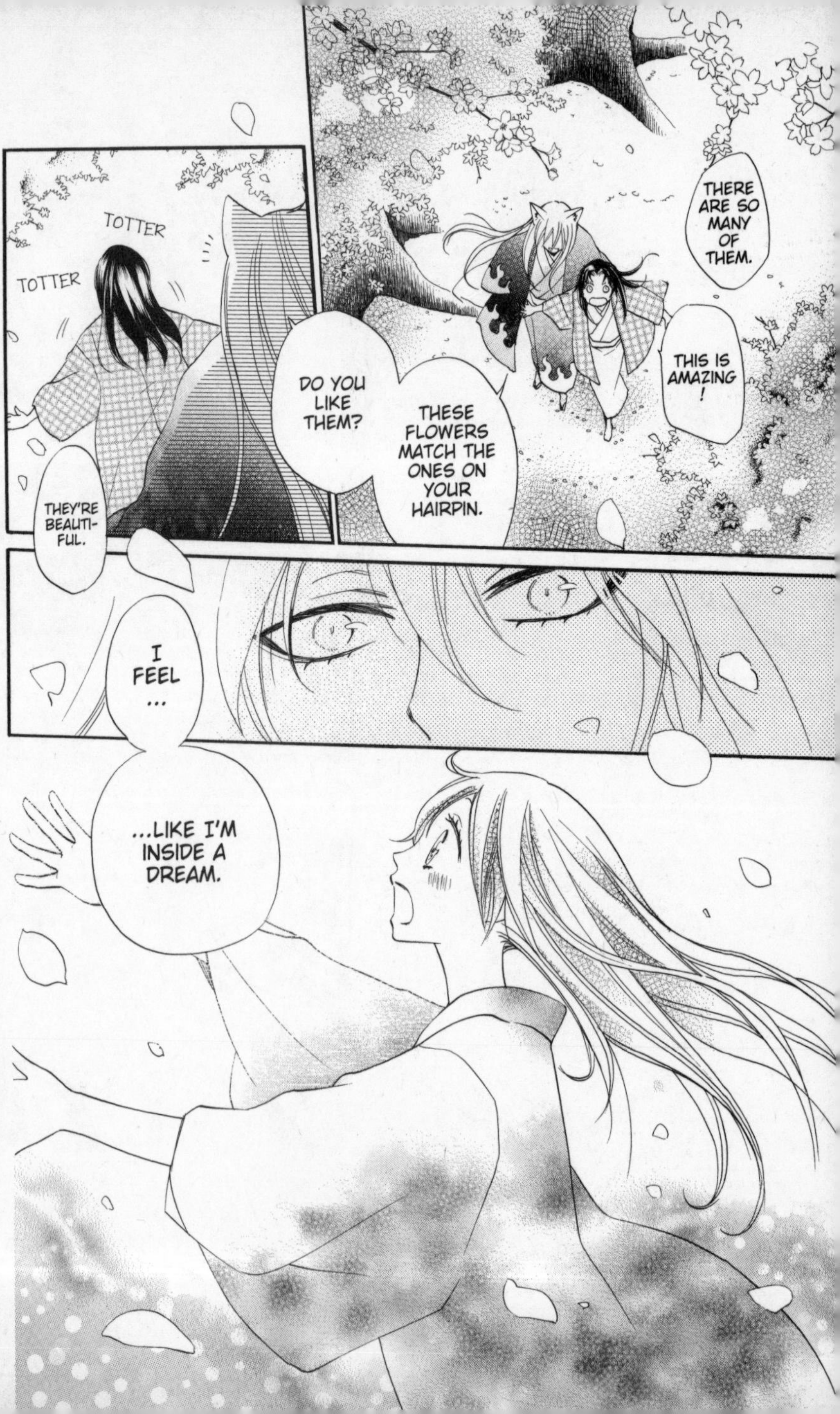
THERE ARE SO MANY OF THEM.
THIS IS AMAZING!
THESE FLOWERS MATCH THE ONES ON YOUR HAIRPIN.
DO YOU LIKE THEM?
TOTTER
TOTTER
THEY'RE BEAUTI-FUL.
I FEEL...
...LIKE I'M INSIDE A DREAM.

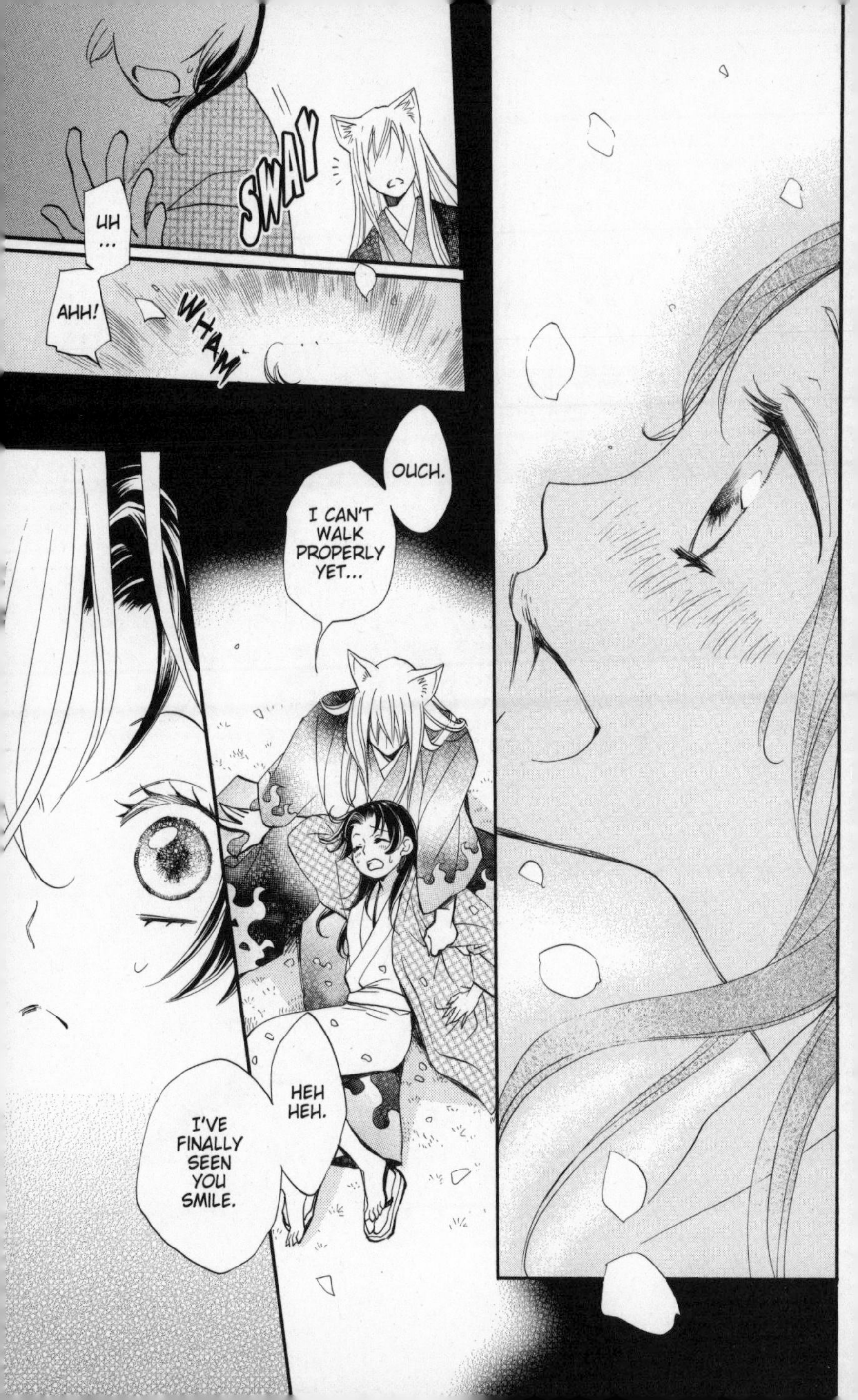
SWAY
UH...
AHH!
WHAM
OUCH.
I CAN'T WALK PROPERLY YET...
HEH HEH.
I'VE FINALLY SEEN YOU SMILE.

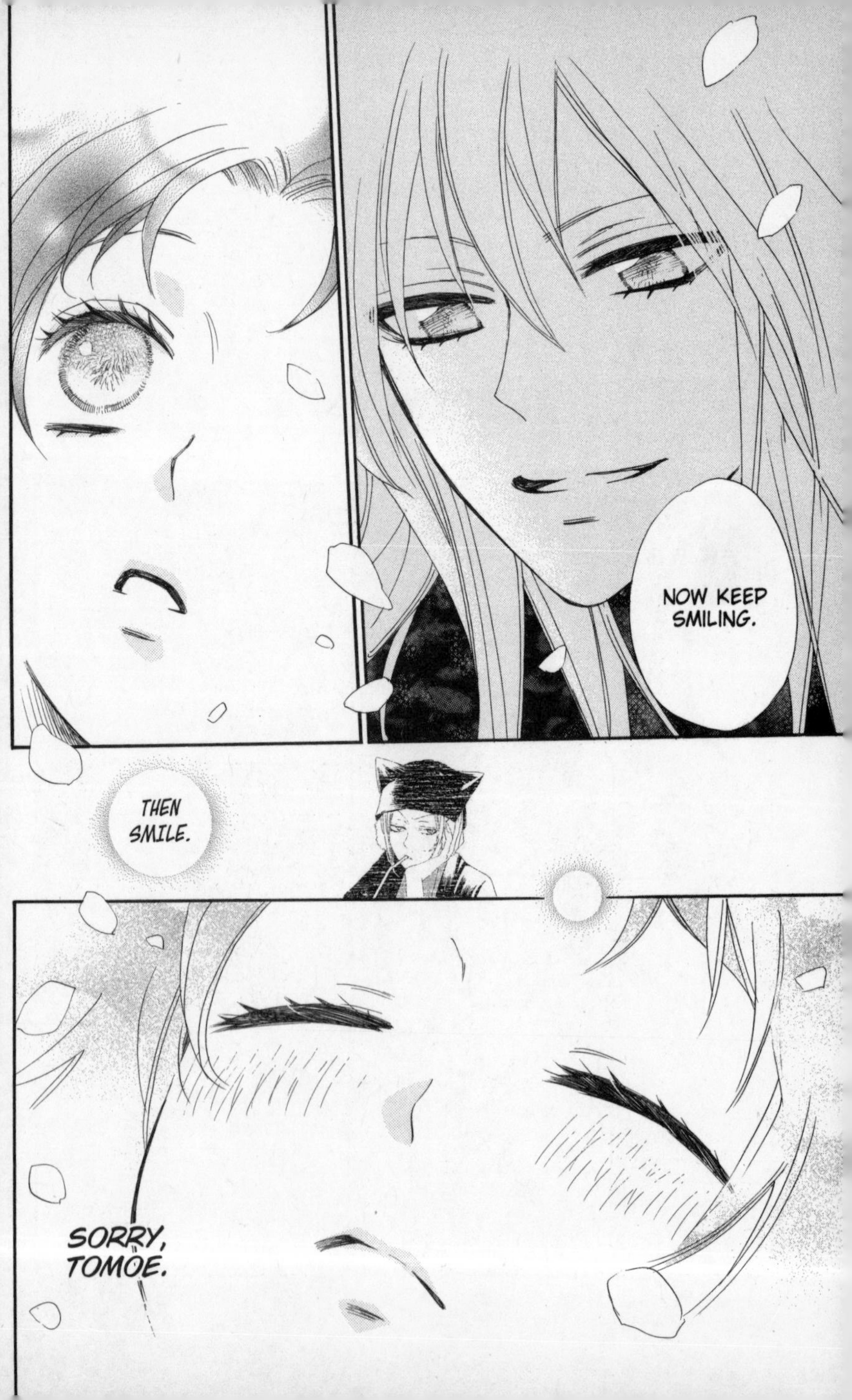
NOW KEEP SMILING.
THEN SMILE.
SORRY, TOMOE.

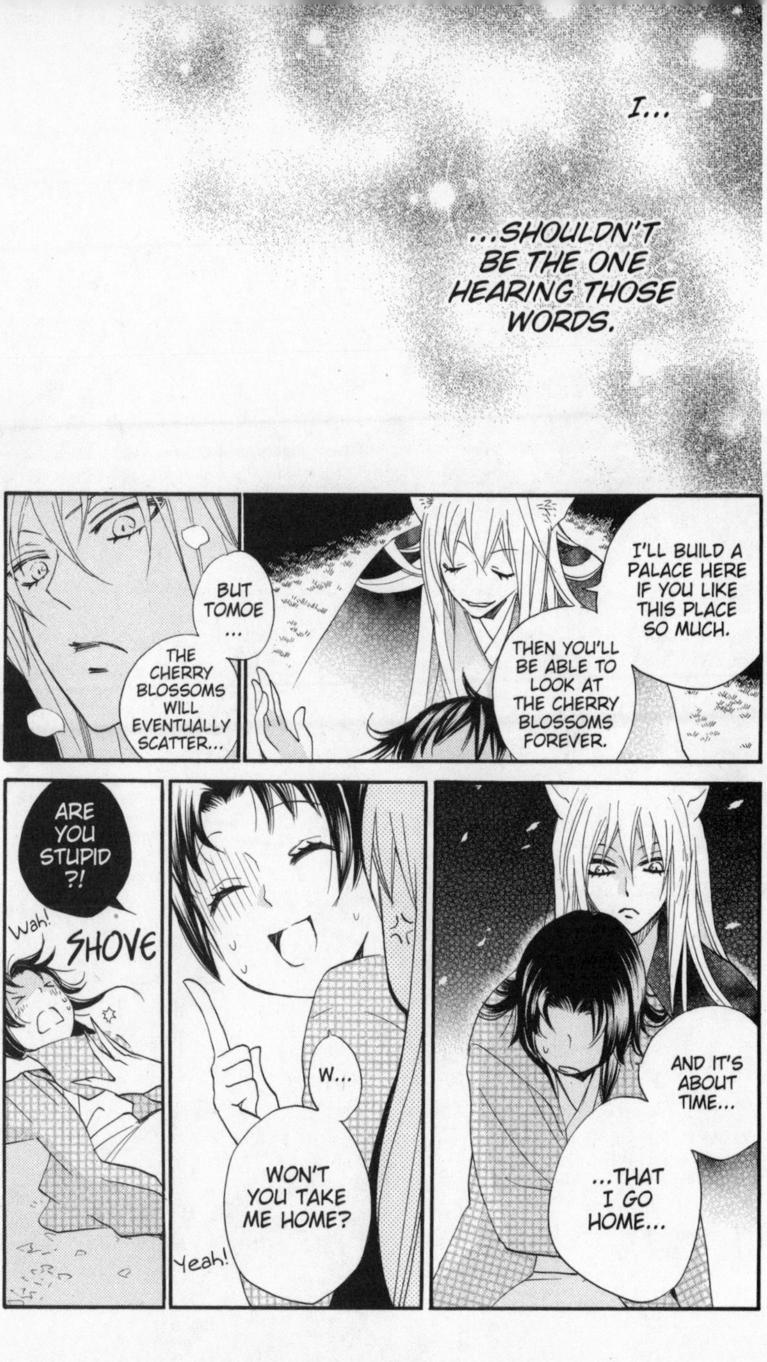
I...
...SHOULDN'T BE THE ONE HEARING THOSE WORDS.
I'LL BUILD A PALACE HERE IF YOU LIKE THIS PLACE SO MUCH.
THEN YOU'LL BE ABLE TO LOOK AT THE CHERRY BLOSSOMS FOREVER.
BUT TOMOE ...
THE CHERRY BLOSSOMS WILL EVENTUALLY SCATTER...
AND IT'S ABOUT TIME...
...THAT I GO HOME...
W...
WON'T YOU TAKE ME HOME?
Yeah!
ARE YOU STUPID ?!
SHOVE
Wah!

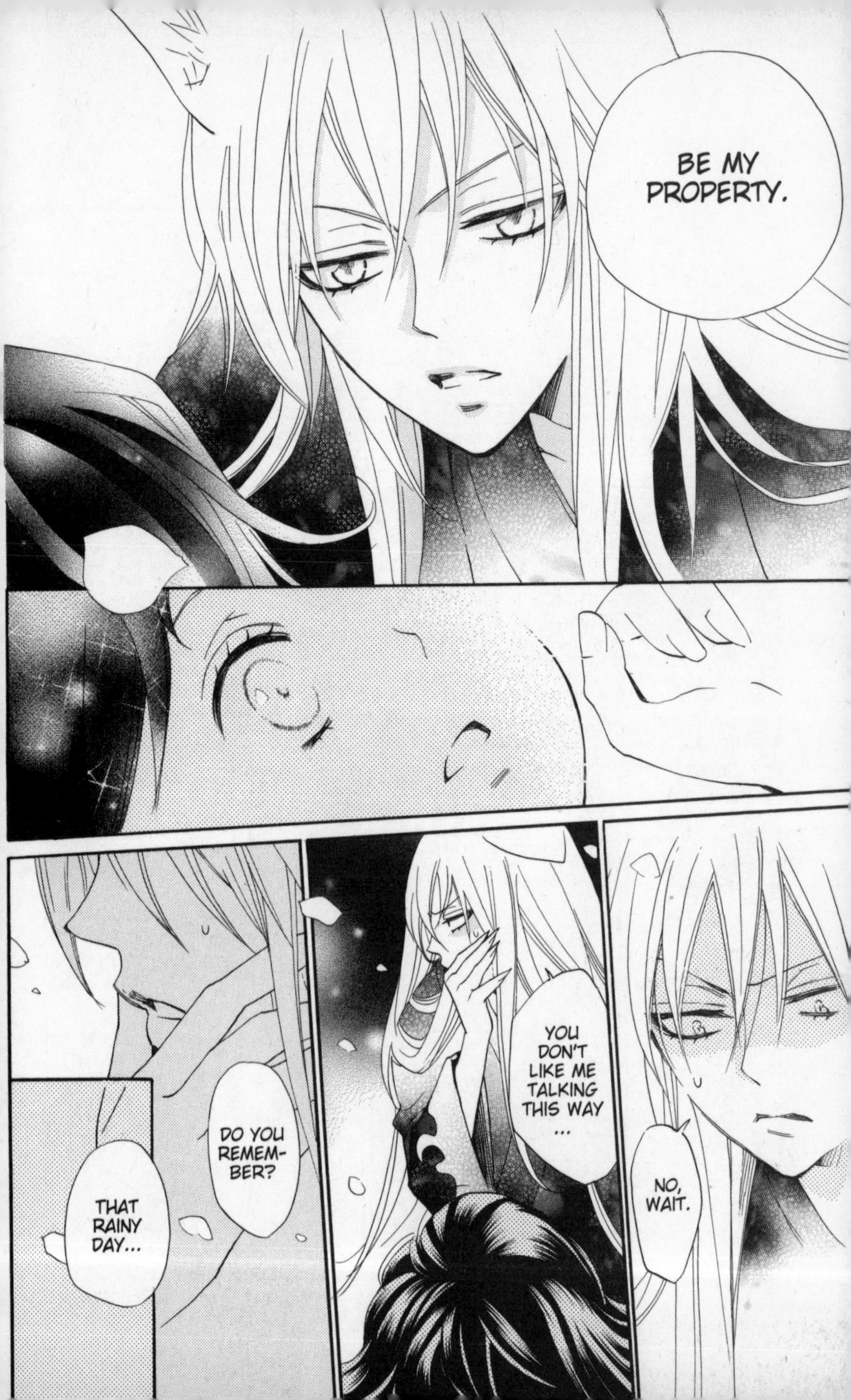
BE MY PROPERTY.
NO, WAIT.
YOU DON'T LIKE ME TALKING THIS WAY ...
DO YOU REMEMBER?
THAT RAINY DAY...

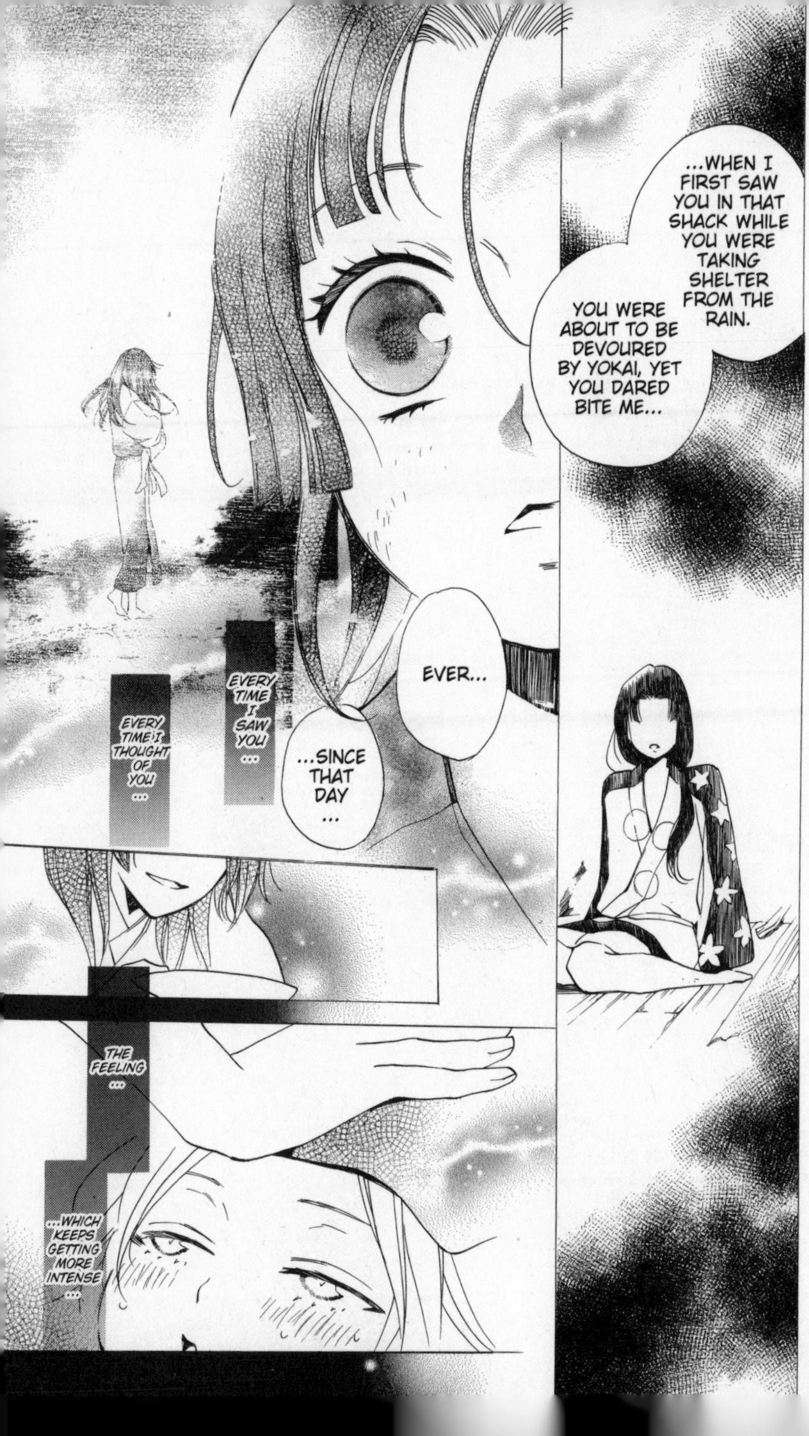
...WHEN I FIRST SAW YOU IN THAT SHACK WHILE YOU WERE TAKING SHELTER FROM THE RAIN.
YOU WERE ABOUT TO BE DEVOURED BY YOKAI, YET YOU DARED BITE ME...
EVER...
...SINCE THAT DAY...
EVERY TIME I SAW YOU...
EVERY TIME I THOUGHT OF YOU...
THE FEELING...
...WHICH KEEPS GETTING MORE INTENSE...

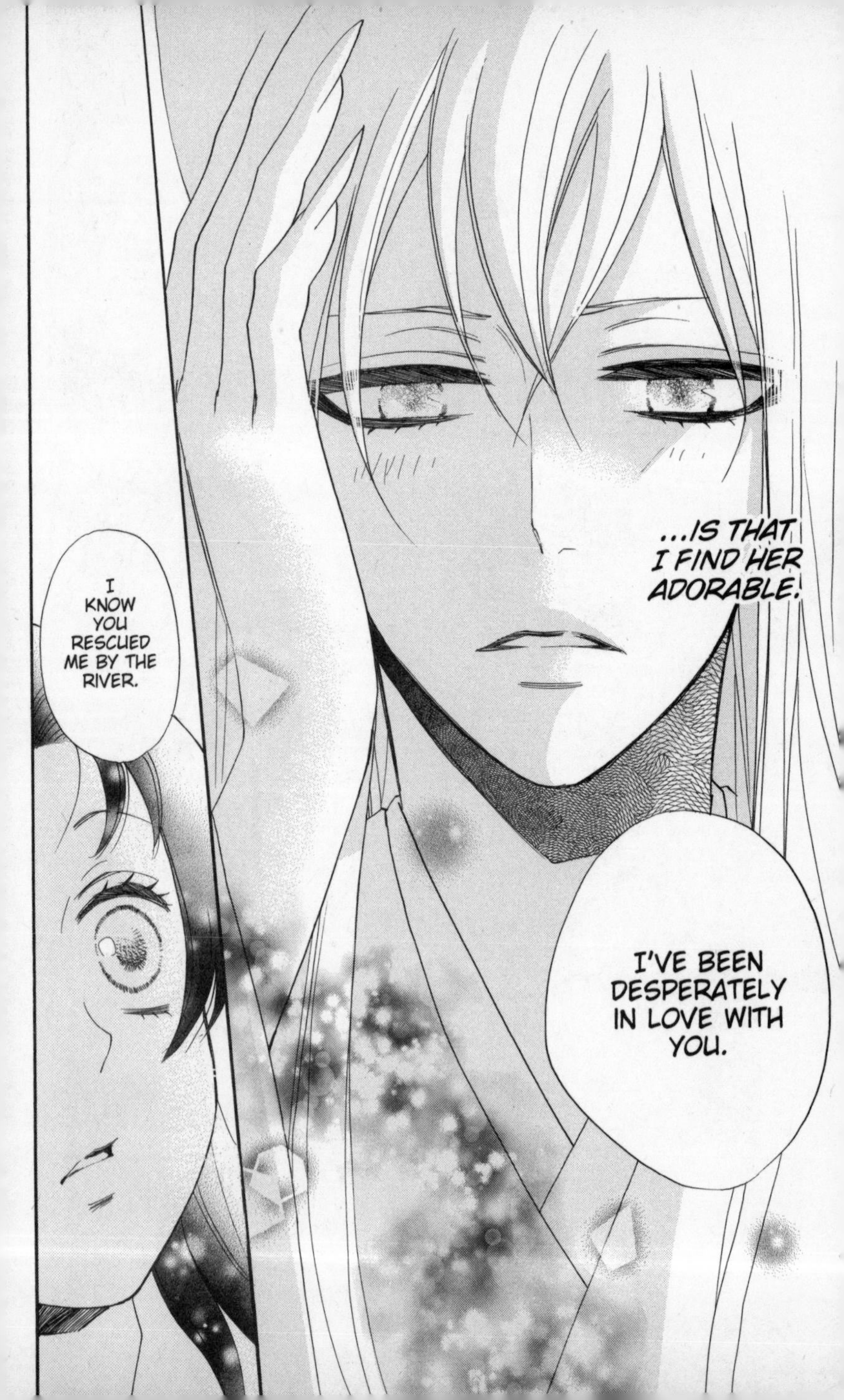
...IS THAT I FIND HER ADORABLE.
I'VE BEEN DESPERATELY IN LOVE WITH YOU.
I KNOW YOU RESCUED ME BY THE RIVER.

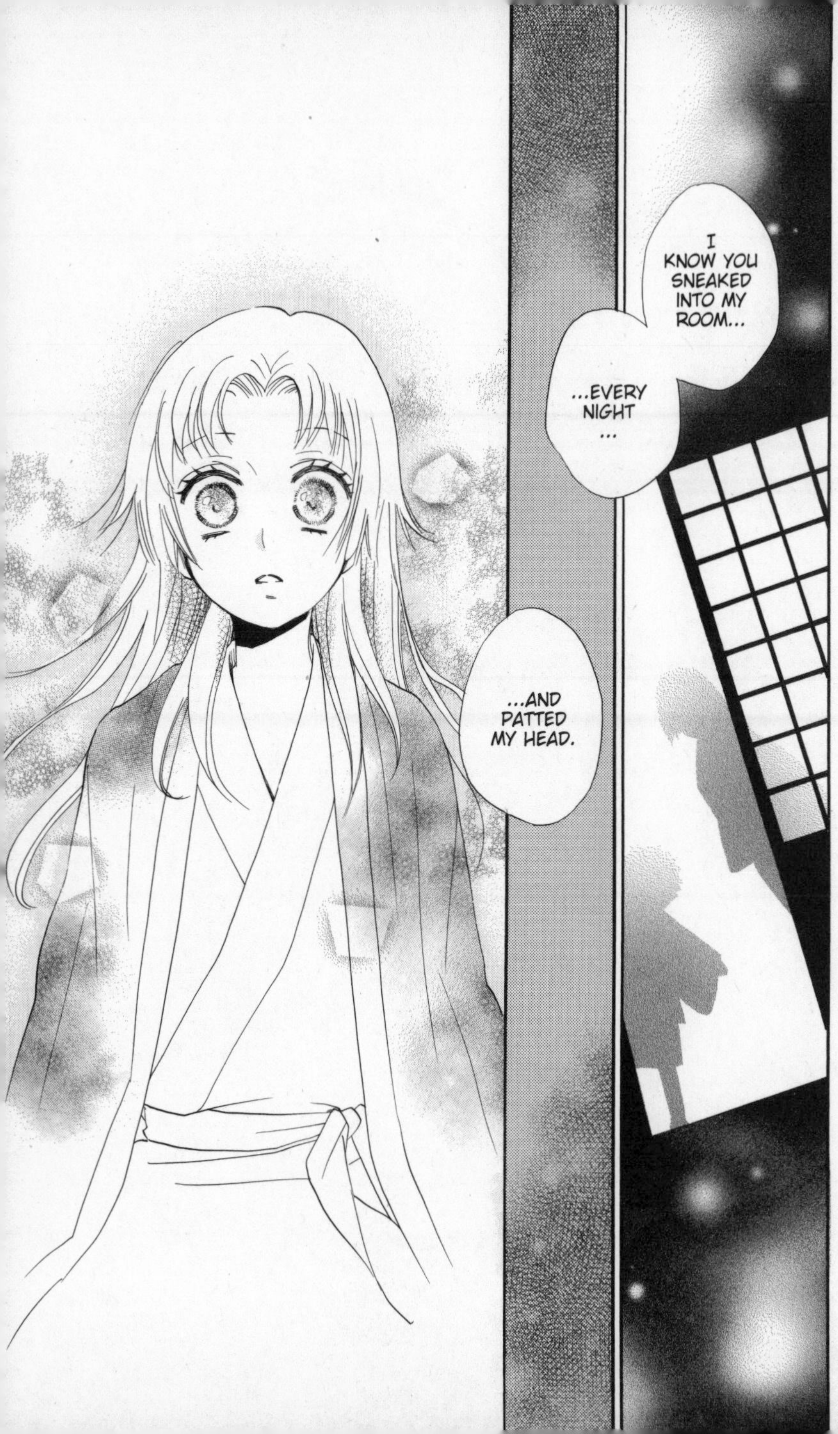
I KNOW YOU SNEAKED INTO MY ROOM...
...EVERY NIGHT ...
...AND PATTED MY HEAD.

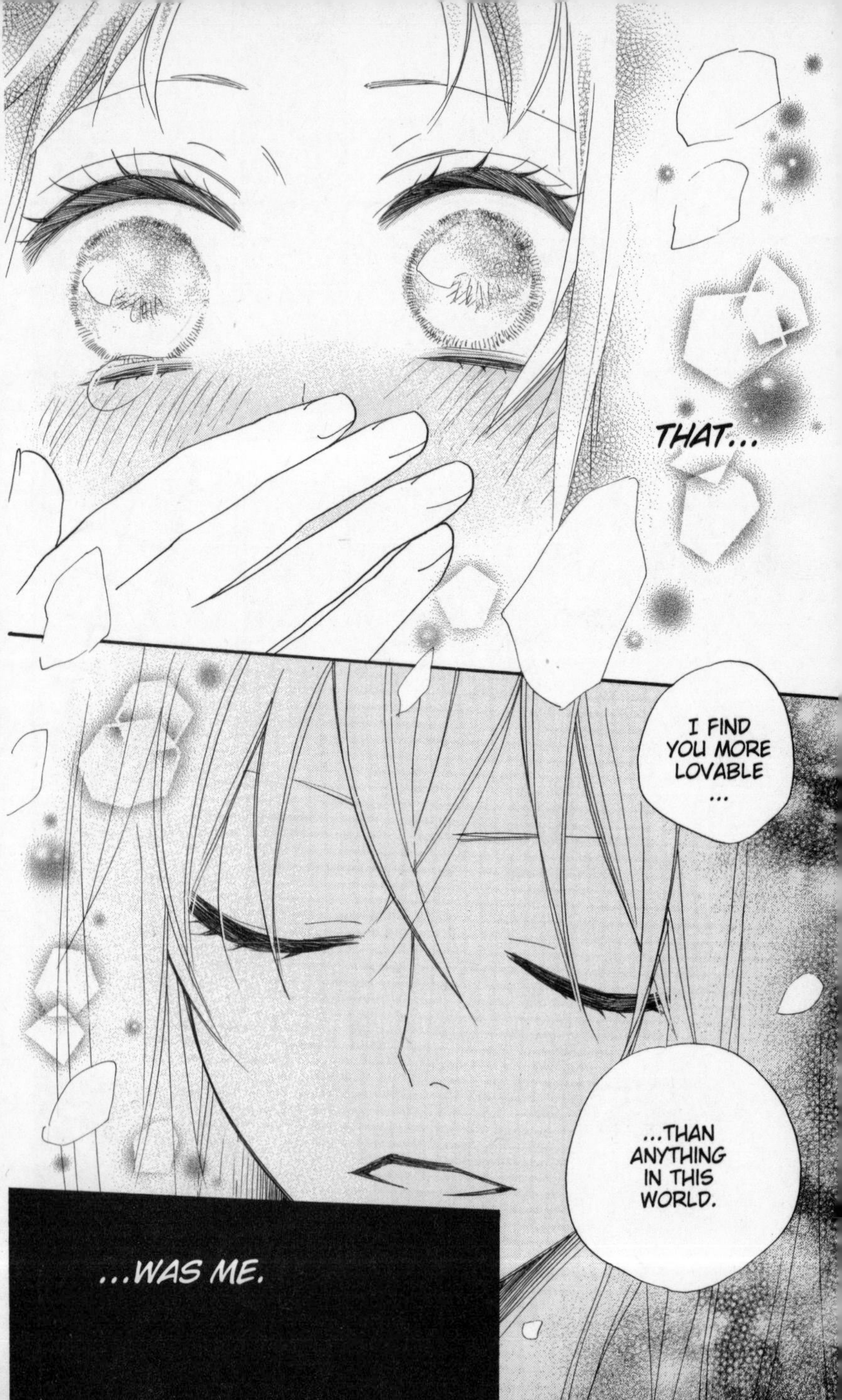
THAT...
I FIND YOU MORE LOVABLE ...
...THAN ANYTHING IN THIS WORLD.
...WAS ME.

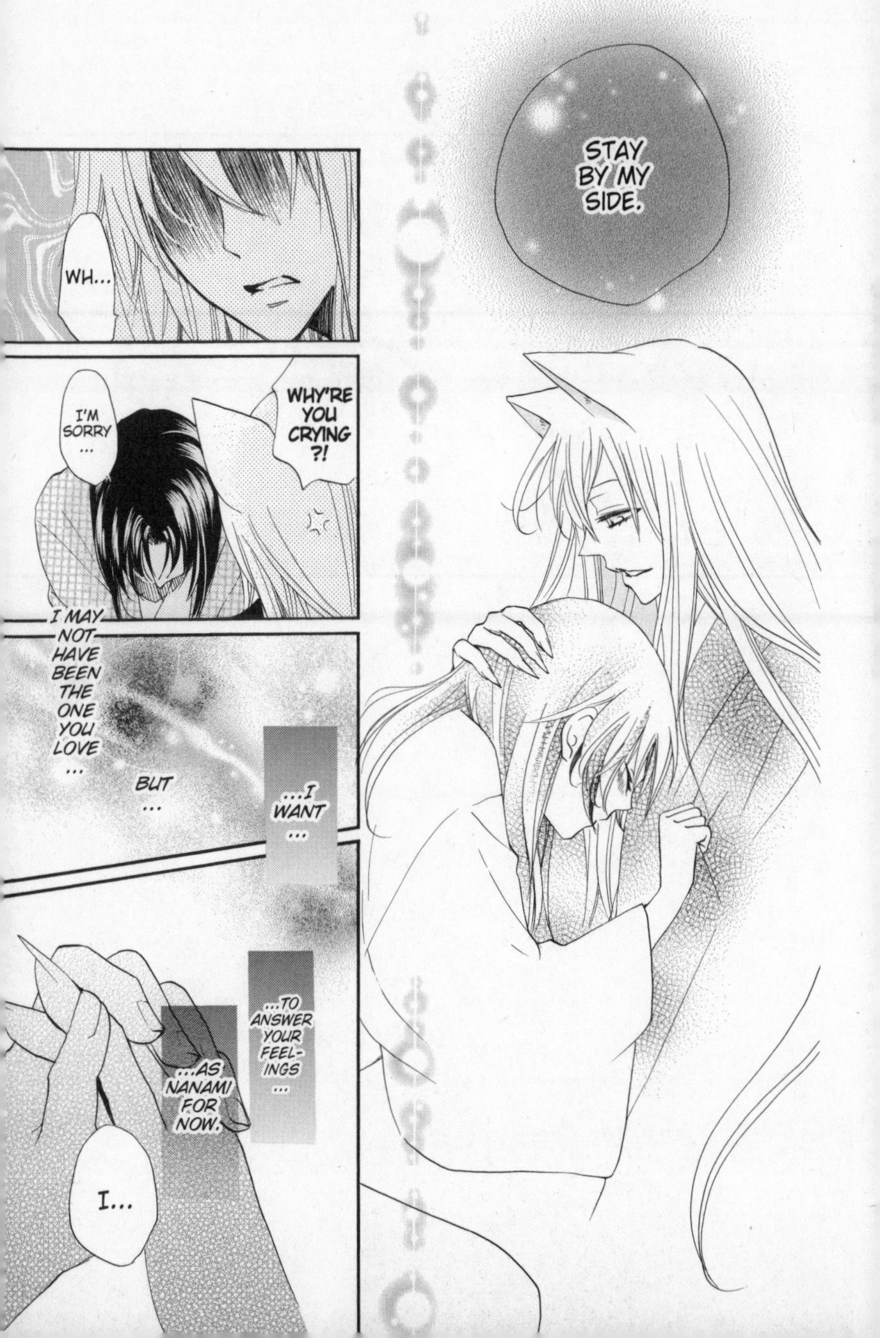
STAY BY MY SIDE.
WH...
WHY'RE YOU CRYING ?!
I'M SORRY ...
I MAY NOT HAVE BEEN THE ONE YOU LOVE ...
BUT ...
...I WANT ...
...TO ANSWER YOUR FEEL- INGS ...
...AS NANAMI FOR NOW.
I...

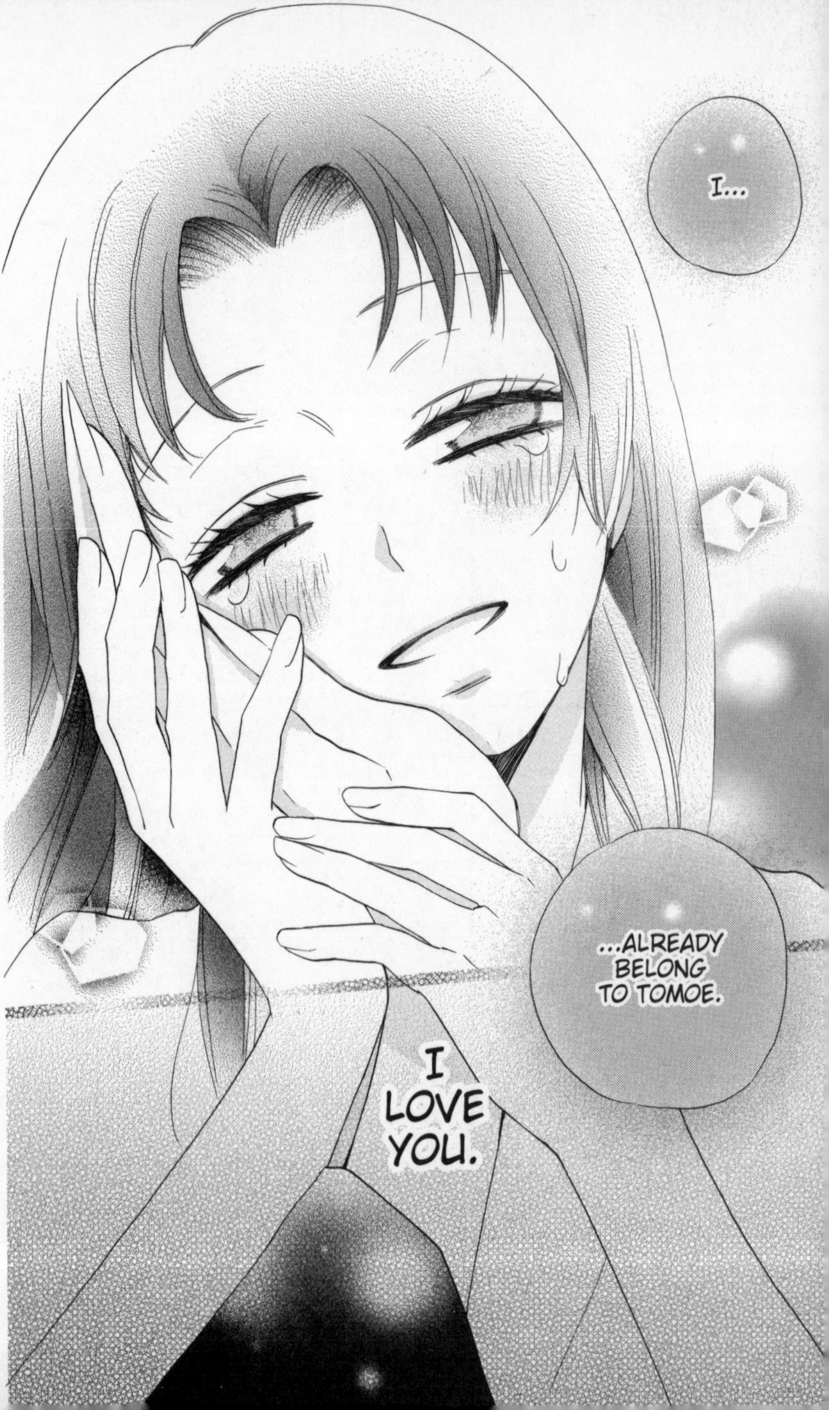
I...
...ALREADY BELONG TO TOMOE.
I LOVE YOU.

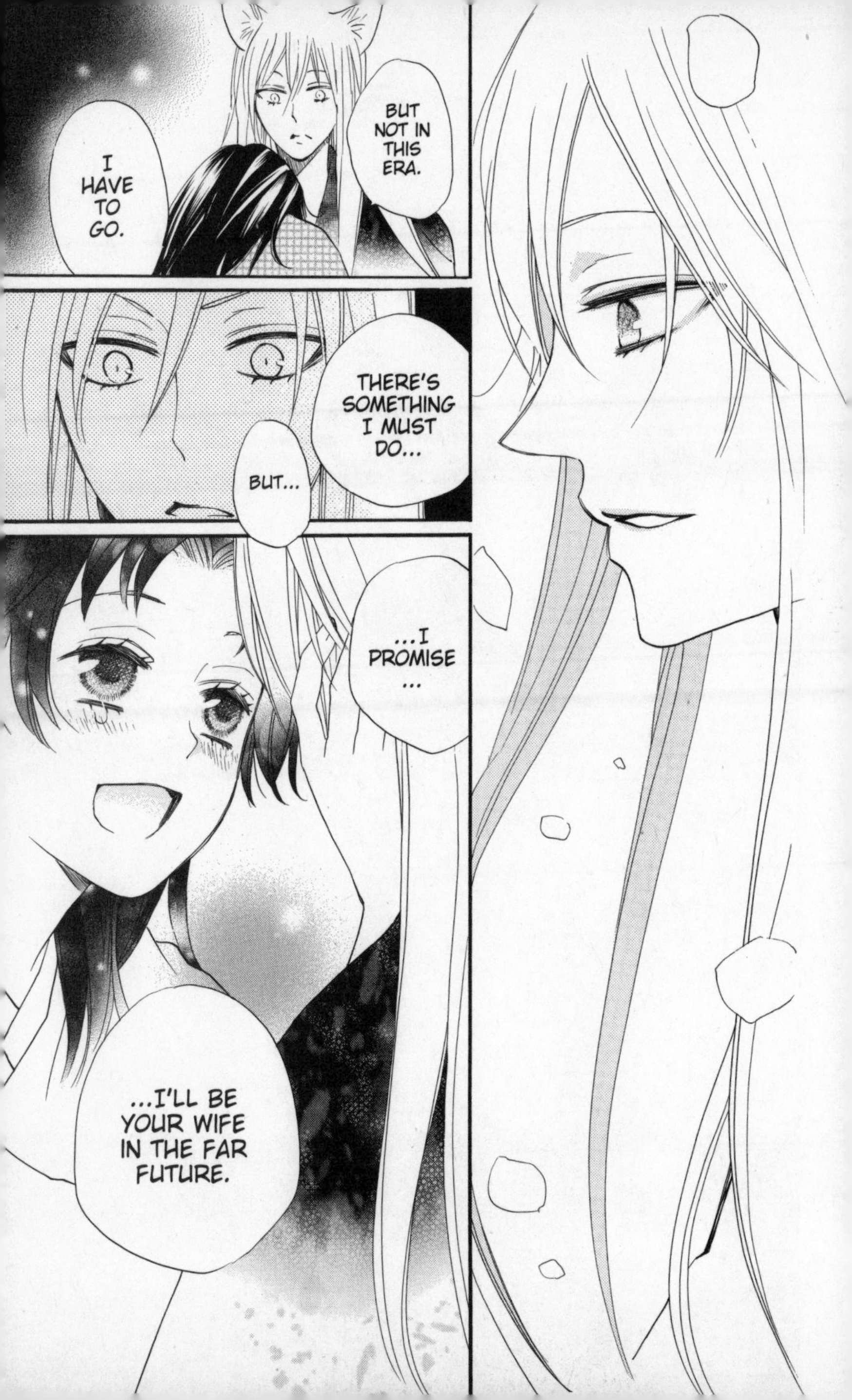
BUT NOT IN THIS ERA.
I HAVE TO GO.
THERE'S SOMETHING I MUST DO...
BUT...
...I PROMISE...
...I'LL BE YOUR WIFE IN THE FAR FUTURE.

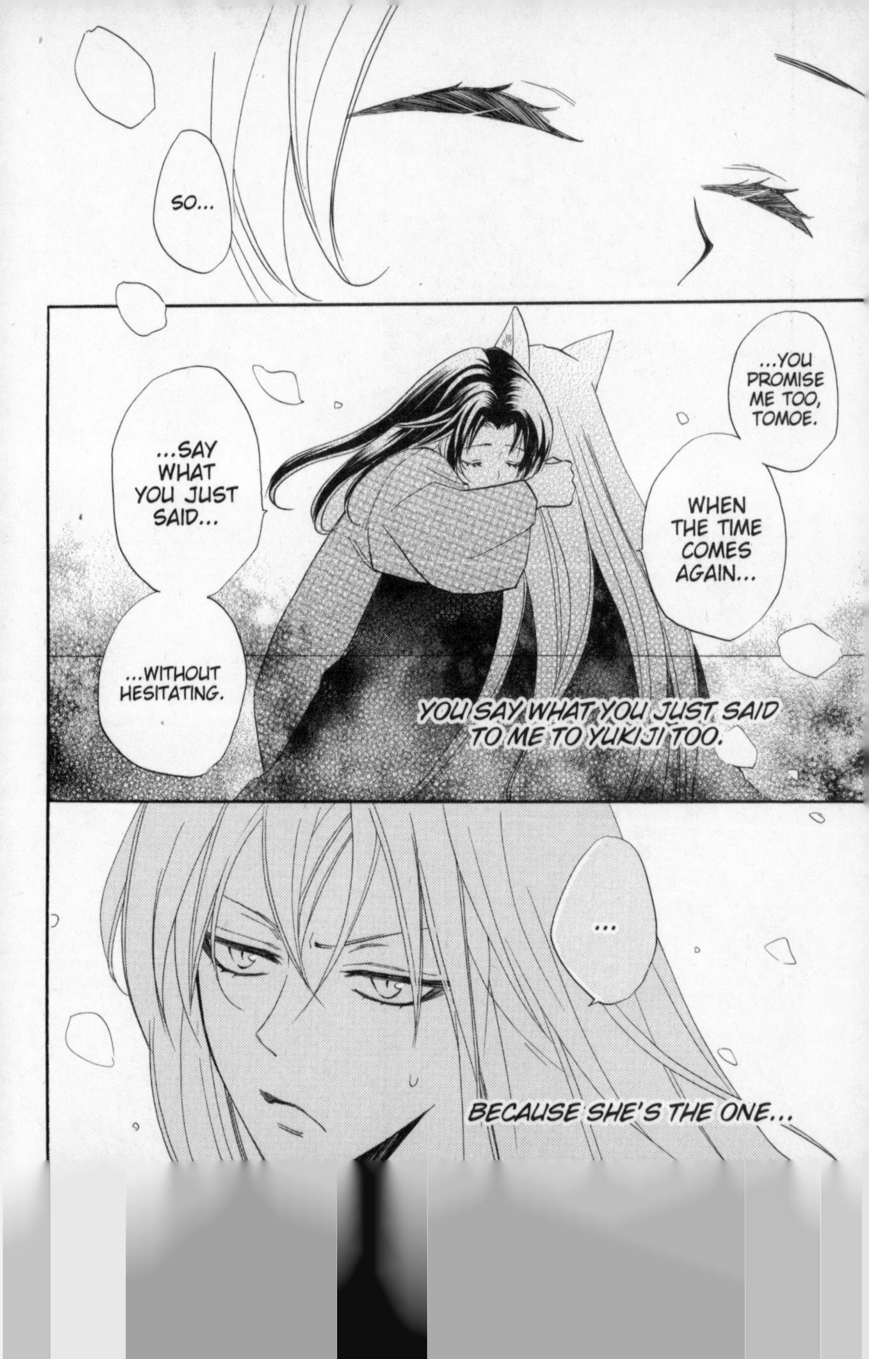
SO...
...YOU PROMISE ME TOO, TOMOE.
WHEN THE TIME COMES AGAIN...
...SAY WHAT YOU JUST SAID...
...WITHOUT HESITATING.
YOU SAY WHAT YOU JUST SAID TO ME TO YUKIJI TOO.
...
BECAUSE SHE'S THE ONE...

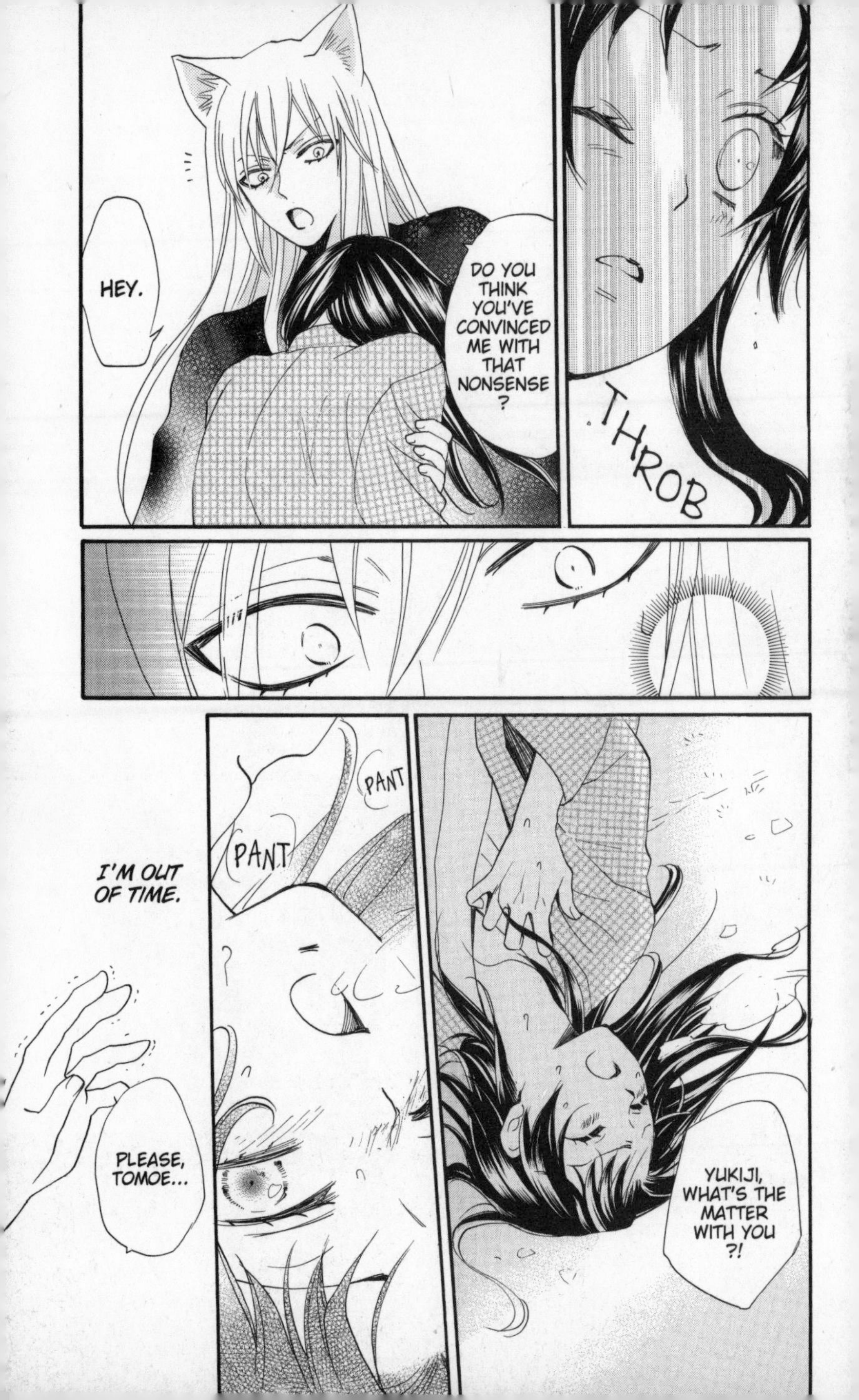
THROB
HEY.
DO YOU THINK YOU'VE CONVINCED ME WITH THAT NONSENSE?
YUKIJI, WHAT'S THE MATTER WITH YOU?!
PANT
PANT
I'M OUT OF TIME.
PLEASE, TOMOE...

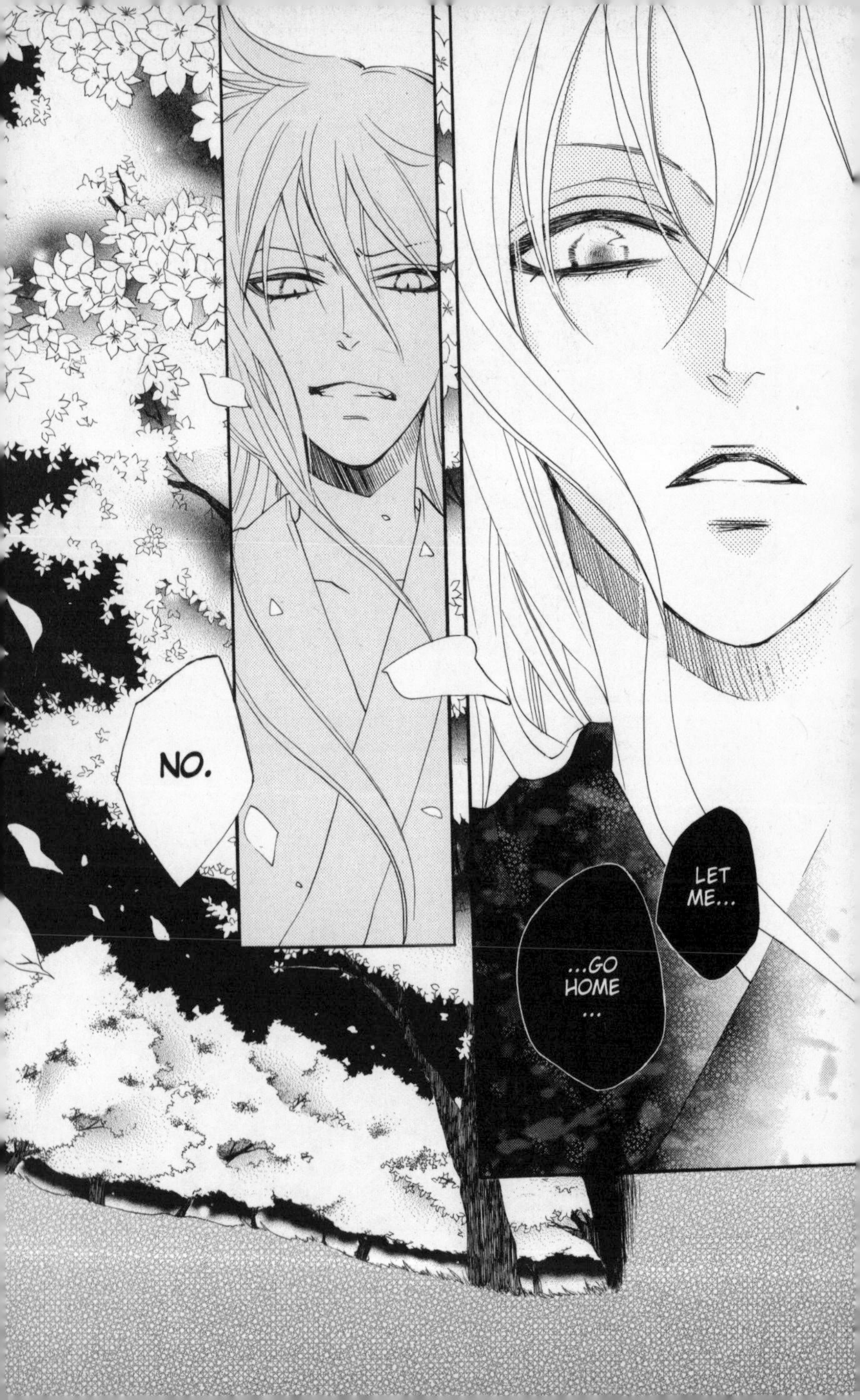
LET ME...
...GO HOME ...
NO.

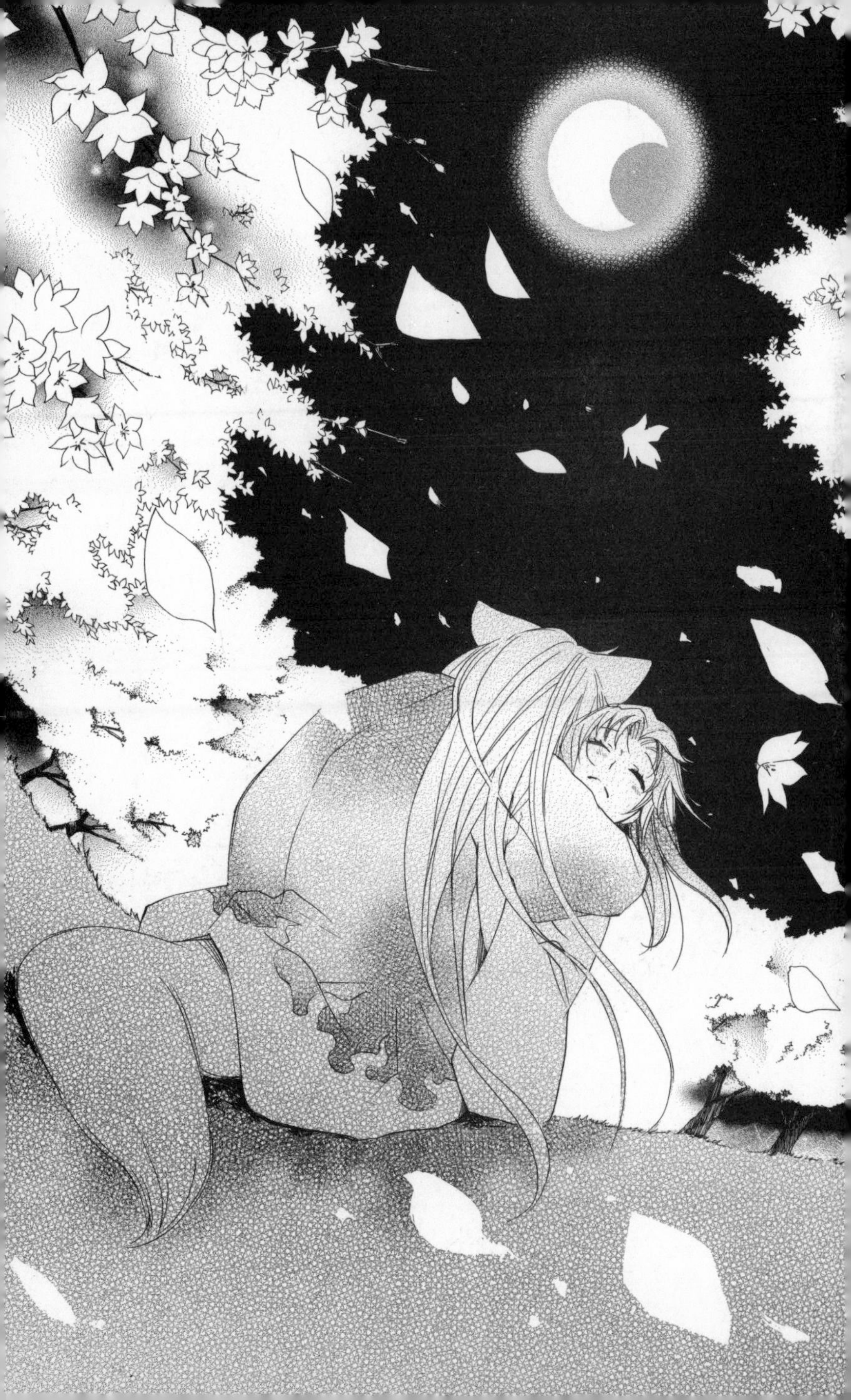

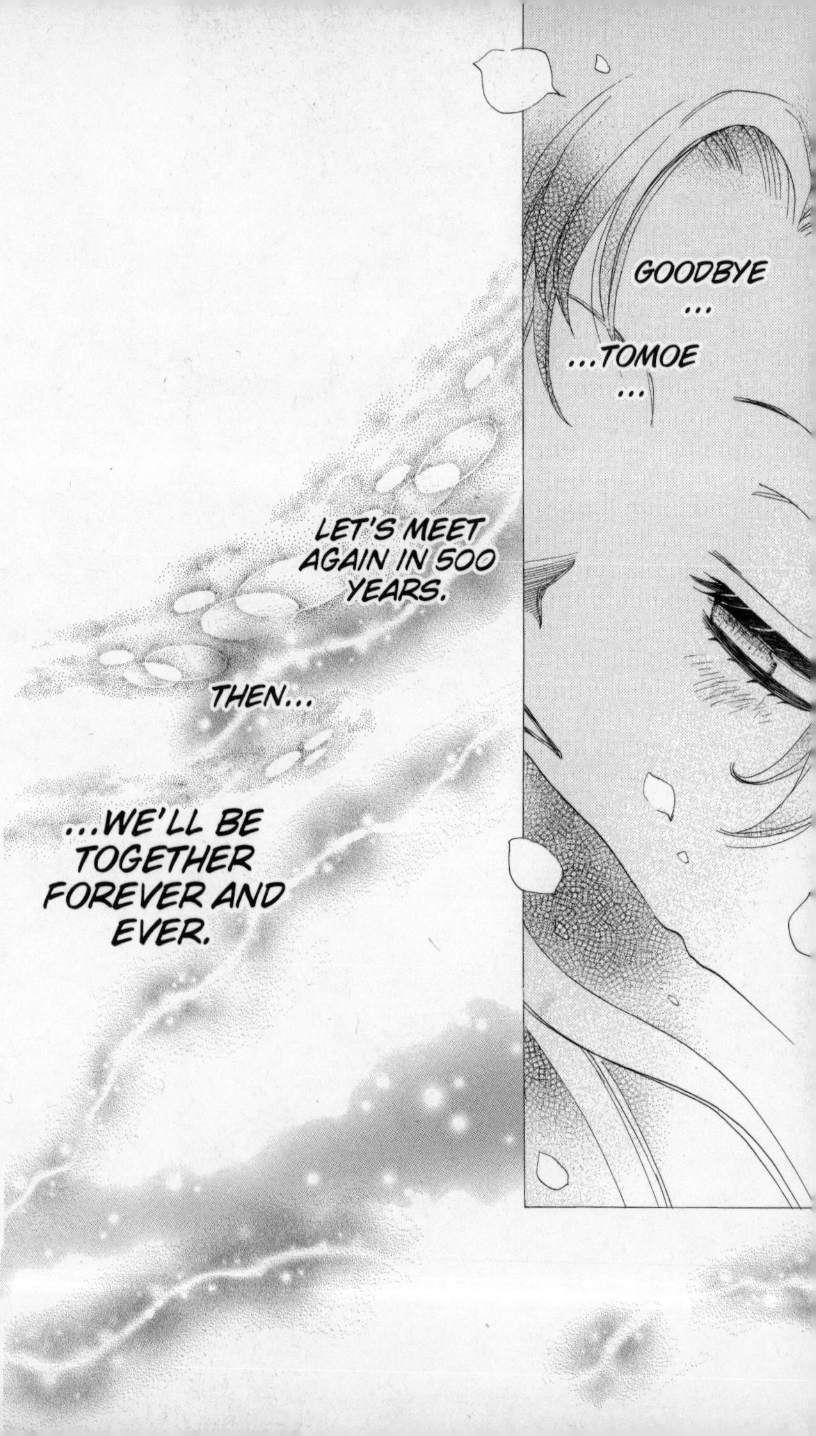
GOODBYE ...
...TOMOE ...
LET'S MEET AGAIN IN 500 YEARS.
THEN...
...WE'LL BE TOGETHER FOREVER AND EVER.

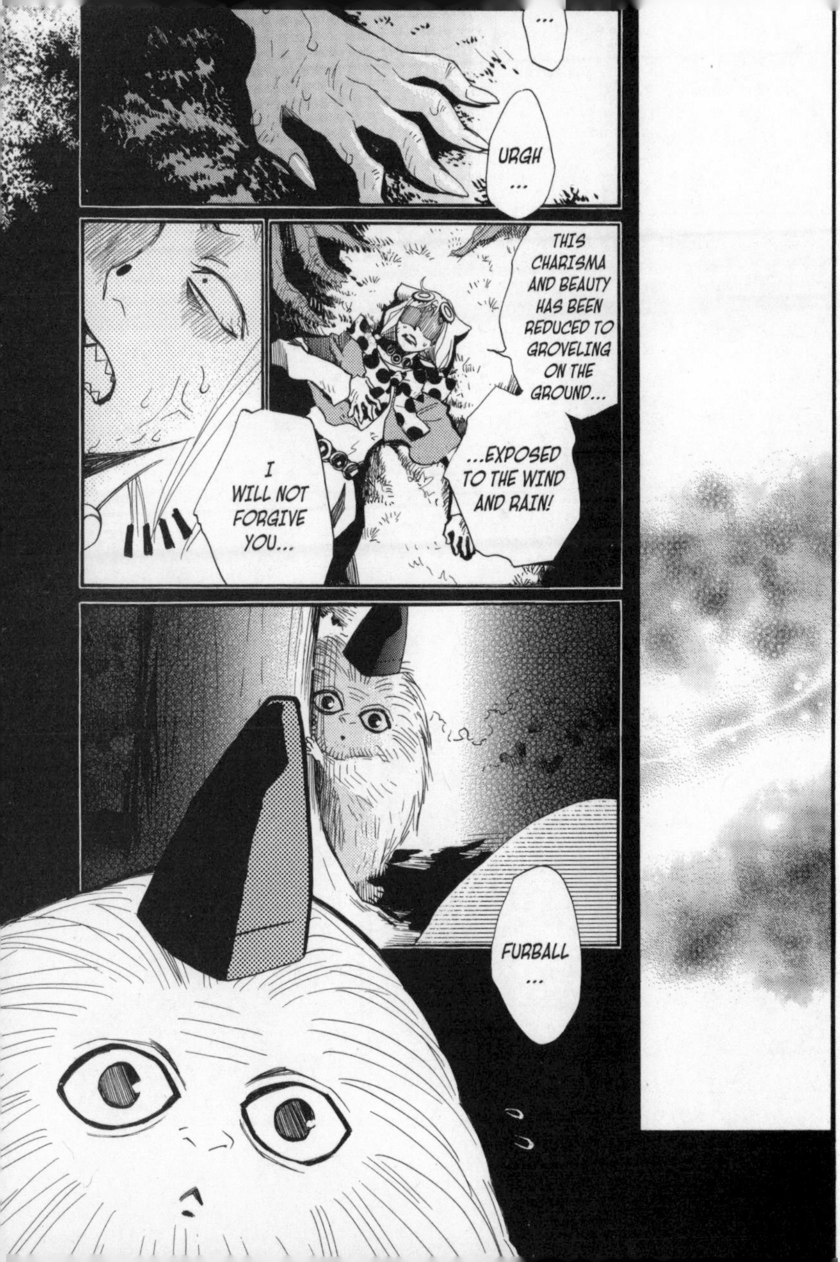
...
URGH ...
THIS CHARISMA AND BEAUTY HAS BEEN REDUCED TO GROVELING ON THE GROUND...
...EXPOSED TO THE WIND AND RAIN!
I WILL NOT FORGIVE YOU...
FURBALL ...

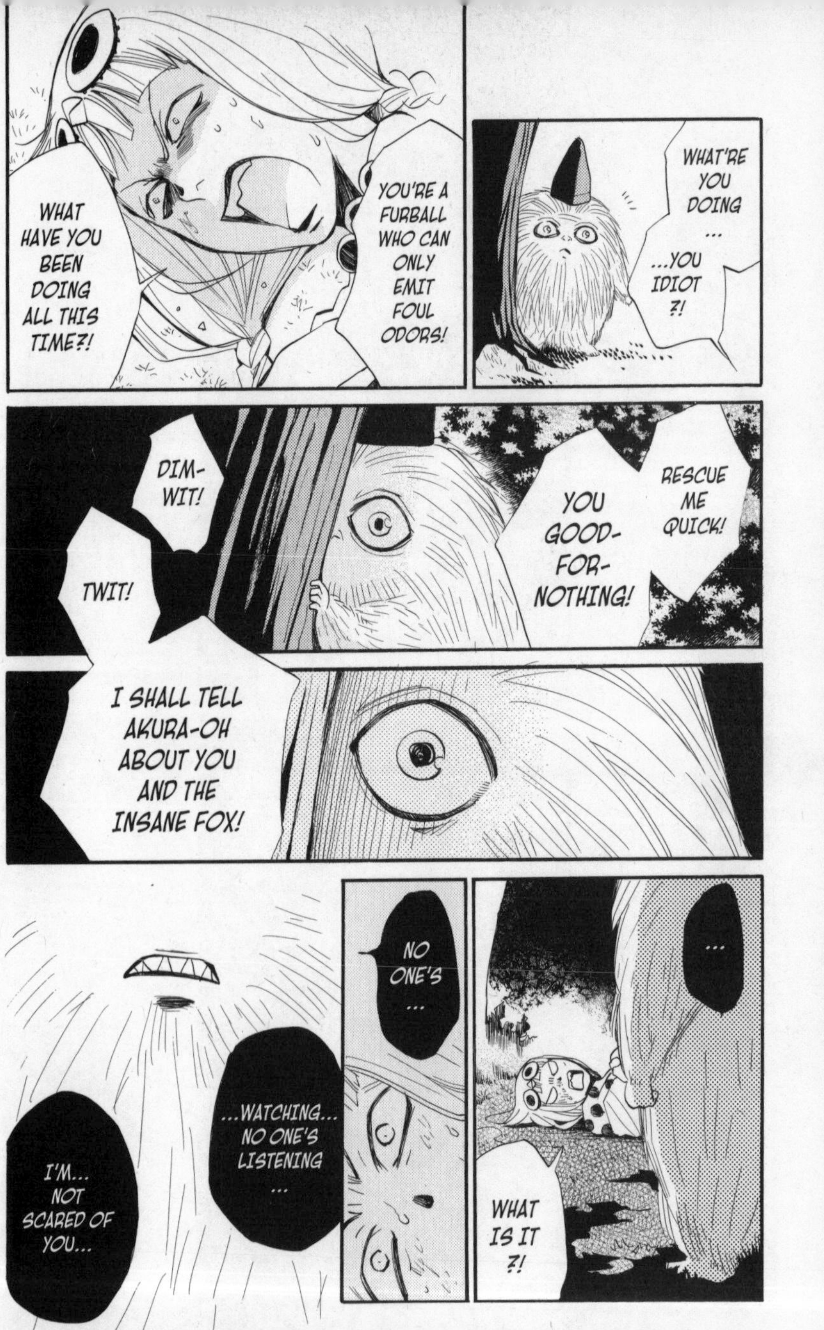
WHAT'RE YOU DOING … …YOU IDIOT ?!
YOU'RE A FURBALL WHO CAN ONLY EMIT FOUL ODORS!
WHAT HAVE YOU BEEN DOING ALL THIS TIME?!
RESCUE ME QUICK!
YOU GOOD-FOR-NOTHING!
DIM-WIT!
TWIT!
I SHALL TELL AKURA-OH ABOUT YOU AND THE INSANE FOX!
…
WHAT IS IT ?!
NO ONE'S …
…WATCHING… NO ONE'S LISTENING …
I'M… NOT SCARED OF YOU…

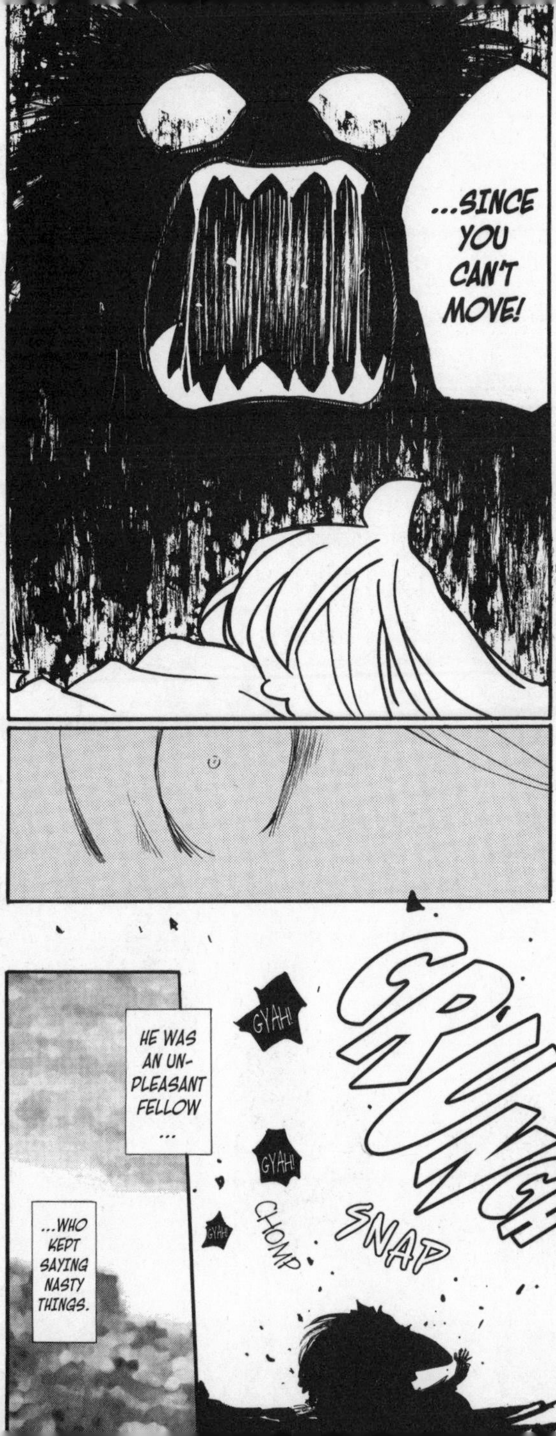
...SINCE YOU CAN'T MOVE!
CRUNCH!
GYAH!
HE WAS AN UN-PLEASANT FELLOW ...
GYAH!
SNAP
CHOMP
GYAH
...WHO KEPT SAYING NASTY THINGS.

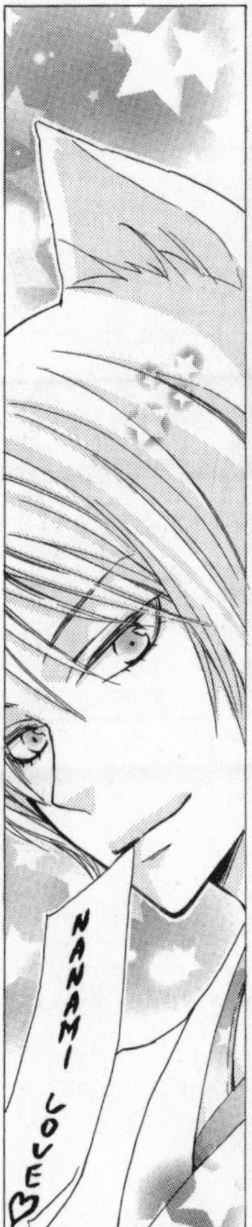
NANAMI LOVE ♡
I love Kamisama Kiss ♡
~Yukichi Nakamura

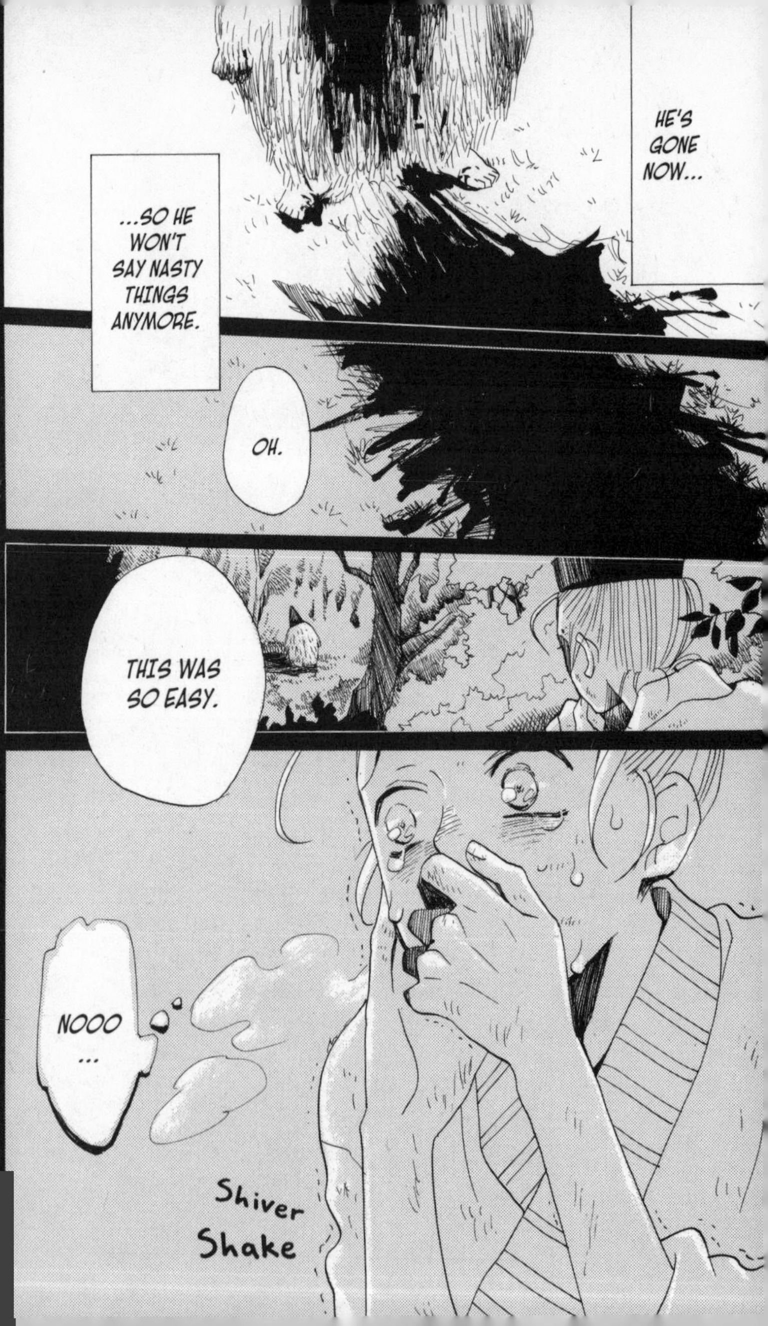
HE'S GONE NOW...
...SO HE WON'T SAY NASTY THINGS ANYMORE.
OH.
THIS WAS SO EASY.
NOOO ...
Shiver Shake

Kamisama Kiss
Chapter 95

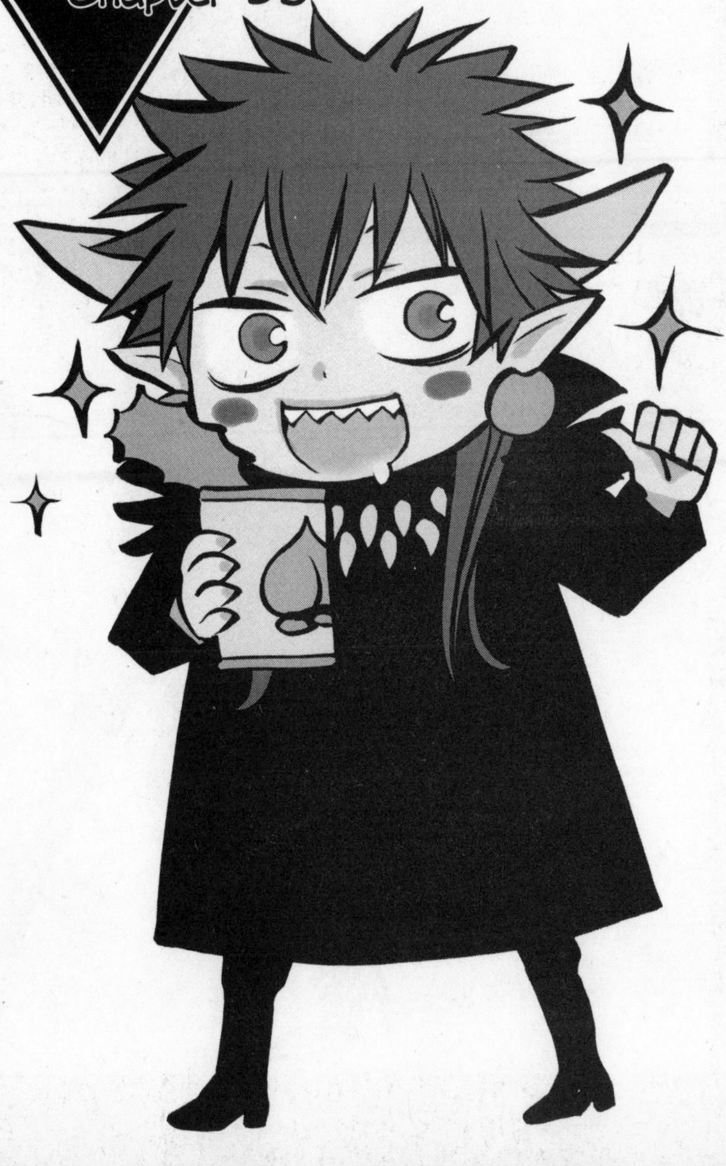

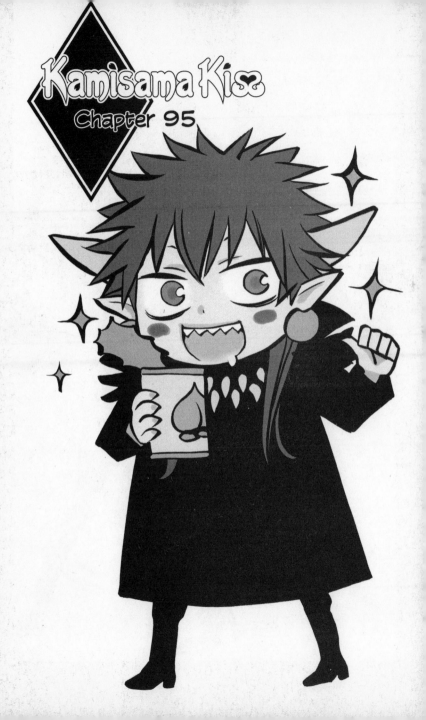

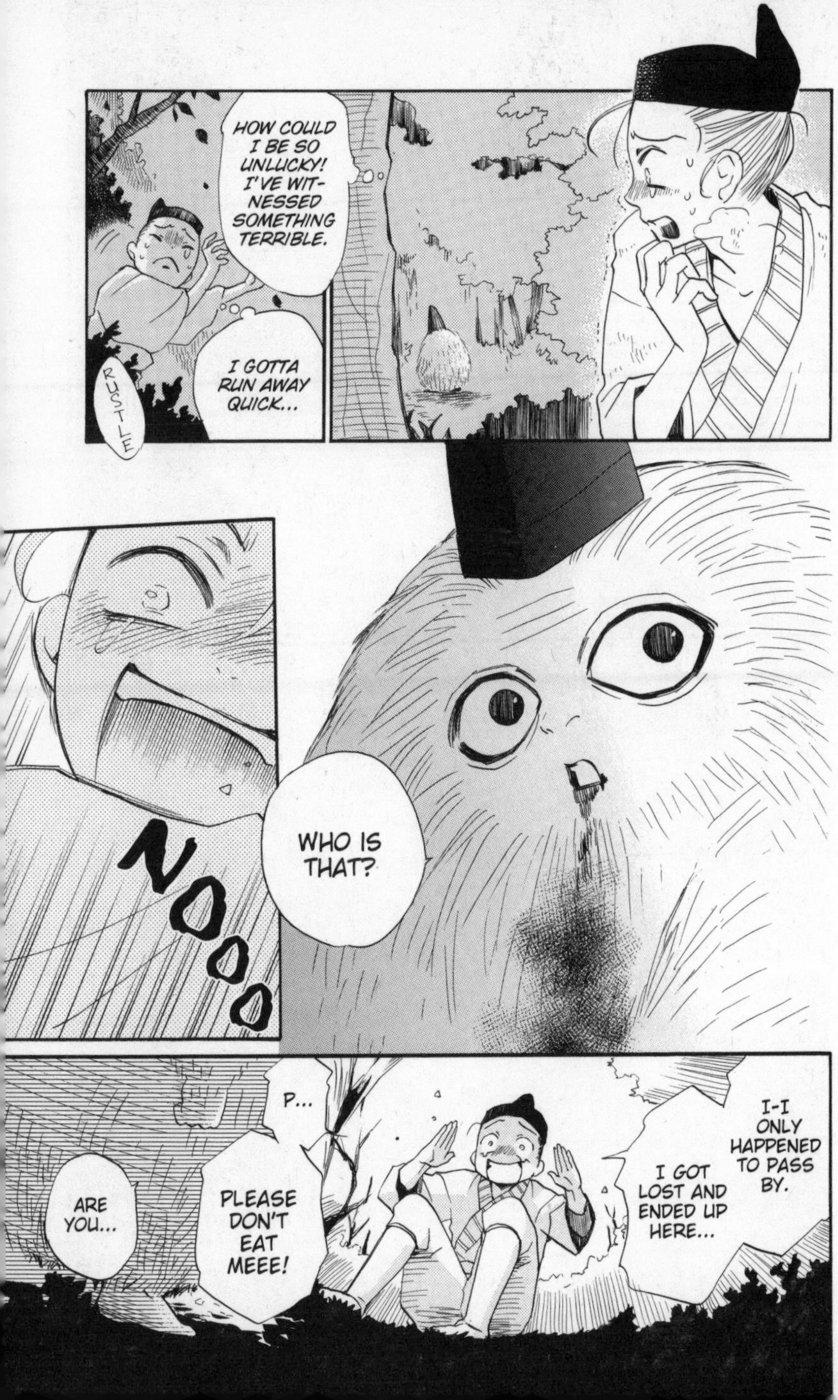
HOW COULD I BE SO UNLUCKY! I'VE WIT-NESSED SOMETHING TERRIBLE.
I GOTTA RUN AWAY QUICK...
RUSTLE
WHO IS THAT?
NOOO
I-I ONLY HAPPENED TO PASS BY.
I GOT LOST AND ENDED UP HERE...
P...
PLEASE DON'T EAT MEEE!
ARE YOU...

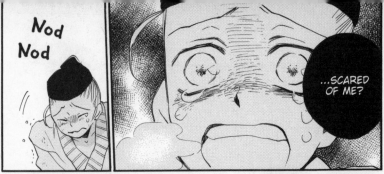

Nod
Nod

...SCARED OF ME?

GOOD.

THEN I'LL LET YOU GO.

HOWEVER, DON'T YOU SAY ANYTHING ABOUT WHAT YOU SAW TODAY.

IF YOU BABBLE EVEN ONE WORD ABOUT THIS, I'LL DEVOUR YOU HEAD FIRST.

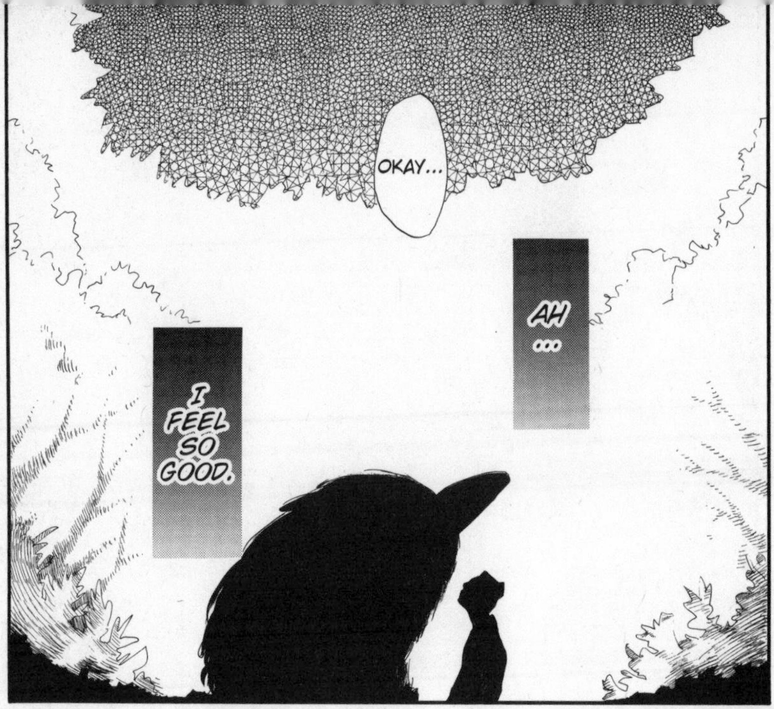
OKAY...
AH...
I FEEL SO GOOD.

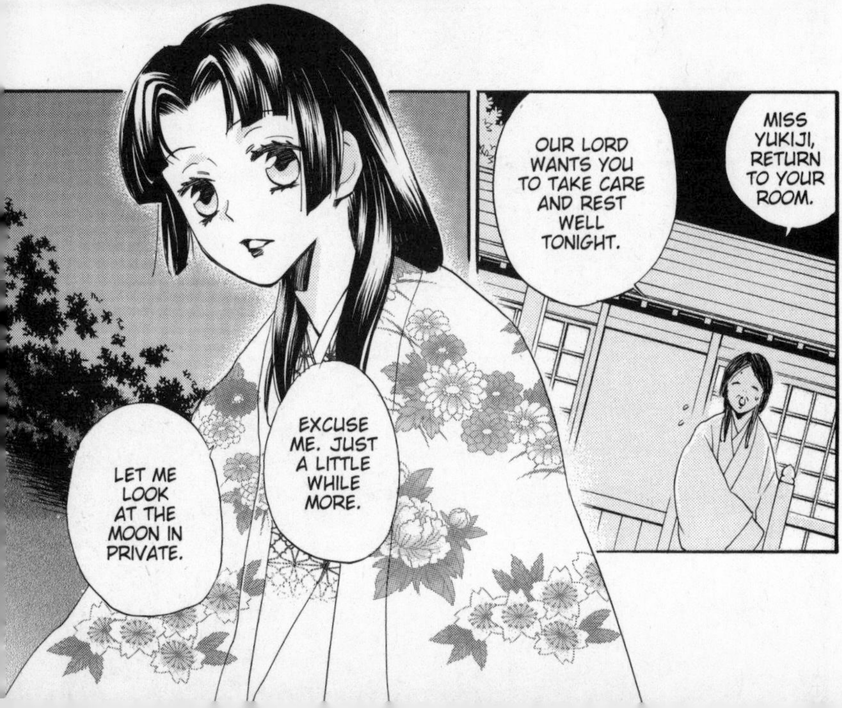
MISS YUKIJI, RETURN TO YOUR ROOM.
OUR LORD WANTS YOU TO TAKE CARE AND REST WELL TONIGHT.
EXCUSE ME. JUST A LITTLE WHILE MORE.
LET ME LOOK AT THE MOON IN PRIVATE.

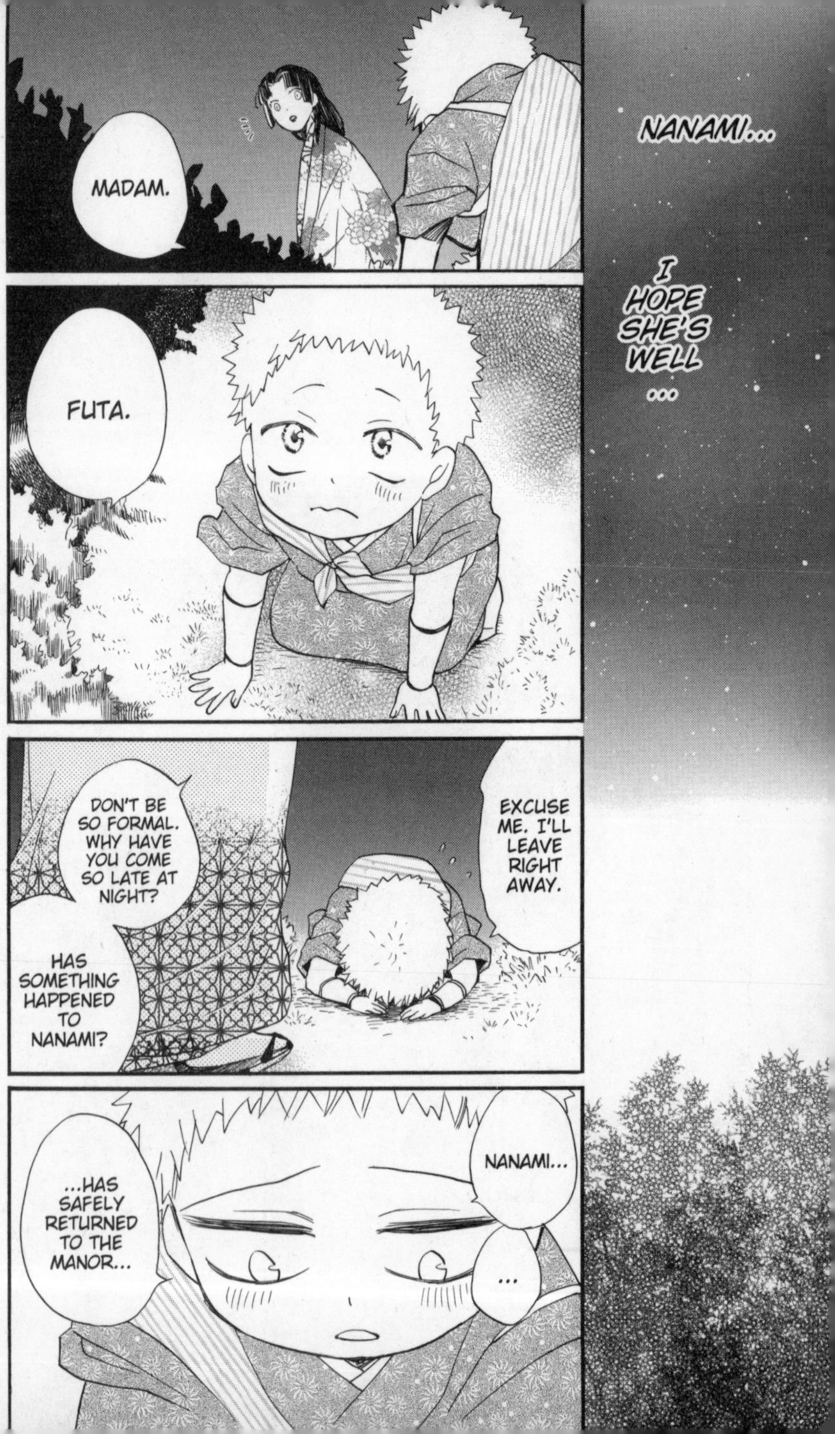
NANAMI...
I HOPE SHE'S WELL...
MADAM.
FUTA.
EXCUSE ME. I'LL LEAVE RIGHT AWAY.
DON'T BE SO FORMAL. WHY HAVE YOU COME SO LATE AT NIGHT?
HAS SOMETHING HAPPENED TO NANAMI?
NANAMI...
...HAS SAFELY RETURNED TO THE MANOR...
...

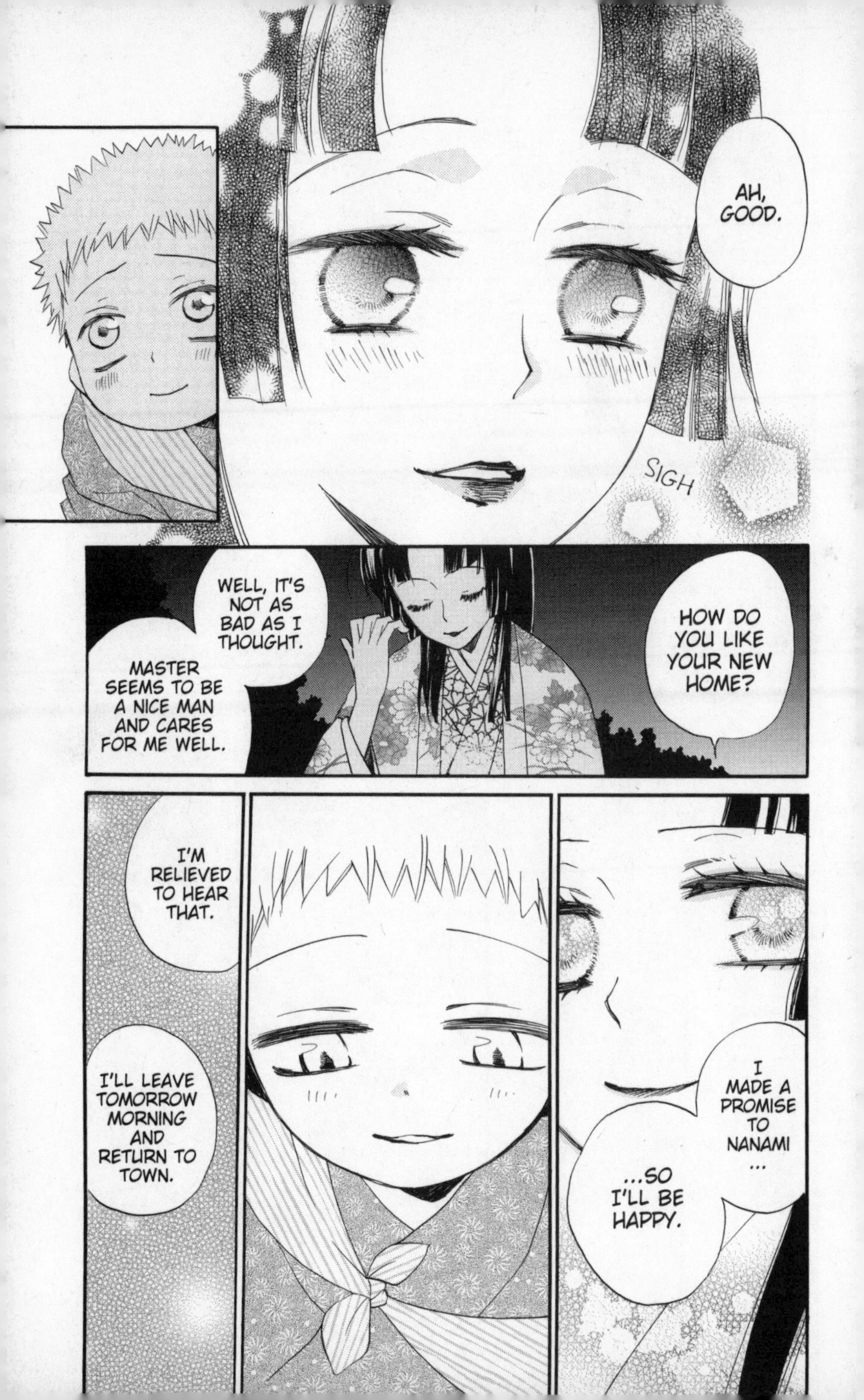
AH, GOOD.
SIGH
HOW DO YOU LIKE YOUR NEW HOME?
WELL, IT'S NOT AS BAD AS I THOUGHT.
MASTER SEEMS TO BE A NICE MAN AND CARES FOR ME WELL.
I MADE A PROMISE TO NANAMI...
...SO I'LL BE HAPPY.
I'M RELIEVED TO HEAR THAT.
I'LL LEAVE TOMORROW MORNING AND RETURN TO TOWN.

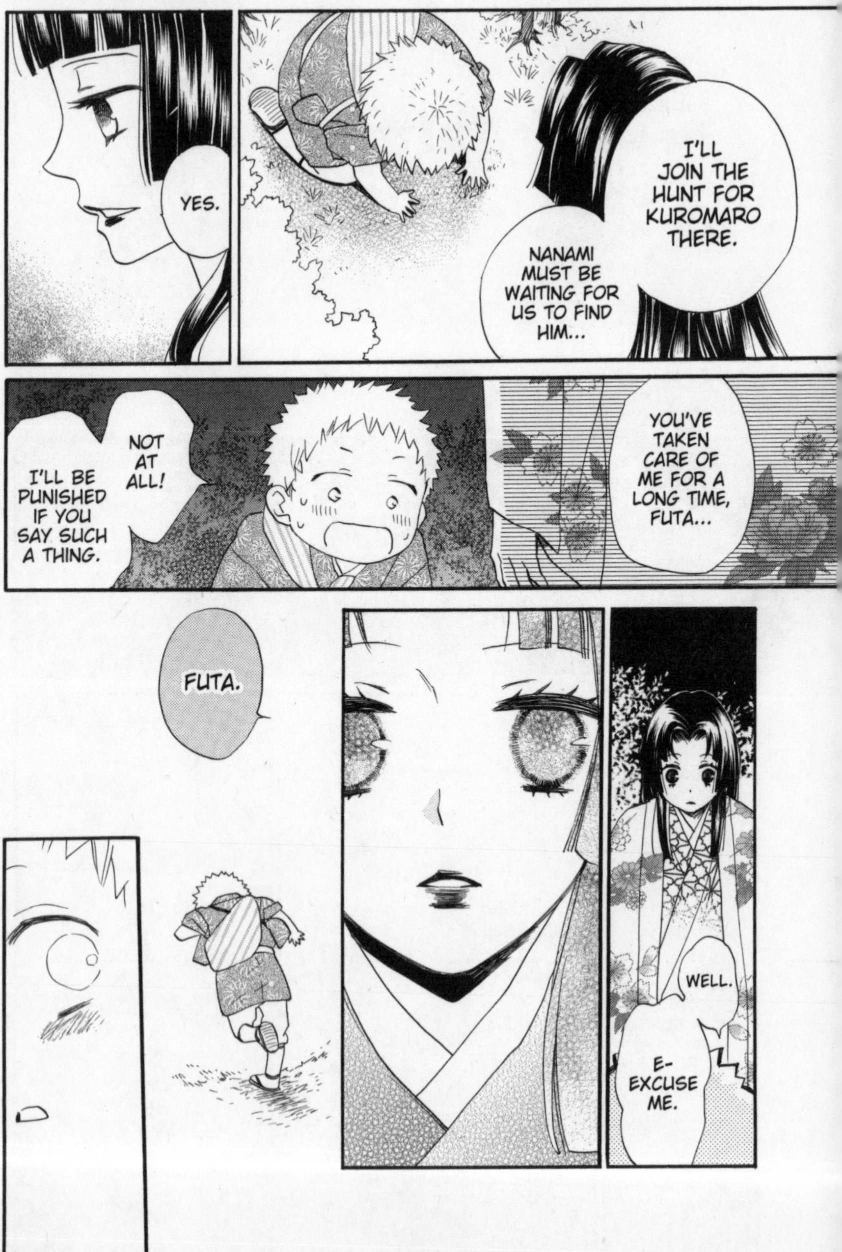
I'LL JOIN THE HUNT FOR KUROMARO THERE.
NANAMI MUST BE WAITING FOR US TO FIND HIM...
YES.
YOU'VE TAKEN CARE OF ME FOR A LONG TIME, FUTA...
NOT AT ALL!
I'LL BE PUNISHED IF YOU SAY SUCH A THING.
WELL.
E-EXCUSE ME.
FUTA.

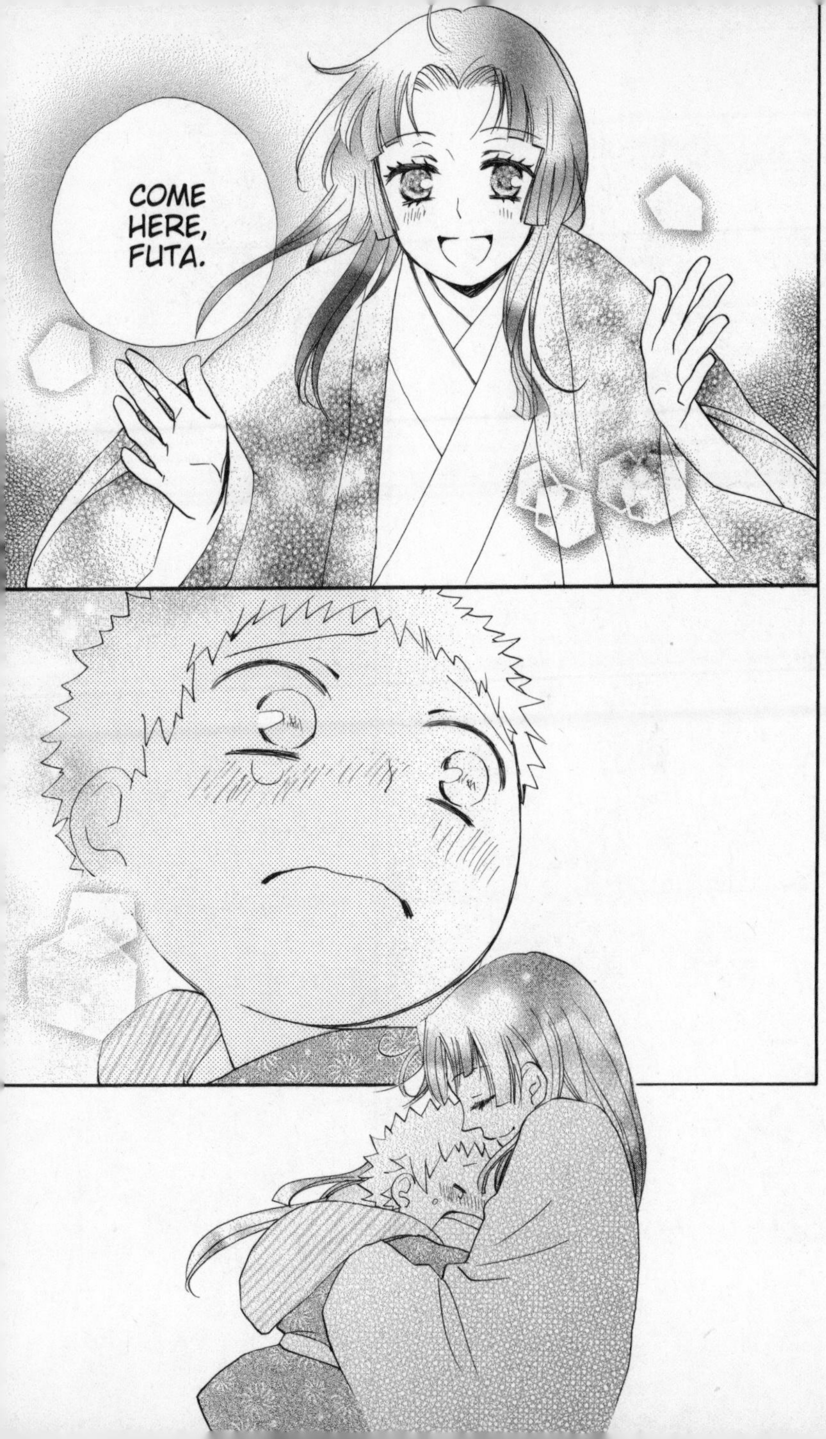
COME HERE, FUTA.

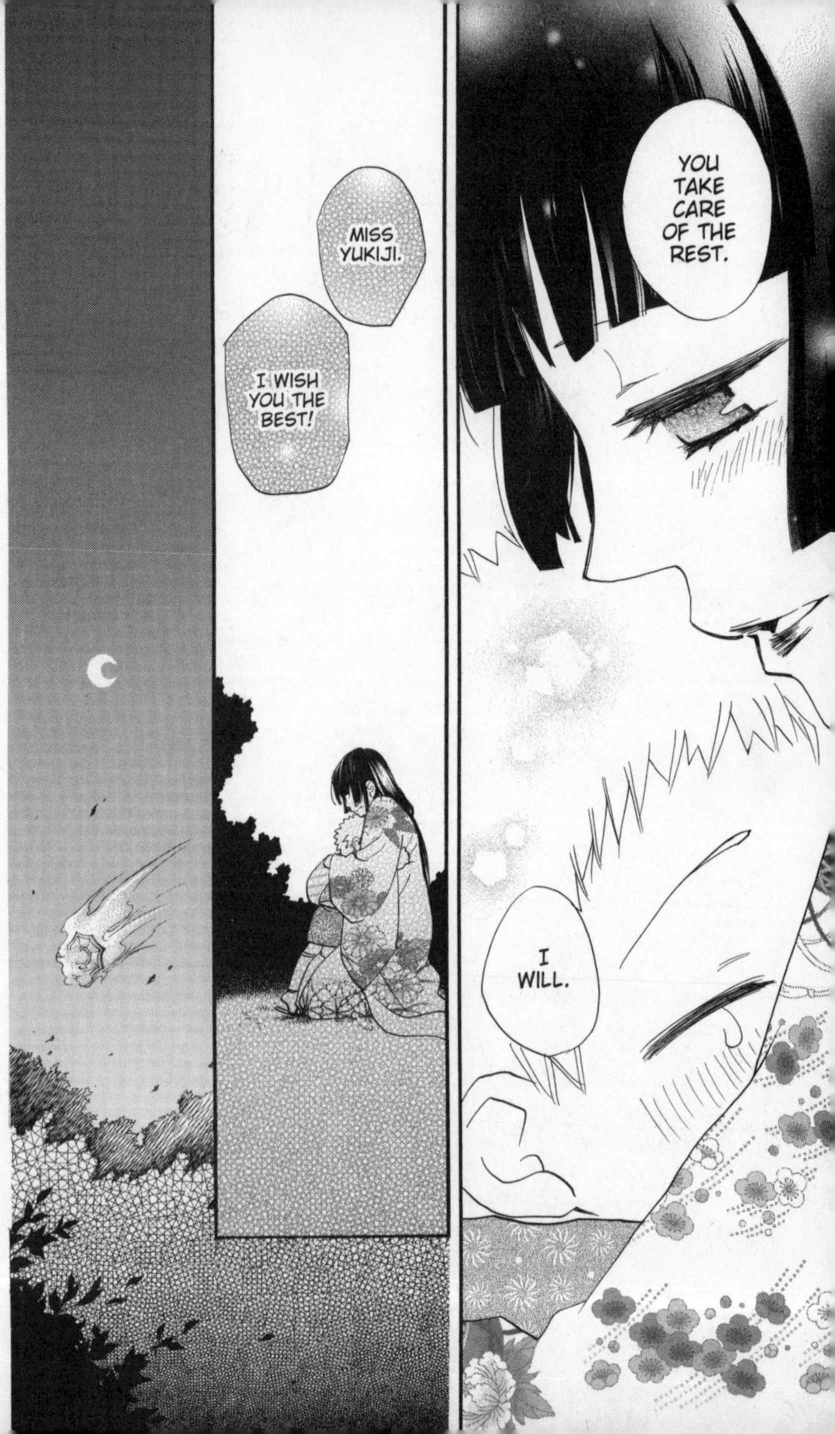
YOU TAKE CARE OF THE REST.
I WILL.
MISS YUKIJI.
I WISH YOU THE BEST!

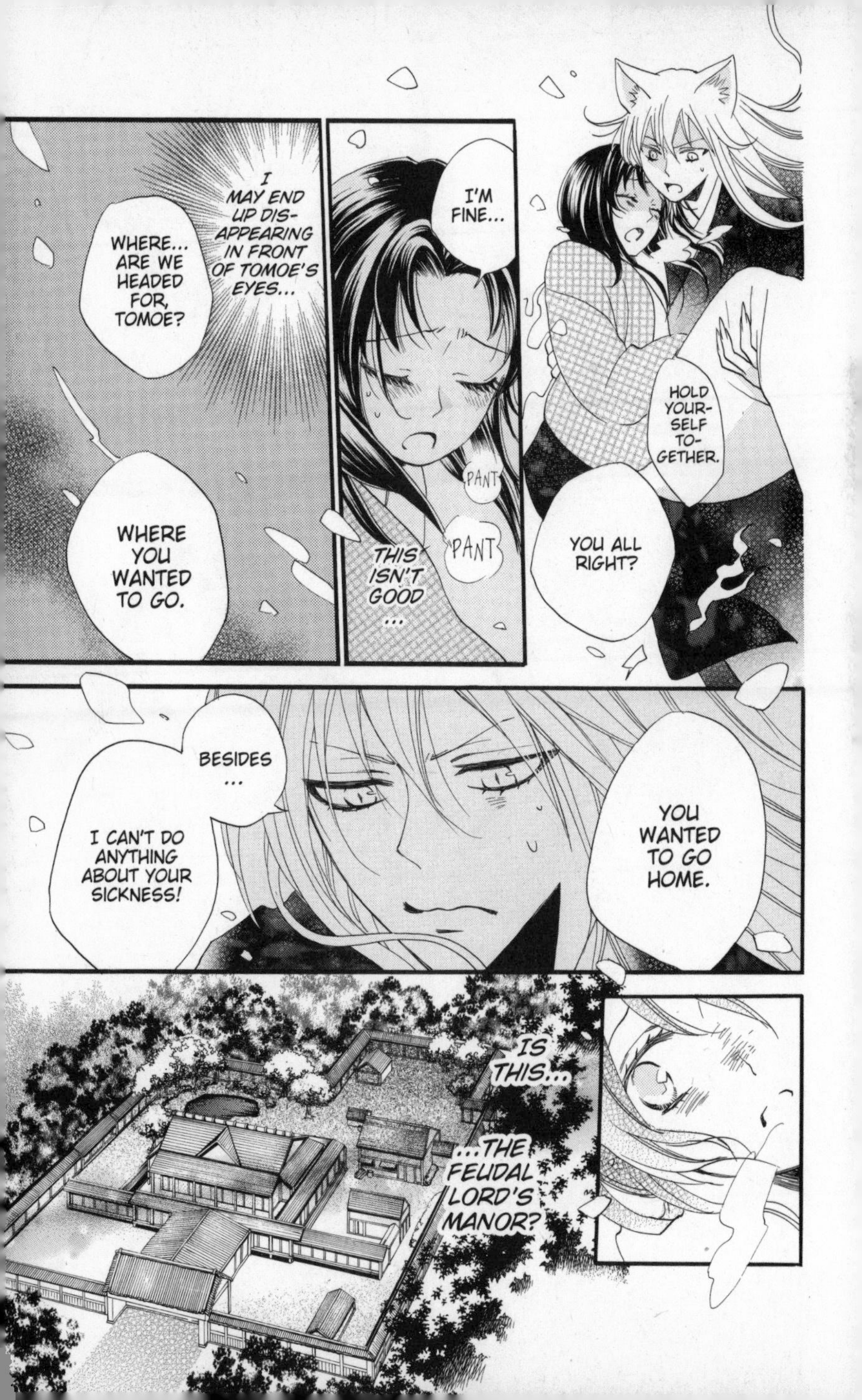

HOLD YOURSELF TOGETHER.
YOU ALL RIGHT?
I'M FINE...
PANT
PANT
THIS ISN'T GOOD...
I MAY END UP DISAPPEARING IN FRONT OF TOMOE'S EYES...
WHERE... ARE WE HEADED FOR, TOMOE?
WHERE YOU WANTED TO GO.
YOU WANTED TO GO HOME.
BESIDES...
I CAN'T DO ANYTHING ABOUT YOUR SICKNESS!
IS THIS...
...THE FEUDAL LORD'S MANOR?

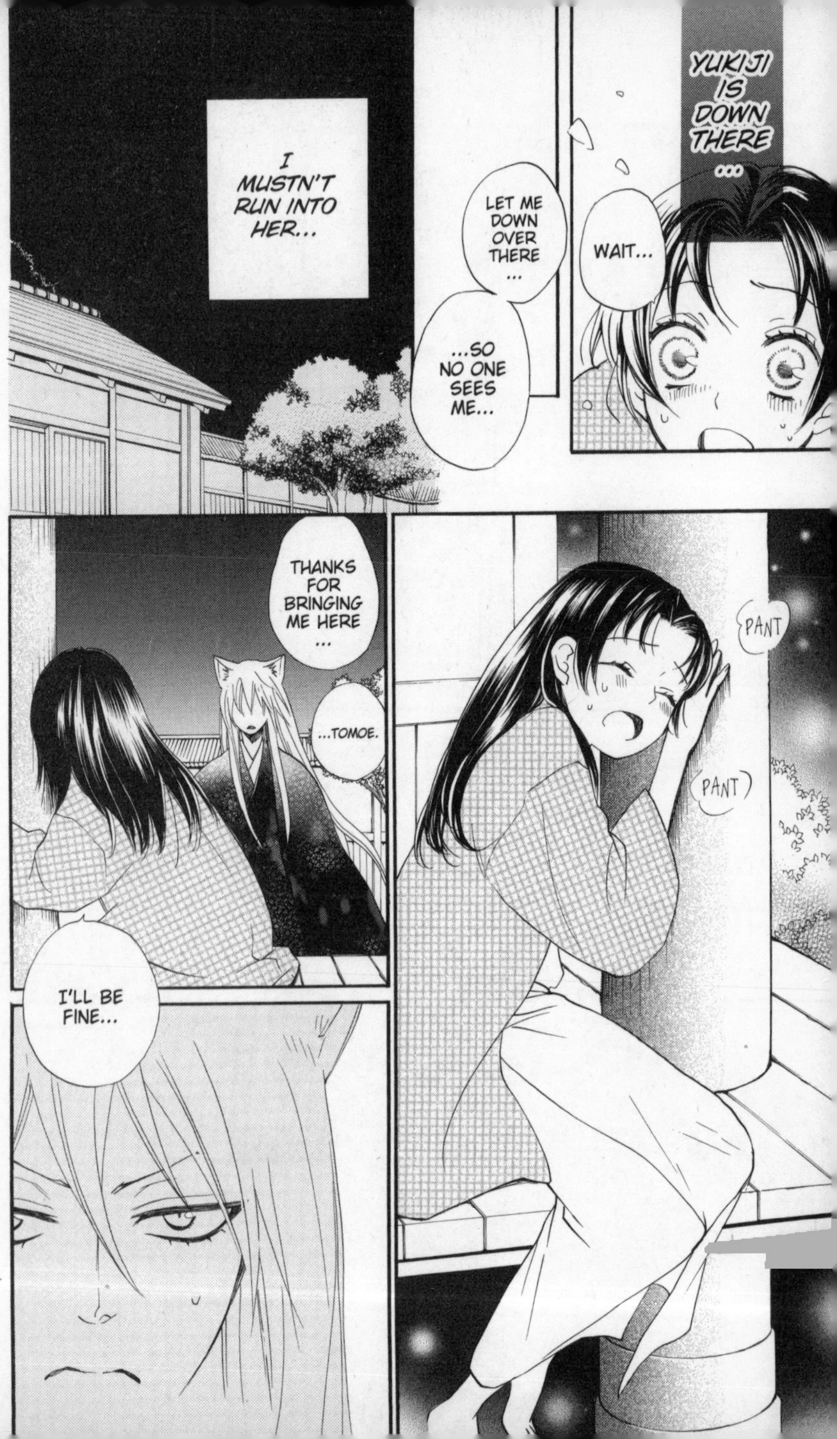
YUKIJI IS DOWN THERE...
WAIT...
LET ME DOWN OVER THERE...
...SO NO ONE SEES ME...
I MUSTN'T RUN INTO HER...
PANT
PANT
THANKS FOR BRINGING ME HERE...
...TOMOE.
I'LL BE FINE...

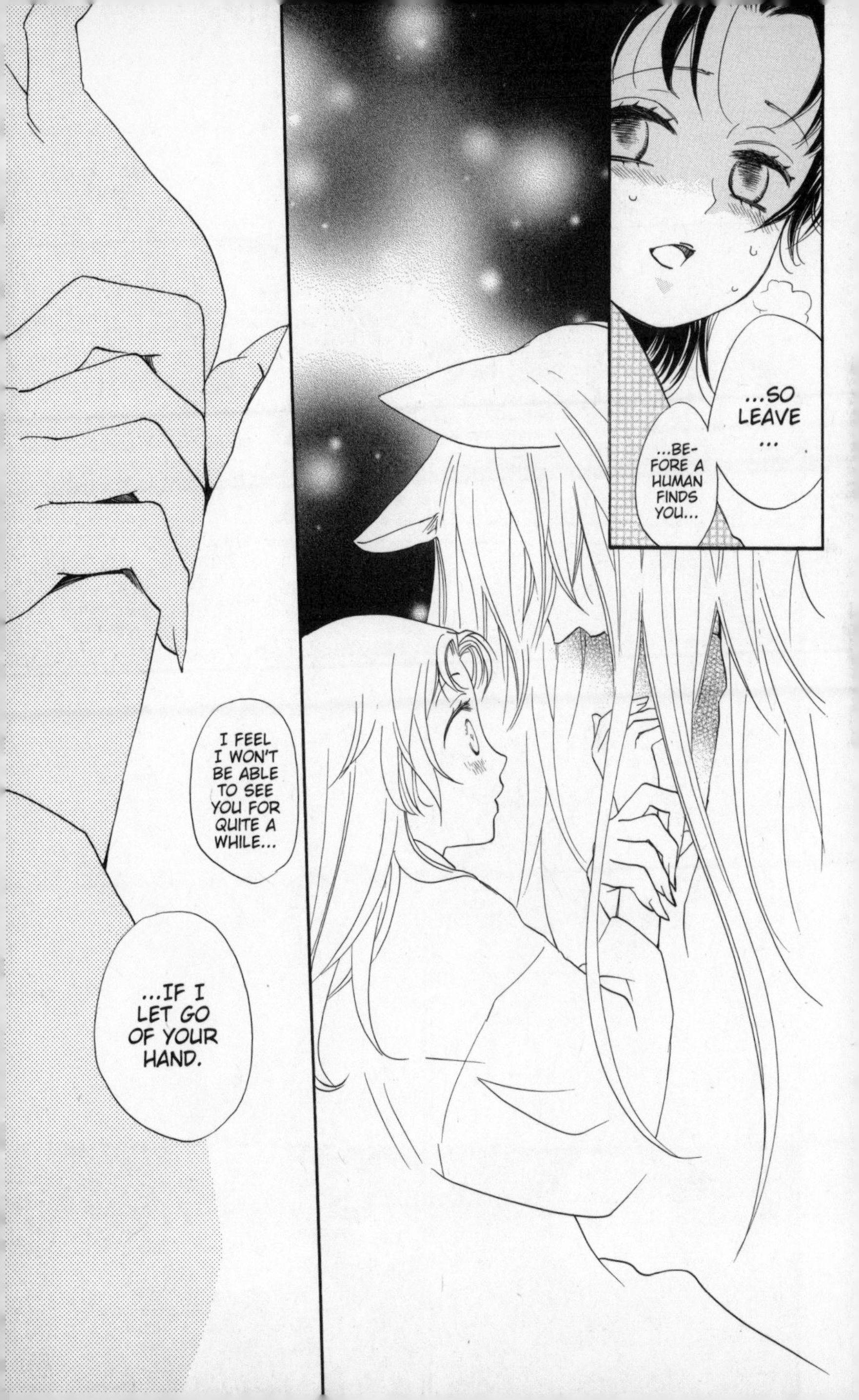
...SO LEAVE ...
...BE-FORE A HUMAN FINDS YOU...
I FEEL I WON'T BE ABLE TO SEE YOU FOR QUITE A WHILE...
...IF I LET GO OF YOUR HAND.

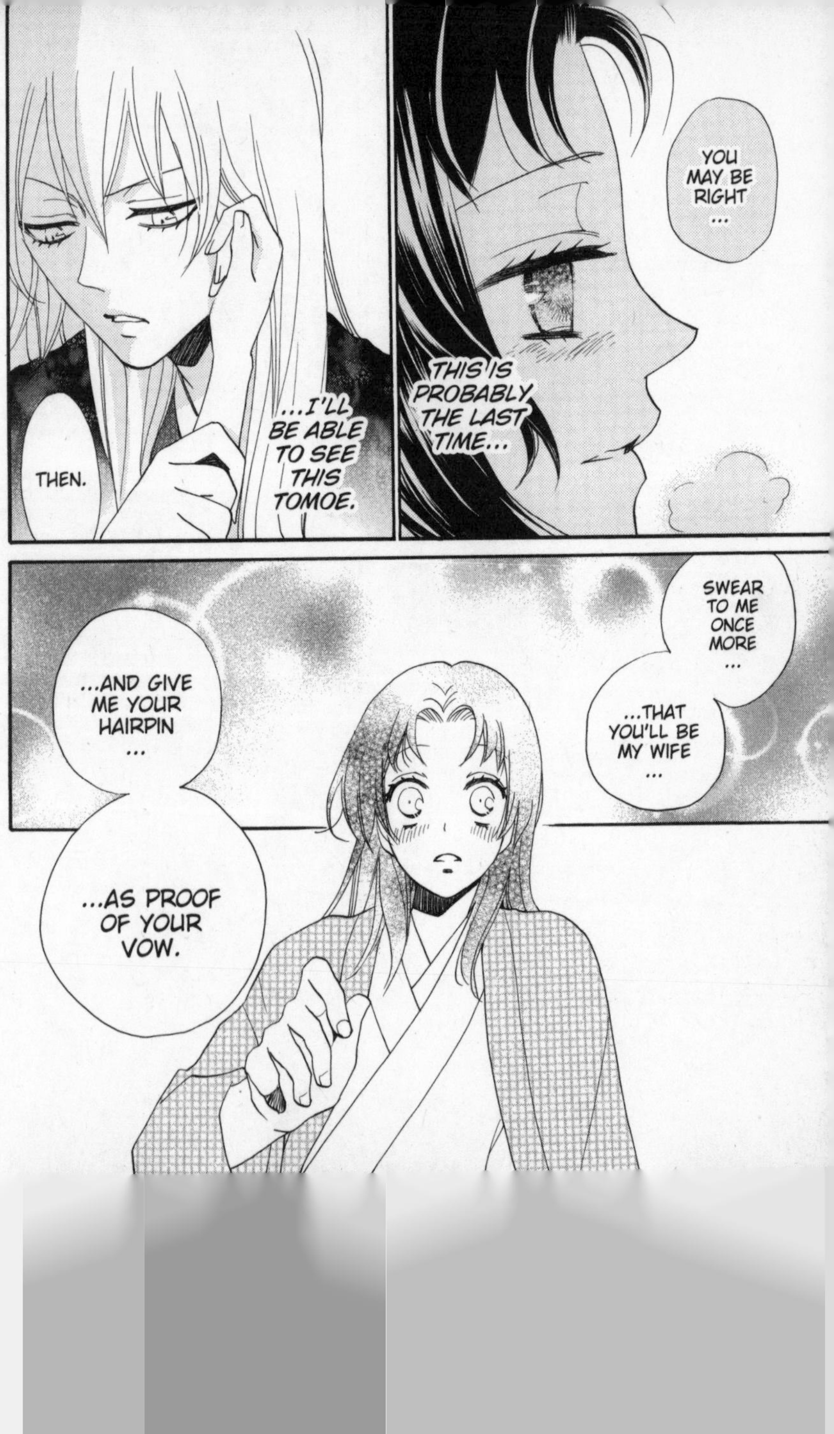
YOU MAY BE RIGHT ...
THIS IS PROBABLY THE LAST TIME...
...I'LL BE ABLE TO SEE THIS TOMOE.
THEN.
SWEAR TO ME ONCE MORE ...
...THAT YOU'LL BE MY WIFE ...
...AND GIVE ME YOUR HAIRPIN ...
...AS PROOF OF YOUR VOW.

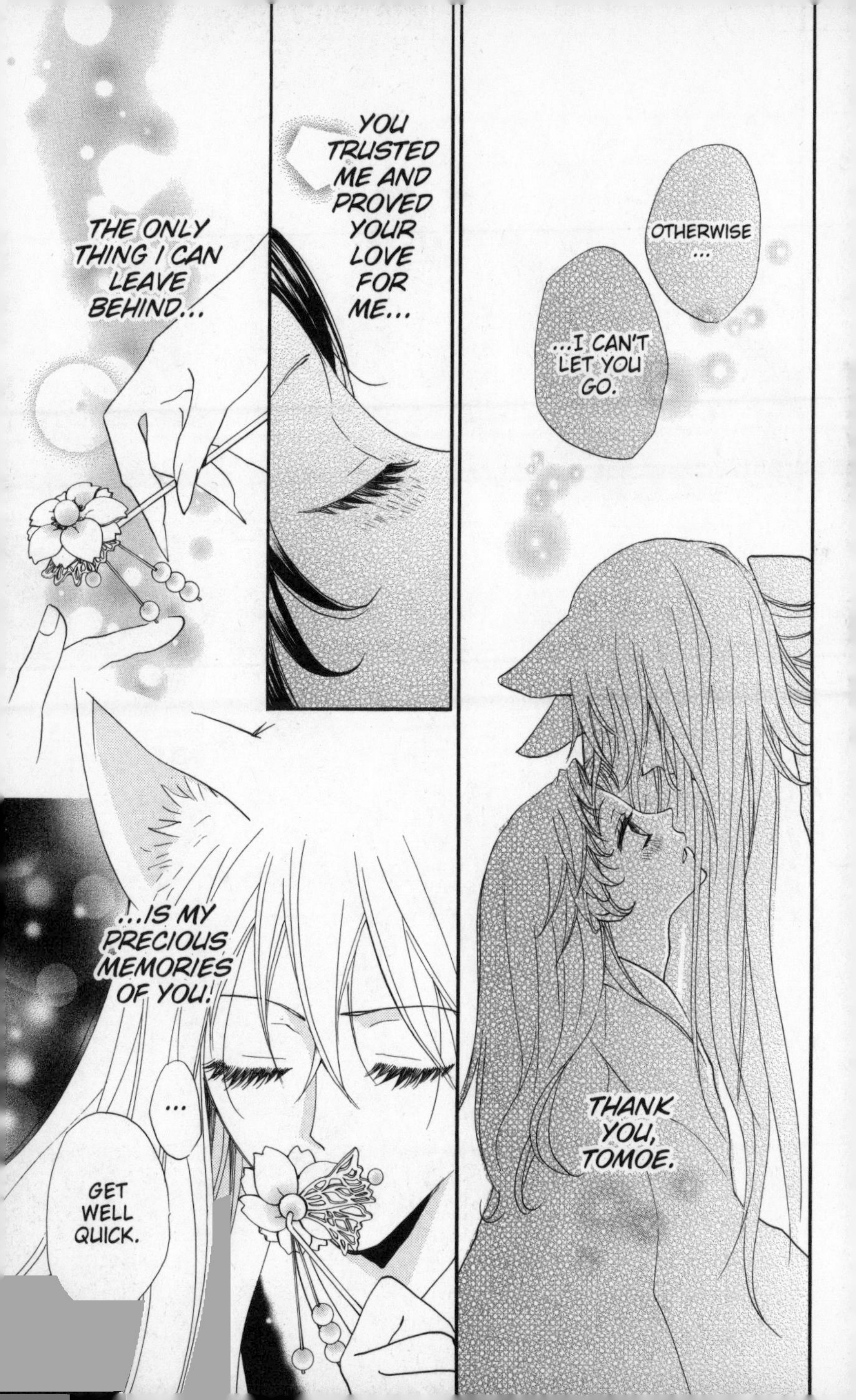
OTHERWISE...
...I CAN'T LET YOU GO.
THANK YOU, TOMOE.
YOU TRUSTED ME AND PROVED YOUR LOVE FOR ME...
THE ONLY THING I CAN LEAVE BEHIND...
...IS MY PRECIOUS MEMORIES OF YOU!
...
GET WELL QUICK.

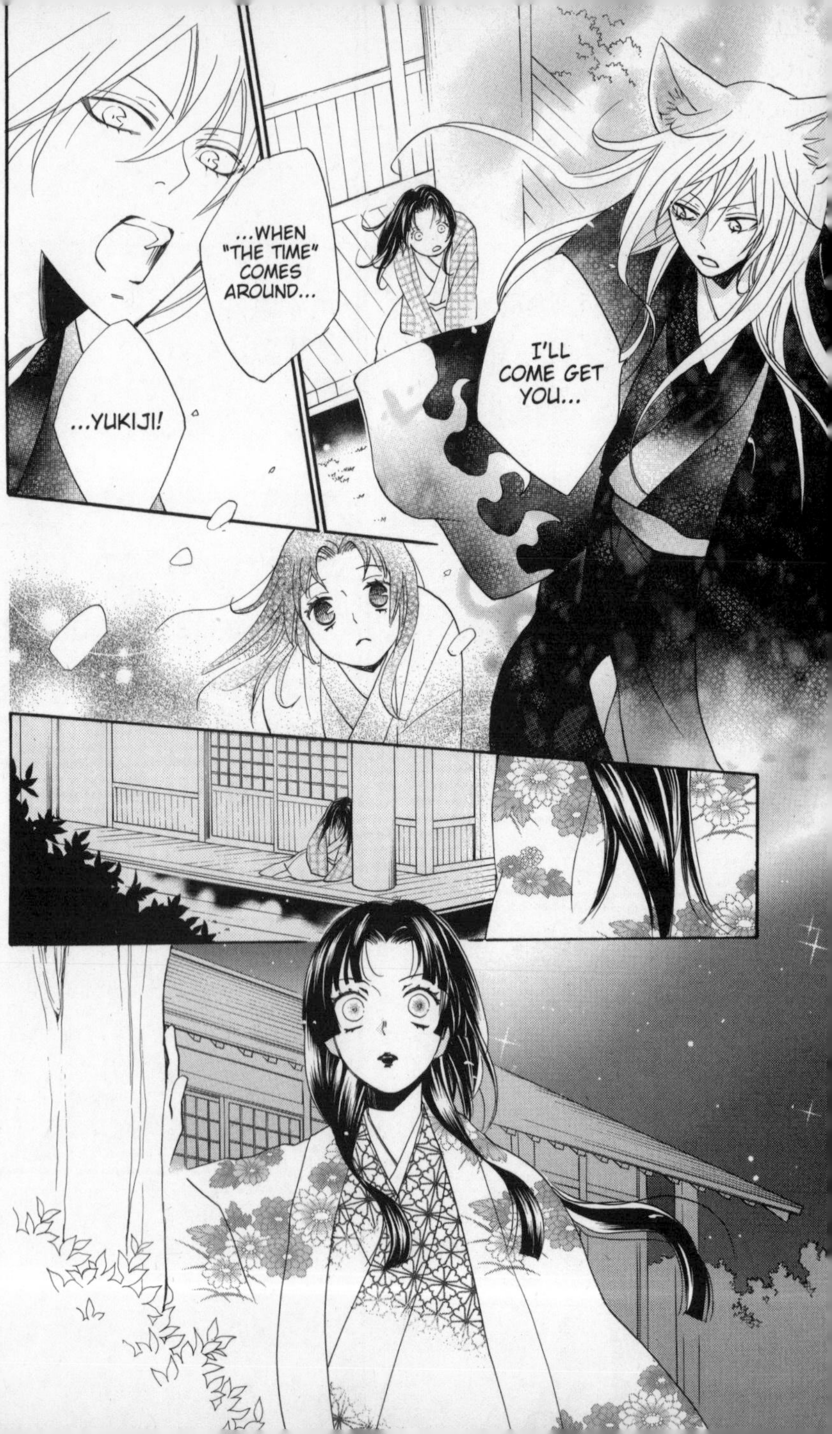
I'LL COME GET YOU...
...WHEN "THE TIME" COMES AROUND...
...YUKIJI!

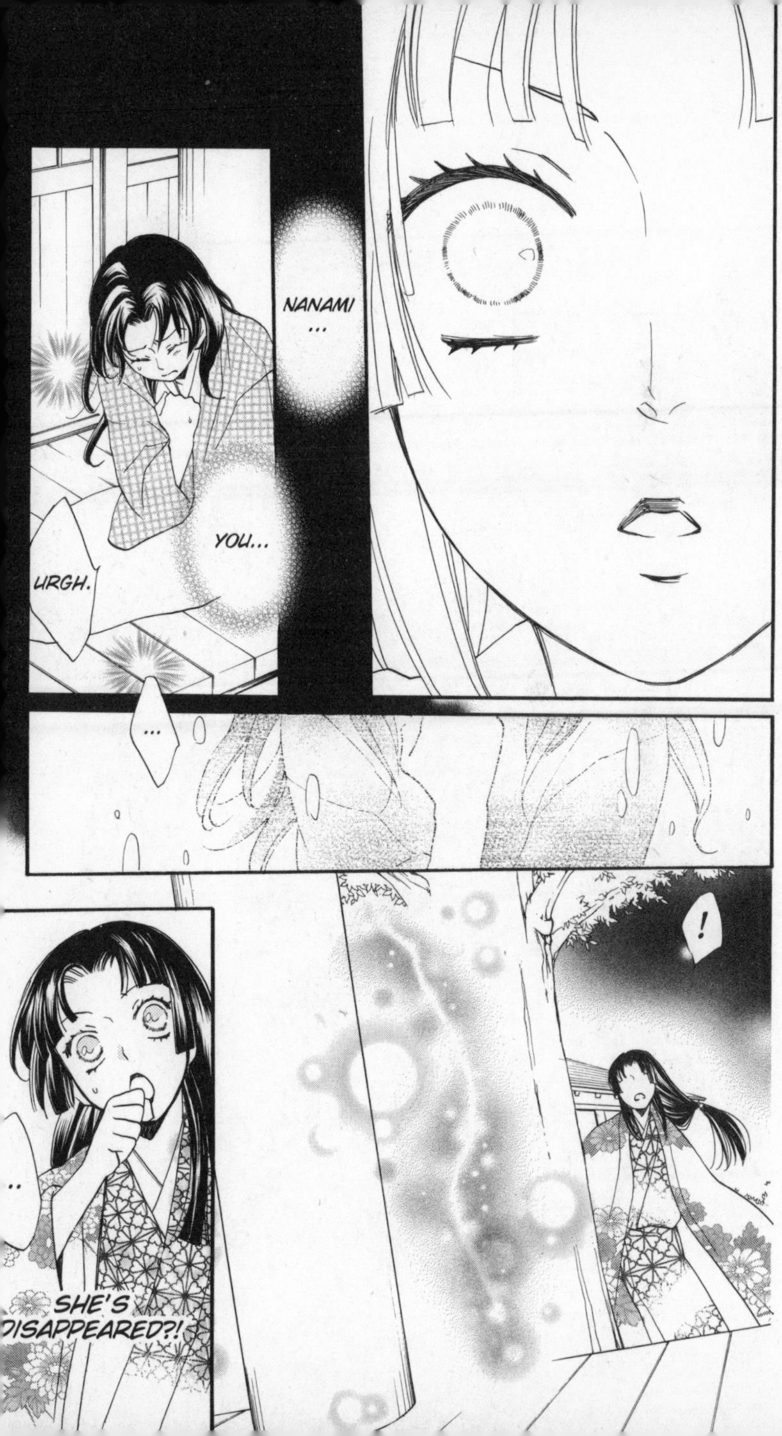
NANAMI ...
YOU...
URGH.
...
!
...
SHE'S DISAPPEARED?!

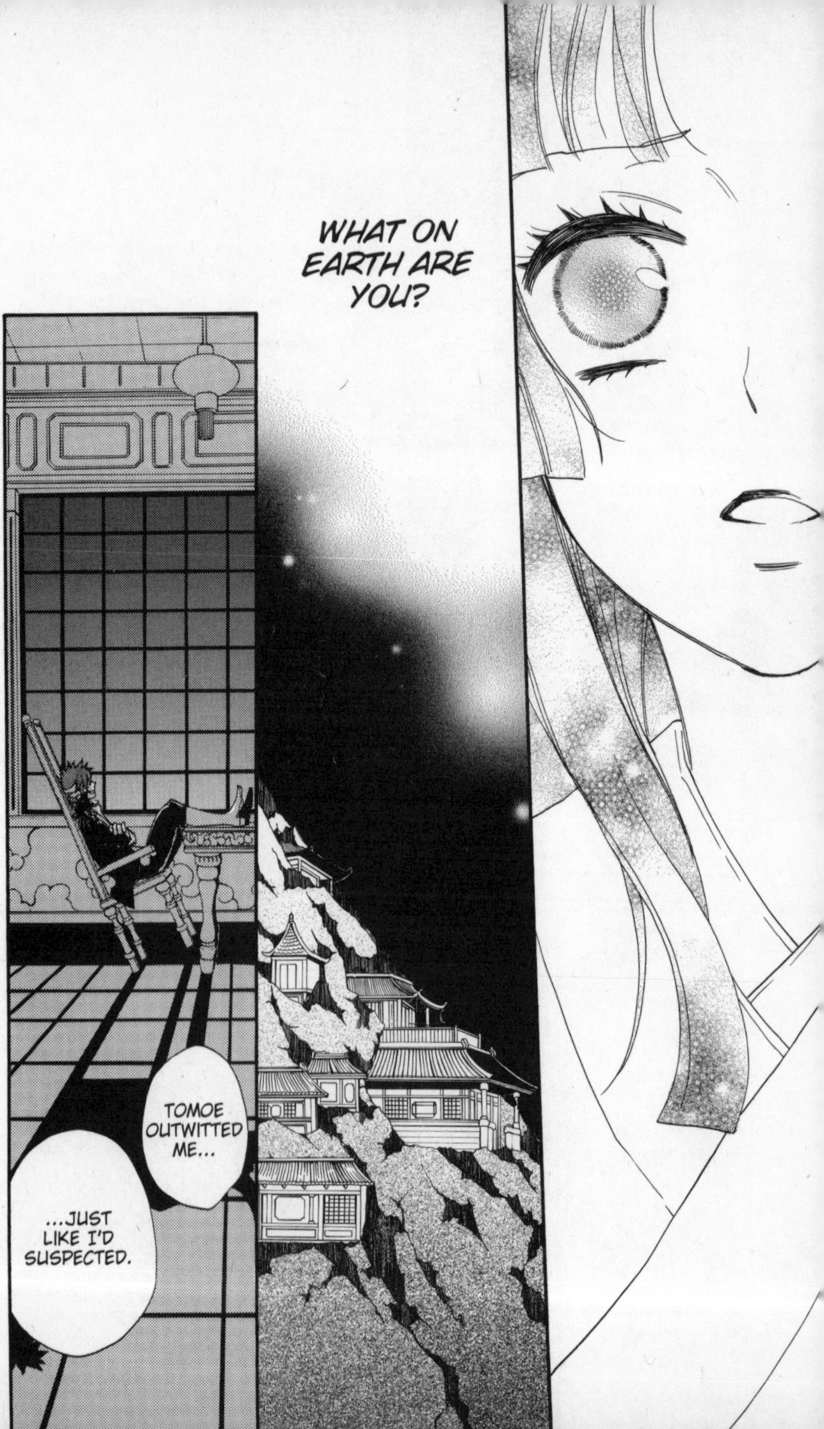
WHAT ON EARTH ARE YOU?
TOMOE OUTWITTED ME...
...JUST LIKE I'D SUSPECTED.

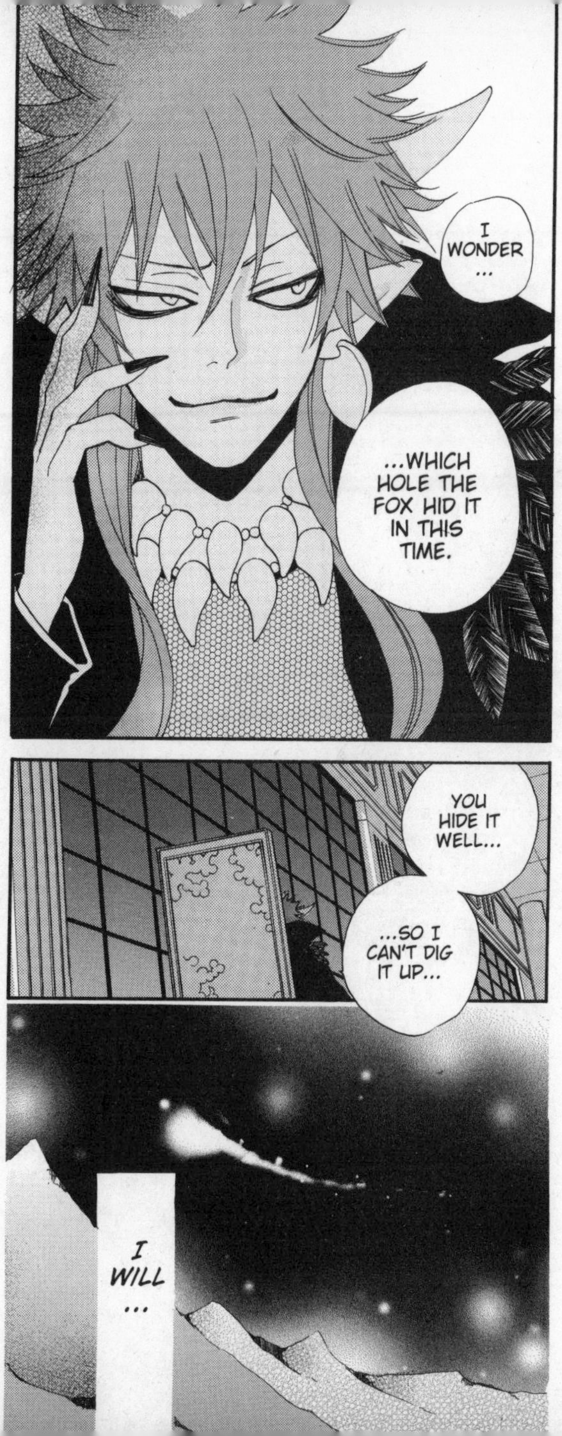
I WONDER ...
...WHICH HOLE THE FOX HID IT IN THIS TIME.
YOU HIDE IT WELL...
...SO I CAN'T DIG IT UP...
I WILL ...

I had Yukichi Nakamura draw a sidebar!!

The lucidity of her drawing!

Thank you Yukichi-san!!

Love Love♥

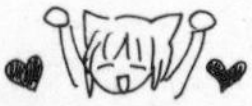

Thank you for reading this far!

If you have any comments and thoughts about volume 16, do let me hear you.

The address is...!

Julietta Suzuki
c/o Shojo Beat
VIZ Media, LLC
P.O. Box 77010
San Francisco
CA 94107

I hope we'll be able to meet again in the next volume...!

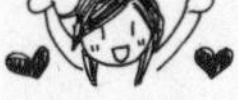

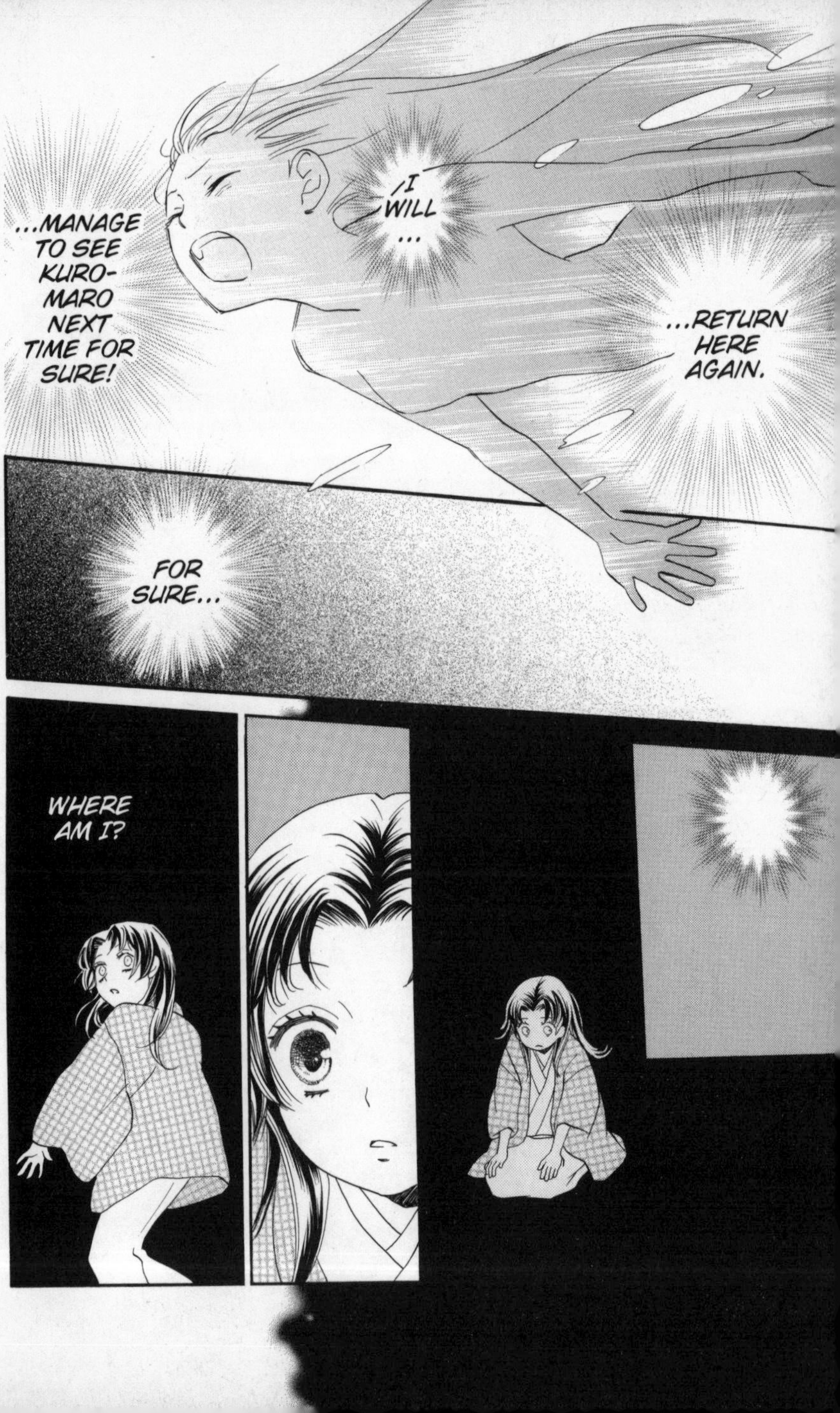
I WILL ...
...RETURN HERE AGAIN.
...MANAGE TO SEE KURO-MARO NEXT TIME FOR SURE!
FOR SURE...
WHERE AM I?

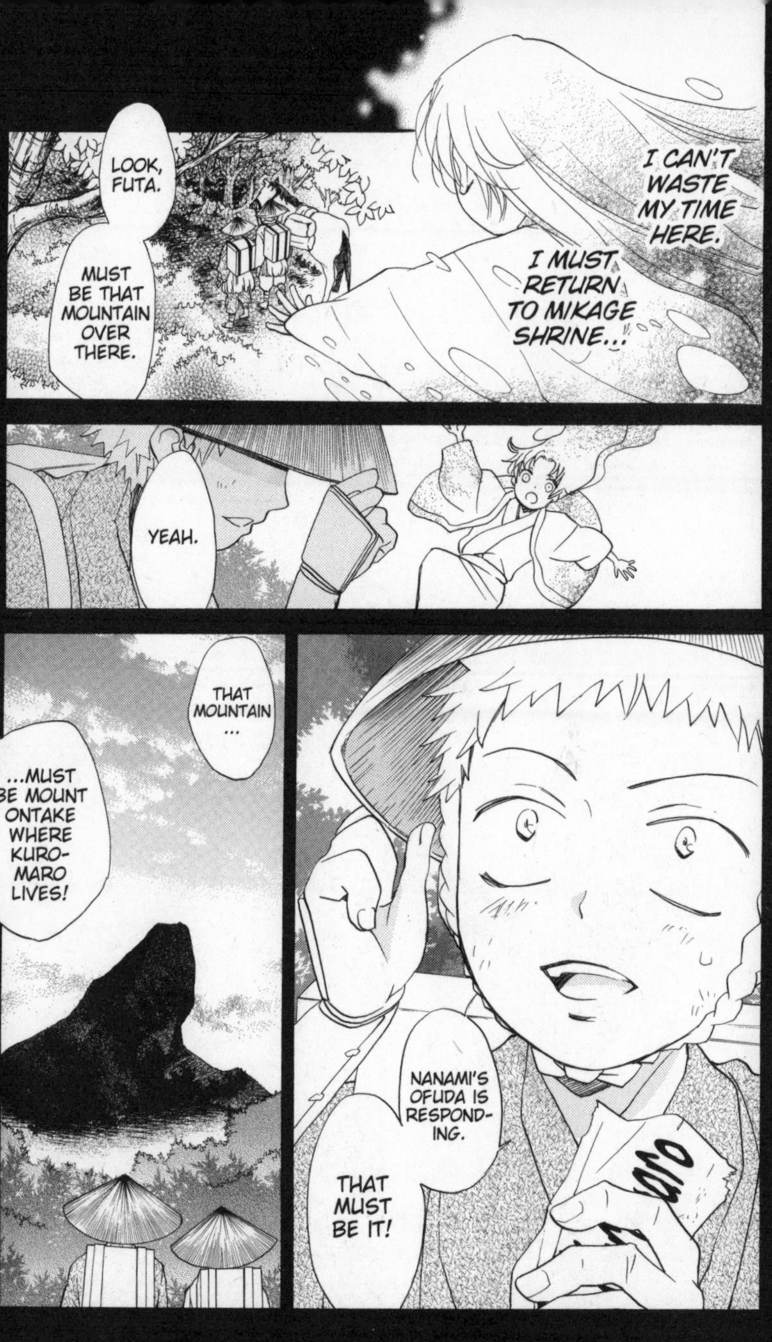
I CAN'T WASTE MY TIME HERE.
I MUST RETURN TO MIKAGE SHRINE...
LOOK, FUTA.
MUST BE THAT MOUNTAIN OVER THERE.
YEAH.
NANAMI'S OFUDA IS RESPOND-ING.
THAT MUST BE IT!
THAT MOUNTAIN ...
...MUST BE MOUNT ONTAKE WHERE KURO-MARO LIVES!

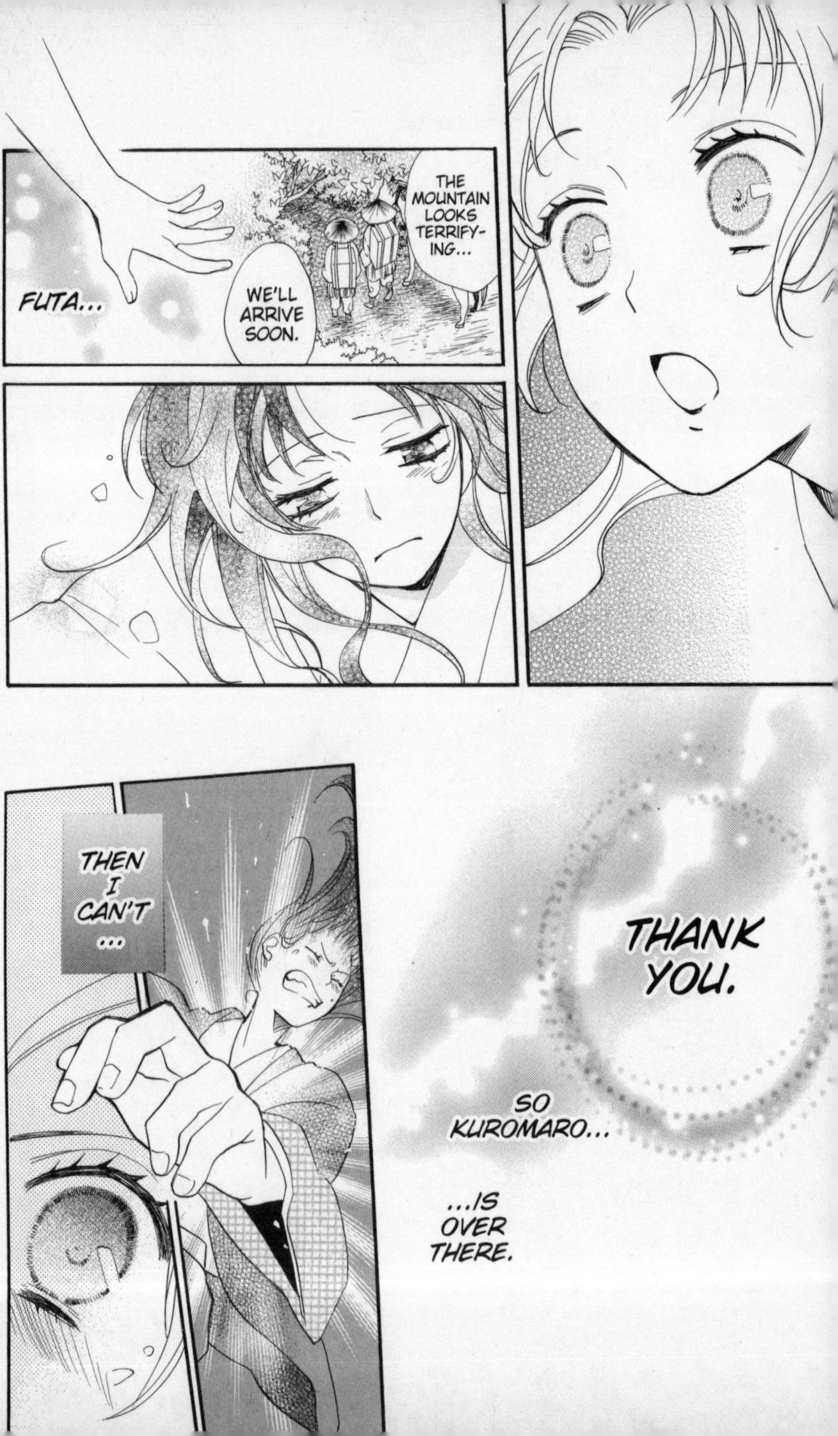
THE MOUNTAIN LOOKS TERRIFYING...
WE'LL ARRIVE SOON.
FUTA...
THANK YOU.
SO KUROMARO...
...IS OVER THERE.
THEN I CAN'T...

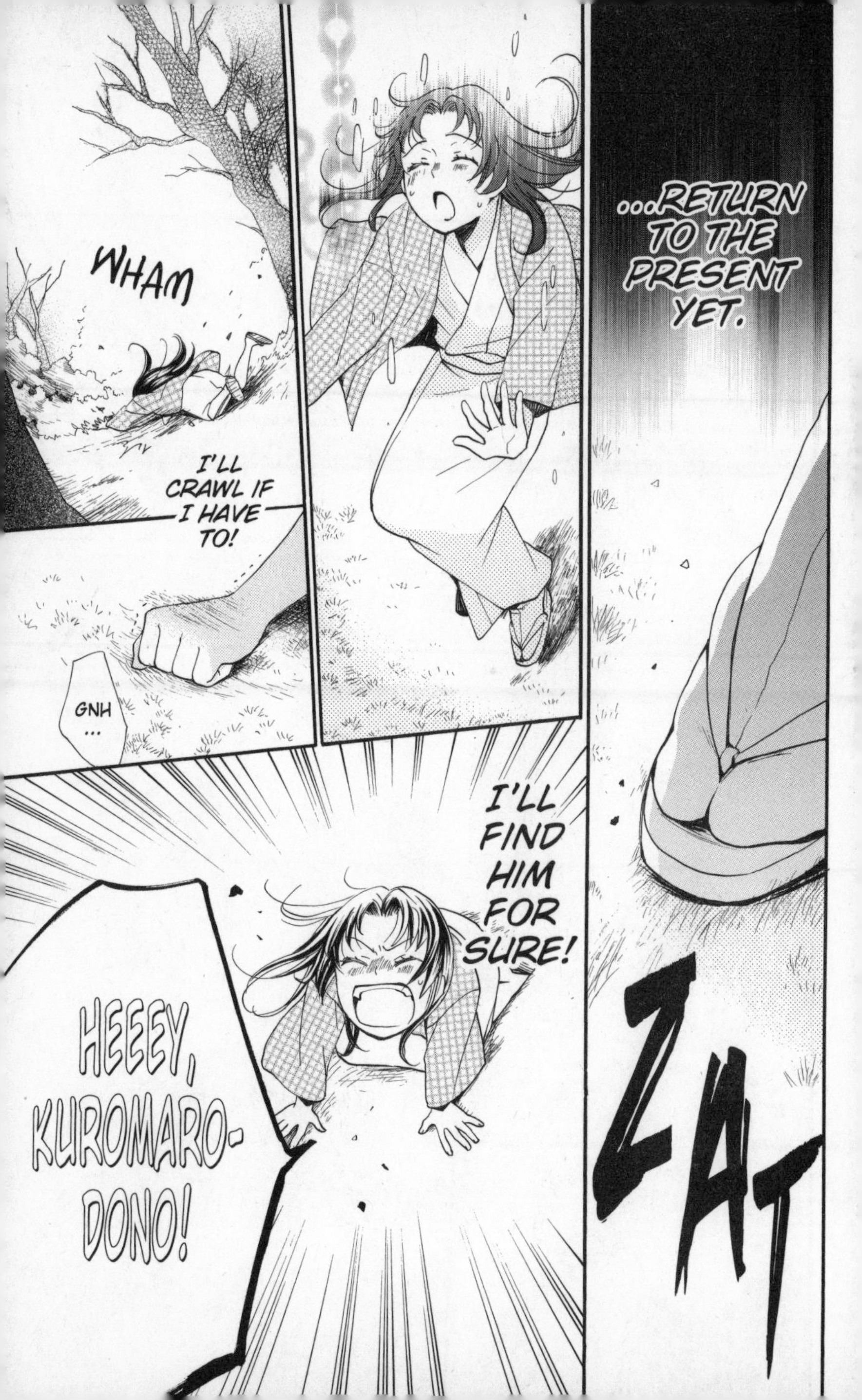
...RETURN TO THE PRESENT YET.
ZAT
WHAM
I'LL CRAWL IF I HAVE TO!
GNH...
I'LL FIND HIM FOR SURE!
HEEEY, KUROMARO-DONO!

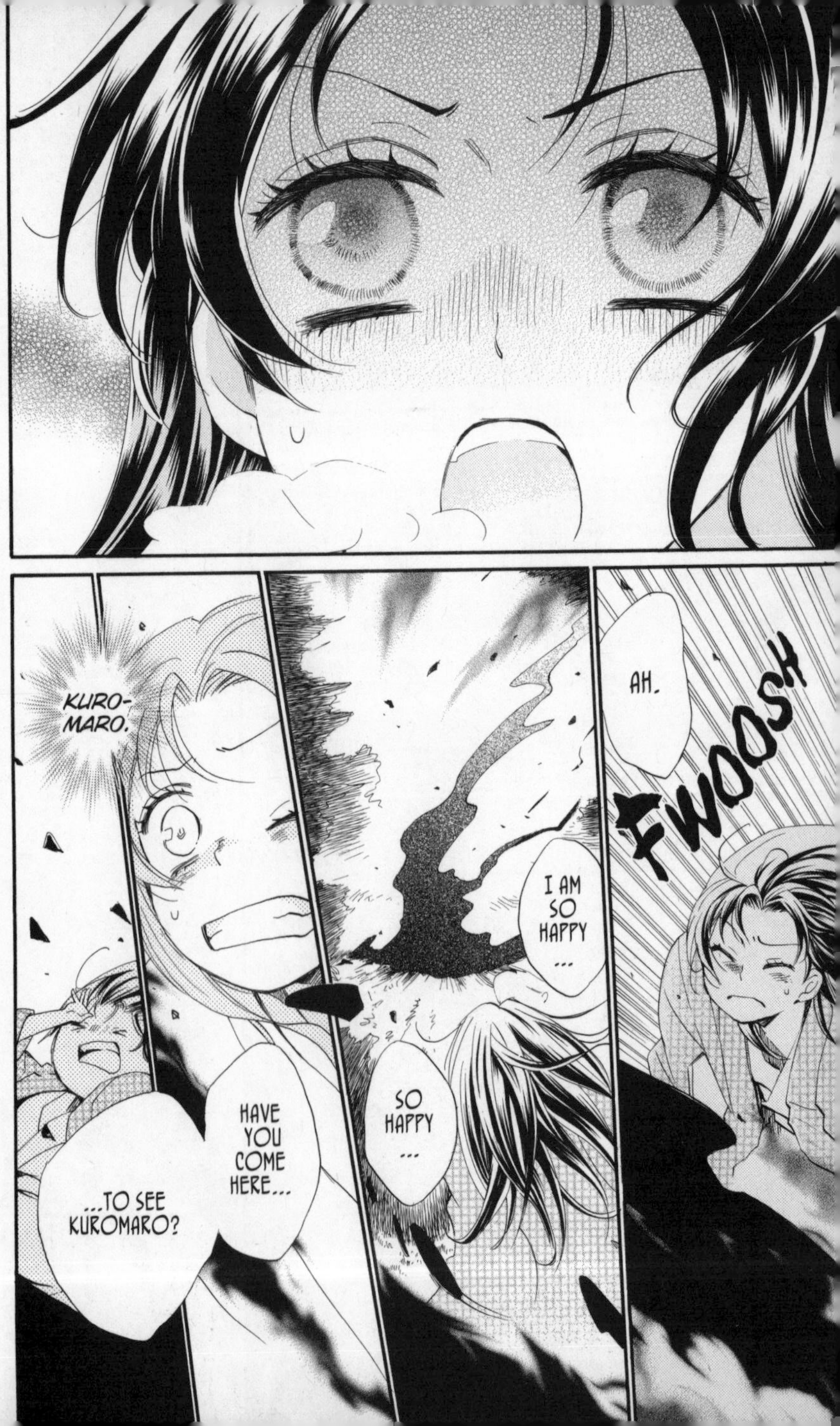
AH.
FWOOSH
I AM SO HAPPY ...
SO HAPPY ...
KURO-MARO.
HAVE YOU COME HERE...
...TO SEE KUROMARO?

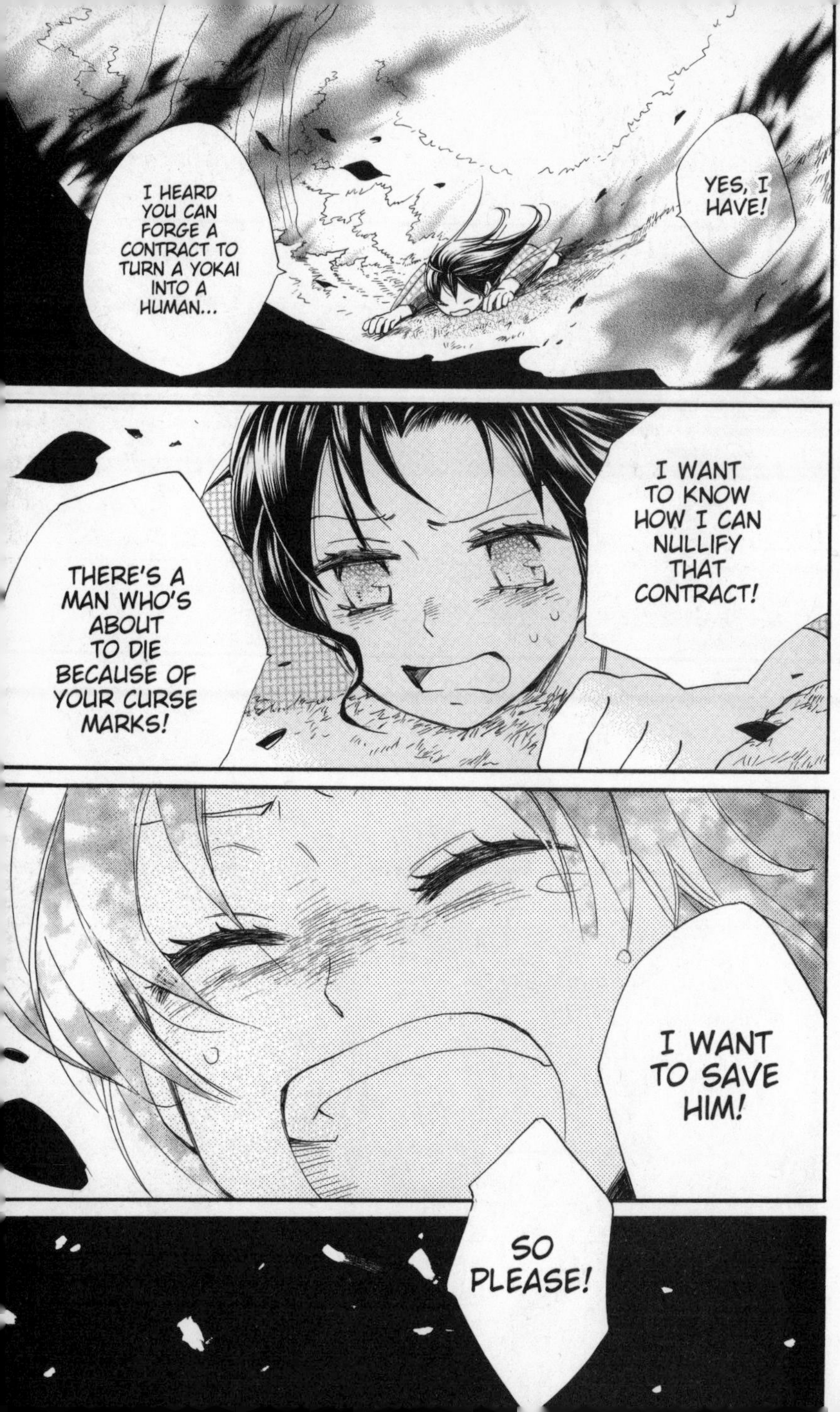
YES, I HAVE!
I HEARD YOU CAN FORGE A CONTRACT TO TURN A YOKAI INTO A HUMAN...
I WANT TO KNOW HOW I CAN NULLIFY THAT CONTRACT!
THERE'S A MAN WHO'S ABOUT TO DIE BECAUSE OF YOUR CURSE MARKS!
I WANT TO SAVE HIM!
SO PLEASE!

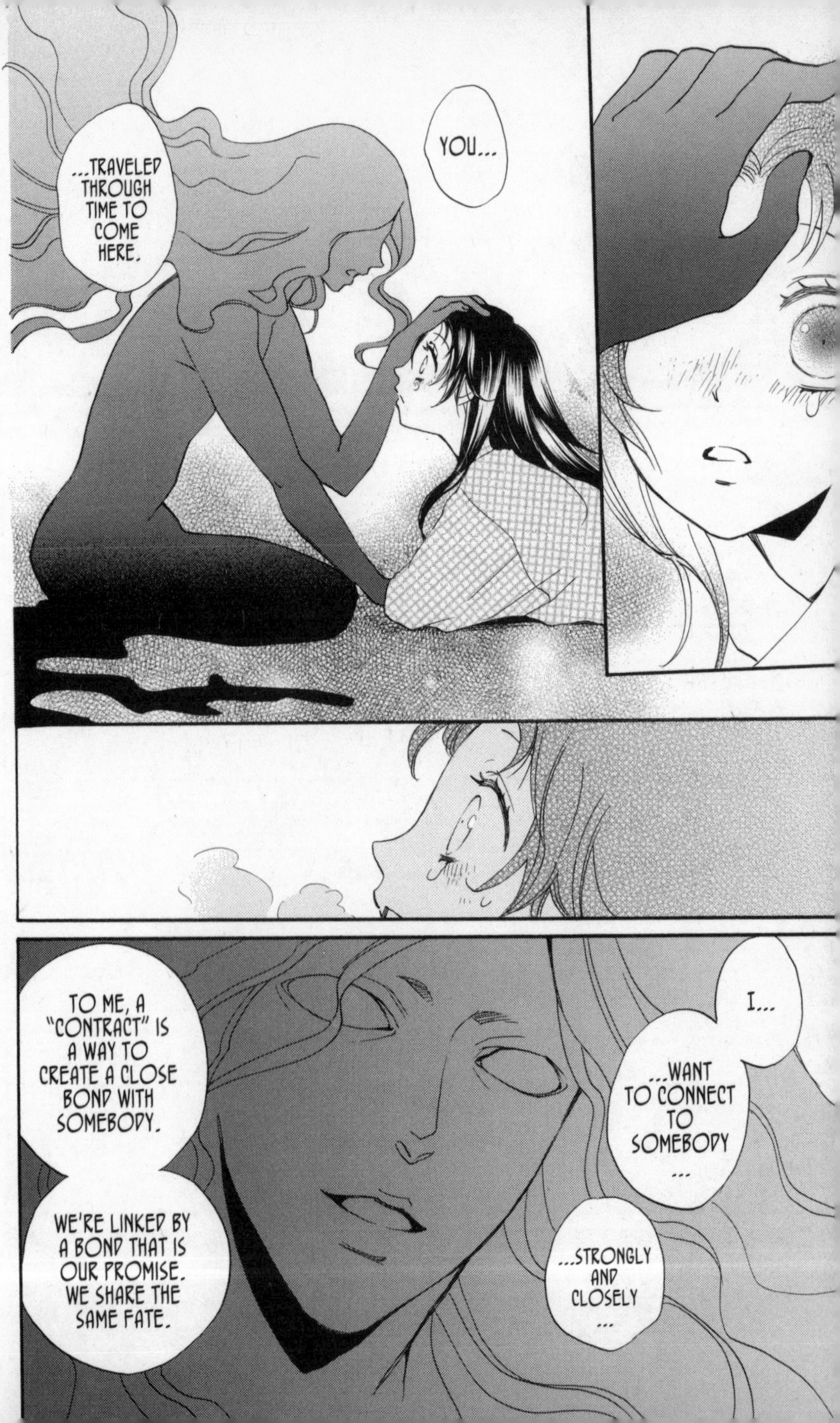
YOU...
...TRAVELED THROUGH TIME TO COME HERE.
I...
...WANT TO CONNECT TO SOMEBODY ...
...STRONGLY AND CLOSELY ...
TO ME, A "CONTRACT" IS A WAY TO CREATE A CLOSE BOND WITH SOMEBODY.
WE'RE LINKED BY A BOND THAT IS OUR PROMISE. WE SHARE THE SAME FATE.

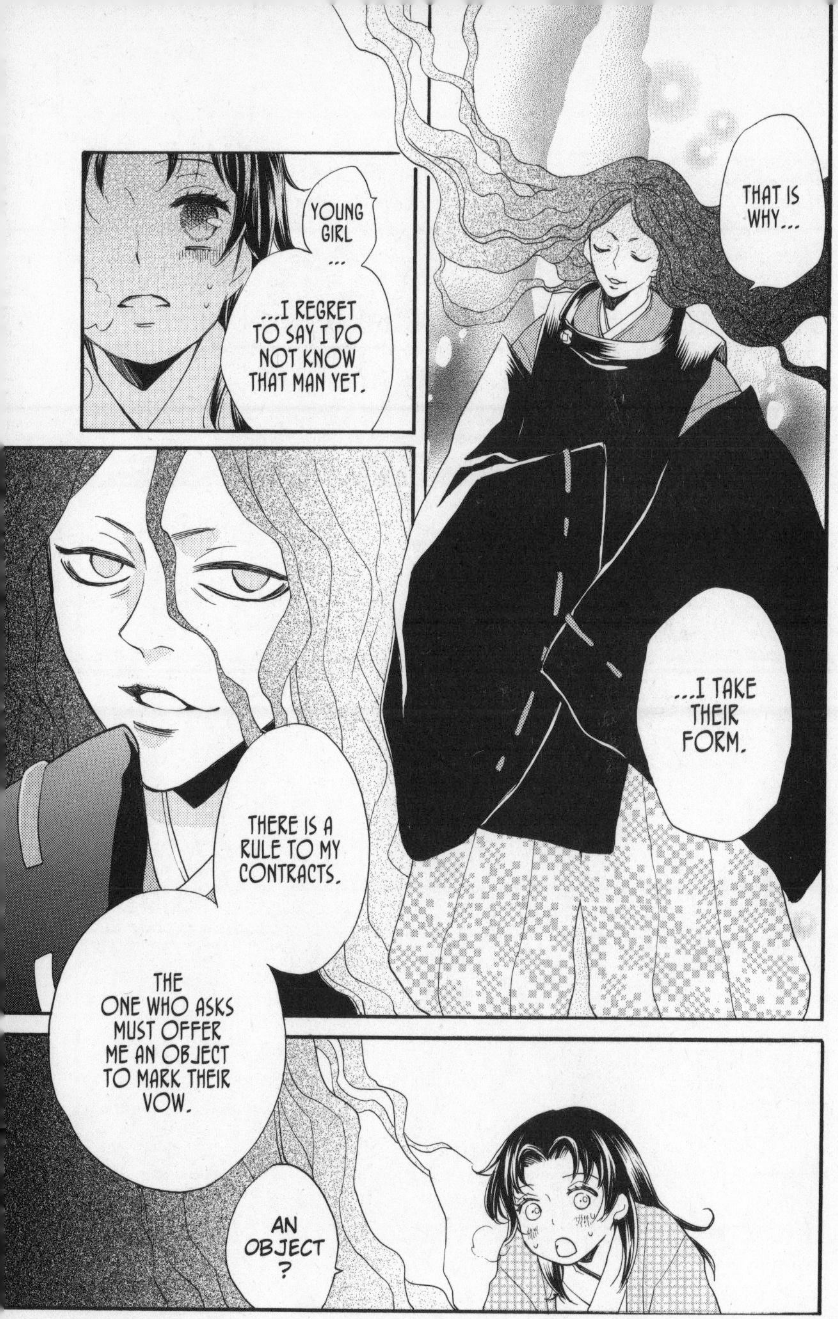
THAT IS WHY...
...I TAKE THEIR FORM.
YOUNG GIRL ...
...I REGRET TO SAY I DO NOT KNOW THAT MAN YET.
THERE IS A RULE TO MY CONTRACTS.
THE ONE WHO ASKS MUST OFFER ME AN OBJECT TO MARK THEIR VOW.
AN OBJECT?

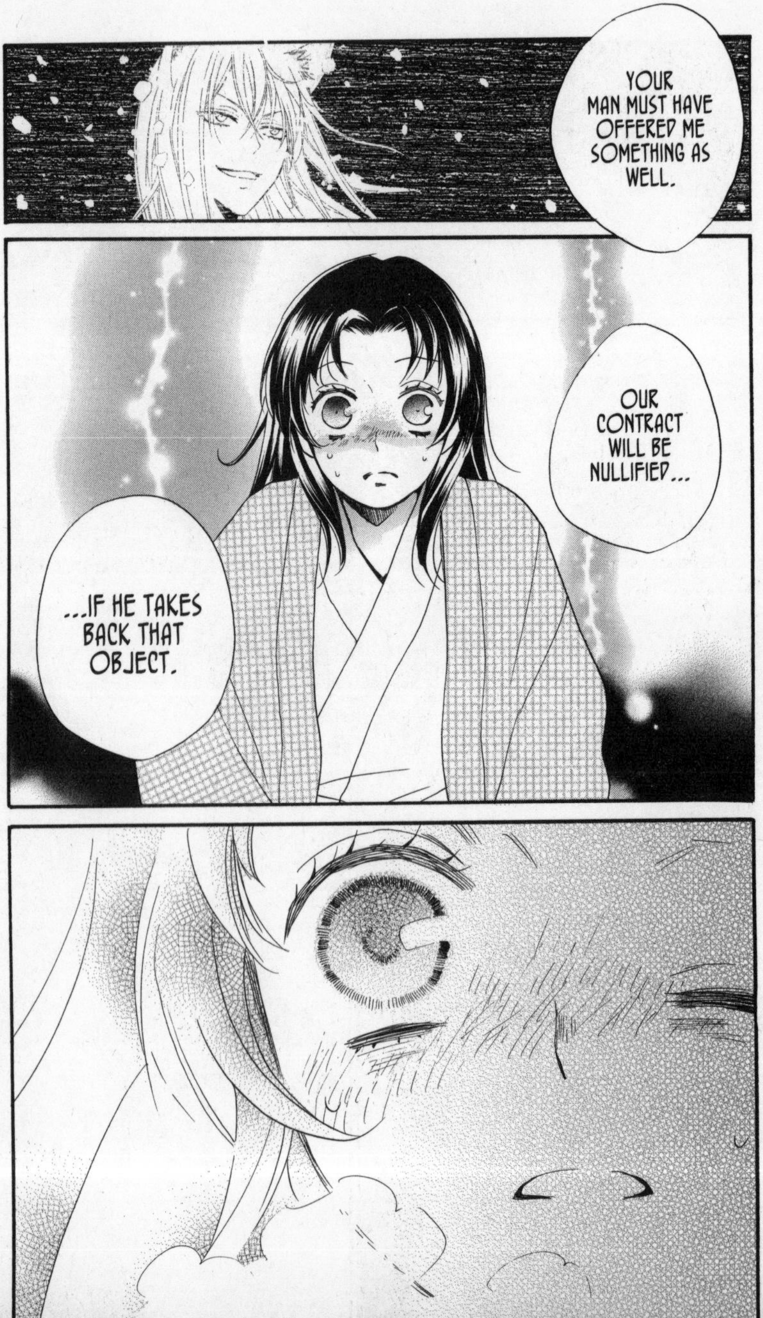
YOUR MAN MUST HAVE OFFERED ME SOMETHING AS WELL.
OUR CONTRACT WILL BE NULLIFIED...
...IF HE TAKES BACK THAT OBJECT.

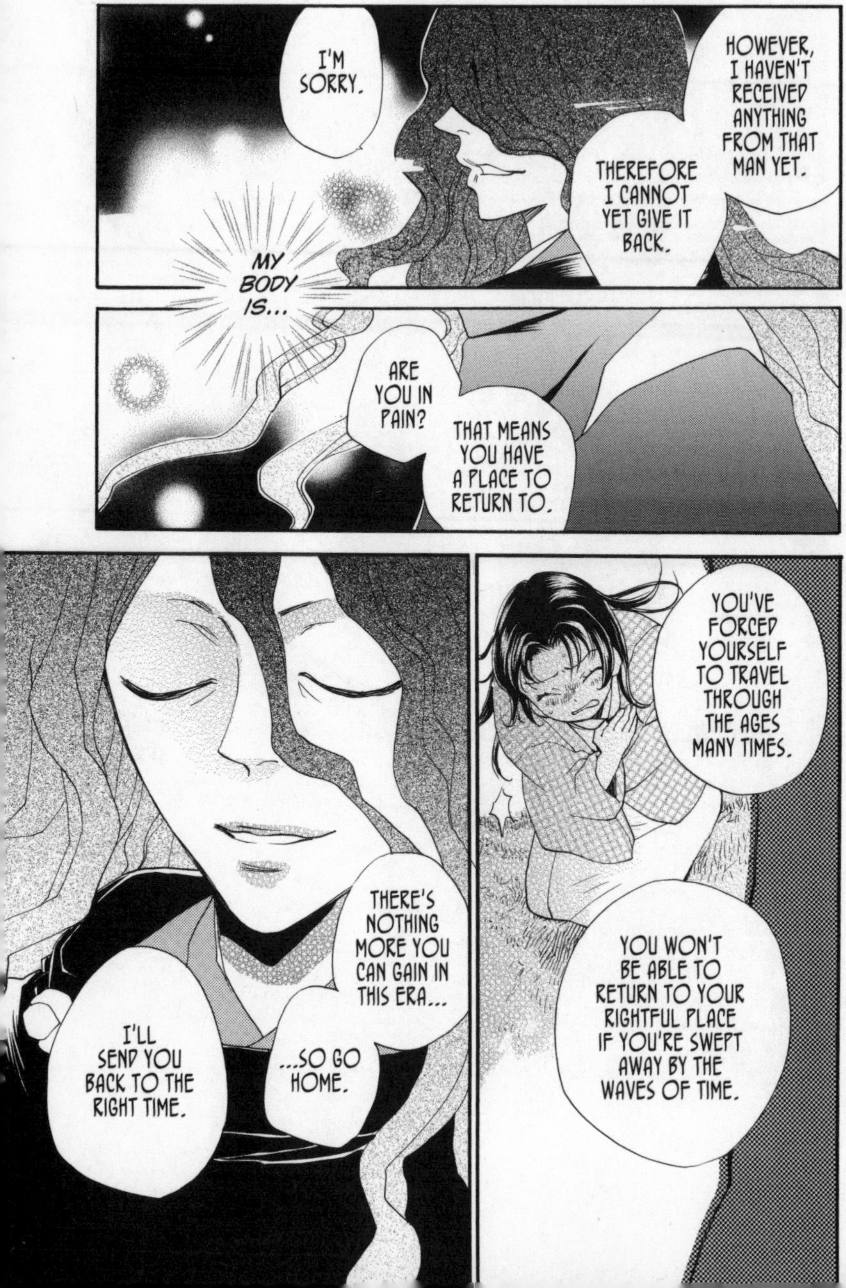
HOWEVER, I HAVEN'T RECEIVED ANYTHING FROM THAT MAN YET.
THEREFORE I CANNOT YET GIVE IT BACK.
I'M SORRY.
MY BODY IS...
ARE YOU IN PAIN?
THAT MEANS YOU HAVE A PLACE TO RETURN TO.
YOU'VE FORCED YOURSELF TO TRAVEL THROUGH THE AGES MANY TIMES.
YOU WON'T BE ABLE TO RETURN TO YOUR RIGHTFUL PLACE IF YOU'RE SWEPT AWAY BY THE WAVES OF TIME.
THERE'S NOTHING MORE YOU CAN GAIN IN THIS ERA...
...SO GO HOME.
I'LL SEND YOU BACK TO THE RIGHT TIME.

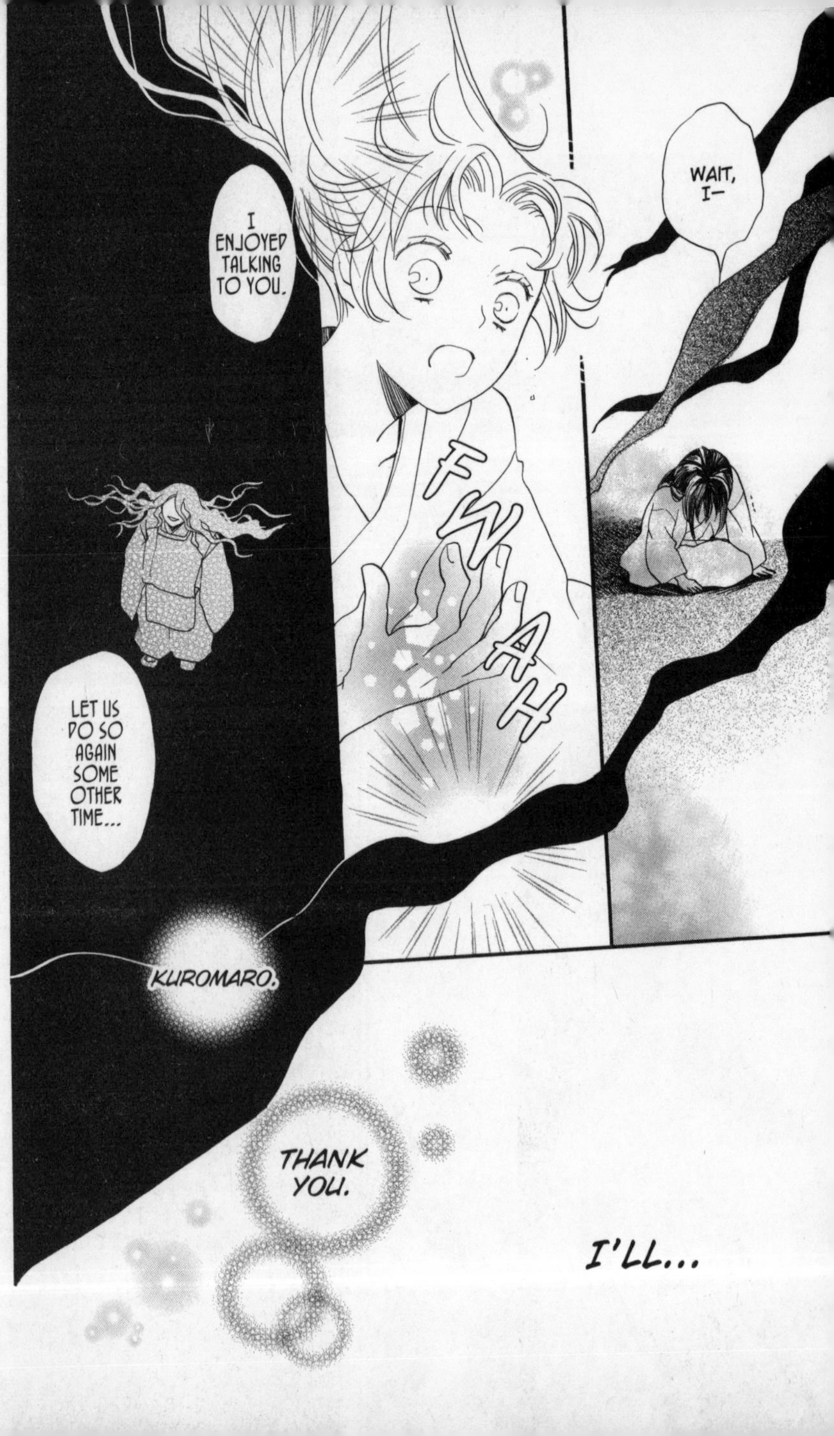
WAIT, I—
FWAH
I ENJOYED TALKING TO YOU.
LET US DO SO AGAIN SOME OTHER TIME...
KUROMARO.
THANK YOU.
I'LL...

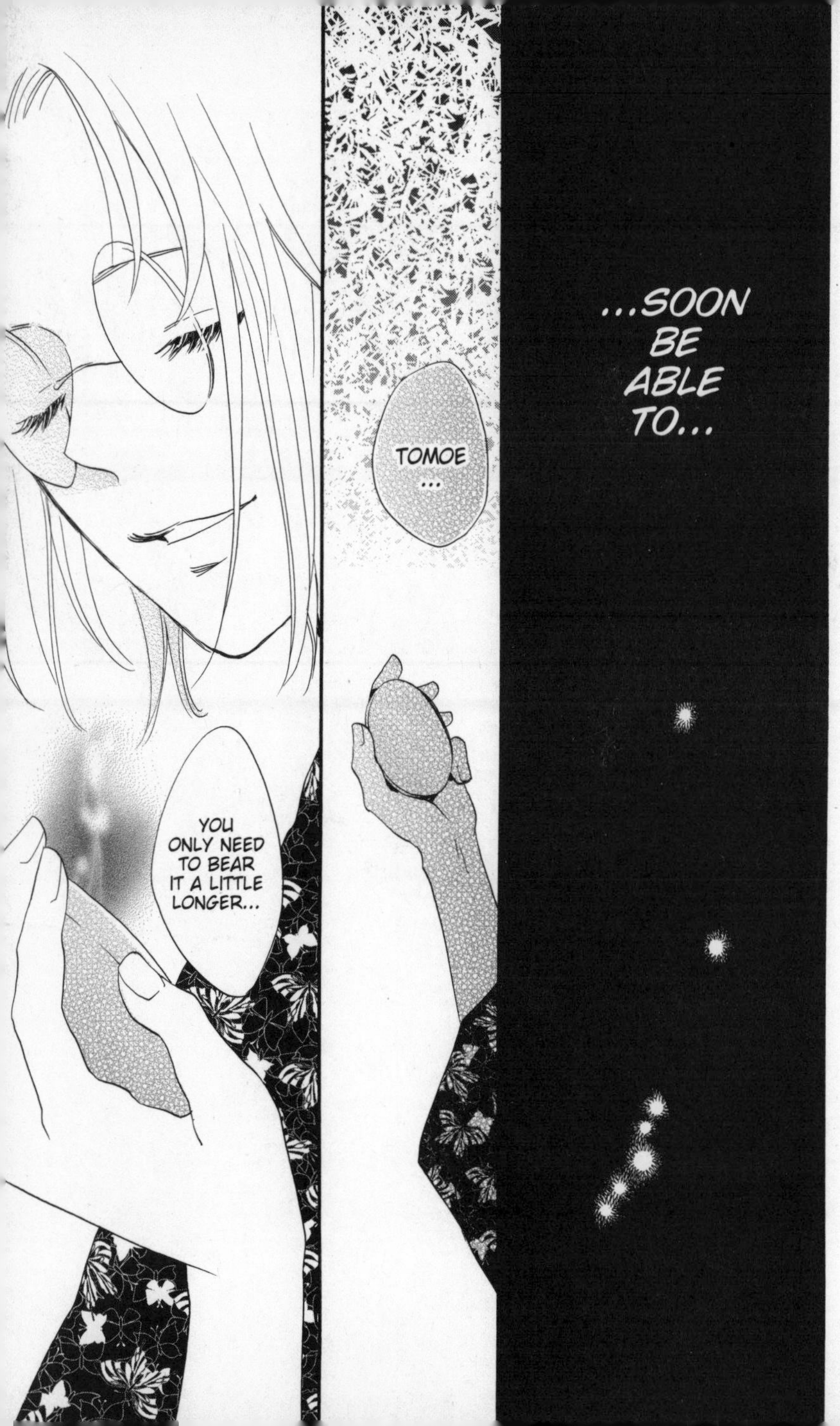
...SOON BE ABLE TO...
TOMOE ...
YOU ONLY NEED TO BEAR IT A LITTLE LONGER...

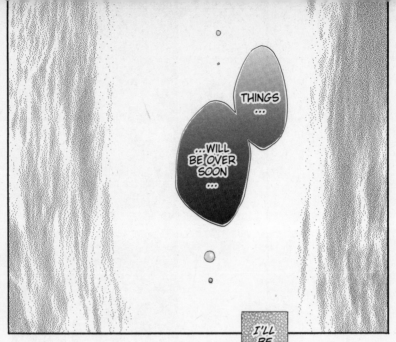

THINGS
...

...WILL
BE OVER
SOON
...

I'LL
BE
ABLE
TO
SAVE
TOMOE
...

...SOON
...

*End of
Kamisama Kiss 16*

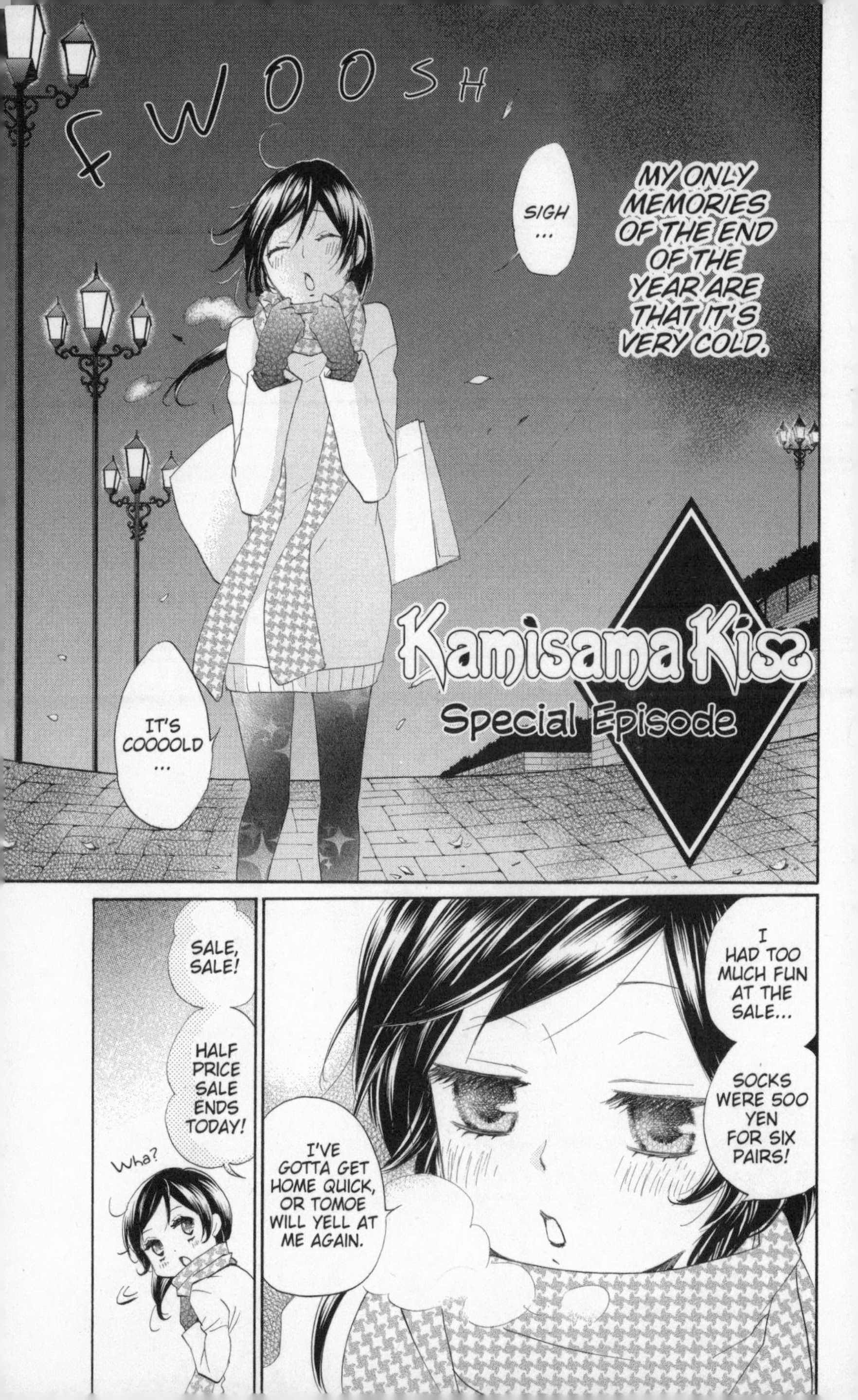
MY ONLY MEMORIES OF THE END OF THE YEAR ARE THAT IT'S VERY COLD.
FWOOSH
SIGH...
Kamisama Kiss
Special Episode
IT'S COOOOLD...
I HAD TOO MUCH FUN AT THE SALE...
SOCKS WERE 500 YEN FOR SIX PAIRS!
I'VE GOTTA GET HOME QUICK, OR TOMOE WILL YELL AT ME AGAIN.
SALE, SALE!
HALF PRICE SALE ENDS TODAY!
Wha?

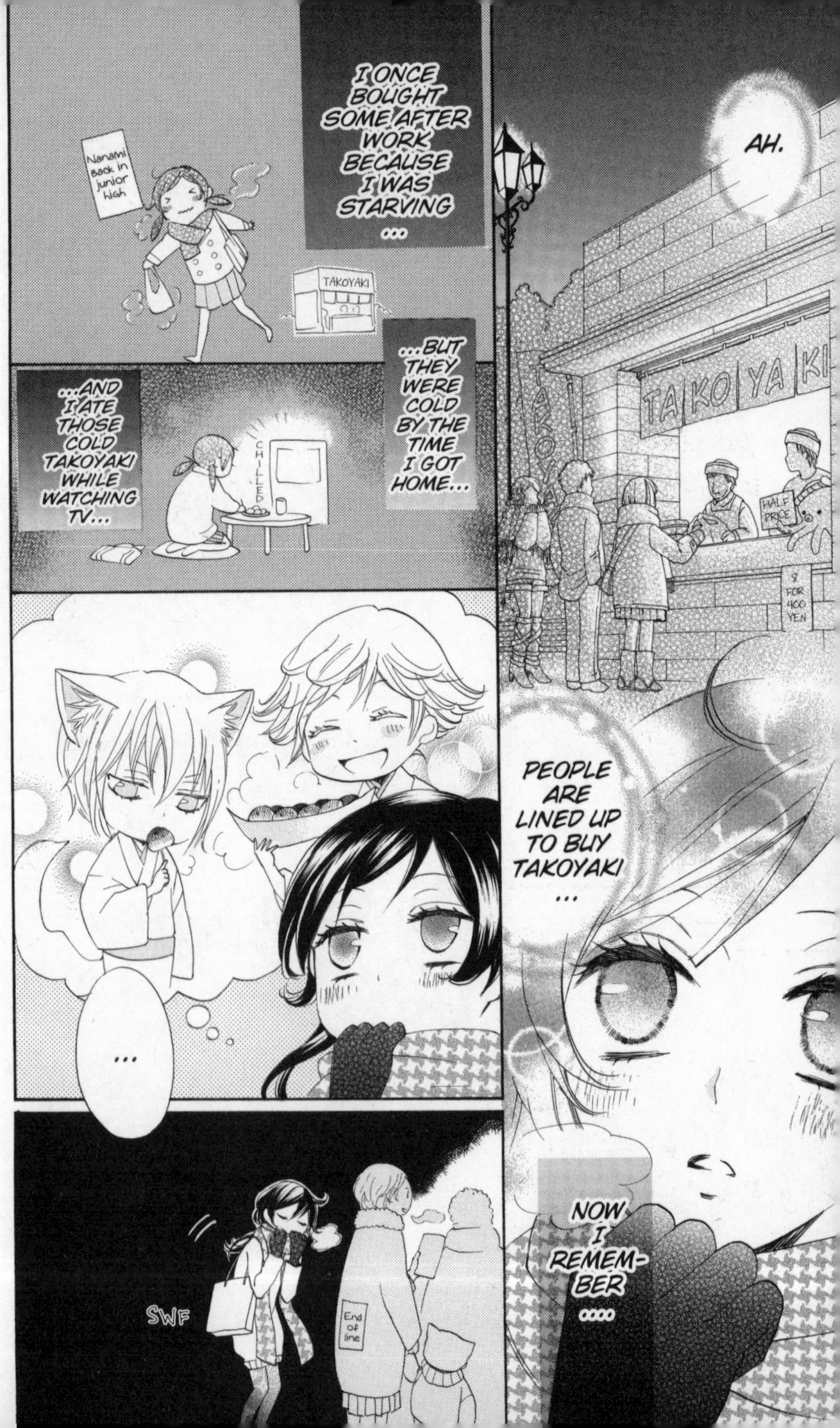
AH.
TAKOYAKI
TA KO YA KI
HALF PRICE
8 FOR 400 YEN
PEOPLE ARE LINED UP TO BUY TAKOYAKI ...
NOW I REMEMBER ....
I ONCE BOUGHT SOME AFTER WORK BECAUSE I WAS STARVING ...
Nanami Back in junior high
TAKOYAKI
...BUT THEY WERE COLD BY THE TIME I GOT HOME...
...AND I ATE THOSE COLD TAKOYAKI WHILE WATCHING TV...
CHILLED
...
SWF
End of line

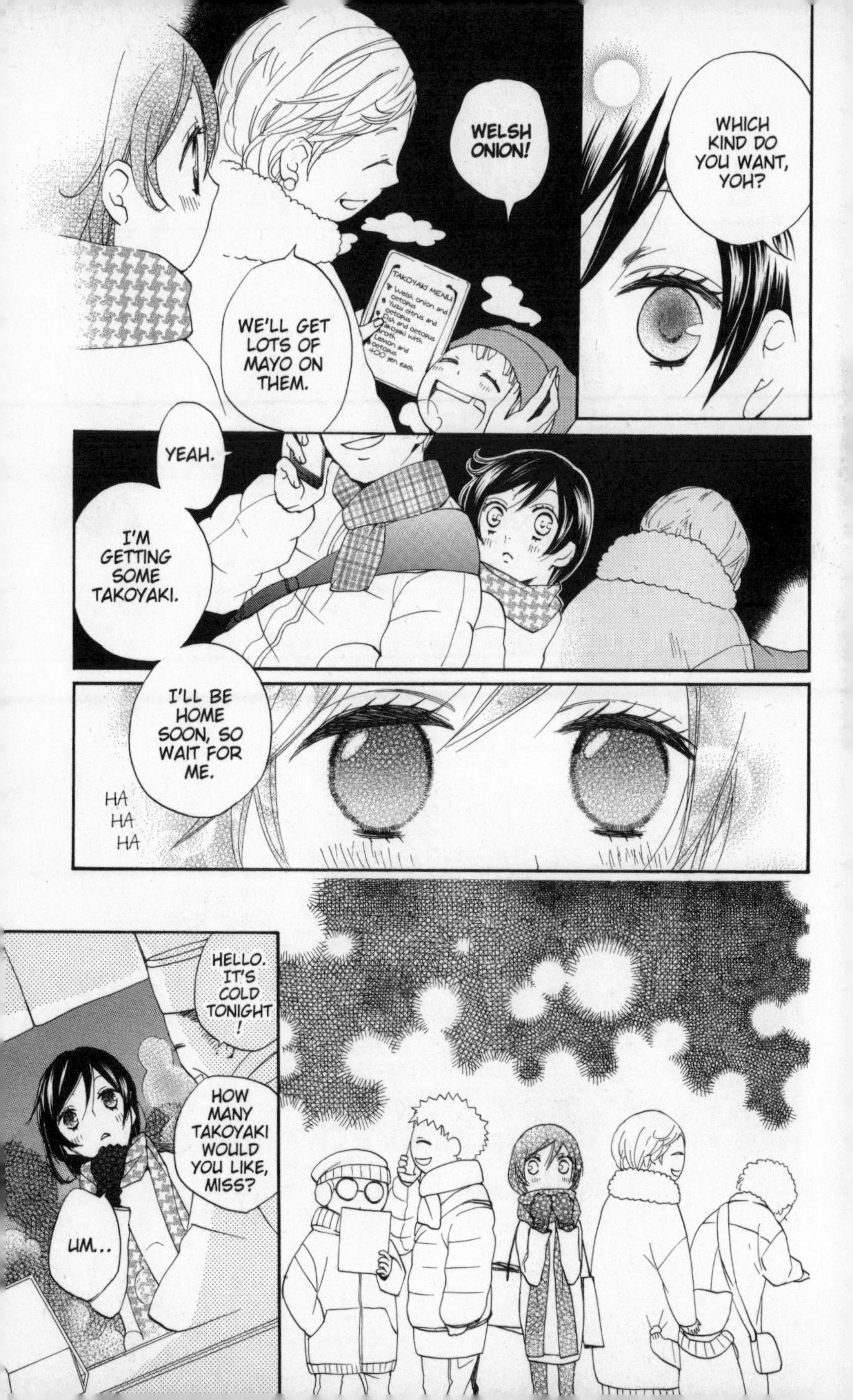
WHICH KIND DO YOU WANT, YOH?
WELSH ONION!
TAKOYAKI MENU
Welsh onion and octopus
Yuzu citrus and octopus
Fish and octopus
Takoyaki with broth
Lemon and octopus
400 yen each
WE'LL GET LOTS OF MAYO ON THEM.
YEAH.
I'M GETTING SOME TAKOYAKI.
I'LL BE HOME SOON, SO WAIT FOR ME.
HA HA HA
HELLO. IT'S COLD TONIGHT!
HOW MANY TAKOYAKI WOULD YOU LIKE, MISS?
UM...

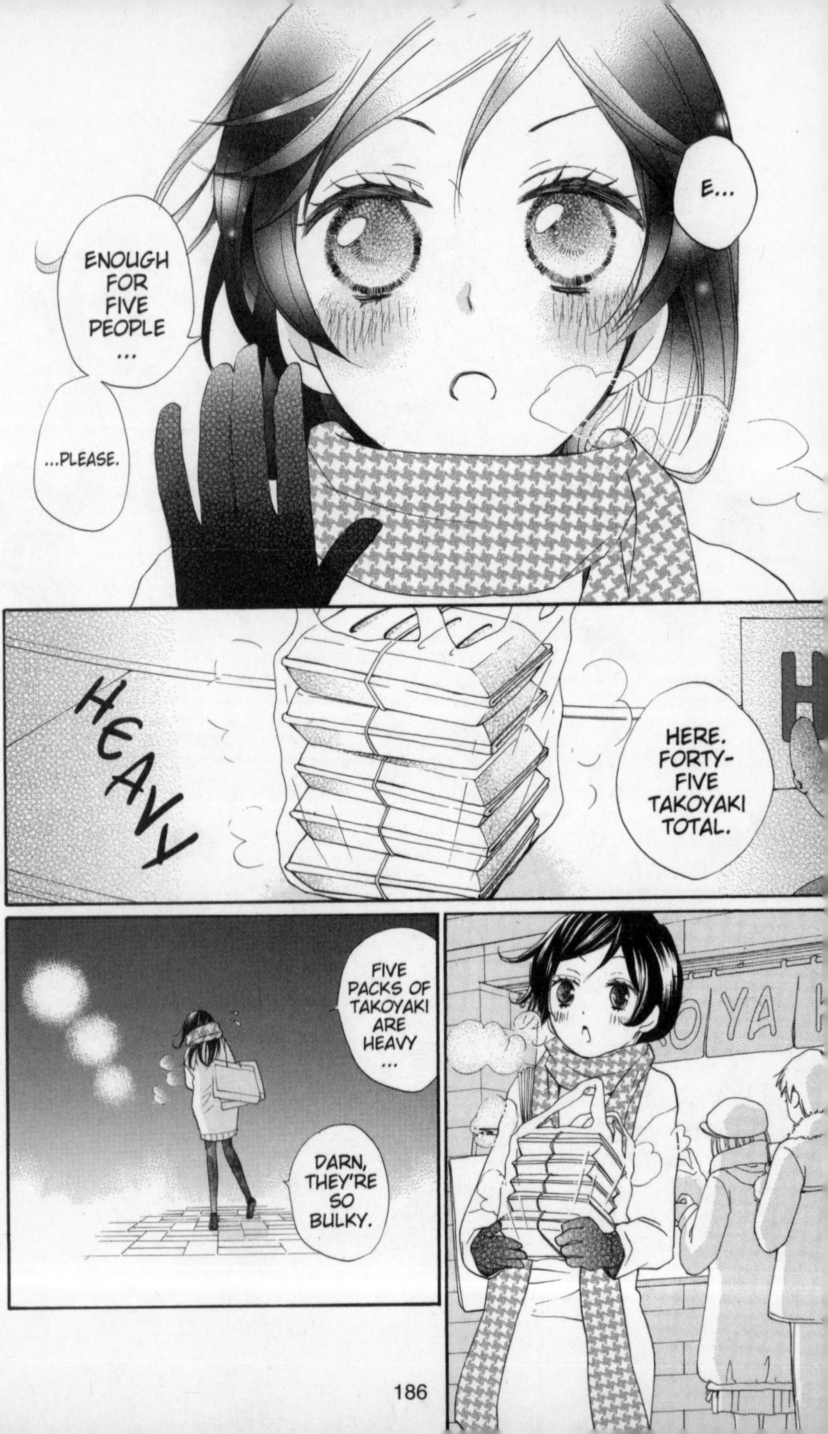
E...
ENOUGH FOR FIVE PEOPLE ...
...PLEASE.
HERE. FORTY-FIVE TAKOYAKI TOTAL.
HEAVY
FIVE PACKS OF TAKOYAKI ARE HEAVY ...
DARN, THEY'RE SO BULKY.

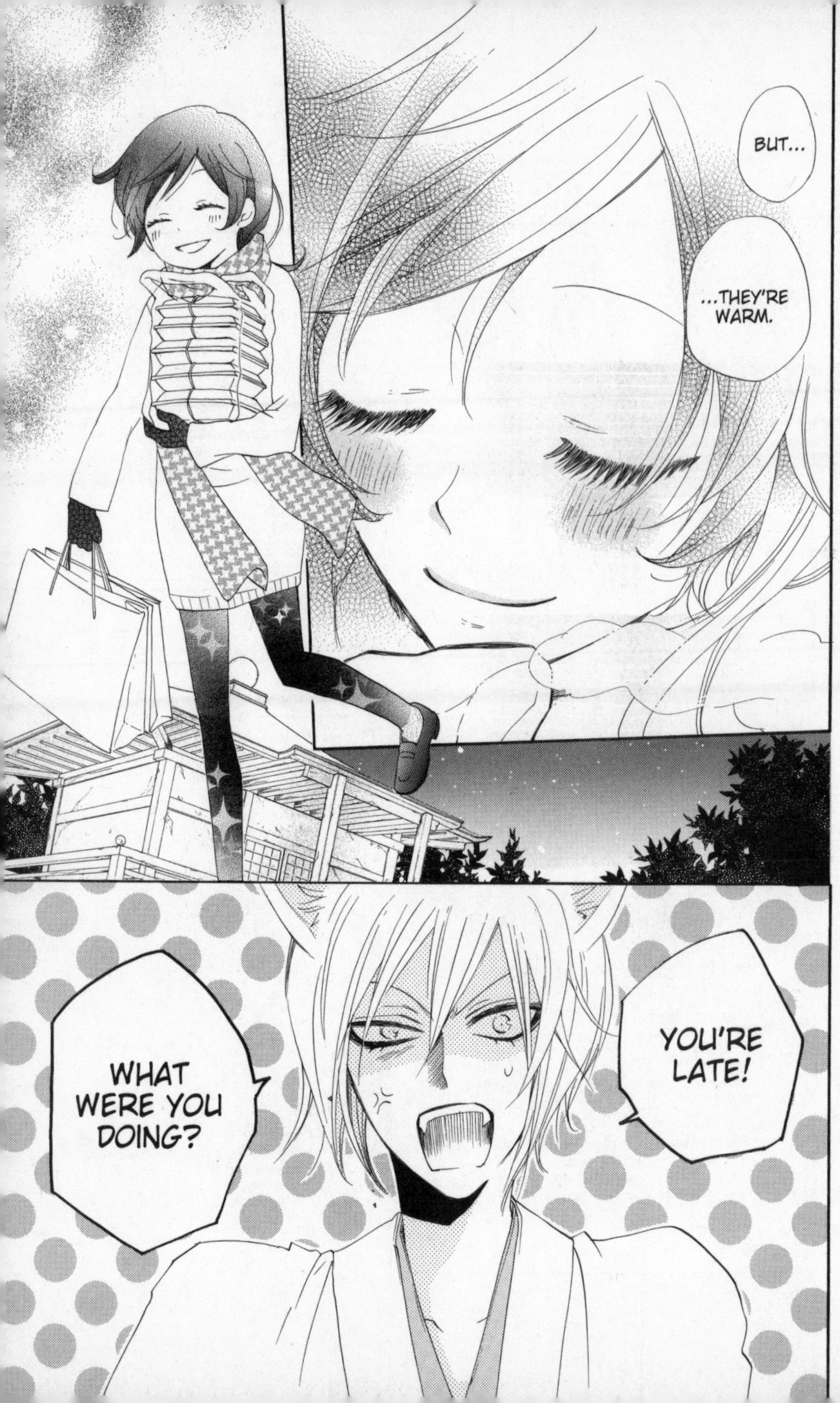
BUT...
...THEY'RE WARM.
YOU'RE LATE!
WHAT WERE YOU DOING?

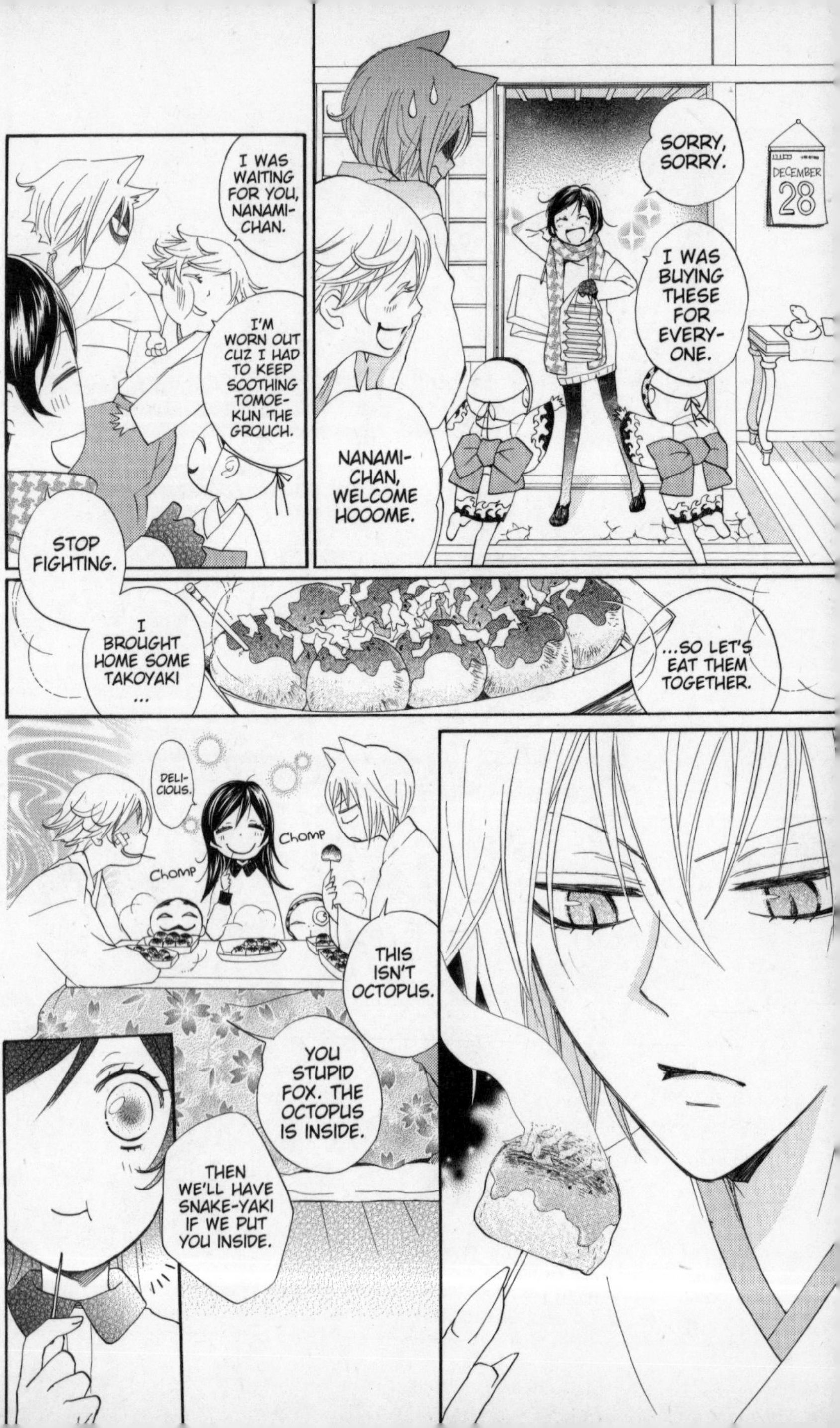
SORRY, SORRY.
DECEMBER 28
I WAS BUYING THESE FOR EVERY-ONE.
NANAMI-CHAN, WELCOME HOOOME.
I WAS WAITING FOR YOU, NANAMI-CHAN.
I'M WORN OUT CUZ I HAD TO KEEP SOOTHING TOMOE-KUN THE GROUCH.
STOP FIGHTING.
I BROUGHT HOME SOME TAKOYAKI ...
...SO LET'S EAT THEM TOGETHER.
DELI-CIOUS.
Chomp
Chomp
THIS ISN'T OCTOPUS.
YOU STUPID FOX. THE OCTOPUS IS INSIDE.
THEN WE'LL HAVE SNAKE-YAKI IF WE PUT YOU INSIDE.

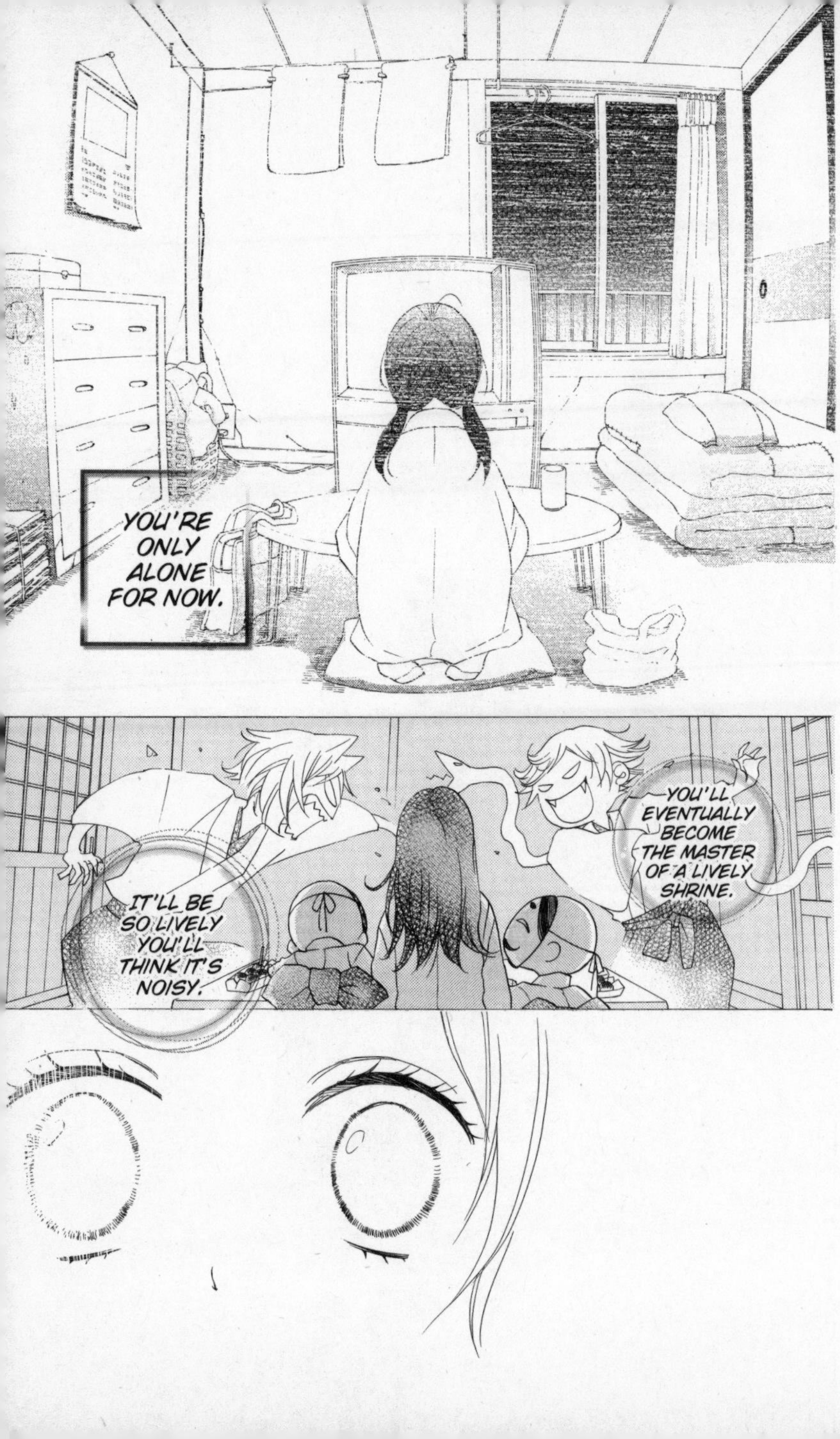
YOU'RE ONLY ALONE FOR NOW.
YOU'LL EVENTUALLY BECOME THE MASTER OF A LIVELY SHRINE.
IT'LL BE SO LIVELY YOU'LL THINK IT'S NOISY.

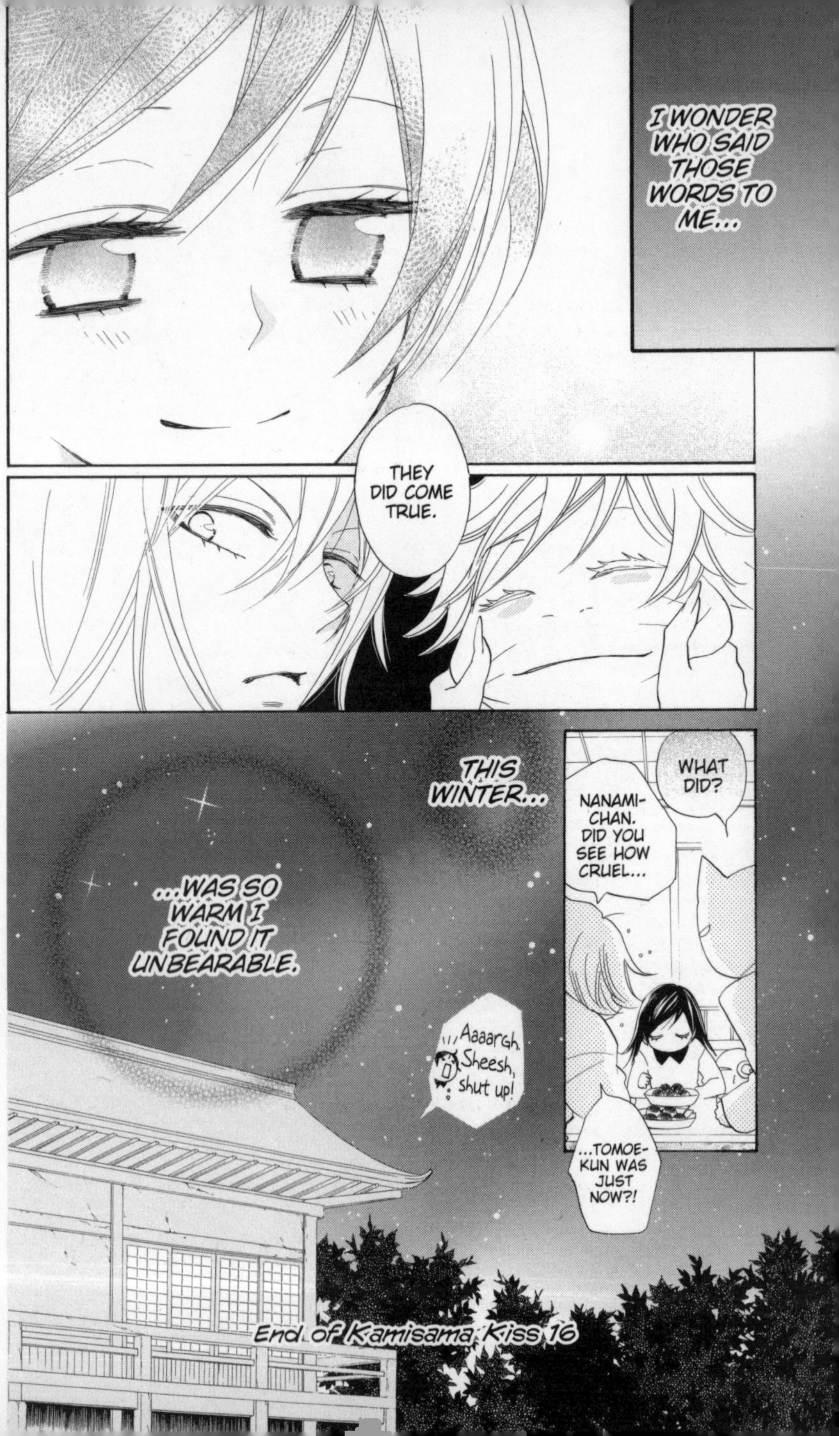
I WONDER WHO SAID THOSE WORDS TO ME...
THEY DID COME TRUE.
WHAT DID?
NANAMI-CHAN. DID YOU SEE HOW CRUEL...
...TOMOE-KUN WAS JUST NOW?!
THIS WINTER...
...WAS SO WARM I FOUND IT UNBEARABLE.
Aaaargh. Sheesh, shut up!
End of Kamisama Kiss 16

The Otherworld

Ayakashi is an archaic term for yokai.

Kami are Shinto deities or spirits. The word can be used for a range of creatures, from nature spirits to strong and dangerous gods.

Kotodama is literally "word spirit," the spiritual power believed to dwell in words. In Shinto, the words you speak are believed to affect reality.

Onibi-warashi are like will-o'-the-wisps.

Shikigami are spirits that are summoned and employed by *onmyoji* (Yin-Yang sorcerers).

Shinshi are birds, beasts, insects or fish that have a special relationship with a kami.

Tengu are a type of yokai. They are sometimes associated with excess pride.

Tochigami (or *jinushigami*) are deities of a specific area of land.

Yokai are demons, monsters or goblins.

Honorifics

-chan is a diminutive most often used with babies, children or teenage girls.

-dono roughly means "my lord," although not in the aristocratic sense.

-kun is used by persons of superior rank to their juniors. It can sometimes have a familiar connotation.

-san is a standard honorific similar to Mr., Mrs., Miss, or Ms.

-sama is used with people of much higher rank.

Notes

Page 10, panel 1: Post station
The Japanese term is *shukuba*. Post stations existed during the
Edo period and were places where travelers could rest during their
journey.

Page 28, panel 5: Kappa
A *kappa* is a water spirit that mainly haunts rivers. It looks like
a child, is green or red all over, has a plate on its head, a tortoise
shell on its back, and webs on its hands and feet.

Page 36, panel 2: Palanquin
In olden days, a bride was carried in a palanquin to her groom's
family to be married.

Page 111, sidebar: Aka-beko, Okiagari-koboshi
Aka-beko is a traditional toy from Aizu, Fukushima Prefecture. It
means "red cow," and the toy is a red cow with a bobbing head.
Okiagari-koboshi are self-righting dolls.

Julietta Suzuki's debut manga *Hoshi ni Naru Hi* (The Day One Becomes a Star) appeared in the 2004 *Hana to Yume Plus*. Her other books include *Akuma to Dolce* (The Devil and Sweets) and *Karakuri Odette*. Born in December in Fukuoka Prefecture, she enjoys having movies play in the background while she works on her manga.

KAMISAMA KISS
VOL. 16
Shojo Beat Edition

STORY AND ART BY
Julietta Suzuki

English Translation & Adaptation/Tomo Kimura
Touch-up Art & Lettering/Joanna Estep
Design/Yukiko Whitley
Editor/Pancha Diaz

KAMISAMA HAJIMEMASHITA by Julietta Suzuki
© Julietta Suzuki 2013
All rights reserved.
First published in Japan in 2013 by HAKUSENSHA, Inc., Tokyo.
English language translation rights arranged with
HAKUSENSHA, Inc., Tokyo.

The stories, characters and incidents mentioned
in this publication are entirely fictional.

Printed in Canada

Published by VIZ Media, LLC
P.O. Box 77010
San Francisco, CA 94107

10 9 8 7 6 5 4 3 2
First printing, October 2014
Second printing, June 2016

www.viz.com

www.shojobeat.com

PARENTAL ADVISORY
KAMISAMA KISS is rated T for Teen and
is recommended for ages 13 and up. This
volume contains fantasy violence.
ratings.viz.com

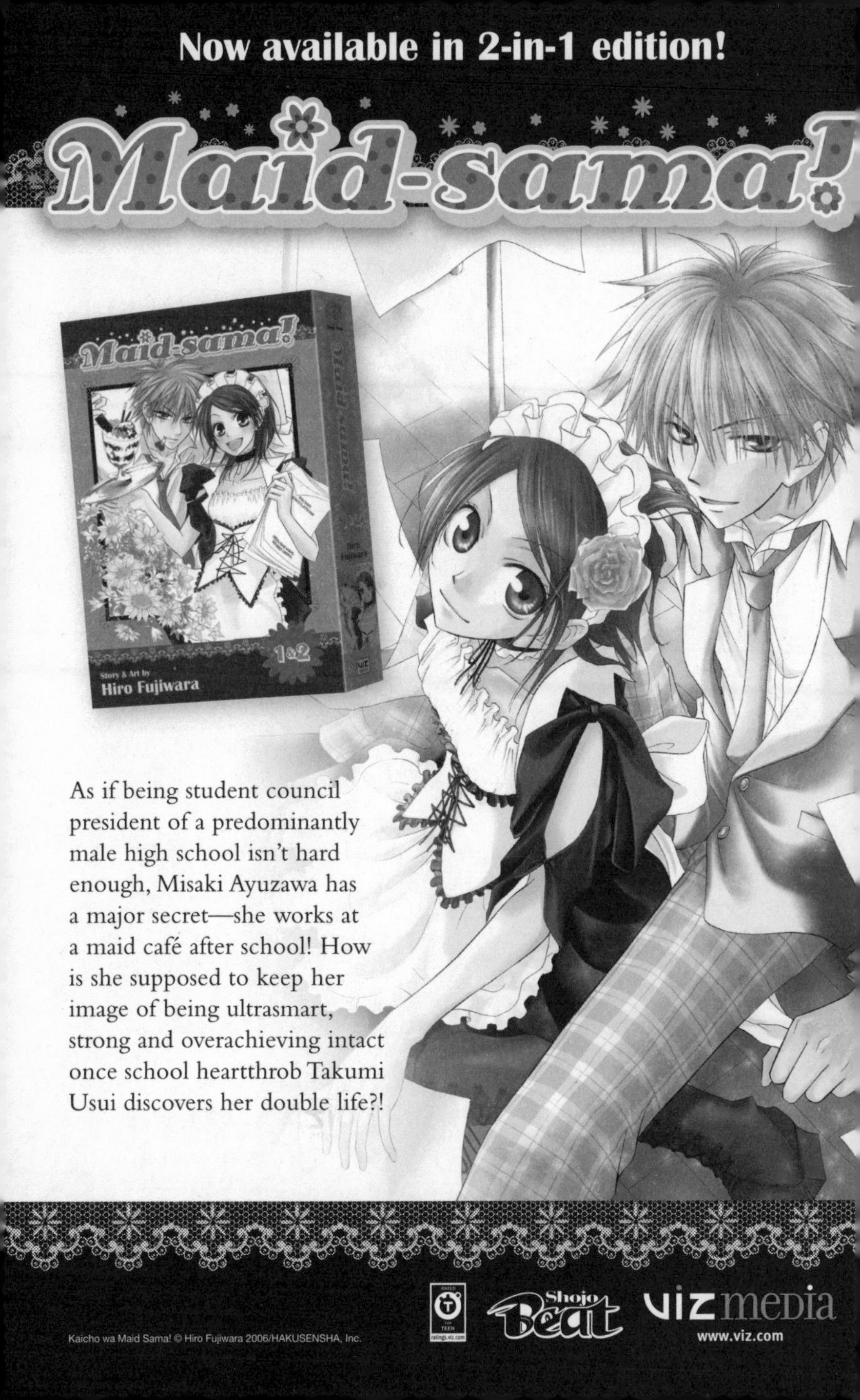

Now available in 2-in-1 edition!
Maid-sama!
Maid-sama!
1&2
Story & Art by
Hiro Fujiwara
As if being student council president of a predominantly male high school isn't hard enough, Misaki Ayuzawa has a major secret—she works at a maid café after school! How is she supposed to keep her image of being ultrasmart, strong and overachieving intact once school heartthrob Takumi Usui discovers her double life?!
Kaicho wa Maid Sama! © Hiro Fujiwara 2006/HAKUSENSHA, Inc.
RATED T FOR TEEN ratings.viz.com
Shojo Beat
VIZ media
www.viz.com

This is the last page.

In keeping with the original Japanese comic format, this book reads from right to left—so action, sound effects, and word balloons are completely reversed. This preserves the orientation of the original artwork—plus, it's fun! Check out the diagram shown here to get the hang of things, and then turn to the other side of the book to get started!